# THE IMITATION OF PAUL

VRIJE UNIVERSITEIT TE AMSTERDAM

# THE IMITATION OF PAUL
## AN EXEGETICAL STUDY

ACADEMISCH PROEFSCHRIFT

TER VERKRIJGING VAN DE GRAAD VAN DOCTOR IN
DE GODGELEERDHEID AAN DE VRIJE UNIVERSITEIT TE
AMSTERDAM, OP GEZAG VAN DE RECTOR MAGNIFICUS
Dr. H. SMITSKAMP, HOOGLERAAR IN DE FACULTEIT DER
LETTEREN IN HET OPENBAAR TE VERDEDIGEN OP VRIJ-
DAG 6 APRIL 1962 OM HALF VIER IN HET WOESTDUIN-
CENTRUM, WOESTDUINSTRAAT 16, TE AMSTERDAM

DOOR

WILLIS PETER DE BOER
GEBOREN TE GRAND RAPIDS, MICHIGAN U.S.A.

WIPF & STOCK · Eugene, Oregon

Wipf and Stock Publishers
199 W 8th Ave, Suite 3
Eugene, OR 97401

The Imitation of Paul
An Exegetical Study
By De Boer, Willis P.
Copyright©1962 by De Boer, Willis P
ISBN 13: 978-1-4982-9367-9
Publication date 3/23/2016
Previously published by J. H. Kok, 1962

*TO GERTRUDE*

# PROPOSITIONS

## I

Paul's references to the imitation of himself are to be understood in the context of the spiritual father-child relationship which exists between himself and his readers, whereby the child brings to expression the Christian way he has seen in his father and knows from him.

## II

Paul's references to the imitation of himself are not to be explained in terms of his readers' reflecting certain "characteristic modalities" of Paul's preaching and way of life, in distinction from the modalities characteristic of the preaching and ways of life of the other apostles and missionaries.

*contra* D. M. Stanley, "'Become Imitators of Me': The Pauline Conception of Apostolic Tradition," *Biblica*, XL (1959), p. 877.

## III

The primary thought in Paul's speaking of his readers as μιμηταί is not that they are obliged to be obedient to him and to act in accordance with his instructions.

*contra* W. Michaelis, μιμέομαι *et al.*, *T.W.N.T.*, IV, pp. 675, 16–676, 2.

## IV

W. Michaelis' assertion: "Die Forderung einer imitatio Christi hat in den paulinischen Aussagen keine Stütze," can not be sustained.

*cf.* W. Michaelis, μιμέομαι *et al.*, *T.W.N.T.*, IV, p. 676, 8–9.

## V

The recurring accent in the various Pauline calls to imitation is on the way of life to which Christ called men in his calls to follow him, namely, the way of humility, self-denial, self-giving, self-sacrifice for the sake of the gospel and the salvation of others.

## VI

Paul's calling his converts to the imitation of himself was a means of nurturing them to the maturity of direct imitation of Christ.

## VII

The Old Testament expressions "walking in God's ways," and "walking after God" or "following God," do not have in mind the idea of imitating God.

    *contra* E. J. Tinsley, *The Imitation of God in Christ*, London: S.C.M. Press, 1960, p. 35.

## VIII

The expression "sons of the prophets" (בני־הנביאים) is to be understood in the sense of a spiritual sonship, indicating the disciples or pupils of the prophets.

    *contra* M. A. van den Oudenrijn, "L'expression 'fils des prophètes' et ses analogies," *Biblica*, VI (1925), pp. 165ff.

## IX

P. Winter correctly proposes that the presence of ἐν in προβεβηκότες ἐν ταῖς ἡμέραις αὐτῶν in Luke 1:7 points to a Hebrew source of the account rather than to an imitation on Luke's part of Septuagintal Greek.

    *cf.* P. Winter, "Some Observations on the Language in the Birth and Infancy Stories of the Third Gospel," *N.T.S.*, I (1954/5), p. 114; and "On Luke and Lucan Sources," *Z.N.W.*, XLVII (1956), p. 222.
    *contra* N. Turner, "The Relation of Luke i and ii to the Hebraic Sources and to the Rest of Luke-Acts," *N.T.S.*, II (1955/6), p. 101.
    P. Benoit, "L'enfance de Jean-Baptist selon Luc I," *N.T.S.*, III (1956/7), p. 173.

## X

The thought that the union of husband and wife in marriage "approaches the state of the original androgynous Adam" is not indicated in Paul's quotation and use of Gen. 2:24 in Eph. 5:31.

    *contra* D. Daube, *The New Testament and Rabbinic Judaism*, London: Athlone Press, 1956, p. 80.

## XI

The reading of καυχήσωμαι in I Cor. 13:3, in spite of its impressive manuscript support, is not be preferred.

## XII

The doctrine of separate resurrections for believers and unbelievers, separated by an intervening reign of Christ, finds no support in I Cor. 15:24 and context.

    *contra* L. S. Chafer, *Systematic Theology*, Dallas (Texas): Dallas Seminary Press, 1948, Vol. IV, pp. 124, 264, 375–76.

## XIII

K. Barth's term "modes of being" (Seinsweisen) for expressing the internal relationships of the Godhead is not to be preferred to the term "persons."

*contra* K. Barth, *Die Kirchliche Dogmatik*, Zollikon-Zürich: Evangelischer Verlag, 1944, Vol. I/1, § 9 (pp. 379ff.).

## XIV

B. Metzger wrongly creates the impression that Jerome's translations of the Apocryphal Books of Tobit and Judith into Latin were done with less care than his translations of the canonical books of the Old Testament.

*cf.* B. Metzger, *An Introduction to the Apocrypha*, New York: Oxford University Press, 1957, p. 179.

## XV

The religious factor in the rise of capitalism in western society is better accounted for in terms of a waning of faith and a breakdown of church control over the lives of men, than, as Max Weber proposed, in terms of the influence and impetus of Calvinism.

## XVI

W. Walker, later cited by H. E. Fosdick, creates the wrong impression of Calvin's attitude in 1537 toward the Athanasian Creed, when Walker says that according to the letter from the pastors of Geneva to the pastors of Berne on about February 20, 1537, Calvin said, "'We swear in the faith of the one God, not of Athanasius, whose creed no true church would ever have approved.'"

*cf.* W. Walker, *John Calvin, the Organizer of Reformed Protestantism, 1509–1564*, New York: Putnam, 1906, p. 197.

H. E. Fosdick, *The Modern Use of the Bible*, New York: Macmillan, 1940, p. 84.

## XVII

The proposed revision of *The Church Order of the Christian Reformed Church (United States and Canada)* ought not to stipulate the following: "The Lord's Supper shall be preceded by a preparatory sermon and followed by an applicatory sermon."

*cf.* Church Order Article 63c, in the *Acts of Synod 1961 of the Christian Reformed Church*, Grand Rapids: Christian Reformed Publishing House, 1961, p. 459.

## XVIII

The forms which the church uses in connection with the administration of the sacraments ought to be liturgically rather than didactically oriented.

## XIX

The gathering of money, if it is to be done during the service of worship, ought to be a liturgically meaningful act. Many Reformed churches presently show little sensitivity to this matter.

## XX

In the worship service kneeling in prayer is liturgically helpful and ought to be encouraged.

# PREFACE

Standing at the point of completing my doctoral study, I take stock of my life. It is a revealing and humbling experience. How much of what I am must be attributed to the influence and good services of others! Quite naturally it is my father and mother who have exercised the most formative influence over my life. During too much of my life I took them for granted. How thankful I am to God for giving them to me, for the good Christian training they have given me, for their continued enjoyment of life and health, and for this opportunity to express publicly the gratitude and love I have for them for all they have meant to me.

In more recent years my closest human associate has been my wife. Here again I enjoy one of God's choicest gifts. Gertrude has willingly shouldered the inconveniences and hard work of living with a family on a very rigorous budget during these more than three years of post-graduate study. She has entered with enthusiasm into the experience of living in another country, learnings its language, and coming to know its people and ways. She offered constant companionship and encouragement in this study project, has shown great patience and understanding during my seasons of tension and frustration, and has given much help with many of the details in preparing this thesis for printing. With profound gratitude to God I dedicate the fruits of my study to her.

The host of people who have given of themselves in my education is too great to permit of personal acknowledgment. I appreciate the efforts of all who have served as my teachers throughout my years of formal schooling. I count it a great privilege to have received my ministerial preparation and training from the faculties of Calvin College and Seminary in Grand Rapids, Michigan. I have further enjoyed a great incentive and challenge to be "a workman that needeth not to be ashamed, handling aright the word of truth" (II Tim. 2:15) from the people I have been privileged to serve as a minister of the Word of God in the Christian Reformed Churches in Washington, D.C., and in Bradenton, Florida. Both my teachers and my parishioners served to whet my appetite for probing the riches of God's Word. To this end I have sought to improve my ability to use the tools and resources available for such work by pursuing graduate study in the field of the New Testament. I am deeply grateful for the funds for further study which were provided to me through the Diamond Jubilee Scholarship and through a portion of the Centennial Missions Scholarship of the Christian Reformed Church. I also express my heartfelt appreciation to the various individuals who have helped in financing this period of study.

## PREFACE

During the past three and one half years I have been very greatly enriched through my study and contacts at the Free University of Amsterdam. The lectures by the various members of the Theological Faculty have shown competent Reformed scholarship in action. The seminars in which the various faculty members have participated in discussing problems of particular interest to the foreign students have proved most helpful and stimulating. I express my appreciation to Prof. Dr. D. S. Attema for his instruction in the Aramaic language and his introduction to Rabbinic literature; and to Prof. Dr. G. C. Berkouwer for his instruction in the History of Doctrine.

The bulk of my study has been under the supervision of Prof. Dr. R. Schippers. To him I owe a special debt of gratitude. He has introduced me to the great breadth of scholarly activity and discussion which is presently occurring in the New Testament field and has given me much guidance in finding my way in it. In directing the work on my dissertation, he has given me what sometimes seemed to be a frightening amount of freedom. At the same time he has reviewed my work with utmost care, often making suggestions which have proved most rewarding in opening new insights or in avoiding pitfalls. I have benefited in my study from his competent scholarship and his keen insight into the problems of the day. It has been a privilege to come to know him as my professor and as a personal friend.

There are so many others who have been of help to me. I express my appreciation to B. M. Mogensen, a theological student in Copenhagen, Denmark, for his help with the Swedish language; to Ds. A. Ferwerda of Amsterdam for the generous use of his ministerial library; to the staffs of the libraries of the Free University and of the Municipal University of Amsterdam for their constant help and co-operation in locating and obtaining the books and articles I needed; to the fellow students who have helped so willingly with proof-reading and many final details in bringing this dissertation to completed form.

These are some of the blessings of which I am the beneficiary. Truly, the Lord has been good to me. May God receive the glory.

## CONTENTS

|  | Page |
|---|---|
| PREFACE | vii |
| INTRODUCTION | xi |

### Chapter One
### PAUL'S WORD FOR IMITATION

| I. | Μιμέομαι in the Greek World | 1 |
| II. | Μιμέομαι in the Jewish World | 8 |
| III. | Μιμέομαι in the New Testament World | 13 |

### Chapter Two
### PAUL'S WORD FOR PERSONAL EXAMPLE

| I. | Τύπος in the Greek World | 17 |
| II. | Τύπος in the Jewish World | 19 |
| III. | Τύπος in the New Testament World | 21 |

### Chapter Three
### THE IDEA OF IMITATION IN THE WORLD OF PAUL

| I. | Imitation in the Greek World | 24 |
| II. | Imitation in the Old Testament | 29 |
| III. | Imitation in the Jewish World | 42 |
| IV. | Imitation in the New Testament World | 50 |
|  | A. The Imitation of Christ | 50 |
|  | B. The Imitation of God | 71 |
|  | C. The Imitation of Other Men | 80 |

### Chapter Four
### THE IMITATION OF PAUL: EXEGETICAL STUDIES

| I. | I Thessalonians 1:6 | 92 |
| II. | II Thessalonians 3:7–9 | 126 |
| III. | I Corinthians 4:16 | 139 |
| IV. | I Corinthians 11:1 | 154 |
| V. | Philippians 3:17 | 169 |

VI. Galatians 4:12 . . . . . . . . . . . . . . . . 188
VII. The Pastoral Epistles (I Timothy 1:16; II Timothy 1:13; 3:10)  196
VIII. Acts 20:35 . . . . . . . . . . . . . . . . . . 201

## Chapter Five
## THE IMITATION OF PAUL: CRITIQUE AND CONCLUSIONS

I. Critique . . . . . . . . . . . . . . . . . . . 206
II. Conclusions . . . . . . . . . . . . . . . . . . 211

ABBREVIATIONS . . . . . . . . . . . . . . . . . 217
BIBLIOGRAPHY . . . . . . . . . . . . . . . . . 219
INDEX OF TEXTS DISCUSSED . . . . . . . . . . . 230
INDEX OF AUTHORS AND EDITORS . . . . . . . . 232

# INTRODUCTION

All of Christendom has heard of the imitation of Christ. Few within Christendom have heard much of the imitation of Paul. Perhaps there is nothing extraordinary about such a state of affairs. After all, Christ fills a far more significant role in Christianity than the Apostle Paul does. And yet, when one looks at the matter purely statistically, it is striking to find that the thought of the imitation of Paul comes to literal expression in the New Testament five times,[1] while the thought of the imitation of Christ is found literally expressed only twice.[2] Furthermore, the only times that the thought of the imitation of Christ comes to literal expression, it comes as an addition to the thought of the imitation of Paul. Paul says: "Be ye imitators of me, even as I also am of Christ" (I Cor. 11:1); and, "Ye became imitators of us, and of the Lord" (I Thess. 1:6). If the thought of the imitation of Christ is to be judged as a highly important thought, then it must at least be admitted that the thought of the imitation of Paul keeps important company. It can hardly be dismissed as a trifling and insignificant concept in the New Testament.

It is further striking to note that the thought of the imitation of Paul is found in the New Testament only on Paul's lips. Paul speaks of the imitation of God,[3] of the imitation of Christ, of the imitation of the churches of Judea,[4] and of the imitation of himself. The statistics again reveal that Paul's thought of the imitation of himself comes to expression more often than his thoughts of the imitation of all the others combined. Can it be that Paul fell victim to the boastful pride which, as Dodd has suggested, was his characteristic temptation?[5] Does Paul have a following of uncritical admirers and devotees who see in him a kind of Christian hero? It is interesting that in connection with the thought of imitation Paul sometimes called special attention to his being an example.[6] In the world in which Paul lived there was often great concern bestowed on being an example and on stimulating the imitation of others. However, this concern was usually part and parcel of a thoroughly moralistic view of life, where man attained to his highest goal through perfecting himself morally. What place is there for urging one's example upon others and for calling for their imitation in a religion of salvation by grace through faith in Jesus Christ? Such questions as these come to mind

---

1  I Cor. 4:16; 11:1; Phil. 3:17; I Thess. 1:6; and II Thess. 3:7—9.
2  I Cor. 11:1; I Thess. 1:6.
3  Eph. 5:1.
4  I Thess. 2:14.
5  C. H. Dodd, "The Mind of Paul: A Psychological Approach," *B.J.R.L.*, XVII (1933), pp. 97ff.
6  *Cf.* Phil. 3:17; II Thess. 3:7—9.

when we become aware of Paul's repeated references to his readers' imitation of him.

There are further questions which arise in connection with the thought of imitating Paul. What is this imitation which Paul seeks? Imitation to modern ears often arouses thoughts of artificiality, slavish copying, non-genuineness, and in regard to human behavior, putting on, and acting. Counsellors today are likely to advise persons to be themselves, rather than to be imitators of someone else. What imitation did Paul have in mind? Was it a general imitation, inclusive of everything; or was there a specific point in which Paul was calling for imitation in his various references to the matter? What is the relation of the imitation of Paul to the imitation of Christ? What accounts for Paul's not simply calling for the imitation of Christ? What was Paul trying to accomplish in calling for the imitation of himself? In our study of the imitation of Paul we shall be in search of the answers to such questions as these.

The literature specifically dealing with the subject of the imitation of Paul is very limited. For this study only two articles have been located which deal with this subject: a study by E. Eidem: "Imitatio Pauli"; [7] and one by D. M. Stanley: "'Become Imitators of Me': The Pauline Conception of Apostolic Tradition." [8] D. van Swigchem has devoted a section of a chapter to it in his dissertation on the missionary character of the local congregation of Christ's church; [9] and some other authors review the matter briefly. [10]

Basic to an understanding of the imitation of Paul is, of course, an understanding of the idea of imitation itself. In this matter the article by W. Michaelis on the Greek word for imitation, μιμέομαι and related forms, in the *Theologisches Wörterbuch zum Neuen Testament* not only provides considerable material for use in the background studies of the word, but also provides considerable occasion for discussion in connection with the exegesis of the various texts. [11] The articles on the various words in the *Theologisches Wörterbuch zum Neuen Testament* by reason of their scope, depth, and comprehensiveness come easily to be regarded as authoritative and as speaking the last word on the subject. It will be abundantly apparent in the progress of this study how much weight has been attached to being able to cite "T.W.N.T." in a certain matter. However, the scholars who have produced these extensive and masterful studies of the various New Testament words would be the last persons to presume that their studies and conclusions should be considered as authoritative or final and not open to review, discussion, and further testing. Michaelis' article on μιμέομαι and its related forms seems to be particularly worthy of further review and testing. The meaning which

---

[7] In *Teologiska Studier Tillägnade Erik Stave*, Uppsala: Almquist & Wiksells, 1922, pp. 67–85.
[8] In *Biblica*, XL, pp. 859–877.
[9] *Het Missionair Karakter van de Christelijke Gemeente volgens de Brieven van Paulus en Petrus*, Kampen: J. H. Kok, 1955, pp. 108–117.
[10] Cf. e.g., S. C. W. Duvenage, *Die Navolging van Christus*, Potchefstroom: Pro Rege – Pers Beperk, 1954, pp. 66–71; E. J. Tinsley, *The Imitation of God in Christ*, London: S.C.M. Press, 1960, pp. 138–140.
[11] W. Michaelis, μιμέομαι, μιμητής, συμμιμητής, *T.W.N.T.*, IV, pp. 661–678.

Michaelis finds in imitation is not a common one. From his studies he concludes that the idea of following an example plays but little role in the meaning of the word as used in the New Testament, and that the dominant idea is that of rendering obedience. [12] The study lying before us must seek to come to some judgment on the validity of Michaelis' interpretation of imitation.

In the first three chapters of our study we shall study various aspects of the background and environment of Paul's speaking of the imitation of himself. In Chapter One we shall study the word which Paul uses in speaking of imitation, μιμέομαι, surveying its usage in the Greek world, in the Jewish world, and in the New Testament world including the writings of the Apostolic Fathers. In Chapter Two we shall do the same thing for Paul's word for personal example, τύπος. In Chapter Three we shall make a survey on a broader basis than simply the use of certain Greek words. Since we shall not be limiting ourselves to the use of Greek words, we can include in Chapter Three a section on the Old Testament along with our surveys of the Greek, the Jewish, and the New Testament worlds. This time we shall attempt to examine the idea of imitation and the idea of being an example, as these pertain particularly to religion and morals, and as they come to expression in a variety of terms or are implicit in various expressions and ideas. In the section on the New Testament we shall look at the subjects of the imitation of Christ, the imitation of God, and the imitation of other men in the New Testament writings. After this background study we shall proceed in Chapter Four to an exegetical study of the various texts and their contexts in which the thought of the imitation of Paul appears. The first five sections of Chapter Four will deal with the texts in which Paul speaks *expressly* of the imitation of himself. The rest of the sections will deal with texts in which the thought is present *in effect*, though not expressly. In Chapter Five we shall offer our judgment of some of the conclusions to which others have come on this subject, and we shall bring the study to a close with a recapitulation and the drawing of our own conclusions.

Perhaps it is appropriate to add a remark or two about the form in which this study is presented. It seems proper to allow those who are being quoted to speak in their own languages as much as possible, rather than attempting always to translate their words into English. At the same time it seems appropriate to try not to be overly burdensome to the readers who are not acquainted with some of these languages. In order to accomplish both these ends, the thesis will be written in the following form. The main train of thought will be presented and carried forward in the English language. However, into this main text will be inserted paragraphs and sections in which there will appear more detailed discussions of various technical points. In these paragraphs, as well as in the footnotes, use will be made of languages other than English, when this is appropriate. These inserted paragraphs will be set off from the main text of the thesis by indentation and compressed type. In order not to break the continuity of the text unduly, some of the shorter

---

12 *Ibid.*, pp. 675, 11 — 676, 2.

discussions will be placed in the footnotes. The bibliography at the end is not to be regarded as a compilation of the books and articles on the subject of the imitation of Paul, but serves as a recapitulation of the works which have been cited in the study. The textual index includes only those texts and passages on which there has been some exegetical discussion. [13]

---

[13] Unless otherwise stated, the following texts and translations are the ones cited in this study:
Hebrew of Old Testament: *Biblia Hebraica*, ed. R. Kittel, 8th ed. by P. Kahle, A. Alt, O. Eissfeldt, Stuttgart: Privilegierte Württembergische Bibelanstalt, 1952.
Greek of Old Testament and Apocrypha: *Septuaginta*, ed. A. Rahlfs, 2 vols., Stuttgart: Privilegierte Württembergische Bibelanstalt, 1943.
Greek of New Testament: *Novum Testamentum Graece*, ed. Eb. Nestle, 23rd ed. by Erw. Nestle and K. Aland, Stuttgart: Privilegierte Württembergische Bibelanstalt, 1957.
Greek and English of Apostolic Fathers: *The Apostolic Fathers*, ed. K. Lake, 2 vols., L.C.L., London: Wm. Heinemann, 1952.
English of Old and New Testaments: *The Holy Bible, American Standard Version*, New York: Thomas Nelson and Sons, 1901.
English of Apocrypha: *The Apocrypha of the Old Testament, Revised Standard Version*, New York: Thomas Nelson and Sons, 1957.

CHAPTER ONE

# PAUL'S WORD FOR IMITATION

"Be ye imitators of me." These are Paul's words. He is the only one in the New Testament Scriptures to speak like this. He is nearly the only one to speak expressly about imitation. Outside of Paul's writings the word μιμέομαι, *imitate*, is found in the New Testament only in Hebrews and III John. However, the word was not an uncommon one in the world of the Apostle Paul. We shall begin our study of the imitation of Paul with a background investigation of μιμέομαι and its related forms. We shall make inquiry into their use in the Greek world, in the Jewish world, and in the New Testament world, including their first usage outside the New Testament writings in the Christian community of the Apostolic Fathers. This will help to recreate the background and environment of Paul's use of them.

## I. Μιμέομαι in the Greek World

The standard Greek lexicons are in agreement in giving *imitate* as the basic meaning of the word μιμέομαι.[1] The lexicons usually distinguish a secondary meaning for the word when it is used regarding the fine arts: *represent, express by means of imitation*. The word μιμέομαι and its related forms [2] can be traced back as far as the sixth century before Christ. It is not to be found in writings of the early epic poets Homer and Hesiod, but from the sixth century on it comes into general usage both in prose and poetry. Interestingly enough, these earliest appearances of the word show it being used in its supposedly derived meaning, for they are speaking of the imitation brought about through the dance and the dramatic exercises of

---

[1] Cf. e.g. H. G. Liddell, and R. Scott, *A Greek-English Lexicon*, (Revised by H. S. Jones), Oxford: Clarendon Press, 1940, *s.v.* (= imitate, represent, portray); A. Bailey, *Dictionnaire Grec-Français*, édition revue par L. Séchan et P. Chantraine, Paris: Librairie Hachette, 1950, s.v. (= imiter); H. Stephanus, *Thesaurus Graecae Linguae*, Paris: Didot, 1848ff., *s.v.* (= Imitor, Sector); F. Passow, *Handwörterbuch der Griechischen Sprache*, 5. Aufl., Leipzig: F. C. W. Vogel, 1841ff., *s.v.* (= nachahmen); W. Pape, *Griechisch-Deutsches Handwörterbuch*, Braunschweig: F. Vieweg, 1880, s.v. (= nachahmen).

[2] The following nouns were formed from the verbal root μιμη-, by the addition of the appropriate suffixes: μιμητής, *imitator* (the agent); μίμησις, *imitation* (the action); and μίμημα, *imitation, copy*, (the result). There were also various adjectival forms (μιμηλός, μιμητέος, μιμητικός, etc.) and various compounds (ἀντιμιμέομαι, ἀπομιμέομαι, συμμιμέομαι etc.). The noun μῖμος, *imitator, mimic, actor*, is also found in a number of compounded forms. Our interest is primarily in μιμέομαι, μιμητής, and συμμιμητής, the forms which appear in the New Testament.

1

the religious ritual.³ Koller finds that the concept *imitation* is not broad enough to account for the widely varied usages of μιμέομαι and its related forms among the Greeks. According to him the word can indeed mean *imitate*, but this is a derived meaning rather than the original and elementary one. The root of the word lies embedded in the ritualistic acting, singing, and dancing of the cult. Koller proposes that the fundamental meaning was *bring to expression by ritualistic dance*, and that the other usages developed from this primal idea.⁴ The essence of the idea is not so much in terms of sameness, complete likeness, exact reproduction, but rather in terms of bringing to expression, representation, portrayal.

Some of the broader reaches of the idea expressed by μιμέομαι are apparent in the writings of the pre-Socratic thinkers. The word was used to describe one of the early steps in the learning process. According to Plutarch, "Democritus [5th-4th century B. C.] declares that we [men] have been their [the animals'] pupils in matters of fundamental importance: of the spider in weaving and mending, of the swallow in homebuilding, of the sweet-voiced swan and nightingale in our imitation of their song (... ἐν ᾠδῇ κατὰ μίμησιν)."⁵ Thus for Democritus the beginnings of culture, art, and technology lie in the imitation of the natural world. Since this reference to Democritus' thought is but a passing one, it is impossible to detect any further clues as to what Democritus saw in this kind of imitation. Perhaps he was simply making the observation that man copies and learns from what he observes in the world of nature around him. However, the possibility can not be excluded that Democritus had in mind some broader and deeper relation between man and the natural world than a copying type of imitation would indicate. This becomes evident from the way μιμέομαι and its related forms are used in writings ascribed to Hippocrates, a contemporary of Democritus. Hippocrates had a different view as to the object which man imitates in his cultural and technical development. In the various techniques of the craftsmen and artisans he saw the copying not of spiders, swallows, and the natural world around man, but the copying of the nature and life of man himself, particularly as his body and its functions reveal it. He spoke of this as "imitating."⁶

Hippocrates does not necessarily mean to say that skilled workers were learning things from a direct observation and study of the human body.

---

3 Cf. *Homeric Hymn to Apollo* 163; Pindar, Fragment 107a (numbering of O. Schroeder, Leipzig, 1900); Aeschylus, Fragment 57 (numbering of A. Nauck, *Tragicorum Graecorum Fragmenta*, Leipzig, 1889). See the discussion of these passages in H. Koller, *Die Mimesis in der Antike*, Bern: A. Francke, 1954, pp. 37—40.

4 "Dabei [i.e. in Koller's study of the word] ergab sich, dass μίμησις 'Nachahmung' bedeuten kann, dass das Wort aber im übrigen ein ganz anderes Bedeutungsfeld besitzt als die Ausdrücke 'Nachahmung', 'imitatio'. *Sein Bedeutungszentrum liegt im Tanz.* μιμεῖσθαι heisst primär: 'durch Tanz zur Darstellung bringen'" (Koller, *Mimesis*, p. 119).

5 Plutarch, "De Sollertia Animalium," § 20, *Moralia* 974a (ed. H. Cherniss and W. C. Helmbold, Vol. XII, L.C.L. London: Wm. Heinemann, 1957, pp. 406,407) = Democritus, Fragment 154, (ed. H. Diels, *Die Fragmente der Vorsokratiker*, Berlin: Weidmannsche Verlagsbuchhandlung. 1952, II, p. 173, 11ff.).

6 φύσιν ἀνθρώπου καὶ βίον ταῦτα μιμεῖται. Hippocrates, ΠΕΡΙ ΔΙΑΙΤΗΣ, I. xii (ed. W. H. S. Jones. Vol. IV, L.C.L., London: Wm. Heinemann, 1931, pp. 250,251).

Neither were they necessarily reproducing what they had first observed. According to Hippocrates' view of cosmology, the human body was "a copy of the whole." [7] In the human body and its functions the pattern and nature of the whole universe was revealed to man. However, man had little consciousness of this fact, even in his instinctive copying of his own bodily functions. Hippocrates laments: "But men do not understand how to observe the invisible through the visible. For though the arts they employ are like the nature of man, yet they know it not. For the mind of the gods taught them to copy (μιμεῖσθαι) their own functions, and though they know what they are doing, yet they know not what they are copying." [8] In view of men's not knowing what they are copying, Hippocrates can hardly have in mind a conscious learning from the body and an intentional imitating of it. Rather he seems to mean that men have learned to do many things, and for each of these things a counterpart can be found in the body and its functions. Men's activities in every sphere reveal the same pattern and form as can be found in the body. This, according to Hippocrates, is what one ought to expect, for all man's activities form a part of the whole and can only be in harmony with the nature of the universe, of which we find a visible copy in man's body. Thus the imitating (μιμέομαι) spoken of points to a similarity which can be detected between various activities of man and his own body. But it also has in mind the deeper relationships which exist here. Man's body contains the pattern and nature of the whole universe. When man's technology imitates his body and its functions, this means that man is bringing to expression and effective practical use the potentialities of the universe, potentialities which have become visible to him in his body. Man in his technology often fails to realize that he is imitating his body, *i.e.* that he is bringing to expression the pattern and nature of the universe of which his body is itself an expression. Man's failure to realize what he is imitating reveals his ignorance and stupidity. Hippocrates pleads with him to learn to observe his body and study it diligently. Thus he can learn the secrets of the universe and with great benefit to himself and others bring them to expression (imitate them) in his technology. The imitation of which Hippocrates was speaking reflects a whole cosmological view of how man and the world are related and how man's potentialities are to be realized.

In the history of Greek thought, imitation was often an important concept for cosmology. Hippocrates was not the first to use the idea of μιμέομαι in this connection. Before him the Pythagoreans were already speaking of things existing by imitation (μιμήσει) of numbers. [9] It is in Plato, however, that we find the exposition and development of this theory of cosmology in such

---

[7] ἀπομίμησιν τοῦ ὅλου. *Ibid.*, I. x (Jones, pp. 246,247).

[8] *Ibid.*, I. xi (Jones, pp. 248,249). In regard to "their own functions," Jones adds the note: "Probably 'the operations of their own bodies,' but Littré translates: 'les opérations divines.'"

[9] See Aristotle, *Metaphysica*, 987b, 10ff. As to what the Pythagoreans meant by this, W. D. Ross, *Aristotle's Metaphysics*, Oxford: Clarendon Press, 1924, Vol. I, p. 163, comments: "It is probably ... that the sixth-century Pythagoreans treated things as 'imitating' number, i.e. as exhibiting numerical relations, while those of the fifth century treated number as the very stuff of which things are made."

a form that it left its imprint on Greek thinking for centuries to follow. One of Plato's discussions of the matter is found in the dialogue *Timaeus*. In this dialogue the objects of the sensual world are seen as "imitations" of the transcendent universal forms or ideas. Plato speaks, for instance, of time imitating eternity (χρόνου ... αἰῶνα μιμουμένου);[10] and the visible object being an imitation (μίμημα) of the eternal model.[11] Man was made as he is in order that he might be able to imitate god.[12] The transcendent idea constitutes the essential nature of the specific sensual object. The object is a representation, an image and likeness (εἰκών) of the idea; it imitates (μιμέομαι) the idea, and is called an imitation (μίμημα) of the idea. The idea is the model and pattern (παράδειγμα). As a representation of the idea the object gives only partial, imperfect, and transient embodiment to the eternal idea. To speak of the object as an imitation carried the connotations of partiality, reduction, and inferiority. Plato was not unaware of this. But he still found the terminology of imitation acceptable and useful in expounding his doctrine of ideas. It is significant that elsewhere he used other terms in expounding the same doctrine. In the *Republic* and *Phaedo*, the chief of the earlier dialogues in which we find this teaching about the ideas, he had spoken of the "participation" (μέθεξις) of sensible things in the forms or ideas, and of the "presence" (παρουσία) of the form in the thing. That Plato could so easily adopt the terminology of imitation in speaking of his doctrine of ideas hints at how much broader the connotations of the term "imitation" were than simply expressing copies and inferior reproductions. There was room for some thought of the idea's being present in the thing and the thing's participating in the idea.[13]

These cosmological views of Plato and the terminology which he developed in expounding them had a far-reaching influence on later Greek thinking. Plato's views were reworked by the later Pythagoreans, and also found their way into the thinking of the Stoics. In Philo we see how they were able to captivate at least certain elements of the Jewish world. There can be no doubt of their currency still in the days of the New Testament. However, there does not appear to be any direct connection between the New Testament usages of μιμέομαι and these Platonic cosmological usages. When the term

---

10 Plato, *Timaeus* 38a (ed. J. Burnet, *Platonis Opera*, Oxford: Clarendon Press, 1905, Vol. IV).
11 *Ibid.*, 48e.
12 Plato illustrates this in regard to man's vision. "God invented it and bestowed it on us that we might perceive the orbits of understanding in the heavens and apply them to the revolutions of our own thought that are akin to them (συγγενεῖς ἐκείναις οὔσας), the perturbed to the imperturbable, might learn to know them and compute them rightly and truly, and so correct the aberrations of the circles in ourselves by imitating the never erring circles of the god (μιμούμενοι τὰς τοῦ θεοῦ πάντως ἀπλανεῖς οὔσας)." *Ibid.*, 47b,c (trans. A. E. Taylor, *Plato: Timaeus and Critias*, London: Methuen and Co., 1929, p. 45).
13 We must leave it to the scholars in Platonic studies to decide how this difference of terminology in Plato's dialogues is to be best accounted for. *Cf. e.g.* A. E. Taylor, *A Commentary on Plato's Timaeus*, Oxford: Clarendon Press, 1928, pp. 27ff.; F. M. Cornford, *Plato's Cosmology*, New York: Liberal Arts Press, 1957, pp. vi ff. Our present interest is only in noting that Plato expounded his doctrine of ideas both in terms of "participation" and "imitation". He apparently did not intend to indicate two substantially different things by the two terms. As Taylor has pointed out (p. 29), Aristotle in his *Metaphysics* (987b 10ff.) saw the difference only as verbal, and not one of content.

imitation became a part of the terminology of a particular cosmological system, it often expressed nothing more than a mechanical process or an ontological relationship. The idea of an active bringing about of imitation on the part of an imitator usually vanished. Neither was there any room for a responsible ethical choice in the matter of imitating.[14] In view of the strong ethical accent in the New Testament passages, the difference of meaning from Plato's cosmological usage is quite apparent.

As we have already stated, the ancient Greeks often described the pursuit of the various fine arts in terms of μιμέομαι. The term does not strike modern ears as being particularly appropriate, at least not if it is to be understood in the sense of imitating, copying, or making exact reproductions. We can see in certain cases how dramatics, painting, sculpture, and perhaps dancing might come to be described as imitating. There are definite possibilities of being imitative here. However, to think of these activities in terms of imitation surely does not enhance their value as real art. In modern times at least, we think of art not as imitative but as creative. Furthermore, we find it much more difficult to apply the thought of art as being basically imitative to music and poetry. And yet, this is precisely the application which the Greeks made. What did they mean in speaking of the arts in terms of μιμέομαι?

In the world of fine arts Plato's name will never be forgotten because of the tirade he made against the poets in his tenth book of *The Republic* (595a ff.). He took a most dim view of the value of their art, and spoke in a most derogatory sense of the poets as being mere imitators.[15] It remains a puzzle what caused Plato to take this position here.[16] Elsewhere his attitude could be quite different.[17] Perhaps Plato was disturbed about some wrong kinds of imitation he saw being stimulated in those around him. Plato recognized that people are bound to imitate what they see and hear, and that in the end these imitations pass into character.[18] Aristotle, on the other hand, sought to rescue poetry from the bad name Plato had given it. He too recognized how natural and universal is the impulse to imitate. He found

---

14 "Je stärker der Mimesis-Begriff an das kosmologische Urbild-Abbild-Schema gebunden ist, desto mehr tritt der von ethischer Verantwortung getragene Gedanke der gehorsamen Befolgung eines Vorbildes zurück" (W. Michaelis, μιμέομαι, et. al., T.W.N.T., IV, p. 663, 50ff.)

15 Plato, The Republic, X, 597ff. (ed. P. Shorey, Vol. II, L.C.L., London: Wm. Heineman, 1946, pp. 426,427). "The imitator knows nothing worth mentioning of the thing he imitates, but that imitation is a form of play, not to be taken seriously, and ... those who attempt tragic poetry, whether iambics or heroic verse are all together imitators" (602b, pp. 446,447). "The creator of the phantom, the imitator, ... knows nothing of the reality but only the appearance" (601b, pp. 442,443). "The mimetic poet sets up in each individual soul a vicious constitution by fashioning phantoms far removed from reality" (605c, pp. 458,459).

16 Koller, *Mimesis*, pp. 67,68 remarks: "Diese Platonische Umbildung des Begriffes [bleibt] ein dialektisches Monstrum, das für die theoretische Weiterbildung der Mimesislehre noch nicht bestimmend wurde. Selbst Platon hält sich nicht weiter daran, abgesehen von je einer Stelle im 'Phaidros' und im 'Sophistes'."

17 *Cf. loc. cit.*

18 "Or have you not observed that imitations, if continued from youth far into life, settle down into habits and (second) nature in the body, the speech, and the thought?" (*Republic* III. 395d (Shorey, Vol. I, pp. 234,235).

this impulse rooted in man's highest nature, *i.e.* his intellectual nature. Aristotle says: "Imitation is natural to man from childhood, one of his advantages over the lower animals being this, that he is the most imitative creature in the world, and learns at first by imitation. And it is also natural for all to delight in works of imitation." [19] Aristotle's view of imitation here is quite different from the derogatory one of Plato. When he proposes that it is natural for everyone to delight in works of imitation, he shows how highly he thinks of imitation. His enthusiasm for imitation suggests that he was thinking of imitation in the sense of the dancer, and now the poet, bringing the harmony and rhythm, and the hidden potentialities and forces of nature to ordered and beautiful expression. [20] Imitation could convey the idea of a creative bringing to expression and portrayal. In the post-Classical period the word again came to have a bad sound, for it was used to describe the slavish copying of the art forms of the classical period. [21] Hence, we see that speaking of the fine arts in terms of imitation could convey some widely varying ideas among the Greeks, and within the range of these ideas it was possible to maintain a lofty view of artistic activity.

The word μιμέομαι was not only used in connection with the more technical and theoretical matters of cosmology or of fine arts. It also described an important part of the learning process. Dio Chrysostom (1st-2nd century A. D.) clearly illustrates what a vital role imitation played here. In his dialogue "On Homer and Socrates" he proposes that Socrates was a pupil of Homer. When this is scoffed at by the person with whom he is talking because Socrates never even saw or met Homer, Dio gains the admission that Socrates was at least a zealous follower (ζηλωτής) of Homer. Then he continues: "Then if a follower, he would also be a pupil (μαθητής). For whoever really follows anyone surely knows what that person was like, and by imitating his acts and words (μιμούμενος τὰ ἔργα καὶ τοὺς λόγους) he tries as best he can to make himself like him. But that is precisely, it seems, what the pupil does—by imitating his teacher and paying heed to him he tries to acquire his art." [22] Here we have a clear instance of μιμέομαι in the sense of doing what one sees others doing, or trying to become like others through reproducing their actions and feelings. This usage of the word from early times on was a very general and popular one, so much so as to suggest that it contained the root idea of the word.

---

[19] Aristotle, *De Poetica*, 1448b (trans. I. Bywater, in *The Works of Aristotle*, ed. W. D. Ross, Vol. XI, Oxford: Clarendon Press, 1952).

[20] *Cf.* Koller, *Mimesis*, pp. 108ff.

[21] Schmid says concerning the post-classical period from about 320 B.C. to 100 A.D.: "Die Fähigkeit, das Charakteristische der Erscheinung bis in die feinsten Einzelheiten hinein zu fassen und auszudrücken, erreicht in Poesie und bildender Kunst zu dieser Zeit ihren Höhepunkt, und dieser Verismus lässt sich durch ethisch-pädagogische Rücksichten keine Grenzen ziehen. Es ist die Blütezeit aller mimischen Gattungen in erzählender, lyrischer und dramatischer Poesie" (W. von Christ, *Geschichte der Griechischen Literatur*, 6. Aufl. [bearb. von W. Schmid u. O. Stählin], München: C. H. Beck, 1920, Vol. II, 1, p. 21. Cf. also p. 462).

[22] Dio Chrysostom, *Discourse* 55. 4,5 (ed. H. L. Crosby, Vol. IV, *L.C.L.*, London: Wm. Heinemann, 1946, pp. 384,385).

In connection with μιμέομαι and the learning processes it is to be noted that the word early found its way into the realm of ethics. There it concerned itself with a vital aspect of man's moral development. Democritus said, "It is necessary either to be good or to imitate goodness"; [23] and again, "It is a grievous thing to imitate evil men and not even to wish to imitate good ones." [24] Xenophon reveals the moral influence that lies behind imitation when he writes about Socrates: "To be sure he never professed to teach this [the desire for goodness]; but by letting his own light shine, he led his disciples to hope that they through imitation of him would attain to such excellence." [25] The same idea is found in Xenophon's account of Antipho's accosting Socrates for his poor example: "Now the professors of other subjects try to make their pupils copy their teachers: if you too intend to make your companions do that, you must consider yourself a professor of unhappiness." [26] Isocrates in his moralistic lectures returns time and again to the imitation theme in counseling his young hearers. In speaking to Demonicus about the virtues of his father Hipponicus, he says, "I have produced a sample of the nature of Hipponicus, after whom you should pattern your life as after an ensample, regarding his conduct as your law, and striving to imitate and emulate your father's virtue; for it were a shame... for children not to imitate the noble among their ancestors." [27] Later Isocrates advises Demonicus: "Pattern after the character of kings, and follow closely their ways." [28] In speaking to the young king Nicocles, Isocrates has the following counsel: "If there are men whose reputations you envy, imitate their deeds"; [29] and then in the words which he has Nicocles speak to his subjects we find, "Be not satisfied with praising good men, but imitate them as well." [30] The Greeks were keenly aware of the power of both good and bad example over the behavior and conduct of others. They recognized the important role which this kind of imitation played.

Hence, we see that μιμέομαι was used in Greek literature in a variety of ways, some of which are still common usages for the word "imitation" in the present day. The use of the word "imitation" to express certain cosmo-

---

23 ἀγαθὸν ἢ εἶναι χρεὼν ἢ μιμεῖσθαι. Democritus, Fragment 39 (Diels, II, p. 155, 5).
24 χαλεπὸν μιμεῖσθαι μὲν τοὺς κακούς, μηδὲ ἐθέλειν δὲ τοὺς ἀγαθούς. *Ibid.*, Frag. 79 (Diels, II, p. 160, 5f.).
25 ἀλλὰ τῷ φανερὸς εἶναι τοιοῦτος ὢν ἐλπίζειν ἐποίει τοὺς συνδιατρίβοντας ἑαυτῷ μιμουμένους ἐκεῖνον τοιούτους γενήσεσθαι. Xenophon, *Memorabilia*, I. 2:3 (ed. E. C. Marchant, L.C.L., London: Wm. Heinemann, 1923, pp. 12,13, and 14,15).
26 εἰ οὖν ὥσπερ καὶ τῶν ἄλλων ἔργων οἱ διδάσκαλοι τοὺς μαθητὰς μιμητὰς ἑαυτῶν ἀποδεικνύουσιν, οὕτω καὶ σὺ τοὺς συνόντας διαθήσεις, νόμιζε κακοδαιμονίας διδάσκαλος εἶναι. *Ibid.*, I. 6:3 (Marchant. pp. 68,69).
27 ... μιμητὴν δὲ καὶ ζηλωτὴν τῆς πατρῴας ἀρετῆς γιγνόμενον· αἰσχρὸν γάρ... τοὺς δὲ παῖδας μὴ μιμεῖσθαι τοὺς σπουδαίους τῶν γονέων. Isocrates, *To Demonicus*, 11 (ed. G. Norlin, L.C.L., London: Wm. Heinemann, 1928, Vol. I, pp. 10,11).
28 Μιμοῦ τὰ τῶν βασιλέων ἤθη καὶ δίωκε τὰ ἐκείνων ἐπιτηδεύματα. *Ibid.*, 36 (Norlin, pp. 26,27).
29 ὧν τὰς δόξας ζηλοῖς, μιμοῦ τὰς πράξεις. Isocrates, *To Nicocles*, 38 (Norlin, pp. 60, 61, 62, 63).
30 μὴ μόνον ἐπαινεῖτε τοὺς ἀγαθοὺς ἀλλὰ καὶ μιμεῖσθε. Isocrates, *Nicocles*, 61 (Norlin, pp. 112,113).

logical relations appears to be a usage peculiar to the Greeks and to those who adopted the idea from them. Neither has a conception of imitation persisted down to our day that would allow one to speak appreciatively of the fine arts as imitations. However, these usages must not be forgotten or ignored. They point to an important aspect of the total meaning and the array of associations found in the Greek μιμέομαι and its related forms. One does violence to the idea which comes to expression in the word by limiting and reducing it to the production of exact likenesses or inferior resemblances. The bringing of something to expression, representation, or portrayal must not be lost from sight. The factor of likeness, similarity, resemblance is of course basic to imitation. But the process of imitation need not be a dull uncreative repetition of something or someone else. Imitation may also include the creative activity of bringing things, ideas, and persons to expression. Imitation was not only a necessary and natural activity for human beings. For the Greeks it was also a most worthwhile one. They stimulated and encouraged it.

## II. Μιμέομαι in the Jewish World

Μιμέομαι and its related words are also found in the Greek writings of the Jewish world. In the Septuagint translation of the Old Testament they appear only infrequently, and then only in the apocryphal books.[31] In the *Wisdom of Solomon* 9:8 the temple is called "a copy (μίμημα) of the holy tent which thou didst prepare from the beginning."[32] In the same book we are told that the potter "competes with workers in gold and silver, and imitates (μιμεῖται) workers in copper; and he counts it his glory that he molds counterfeit gods" (15:9). The imitating and the competing express parallel thoughts in this passage; the meaning is simply that the potters engage themselves in the same kind of misspent toil in forming futile gods (vs. 8) as the various kinds of metalsmiths. Imitation merely expresses a comparison and a similarity in their activities without meaning that the coppersmiths exerted an influence over the potters, or that the potters took the coppersmiths as their examples and learned their art from them. In the *Wisdom of Solomon* we are also told that men imitate (μιμοῦνται) virtue (4:2).[33] The context argues that the way of virtue even when this means giving up hopes of having offspring is superior to entering into unlawful unions (vs. 6) and having a prolific brood (vs. 3). "For in the memory of virtue is immortality, because it is known both by God and by men. When it is present, men imitate it, and they long for it when it has gone; and throughout all time

---

31 The reading of B* in Ps. 30:7 was ἐμίμησας, but this reading has every indication of being a copyist's error for ἐμίσησας, which was the correction made by B¹ and is found in the other manuscripts. The Massoretic Text has שנאתי.

32 This is the only instance of the use of μίμημα in the Septuagint, but it may be found twice in Aquila's translation of the Old Testament: Ezek. 16:61 and 23:14.

33 Codex A and many miniscules have τιμῶσιν instead of μιμοῦνται, *i.e.* "Men honor virtue."

it marches crowned in triumph, victor in the contest for prizes that are undefiled" (vss. 1, 2). Here imitation gives indication of how the virtuous person's influence is felt in the lives of others.

In *IV Maccabees* are the only other places where the words are used in the Septuagint. Here both times they are found on the lips of martyrs. In 9:23 the eldest of the seven Jewish brothers who were martyred before their mother's eyes for not renouncing the Law of Moses calls to his brothers, "Imitate me (μιμήσασθέ με), my brothers; do not desert your post in my trial." [34] In 13:9 we are told that the seven brothers gave one another courage saying, "In brotherly fashion, brothers, let us die on behalf of the Law. Let us emulate (μιμησώμεθα) the Three Youths of Assyria who despised a similar ordeal in the furnace." [35] Thus the idea of the imitation of human conduct is to be found in the Apocrypha, but outside of the passage in *Wisdom of Solomon* 4:2, the instances are only in the very late *IV Maccabees*. The idea of the imitation of God does not appear, at least, not expressly.

The pseudepigraphal literature is quite different on this score. In the *Testament of Benjamin,* Joseph is recommended for imitation (3:1 and 4:1). The *Testament of Asher* 4:3 takes the further step of speaking of the imitation of the Lord: "[The good man] followeth the Lord's example, in that he accepteth not the seeming good as the genuine good." [36] In the *Letter of Aristeas* there is a conversation between a heathen king and his Jewish guests about what makes for a good ruler and leader. Here there are four times that the imitation of God enters the conversation: "You would maintain it [the

---

[34] Translation of M. Hadas, *The Third and Fourth Books of Maccabees,* New York: Harper and Bros., 1953, p. 197.

[35] The story of this Jewish mother and her seven sons. recorded in *II Macc.* 7 and enlarged upon in *IV Macc.* had profound influence on later Jewish and Christian readers. Their calling each other to imitate an example of resolute steadfastness even in the face of death was picked up by more than one Christian writer and applied to the situations of his day. *Cf.* Cyprian's "Exhortation to Martyrdom," Chap. 11, and Origen's "Exhortation to Martyrdom," Chap. 23ff.

[36] ... μιμεῖται Κύριον, μὴ προσδοκώμενος τὸ δοκοῦν καλὸν μετὰ τοῦ ἀληθινοῦ καλοῦ (Greek text: R. H. Charles, *The Greek Versions of the Testaments of the Twelve Patriarchs,* Oxford: Clarendon Press, 1908, p. 177; translation: R. H. Charles, *The Apocrypha and Pseudepigrapha of the Old Testament,* Oxford: Clarendon Press, 1913, Vol. II, p. 344). Michaelis, *T.W.N.T.*, IV, p. 666, 6ff., calls attention to the fact that just two verses later (in vs. 5) we read: "(Good men) walk in zeal for the Lord (ἐν ζήλῳ θεοῦ πορεύονται) and abstain from what God also hateth and forbiddeth by his commandment." In regard to this walking in zeal for the Lord, Michaelis says: "Gott nacheifern = den Herrn nachahmen, das heisst: sich an seine Gebote halten" (ll. 8,9). One wonders what has brought Michaelis to use an equation sign here in regard to the ideas of *nacheifern* and *nachahmen.* It is true that the two ideas are often found together, as Michaelis has noted (p. 664, 21ff; p. 677, 41ff; *cf.*, also Isocrates, *To Demonicus,* 11 (cited above, p. 7, fn. 27). Furthermore, ζῆλος may indicate a zeal in imitating, as A. Stumpff shows from an instance in Plutarch (ζῆλος, *T.W.N.T.*, II, p. 879, 37ff.); after listing other Greek citations he concludes: "Das Wort dient hier durchweg zur Bezeichnung eines edlen ethischen Motivs zur Vervollkommnung des Charakters..." (ll. 42,43). Apparently it is on the basis of this meaning and usage of ζῆλος that Michaelis makes his assertion "Gott nacheifern = den Herrn nachahmen." But is there any indication that the imitation of vs. 3 and the walking in zeal of vs. 5 are here to be equated? The content of the imitation of vs. 3 is specifically stated. The good man does what the Lord does: he differentiates between true good and apparent good. If the reference in vs. 5 to the keeping of God's commandments gives any indication of the specific meaning, usage, and content of the word μιμέομαι, it is certainly a more attenuated one than the statement of Michaelis would lead one to believe.

kingdom] best by imitating (μιμούμενος) the constant gentleness of God"; [37] "for as God is the benefactor of the whole world, so would you, imitating (μιμούμενος) Him, be devoid of offense": [38] chief magistrates ought to be "those who have a hatred of evil and emulate (μιμούμενος) the conduct of their ruler [*i.e.* God]"; [39] and "For just as God benefits all men, so do you in emulation (μιμούμενος) of Him, benefit those subject to you." [40] If there is little evidence of imitation in matters of human conduct in the Old Testament and Apocrypha, the idea has at least established itself in the Pseudepigrapha.

In Philo the use of μιμέομαι and the related words is very common. The influence of Plato's cosmological views on Philo is seen in his very frequent use of μίμημα to express the relation of the earthly realm to its heavenly counterpart. He uses μίμημα in this way more than sixty times. Μιμέομαι and μιμητής on the other hand show the more ordinary Greek usages. While there are instances in which μιμέομαι expresses simply a comparison, as when a sickness creeping through the body "imitates (μιμουμένη) the force of fire working on an abundance of fuel," [41] usually it expresses the imitation of an example. Moses' life is "a well-wrought picture, a piece of work beautiful and godlike, a model for those who are willing to copy it." [42] Imitation is normal for pupils: "Now the first virtue of beginners is to desire that their imperfection may imitate (μιμεῖσθαι) as far as possible the perfection of the teacher." [43] On another occasion Philo distinguishes between the "learner" and the "practicer": "It is a characteristic mark of the learner that he listens to a voice and to words, since by these only is he taught, whereas he who acquires the good through practice, and not through teaching, fixes his attention not on what is said, but on those who say it, and imitates their life (μιμούμενος τὸν ἐκείνων βίον) as shown in the blamelessness of their successive actions." [44] Philo finds imitation following of necessity in loyal children: "Necessarily then do His [God's] loyal children imitate their Father's nature and, with a forwardness that brooks no delay, do what is excellent, and the most excellent deed of all is before aught else to honor God." [45]

Michaelis finds this citation "Beachtenswert." He explains it thus: "die gehorsamen Kinder, indem sie das Wesen des Vaters nachahmen,

---

[37] *Letter of Aristeas* 188 (ed. M. Hadas, *Aristeas to Philocrates*, New York: Harper & Bros., 1951, pp. 174,175).
[38] *Ibid.* 210 (Hadas, pp. 182,183).
[39] *Ibid.* 280 (Hadas, pp. 210,211).
[40] *Ibid.* 281 (*Loc. cit.*).
[41] Philo, *De Specialibus Legibus* IV. 83 (ed. F. H. Colson and G. H. Whitaker, L.C.L., London: Wm. Heinemann, 1929–1941, VIII, pp. 58,59).
[42] παράδειγμα τοῖς ἐθέλουσι μιμεῖσθαι. *De Vita Mosis* I, 158 (Colson and Whitaker, VI, pp. 358,359). Notice the use of τύπον in the next sentence: "Happy are they who imprint... that image (τύπον) in their souls."
[43] *De Sacrificiis Abelis et Caini* 64 (Colson and Whitaker, II, pp. 142,143).
[44] *De Congressu Quaerendae Eruditionis Gratia* 69 (Colson and Whitaker, IV, pp. 492,493).
[45] Δεόντως οὖν μιμούμενοι τὴν τοῦ πατρὸς φύσιν οἱ ὑπήκοοι παῖδες ἀμελλητὶ μετὰ σπουδῆς πάσης τὰ καλὰ δρῶσιν, ὧν ἔργον ἐστὶ κάλλιστον ἡ ἀνυπέρθετος θεοῦ τιμή. *De Sacrificiis Abelis et Caini* 68 (Colson and Whitaker, II, pp. 142,143).

tun notwendig das Gute... [Greek text cited in part], dh indem der
G e h o r s a m erwähnt ist, erhält das Nachahmen den Charakter des
Befolgens der Gebote des Vaters." [46] In view of the conclusions to which
Michaelis comes regarding many of the New Testament passages on
imitation, namely, that the emphasis is on the recognition of authority
and on obedience, [47] it is easy to understand Michaelis' interest in this
present sentence from Philo. However, the question may be raised
whether obedience to the commands of a father really plays as central
a role in the statement here as Michaelis gives it. The passage is from
Philo's treatise, "The Sacrifice of Abel and Cain," an allegorical interpretation of Gen. 4:2—4. Philo explains the underlying philosophical
thought of the terms "Cain" and "Abel" thus: "There are two opposite
and contending views of life, one which ascribes all things to the mind
as our master, whether we are using our reason or our senses, in motion
or at rest, the other which follows God, whose handiwork it believes
itself to be." [48] In connection with Gen. 4:3, "And it came to pass after
some days that Cain brought of the fruits of the earth as a sacrifice to
the Lord," Philo brings several charges against the Cain spirit, among
them that he offered only "after some days." This naturally leads to a
homily on the duty of ready service and of avoiding all delay. In this
connection he dwells on the timelessness of God's actions, which we
should imitate in our worship (sections 64—68). This is contrasted with
Pharaoh's postponement of Moses' prayers on his behalf (section 69),
and in Pharaoh Philo sees an illustration of the human tendency to seek
help in misfortune in every possible earthly remedy rather than turn to
God (sections 70—71). He closes his consideration of the first charge
against the Cain spirit with this summarizing statement: "So then every
imagination which counts that all things are its own possession and
honours itself before God... may know that it stands in danger to be
brought to the judgement-bar for impiety." [49] In the broad context Philo
then is contrasting two basic views of life: the one where man recognizes
God as Creator and himself as his creature (cf. "whose handiwork it
believes itself to be"), the other where man sees himself to be his own
ruler and goal (cf. "all things are its own possession and honours itself
before God"). In such a context to speak of οἱ ὑπήκοοι παῖδες and in
the very next sentence to present their contrast in Pharaoh, who has no
eye for the timeless values displayed in God, suggests that ὑπήκοοι has
in mind a more fundamental relationship than that expressed by obedience
to God's commands. It speaks of the men who recognize themselves as
his creatures and subjects, as over against men who see themselves as
autonomous. [50] The idea indeed includes the obedience to commands,
but it sees the whole matter more broadly than this. Perhaps the
translation by Colson and Whitaker of "loyal children" catches the spirit
of the phrase as well as any.

Nevertheless, Michaelis was quite correct in calling this statement
about imitation from Philo noteworthy. It is noteworthy not so much
for the combination of the ideas of obedience and imitation, but rather

---

[46] T.W.N.T., IV, p. 667, 13—17.
[47] See especially T.W.N.T., IV, p. 675, 1—8.
[48] Sacr. Abel. et Cain. 2 (Colson and Whitaker, II, pp. 94,95).
[49] Ibid. 71 (Colson and Whitaker, II, pp. 148,149).
[50] Cf. the use of ὑπήκοοι as a term for the subject allies of Athens in distinction from the αὐτόνομοι, the independent allies, in Thucydides 7. 57. Philo's words are translated "die unterwürfigen Kinder" by both L. Cohn, Die Werke Philos von Alexandria, Vol. III, Breslau: M. & H. Marcus, 1919, p. 242; and in Bibliothek der griechischen und römischen Schriftsteller über Judentum und Juden, ed. L. Philippson et al., Bd. IV (Philo), Leipzig: Oskar Leinar, 1870, p. 20.

for presenting imitation as a taking on by the children of the nature
and characteristics of their father. Philo is in the midst of his homily
on the duty of ready service. He has been urging the consideration of
how swiftly and immediately God acts: "But the divine Teacher is swifter
than Time.... God spake and it was done—no interval between the
two.... Now even amongst us mortals there is nothing swifter than
a word.... But if the word has proved swifter than all, much more is
it so with Him... [and Philo goes on to reason about God's omnipresence]" (sections 66—68). Then comes the passage about imitation, flowing
naturally from the preceding (cf. οὖν), and emphasizing that loyal children
imitate their Father's nature, do what is excellent ἀμελλητὶ μετὰ σπουδῆς
πάσης, *without hesitation with all haste*, and that the best deed is
ἡ ἀνυπέρθετος θεοῦ τιμή, the *immediate* honoring of God. Philo continues, "But Pharaoh the 'Disperser of the excellent' cannot receive the
vision of timeless values." For when he was plagued by the frogs and
Moses asked him to appoint a time for prayer, "though in that dire
strait he should have said 'Pray for me at once,' he puts it off with the
word 'tomorrow'" (section 69). The thing to which Pharaoh is oblivious,
but which the loyal children have learned from their Father, is his
immediacy of action. This is his characteristic, and the children have
come to have the same characteristic. This is what Philo is speaking
of when he describes them as imitating their Father's nature. Michaelis'
statement, "Die gehorsamen Kinder, indem sie das Wesen des Vaters
nachahmen, tun notwendig das Gute," can only be understood as a
further inference from Philo's words, and not as the point of the
statement in the context in which it stands.[51] His further explanation,
"Indem der G e h o r s a m erwähnt ist, erhält das Nachahmen den
Charakter des Befolgens der Gebote des Vaters," presents a combination
of ideas which is not to the point, when the passage is placed in its original
context. The imitation of this passage is the following of the Father's
nature, not the following of his commands.

The citations from Philo about imitation being normal for pupils, and a
necessity for loyal children, actually had to do with the imitation of God
in the figure of a teacher and father. Philo does not hesitate to speak directly
about the imitation of God. On one occasion he speaks of the Logos imitating
the Father: "The Son thus begotten followed (μιμούμενος) the ways of His
Father, and shaped the different kinds, looking to the archetypal patterns
which the Father supplied."[52] Parents too are imitators of God in their
bringing forth children from non-existence to existence.[53] When Philo speaks
of the lesson "that a man should imitate God as much as may be and leave
nothing undone that may promote such assimilation as is possible,"[54] he

---

[51] Michaelis' citation of the Greek has a remarkable ellipsis which leaves out the crucial words ἀμελλητὶ μετὰ σπουδῆς πάσης (see *T.W.N.T.*, IV, p. 667, 15).

[52] *De Confusione Linguarum* 63 (Colson and Whitaker, IV, pp. 44,45).

[53] *De Decalogo* 111. *Cf.* sect. 107: "The act of generation assimilates (ἐξομοίωσιν) them to God, the generator of the All"; and sects. 119,120: "For parents are the servants of God for the task of begetting children.... Some bolder spirits... say that a father and a mother are in fact gods revealed to sight who copy (μιμούμενοι) the Uncreated in His work as the Framer of life." Apparently the imitation in sects. 111 and 120 is expressive simply of a similarity of action, although something of Platonic cosmological views undoubtedly underlies this similarity.

[54] *De Virtutibus* 168 (Colson and Whitaker, VIII, pp. 266,267). *Cf.* also *De Specialibus Legibus*, IV, 188.

undoubtedly has the passage from Plato's *Theaetetus* in mind, *i.e.* that flying away from earth to heaven is to become "like God, so far as this is possible." [55] Philo sees the imitation of God as a general rule for human conduct: "To imitate God's works is a pious act"; [56] and "what greater good can there be than that they [men] should imitate God." [57]

Philo also uses the substantive μιμητής on several occasions. According to him, ungrateful men ought to become imitators of the animals, who show appreciation of kindnesses offered. [58] Joshua was an imitator of Moses' characteristics. [59] The usages are ordinary and do not add new material.

Josephus' use of these words was according to their common usage. [60] Usually it was a matter of the conscious imitation of some good or bad characteristic or action. Sometimes it was merely the expression of a comparison. Josephus does not speak of an imitation of God.

Thus it becomes apparent that after a total absense of μιμέομαι and its related forms in the Septuagint translation of the canonical Old Testament scriptures, the word has come to be used with considerable frequency in later Jewish writings. Under the influence of Greek philosophy it is sometimes found expressing cosmological relations; sometimes also it expresses a simple comparison or likeness. But a very frequent and common usage is in connection with the processes of human development, where one person, being under the influence of another, or at least in acquaintance with another, seeks to become like that person in a certain respect. He imitates him.

### III. Μιμέομαι in the New Testament World

It is not necessary at this point in our study to give more than the briefest survey of the use of the word in the New Testament, since in the progress of our study we shall have occasion to look more thoroughly at all of these texts. Μιμέομαι and two related forms (μιμητής and συμμιμητής) are found eight times in the letters of Paul, two times in the epistle to the Hebrews, and once in John's third epistle. [61] The command in III John 11 is the most

---

55   *Theaetetus* 176a,b. *Cf.* below, p. 27. In *De Fuga et Inventione* 63 Philo quotes this passage from Plato, naming the treatise.
56   *Legum Allegoriae* 48 (Colson and Whitaker I, pp. 176,177).
57   *De Specialibus Legibus* IV, 73 (Colson and Whitaker VIII, pp. 52,53).
58   *De Decalogo* 114.
59   *De Virtutibus* 66.
60   Michaelis, *T.W.N.T.*, IV. p. 668, 5ff.
61   In I Peter 3:13 the reading of μιμηταί is found only in the late Koine family of texts, as over against ζηλωταί with support from all the rest of the textual tradition. Keil offers a likely explanation of the divergence: "Warscheinlicher ist die Vermutung, dass man τοῦ ἀγαθοῦ wegen des Artikels im Unterschieden von dem artikellosen ἀγαθόν v. 11 für den Genitiv Maskul. hielt, wie mit älteren Ausll., *Lorinus, Aretius* u. A. noch Wiesg. [*i.e.* Wiesinger] meinte, dass wol Christus darunter verstanden werden könte, wozu dann ζηλωταί nicht passte, so dass es nach Stellen wie Eph. 5:1, I Thess. 1:6 in μιμηταί geändert wurde (Huth.) [*i.e.* Huther]. (C. F. Keil, *Commentar über die Briefe des Petrus und Judas*, Leipzig: Dörffling und Franke, 1883, p. 115, fn.1). *Cf.* also S. Greijdanus, *De Brieven van de Apostelen Petrus en Johannes,*

abstract and general of the New Testament references. John admonishes Gaius: "Imitate not (μὴ μιμοῦ) that which is evil but that which is good." However, in spite of the general terms, there can be little doubt that John has in mind human conduct as exemplified by certain persons which he is recommending.[62] In Hebrews 6:12 the author expresses his great desire for his readers in the following words: "that ye be not sluggish, but imitators (μιμηταί) of them who through faith and patience inherit the promises." In Heb. 13:7 there is the exhortation: "Considering the issue of their life, imitate (μιμεῖσθε) their faith." Hence it is clear that in these non-Pauline passages imitation has to do with bringing to expression in one's life something he has witnessed in another.

In the letters of Paul the reference is six times to the imitation of Paul himself, or of Paul together with his associates: I Cor. 4:16; 11:1; Phil. 3:17; I Thess. 1:6; and II Thess. 3:7,9. In two of these passages the imitation of Christ also comes to the fore: "Be ye imitators of me, even as I also am of Christ" (I Cor. 11:1); and "Ye became imitators of us, and of the Lord" (I Thess. 1:6). These are the only places in the New Testament where the imitation of Christ is literally expressed. Paul also has a command to imitate God (Eph. 5:1). Then in I Thess. 2:14 he speaks of being imitators of the churches of Judea. Thus Paul too speaks of imitation in connection with human conduct. To what extent it is simply expressive of a comparison or a likeness, and to what extent it expresses an activity of bringing to expression in one's life what has been witnessed in another must be further studied and clarified. But at least there appear to be no Greek cosmological concepts at work here.[63]

The writings of the Apostolic Fathers which have come down to us show that in the days immediately following the writing of the New Testament books the thought expressed in the word μιμέομαι had become much more common in the Christian community. As over against 11 times in the whole New Testament, the word (and its cognates, including the rare ἀντιμιμέομαι) is found 18 times in the writings of the Apostolic Fathers, a body of writings about half the size of the New Testament. Ignatius comments on how disastrous it would be if God were to imitate our actions (*To the Magnesians* 10:1). He also admonishes to take care not to imitate (ἀντιμιμήσασθαι) the conduct of the opponents of Christianity (*To the Ephesians* 10:2). Several times exemplary men are held up for imitation: the prophets and famous men of old (*I Clement* 17:1); Polycarp, "whose martyrdom all desire to imitate"

---

en de Brief van Judas, K.N.T., Amsterdam: H. A. van Bottenburg, 1929, p. 134, who calls attention to the fact that the preceding context (2:21ff.) speaks of Jesus as example. In this textual divergence we again see the close relationship of ζηλωτής and μιμητής as noted above, fn. 36.

[62] See discussion of passage below, p. 85.

[63] Schoeps refers to Paul's use of the "aus platonischem Sprachgebrauch stammende μιμεῖσθαι" (H. J. Schoeps, "Von der Imitatio Dei zur Nachfolge Christi," *Aus Frühchristlicher Zeit*, Tübingen: J. C. B. Mohr (Paul Siebeck). 1950, p. 293). However, μιμέομαι was in common usage in the Greek language both before and after Plato. Plato's references to men being μιμηταί is usually in the sense of their being producers of an imitation rather than the real thing, and the tone in which Plato speaks of this is usually derogatory (*cf. Sophists* 235a, 268c; *Gorgias* 513b; *Statesman* 303c; *Republic* X, 597ff.).

(*Martyrdom of Polycarp* 19:1, *cf.* 1:2); Burrhus, who was "a pattern (ἐξεμπλάριον) of the ministry of God" (Ignatius, *To the Smyrnaeans* 12:1). However, it is the imitation of God, the Lord, or Jesus Christ which has really come to its own in these writings: *cf.* *Diognetus* 10:4 (twice),5,6; Ignatius, *To the Ephesians* 1:1 (where the imitation of God probably refers to Christ; *cf.* in the same verse: "the blood of God"); 10:3; *To the Philadelphians* 7:2 ("Be imitators of Jesus Christ, as was he also of his Father"); *To the Romans* 6:3 ("Suffer me to follow the example [μιμητὴν εἶναι] of the passion of my God" = Christ); *To the Trallians* 1:2; Polycarp, *To the Philippians* 1:1; [64] 8:2; and *Martyrdom of Polycarp* 17:3. An interesting phenomenon in the Apostolic Fathers is the connection which has developed between imitation and martyrdom: *e.g.*, "the martyrs we love as disciples and imitators of the Lord" (*Mart. Pol.* 17:3); *cf.* 19:1; Ign., *Rom.* 6:3, etc. It is also interesting to note that in this relatively frequent reference to imitation no one has followed Paul's example and called for the imitation of himself.

\* \* \*

From the foregoing survey of the use of the word μιμέομαι and its related forms it becomes evident that Paul was introducing no new idea or terminology when he chose to use it in his letters. He had well-established Greek usage behind him, as well as the use of the term in the Greek writings which the Jewish community had produced. There was a breadth of content in the Greek word which can not be subsumed under the idea of imitation in the sense of merely producing the same thing or a likeness. At its root the word carried the thought of bringing to expression, representation, and portrayal. While this thought was by no means prominent in much Greek usage of the word, the possibility that it hovered in the background of the word by way of the array of associations which a usage of the word brought may not be disregarded. From early times the Greeks had noticed that an essential part of the growth and educational process in human beings is by the process of imitation. This applied not alone in developing mechanical skills, but fully as much in the development of character and in the formation of one's customs, ways, and way of life. In the process of developing by way of imitation parents and teachers played a most important role as example. In some of the Jewish writings current in Paul's day there was no hesitation to recommend God as an example to be imitated. God is then usually held up in terms of moral perfection and pre-eminence, and the accent is strongly moralistic. When Paul spoke of the imitation of God, his terminology was not new, but the point he was making may not have been the same. Whether it was an innovation when Paul spoke of the imitation of Christ or not is something

---

[64] δεχαμένοις τὰ μιμήατα τῆς ἀληθοῦς ἀγάπης; the meaning of the phrase is not clear. Lightfoot's translation and explanation is reasonable: "'*since ye welcomed those copies of the true Love*'. The reference is doubtless to Ignatius and his companions, to whom the Philippians showed attention when halting there on their way to Rome; . . . . They were imitators of Christ who is the true Love" (J. B. Lightfoot, *The Apostolic Fathers*, Part II, Vol. III, London: Macmillan, 1889, p. 322).

we shall probably never know. At least the earliest records we presently have of the expression are in Paul. It was a thought which took hold in the minds of the young Christians and was to come to very widespread usage after Paul's time. However, when it came to speaking of imitation, Paul spoke most often about the imitation of himself. The words were all common enough; and yet there was nothing common about using them in such personal reference. Why did Paul place such emphasis on the imitation of himself? Was Paul's appeal as moralistic as many of the Greek and Jewish appeals to imitation were? These matters call for further investigation.

CHAPTER TWO

## PAUL'S WORD FOR PERSONAL EXAMPLE

In Paul's letters the term τύπος three times appears in close connection with the idea of imitation. Twice Paul refers to himself as being a τύπος for his readers to imitate: II Thess. 3:9 and Phil. 3:17. Once he speaks of the Thessalonians as being a τύπος to others now that they had become imitators of him: I Thess. 1:6,7. Τύπος is an essential part of the whole train of Paul's thought on imitation. We shall again seek to recapture the background and environment of the word as used by Paul by taking note of its usage in the Greek world, in the Jewish world, and in the New Testament world.

### I. Τύπος in the Greek World

In classical times, as well as in New Testament times, τύπος expressed a variety of ideas. Probably we approach the meaning of the word better by way of the verb τυπόω, *to form by impressing*, than by way of τύπτω, *to strike a blow*.[1] Basically τύπος was a form used to give shape to something, a hollow mold.[2]

> The root form of τύπος has often been traced to τύπτω, *to beat, strike*, thus making τύπος in its basic form *a blow*.[3] Evidence for this latter position is usually found in the words of the Oracle as quoted by Herodotus. The Oracle says that the bones of Orestes will be found where "... τύπος ἀντίτυπος καὶ πῆμ' ἐπὶ πήματι κεῖται."[4] The bones were eventually found in the courtyard of a blacksmith shop, and Herodotus' solution of the riddle is that the anvil and hammer (τὸν ἄκμονα καὶ τὴν σφῦραν) are the τύπος ἀντίτυπος and the forged iron the anguish laid upon anguish.[5] The idea *blow* is found by some in this use of τύπος: *e.g.* "blow against blow";[6] "shock and counter-

---

1 B. Rigaux, *St. Paul: Épitres aux Thessaloniciens*, E.B., Paris/Gembloux: Gabalda, Duculot, 1956, p. 384.

2 A. von Blumenthal, "ΤΥΠΟΣ und ΠΑΡΑΔΕΙΓΜΑ," *Hermes, Zeitschrift für Klassische Philologie*, LXIII (1928), p. 395.

3 Liddell-Scott, *Lexicon*, *s.v.*; Pape, *Handwörterbuch*, *s.v.* (= Schlag); Stephanus, *Thesaurus*, *s.v.* (= ictus).

4 Herodotus, I. 67 (ed. A. D. Godley, Vol. I, *L.C.L.*, London: Wm. Heinemann, 1931, pp. 80,81): "Shock makes answer to shock, and anguish is laid upon anguish."

5 *Ibid.* I. 68 (Godley, pp. 82,83).

6 Liddell-Scott, *Lexicon*, *sub* ἀντίτυπος.

shock."[7] It is interesting to notice the details of Herodotus' explanation. He states that the τύπος ἀντίτυπος are the anvil and hammer; he states them in that order. In the light of a careful study of the context Blumenthal has concluded that the Greek text must originally have read τύπος ἀντιτύπῳ;[8] and in the light of his study of τύπος, its related forms, and its composite forms (including ἀντίτυπος), he concludes that the idea expressed is *form* rather than *blow*. He would translate the Oracle, "Wo Form auf Abbild liegt und Leid auf Leid."[9] Interestingly enough, the old translation of Rev. W. Beloe already had it this way: "Where form to form with mutual strength replies."[10] The evidence Blumenthal gathers points in the direction of *hollow mold* as being the basic idea of τύπος. Possibly there is some specific kind of mold at the basis of the word. In view of a possible clue which he discovers, Blumenthal conjectures, "Ich möchte vermuten... dass τύπος zuerst 'Brotform' war. Doch das lässt sich nicht beweisen."[11]

By a very natural transition τύπος came to be used not only for "the form", but for "the thing formed". The latter became a very common and widespread usage. Τύπος was used for the impression of a seal, the stamp on a coin, the print of something (footprint, imprint of teeth), an engraved mark, printed letters, castings, replicas made in a mold, poured images and statues. The step was but a slight one to expand the meaning of τύπος to anything that was a copy or reproduction, regardless of whether a specific mold had been used or not, such as figures worked in relief by modelling or sculpture, carved figures, images, idols. Another expansion of the basic idea is found in the use of τύπος for rough, crude, unfinished shape or form, as when Empedocles proposed in connection with the origin of man that "undifferentiated forms (τύποι) rose from the earth."[12] Such a usage may have developed from thinking of a statue as already having its fixed form to a certain extent when it was merely a roughly hewn block of marble fresh from the quarry.[13] Thus, τύποι might be mere sketches, rough drafts, things in outline form, the general idea of a thing. The thing itself could be reduced to its bare outline, its τύπος. However, the τύπος is not necessarily of lesser significance than the thing itself. As over against the entirety of the thing, where encumbrances and unessential parts abound, the τύπος reveals the essential form.[14] Hence, τύπος may express the idea of the pattern, model, archetype, norm of a thing. In Plato's *Republic* there is a dialogue over education and over what kind of poetry ought to be permitted for the

---

[7] Godley, *Herodotus*, p. 83; cf. also "coup et contra-coup", Ph.-E. Legrand, *Herodotus, Histoires*, Livre 1, Paris: Société d'Édition "Les Belles Lettres," 1956, p. 71.
[8] Blumenthal, *Hermes*, LXIII, p. 393.
[9] *Ibid.*, p. 409.
[10] W. Beloe, *Herodotus*, Vol. I, London: 1825, p. 48.
[11] Blumenthal, *Hermes*, LXIII, p. 395.
[12] Empedocles 62,4. (Translation of Liddell-Scott, *sub* τύπος VI, 2.)
[13] Blumenthal, *Hermes*, LXIII, pp. 404,405.
[14] J. E. Heyde, "Typus — Ein Beitrag zur Bedeutungsgeschichte des Wortes Typus," *Forschungen und Fortschritte*, XVII (1941), p. 220: "Τύπος heisst m.E. also einerseits mehr abwertend (im Gegensatz zum Ganzen des Dinges) blosser Umriss (Nachbild), anderseits mehr aufwertend (im Gegensatz zum Unwesentlichen am Dinge) Muster (Vorbild)."

young.[15] The word τύπος enters the discussion repeatedly: "To founders (of a state) it pertains to know the patterns (τύπους) on which poets must compose their fables";[16] "the patterns (οἱ τύποι) or norms of right speech about the gods, what would they be";[17] "this then ... will be one of the laws and patterns (νόμων τε καὶ τύπων) concerning the gods to which speakers and poets will be required to conform";[18] "by all means, ... I accept these norms (τύπους), and would use them as canons and laws."[19] Τύπος thus may have definite normative implications.

Τύπος is also used in regard to a model, pattern, or standard for human behavior. It may designate a person or persons who are in a position which makes them an example to others and who set the standard or establish the pattern of the way of life for others. For instance, a fragment from the writings of Democritus tells us that "those who fail to follow the pattern (τύπος) of diligence and thrift of the fathers are wont to come to ruin."[20] The element of example is very clear in the inscription found at Nemrud Dagh in which Antiochus I, a king of Commagene in the first century before Christ, says: "I have exhibited to the youth ... an example (τύπον) of the piety which a devout person shows toward the gods and his ancestors."[21] It is with this use of τύπος to express an example that we shall be the most concerned in the pursuit of this present study.

The range of meanings of the word τύπος finally reduces to two basic ones: "the form" and "the thing formed."[22] As a "form" it may be a mold, die, archetype, pattern, model, example. As a "thing formed" it may be an impression, molding, replica, sculpture, image. The usage of the word for such general concepts as shape, over-all form, outline stands between these two areas of meaning, but may point in the direction of either or both of them.

## II. Τύπος in the Jewish World

The same variety of meanings for τύπος that is found in the Greek world is found in the Greek language used by the Jewish community. Τύπος is found only twice in the Septuagint translation of the Old Testament, but these two instances clearly show the two basic usages of the word. In Amos 5:26 it is "the thing formed," an image: "Yea, ye have borne the tabernacle of your king and the shrine of your images (τύπους), the star of your god,

---

15 Book II, Section XVII ff.
16 Plato, *The Republic,* 379a (Shorey, I, pp. 182,183).
17 *Loc. cit.* (οἱ τύποι περὶ θεολογίας τίνες ἂν εἶεν).
18 *Ibid.* 380c (Shorey, pp. 188,189).
19 *Ibid.* 383c (Shorey, pp. 198,199).
20 οὗτοι, ἤν ἁμάρτωσι τοῦ πατρικοῦ τύπου τοῦ ἐπιμελέος καὶ φειδωλοῦ, φιλέουσι διαφθείρεσθαι. Democritus 228. (Diels, II, p. 191).
21 τύπον δὲ εὐσεβείας, ἣν θεοῖς καὶ προγόνοις εἰσφέρειν ὅσιον, ἐγὼ παισὶν ... ἐκτέθεικα. *Orientis Graeci Inscriptiones Selectae* 383, 212f. (ed. W. Dittenberger, Leipzig: S. Hirzel, 1903, Vol. I, p. 603).
22 *Cf.* K. J. Woollcombe, "The Biblical Origins and Patristic Development of Typology," in *Essays on Typology,* (Studies in Biblical Theology, No. 22), London: SCM Press, 1957, p. 61.

which ye made to yourselves." In Exod. 25:39(40) it is "the form", the pattern; God tells Moses to be sure to make these things "after their pattern (τύπον), which hath been showed thee in the mount."

In the Apocrypha and Pseudepigrapha there are also instances where τύπος is used in these well-established senses. *III Macc.* 3:30 tells us that "such was the form (τύπος) of the letter that was written." In *IV Macc.* 6:19 we read the warning lest "we should prove to be a model (τύπος) of impiety to the young by setting an example for the eating of forbidden food."[23] Thus far the Jewish writers are using the word in the same general way as the Greek writers.

In Josephus the usage of τύπος does not seem to go beyond the ordinary range of meanings found in the Greek writers. In Philo also the ordinary usages occur.[24] But sometimes in Philo τύπος is found with a new content related to Philo's philosophic views. He proposed that God not only created the world, but that before creating the world he created a pattern according to which the world was to be made. Philo compared God's activity to that of an architect who plans a city before he begins the building of it. All the different parts become stamped on his mind as an impression of a seal is stamped on wax. He builds the city according to the pattern which he has in his mind. So was it with God also. "When he was minded to found the one great city, God conceived beforehand the models (τύπους) of its parts, and out of these he constituted and brought to completion a world discernible only by the mind, and then with that for a pattern, the world which our senses perceive."[25] Hence, God created a pattern-world and a perceptible world. The perceptible world is well-known to us because of the information we constantly receive from our senses. However, the pattern-world can also be known to us, for in creating man, God followed the pattern of the Logos, the archetype of rational existence.[26] Since we are rational and have a mind, we may discern the τύποι, the archetypal patterns existing in the world of ideas. It was one of these patterns which God showed to Moses and impressed on his mind while he was on Mt. Sinai, so that afterwards Moses could have the tabernacle constructed precisely according to that pattern.[27] Thus we see that Philo, influenced as he was by Plato, gives expression to certain ideas about cosmology in which τύπος is a pattern or model with definite cosmological content.

---

[23] Hadas, *Maccabees*, p. 179.
[24] *Cf.* the interesting instance of τύπος used with μιμέομαι, cited above, p. 10, fn. 42.
[25] *De Opificio Mundi* 19 (Colson and Whitaker, I, pp. 16,17).
[26] *De Specialibus Legibus* III, 207: For it is the mind of man which has the form of God, being shaped in conformity with the ideal archetype, the Word that is above all." (Colson and Whitaker, VII, pp. 604,605).
[27] *De Vita Mosis* II, 76: "So the shape (τύπος) of the model was stamped upon the mind of the prophet, a secretly painted or moulded prototype, produced by immaterial and invisible forms; and then the resulting work was built in accordance with that shape (πρὸς τὸν τύπον) by the artist impressing the stampings upon the material substances required in each case" (Colson and Whitaker, VI, pp. 486,487).

## III. Τύπος in the New Testament World

It was against this whole background and in such an environment of word-usage that the various New Testament writers chose τύπος to express their thoughts. Since their language was essentially popular, their use of individual words shows the freedom and variety that are usually found in the speech current among common people. Actually among the fifteen times that the word τύπος is used in the New Testament, there is a good cross section of the common Greek usages of the word. In John 20:25 there is the elementary meaning of a mark or impression made by a hard substance upon a softer one: "Except I shall see in his hands the print (τύπον) of the nails, and put my finger into the print (τύπον) of the nails...." In Acts 7:43 (quoting Amos 5:26) it is an image; in Acts 7:44 and Heb. 8:5 (both quoting Exod. 25:40), it is again the pattern or model of the tabernacle. There is the letter of Claudias Lysias about the Apostle Paul which was written "after this form" (τὸν τύπον τοῦτον) (Acts 23:25). The expression undoubtedly seeks to convey the thought that the essence of the letter has been reproduced in what the author of Acts has included in his account.[28] In Rom. 6:17 we read of the "form of teaching" (τύπον διδαχῆς) to which the Romans had been delivered and to which they had become obedient. The expression has been variously understood. Some have read τύπος here in the sense of an outline or summary and have seen in this verse an indication of an early form of Christian catechism or creed.[29] However, it is possible to read it also as expressing simply the basic idea of form or mould. Thus Beare proposes that Paul is thinking of "the Didache which belongs to the Gospel, the teaching concerning the way of life which is worthy of the Gospel of Christ, considered as a mould which gives to the new life its appropriate shape or pattern."[30] The most prominent use of τύπος in the New Testament is in the sense of a personal example, a pattern of human behavior personally mediated and exercising a formative influence over those coming in contact with it:

---

[28] Bauer proposes that it is perhaps preferable to think of the *content* here than of the *form* (of expression). (W. Bauer, *Griechisch-deutsches Wörterbuch zu den Schriften des Neuen Testaments und der übrigen Urchristlichen Literatur*, 5. Aufl., Berlin: Alfred Töpelmann, 1958, *sub* τύπος 4). Grosheide undoubtedly catches the sense of the expression when he proposes that it indicates "dat Lukas den brief niet letterlijk kent, ... maar weet toch ... wat er ongeveer in stond." (F. W. Grosheide, *De Handelingen der Apostelen*, K.N.T., Amsterdam: H. A. van Bottenburg, 1948, Vol. II, p. 320).

[29] Cf. e.g., J. Kürzinger, "Τύπος διδαχῆς und der Sinn von Röm 6,17f," *Biblica*, XXXIX (1958), pp. 172f.

[30] F. W. Beare, "On the Interpretation of Romans VI. 17," *N.T.S.*, V (1958—59), p. 210. Beare states further: "The Christian Didache, when it is followed with a wholehearted obedience, imparts to our lives a specific character and pattern, moulding them into the likeness of Christ.... The Apostle thinks of the Christian life as disciplined and ordered in keeping with clear and concrete instruction given by precept and example. Such teaching is here conceived as a die or pattern which shapes the whole of the life which yields to it, in conformity with the will of God" (pp. 209,210). This understanding of τύπος is also found in L. B. Radford, "Some New Testament Synonyms: Δεῖγμα, ὑπόδειγμα, τύπος, ὑποτύπωσις, ὑπογραμμός," *The Expositor*, 5th Series, VI (1897), pp. 381,382. (The article by E. K. Lee, "Words denoting 'Pattern' in the New Testament," *N.T.S.*, VIII [1961/62], pp. 166—173, reproduces Radford's article almost totally and literally!)

Phil. 3:17; I Thess. 1:7; II Thess. 3:9; I Tim. 4:12; Tit. 2:7; I Pet. 5:3.[31] It is difficult to decide which of two senses is the correct one for τύπος in I Cor. 10:6. Commentators are divided as to whether it is an illustration of wrong conduct taken from history and thus is to be understood as an example in the sense of a warning,[32] or whether it is an instance of Paul's specific "typological" use of τύπος.[33] In Rom. 5:14, however, there is little room for doubt that Paul uses τύπος in some special and technical "typological" sense. Adam is called the type (τύπος) of Christ, or literally, "the figure of him that was to come" (τύπος τοῦ μέλλοντος). Here τύπος gives expression to a genuine historical correspondence which Paul found between Adam and Christ, whereby Adam in a certain sense was a prefigurement and anticipation of the fulfillment of the work of redemption wrought by Christ.[34] Hence the range of usage for τύπος in the New Testament is from the elementary sense of a mark to the highly refined technical sense of a biblical doctrinal type. But the most constantly recurring usage in the New Testament is that of a pattern for human conduct or a personal example.

In the Apostolic Fathers the word τύπος comes into very abundant usage. This is especially true in *The Epistle of Barnabas* and *The Shepherd of Hermas*, where the use is almost exclusively in a symbolical typological sense.[35] In *Hermas* there is also an instance of usage in the basic sense of

---

[31] The A.S.V. consistently translates τύπος with the archaic *ensample* in each of these instances. The K.J.V. used *ensample* for four of the passages, but translated I Tim. 4:12 with *example*, and Tit. 2:7 with *pattern*. The R.S.V. has used *example* in each instance except Tit. 2:7, where it uses *model*. The N.E.B. has used *example* in each instance except I Thess. 1:7, where it uses *model*.

[32] Here the A.S.V. and the K.J.V. use *example*. The R.S.V. uses *warning*: "Now these things are warnings for us, not to desire evil as they did"; the N.E.B. translates it "symbols to warn us."

[33] Among those understanding it as *example* are J. Calvin, *Commentarius in Epistolam Pauli ad Corinthios I* (in *Ioannis Calvini Opera Quae Supersunt Omnia*, ed. G. Baum, E. Cunitz, E. Reuss, Vol. XLIX. Brunsvigae: C. A. Schwetschke, 1892) *sub loc., cf.* also *sub* vs. 11; Radford, Expositor, 5th Ser., VI, pp. 382,383; A. Robertson and A. Plummer, *First Epistle of St. Paul to the Corinthians*, I.C.C., Edinburgh: T. & T. Clark, 1911, *sub loc.*; H. Lietzmann, *An die Korinther I–II*, H.N.T., Tübingen: J. C. B. Mohr (Paul Siebeck), 1931, *sub loc.*, in the sense of *Warnung*; J. Moffatt, *The First Epistle of Paul to the Corinthians*, M.N.T.C., London: Hodder & Stoughton, 1954, *sub loc.* Among those proposing a typological meaning here are P. Bachmann, *Der erste Brief des Paulus an die Korinther*, K.z.N.T., Leipzig: A. Deichert, 1905, *sub loc.*; E.-B. Allo, *St. Paul. Première Épître aux Corinthiens*, E.B., Paris: J. Gabalda, 1934, *sub loc.*; H.-D. Wendland, *Die Briefe an die Korinther*. N.T.D., Göttingen: Vandenhoeck & Ruprecht, 1956, *sub loc.*; F. W. Grosheide, *De Eerste Brief aan de Kerk te Korinthe*, C.N.T., Kampen: J. H. Kok, 1957, *sub loc.*, (who also adds: "De betekenis van τύπος sluit dus nauw aan bij die van voorbeeld" [p. 263]). On the other hand, J. Héring, *La première Épître de Saint Paul aux Corinthiens*, C.d.N.T., Neuchâtel: Delachaux & Niestlé S.A., 1949, *sub loc.*, seeks a third possibility in "une empreinte, d'où le sens de *signe* ou *image*." The matter seems to be determined largely by what specific view one has of typology and how extensive its boundaries are. Since the matter is not germane to our present study, it will not be further pursued.

[34] Throughout the history of Biblical study and exegesis the matter of typology has caused much difference of opinion and has called forth much debate, discussion, and study. Bibliographies of the more recent literature on the subject may be found in L. Goppelt, *Typos, Die typologische Deutung des Alten Testaments im Neuen*, Gütersloh: C. Bertelsmann, 1939, pp. 250–255, and in J. Daniélou, *Sacramentum Futuri. Études sur les Origines de la Typologie Biblique*, Paris: Beauchesne et ses Fils, 1950, pp. vii–ix. The recent study of G. W. H. Lampe and K. J. Woollcombe, *Essays in Typology*, London, SCM Press, 1957, has no bibliography.

[35] *Barnabas* 6:11; 7:3,7,10,11; 8:11; 12:2,5,6,10; 13:5; *Hermas, Similitude* 2:2; *Vision* 3:11:4; 4:1:1; 4:2:5; 4:3:6.

a mark, *i.e.* the holes left in the ground after the stones have been removed (*Similitude* 9. 10. 1,2). In *Barnabas* 19:7 and *Didache* 4:11 there are commands to slaves to obey their masters who are a representative or type of God. In Ignatius, *To the Trallians* 3:1 this same expression is used of the bishop: "Likewise let all respect the deacons as Jesus Christ, even as the bishop is also a type of the Father (τύπον τοῦ πατρός) and the presbyters as the council of God and the college of Apostles." In Ignatius, *To the Magnesians* 6:1 (twice) there is a textual problem which makes it uncertain whether he is saying that the bishop rules in the place (τόπον) of God, or as a representative (τύπον) of God. In the next verse we read, "Let there be nothing in you which can divide you, but be united with the bishop and with those who preside over you as an example and lesson of immortality (εἰς τύπον καὶ διδαχὴν ἀφθαρσίας)." Lightfoot notes that "the idea of ἀφθαρσία in Ignatius ... is not merely immortality, but moral incorruption as carrying with it immortal life." [36] This passage then points to the bishop not merely as a representative of spiritual authority but as an instance of moral virtue and a portrayal of a way of life which can serve as instruction to the people under him and can exercise an influence over them. This is as close as the Apostolic Fathers come to speaking of a personal example when using τύπος. It becomes apparent that after the New Testament writings τύπος was becoming an important word for typology and for the position of the bishop, but that it did not continue to play an important role in expressing personal example. This role was performed by other words. [37]

\* \* \*

Within the whole complex of ideas expressed by τύπος, that of *personal example* has a natural place. In the world of the New Testament and in the New Testament itself it was a well-established and well-accepted usage. The fact that upon occasion in the New Testament it is very closely connected to the idea of imitation serves as further confirmation of this usage. That a man as self-effacing and humble as the Apostle Paul should be found pointing to himself as an example is remarkable, but there is every indication that he intended to do precisely that. What Paul found to be exemplary and what he sought to accomplish in urging the imitation of himself and his example on his readers can only be determined by a careful study of the various passages. There is no escaping the strong moralistic accent in the instances we have located of τύπος as personal example in the Greek and Hellenistic Jewish literature. Is that the accent also in Paul?

---

[36] Lightfoot, *Apost. Fathers*, Part II, Vol. II, p. 121.
[37] *Cf.* below, p. 83. That τύπος remained in circulation in the sense of example is clear from the Lexicon of Hesychius (5th cent. A.D.) where τύπος is given as a synonym and explanatory word for ὑπογραμμός. See *Hesychii Alexandrini Lexicon*, ed. M. Schmidt, Jenae; Sumptibus Frederici Maukii, 1858ff. *sub* ὑπογραμμός.

CHAPTER THREE

# THE IDEA OF IMITATION IN THE WORLD OF PAUL

The foregoing studies of μιμέομαι and τύπος have surveyed the range of meanings and usages found in these words in pre-New Testament and New Testament times. We shall now review this same period on a broader basis. In this chapter we shall not limit ourselves to instances where the specific words are found, but shall attempt to examine the idea of imitation and of being an example particularly in the area of religion and morals as it comes to expression in other ways or is implicit in various expressions and ideas. All this is part of the larger context surrounding Paul's speaking of the imitation of himself or of his being an example.

## I. Imitation in the Greek World

The classical world was well aware of the power of example over the lives of men. Aristotle with all his ability and love for philosophy had no delusions about what limited success philosophical argumentation had in persuading most men. He proposed that in arguing a point one ought to resort to frequent use of example (παράδειγμα) to make the argument more convincing and compelling upon his hearers.[1] He recognized that most men feel the impact of the particular, the concrete, the vivid and personal, while the general, the universal, the abstract, and the impersonal fail to grip them. The whole classical world showed its agreement with him. They made great strides in the development of philosophical theorizing. But at the same time they had the highest respect for anecdotes, fables, illustrative material, and the lessons of experience and history. In fact, they recorded history not simply for the record. They saw history as providing the examples from which men must learn. Thucydides said of the history which he wrote that it is "a true picture ... of like events which may be expected to happen hereafter in the order of things."[2] Cicero found that it "sheds light upon reality, gives life to recollection, and guidance to human existence."[3] Quintilian warned against too one-sided a concentration on philosophy:

---

[1] Aristotle, *Rhetorica* 1394a; cf. 1356b, 1418a.
[2] Thucydides I. 22 (trans. B. Jowett, Vol. I, Oxford: Clarendon Press, 1900, p. 16).
[3] Cicero, *De Oratore* II. ix. 36 (ed. E. W. Sutton and H. Rackham, L.C.L.. London: Wm. Heinemann, 1959, pp. 224,225).

It is desirable that we should not restrict our study to the precepts of philosophy alone. It is still more important that we should know and ponder continually all the noblest sayings and deeds that have been handed down to us from ancient times. And assuredly we shall nowhere find a larger or more remarkable store of these than in the records of our own country. Who will teach courage, justice, loyalty, self-control, simplicity, and contempt of grief and pain better than men like Fabricius, Curius, Regulus, Decius, Mucius, and countless others? For if the Greeks bear away the palm for moral precepts, Rome can produce more striking examples of moral performance, which is a far greater thing. [4]

As philosophy took a more popular turn in Cynicism and Stoicism and sought to make its impact on all classes of men, the slaves, the uneducated, and the man on the street included, the diatribe developed as a rhetorical form with which to confront men and engage them in thinking. One of the characteristics of this kind of reasoning with men was its generous use of examples from legend and history.[5] The examples and experiences of men were considered of great importance and were put to wide usage in the Greek and Roman world.

In the ancient world there was also a great appreciation of the importance and influence of a close personal example. They recognized that under almost every circumstance the older, more experienced, and more advanced serve as a pattern for the younger, less experienced, and less advanced to follow. This fact gave some leaders a sense of great responsibility toward the people over whom they ruled. Xenophon tells us that Cyrus "believed that he could in no way more effectively inspire a desire for the beautiful and the good than by endeavoring, as their sovereign, to set before his subjects a perfect model of virtue in his own person." [6] He had considerable success in this, at least with regard to his religious practices, for "the rest of the Persians also imitated (ἐμιμοῦντο) him from the first; for they believed that they would be more sure of good fortune if they revered the gods just as he did who was their sovereign and the most fortunate of all." [7] Aristotle advised Alexander along the same lines: "You must realize that the model set before most men is either the law or else your life and the expression of your reason." [8]

However, there was no area where the influence of one person over others was more recognized and sought after than that of the teacher or wise man over his own pupils. The system which developed whereby the pupils came to live with the teacher, accompanying him on all kinds of occasions, was conducive to the fullest working of the imitation processes. An education under this system went far beyond the mere learning of subject matter.

---

4 Quintilian, *Institutio Oratoria* XII. ii. 29,30 (ed. H. E. Butler, Vol. IV, L.C.L., London: Wm. Heinemann, 1958, pp. 398,399).

5 R. Bultmann, *Der Stil der paulinischen Predigt und die kynisch-stoische Diatribe*, Göttingen: Vandenhoeck & Ruprecht, 1910, pp. 50ff.

6 Xenophon, *Cyropaedia* VIII. i. 21 (ed. W. Miller, Vol. II, L.C.L., London: Wm. Heinemann. 1914, pp. 316,317).

7 *Ibid.* VIII. i. 24 (Miller, *loc. cit.*).

8 Aristotle, *Rhetorica ad Alexandrum* 1420b (trans. E. S. Forster, in *The Works of Aristotle*, ed. W. D. Ross, Vol. XI, Oxford: Clarendon Press, 1952).

Xenophon tells us: "Socrates was so useful in all circumstances and in all ways, that any observer gifted with ordinary perception can see that nothing was more useful than the companionship of Socrates, and time spent with him in any place and in any circumstances. The very recollection of him in absence brought no small good to his constant companions and followers; for even in his light moods they gained no less from his society than when he was serious." [9] The instruction of the pupil came fully as much from the actions and deeds of the teacher as from his words. [10] Seneca gives a striking testimony to the power of the teacher's example when he writes to Lucilius:

> Of course, however, the living voice and the intimacy of a common life will help you more than the written word. You must go to the scene of action, first, because men put more faith in their eyes than in their ears, and second, because the way is long if one follows precepts, but short and helpful, if one follows patterns [per exempla]. Cleanthes could not have been the express image of Zeno, if he had merely heard his lectures; he shared in his life, saw into his hidden purposes, and watched him to see whether he lived according to his own rules. Plato, Aristotle, and the whole throng of sages who were destined to go each his different way, derived more benefit from the character than from the words of Socrates. It was not the class-room of Epicurus, but living together under the same roof, that made great men of Methodorus, Hermarchus, and Polyaenus. [11]

In the ancient classical world the close association with and imitation of the teacher was encouraged.

There was another facet of life in which imitation and its related ideas played a major role in the Graeco-Roman world. Imitation was an important process in religious development and in the attainment of the ideal state of existence for man. Among the Greeks Plato developed the concept of imitation in its religious aspects most fully. In this he followed the lead given him by Pythagoras. Pythagoras had made the phrase "Follow God" [12] a precept in his system, and had proposed that the chief end of man is to become like God. [13] Plato conceived of God as the author of all good, and since God is

---

9 Xenophon, *Memorabilia* IV. i. 1 (Marchant, pp. 264,265).
10 *Ibid.* IV. iii. 18,25; cf. I. ii. 17.
11 Seneca, *Ad Lucilium Epistulae Morales* VI. 5–7 (ed. R. M. Gummere, Vol. I, L.C.L., London: Wm. Heinemann, 1953, pp. 26—29).
12 The original meaning of the expression "to follow the gods" is apparently to be found in the primitive cultic idea that man best succeeds in uniting himself with the deity by imitating the actions and deeds of the deity. Cf. E. G. Gulin, „Die Nachfolge Gottes," *Studia Orientalia*, I (1925), p. 45.
13 Concerning the Pythagorean teaching on imitation, J. Burnet, "Pythagoras and Pythagoreanism," *E.R.E.*, X, p. 526a, says: "If we may also regard the famous description of the true philosopher in the *Theaetetus* (176 B-D) as inspired by Pythagorean teaching, we may go a step further and attribute to Pythagoras the doctrine that the end of man is to become like God (ὁμοίωσις τῷ θεῷ). We are not able to prove this indeed, but it is so far confirmed by the fact that Aristoxenus makes 'the following of God' (τὸ ἀκολουθεῖν τῷ θεῷ) the keynote of the Pythagorean system as expounded by him; and an unknown writer excerpted by Stobaeus (*Ecl.* ii. 249, 8 Wachsmuth; cf. Aristoxenus ap. Iambl. *Vita Pyth.* 137) gives 'Follow God' (ἕπου θεῷ) as a Pythagorean precept, and calls attention to the agreement of Plato with it."

free of all envy (a most divisive force among men), God wishes to have all things become as like himself as possible.[14] Such possibilities of likeness exist for man since God is a soul, and he has given man a soul. It is man's highest calling to follow after God and to become like him.[15]

For Plato the becoming like God provided the way of escape from all the evils of this world and this life. In his classic statement of the doctrine he has Socrates say:

> But it is impossible that evils should be done away with, ... for there must always be something opposed to the good; and they cannot have their place among the gods, but must inevitably hover about mortal nature and this earth. Therefore, we ought to try to escape from earth to the dwelling of the gods as quickly as we can; and to escape is to become like God, so far as this is possible; and to become like God is to become righteous and holy and wise.... God is in no wise and in no manner unrighteous, but utterly and perfectly righteous, and there is nothing so like him as that one of us who in turn becomes most nearly perfect in righteousness.[16]

The close relationship between imitation and becoming alike for Plato can be detected in the following statement of how "acting alike" results in "becoming alike":

> Two patterns ... are set up in the world, the divine, which is most blessed, and the godless, which is most wretched. But these men do not see that this is the case, and their silliness and extreme foolishness blind them to the fact that through their unrighteous acts they are made like the one and unlike the other. They therefore pay the penalty for this by living a life that conforms to the pattern they resemble.[17]

This latter statement also betrays the eudaemonistic motive which Plato has for the imitation of God. God is the supremely happy being, as perfect ethically as physically. In so far as man becomes like God through imitating

---

14 πάντα ὅτι μάλιστα ... παραπλήσια ἑαυτῷ (*Timaeus*, 29e). A. E. Taylor offers a helpful commentary on this thought and its relation to imitation. He says that Plato's later writings show a development of the thoughts that "in the end *all* that happens is due to the agency of souls and that the supreme soul, God, is perfectly wise, and therefore. in virtue of the Socratic doctrine that virtue is knowledge, perfectly good.... It is the activity of soul, acting for the sake of what it believes to be good, by which the actual course of nature is made an approximate, though never a complete realization of good, an 'imitation' of the perfect order of the Forms.... The world is not perfect, it is not as good as God Himself, but only 'as like Him as may be'.... [This] means that since the world *is* not God, but something derived from and dependent on God, it cannot be as good as God Himself. If it were, there would be no distinction between God and the world; the world would just be God over again. Plato is no 'Pantheist'." A. E. Taylor, *A Commentary on Plato's Timaeus*, Oxford: Clarendon Press, 1928, pp. 77,78.

15 *Cf. Phaedrus* 248a, where Socrates describes the struggle of the soul "which best follows after God and is most like him" (ed. H. N. Fowler, L.C.L., London: Wm. Heinemann, 1928, pp. 476,477).

16 *Theaetetus* 176a,b,c (ed. H. N. Fowler, L.C.L., London: Wm. Heinemann, 1921, pp. 126—129).

17 *Ibid.* 176e, 177a (Fowler, pp. 130,131). For further evidence that ὁμοίωσις in Plato includes the idea of imitation, *cf.* P. A. Heitmann, *Imitatio Dei* (Studia Anselmiana, No. 10), Rome: Herder, 1940, pp. 21ff.

him, he too can enjoy such perfection and happiness.[18] The whole doctrine of imitating deity became highly refined and fully developed philosophically in Plato. Gulin detects the primitive cultic idea at work here nevertheless. It is still the idea that by reproducing the motions and actions of deity one comes to participate in the being and essence of the deity.[19]

For the Stoics too this following of God played an important role. Epictetus tells us that Zeno, the founder of the Stoic school, said, "To follow the gods is man's end."[20] Epictetus characterizes the true Stoic as "a man who has set his heart upon changing from a man into a god, and although he is still in this paltry body of death, does none the less have his purpose set upon fellowship with Zeus."[21] According to Seneca the relationship between man and God is more than one of friendship: "Rather there is a tie of relationship and a likeness, since in truth, a good man differs from God in the element of time only; he is God's pupil, his imitator, and true offspring."[22] Epictetus explains that we become like God by imitation: "The man who is going to please and obey them (the gods) must endeavor as best he can to resemble (ἐξομοιοῦσθαι) them. If the deity is faithful, he also must be faithful; ... if highminded, he also must be highminded, and so forth; therefore, in everything he says and does, he must act as an imitator (ζηλωτὴν) of God."[23] Cicero in explicating Socrates' views speaks of the easy way of return to God that there is at death for the souls which "in the bodies of men had followed the life of the gods."[24] In short, the imitation of God was a most familiar ethical maxim for the Stoics, presenting the way of escape from the troubles and threats which men everywhere experience.

With both Platonism and Stoicism abroad in the hellenistic world, the idea of imitation was a very current one. Thoroughly intertwined with it were the concepts of following God and becoming like him. For the Greeks imitating, following, becoming like God was the way to man's goal and highest good. It was the way that man attained divinity.

---

18 Heitmann, *Imit. Dei*, p. 29.

19 "Die Art und Weise, in der Platon die Nachfolge und das Ä h n l i c h w e r d e n mit Gott hier als Synonyma gebraucht hat, zeigt uns, dass hier die primitive Auffassung von der kultischen Nachahmung Gottes als ein Mittel zur Erreichung der Gottähnlichkeit noch nachwirkt. Im Kulte ahmte man Gott nach, imitierte ihn, und dabei hatte man das Gefühl, wie ein Gott zu werden. Platon hat hier diese Auffassung nur vergeistigt und ethisiert. Er meint, dass d i e Seele am meisten Gott ähnelt, die seinem Willen nachgefolgt ist" (Gulin, *Stud. Orient.*, I, p. 46).

20 "τέλος ἐστὶ τὸ ἕπεσθαι θεοῖς." Epictetus, *The Discourses* I. xx. 15 (ed. W. A. Oldfather, Vol. I, *L.C.L.*, London: Wm. Heinemann, 1926, pp. 140,141). Epictetus himself makes the same statement, but uses the verb ἀκολουθεῖν: I. xxx. 4.

21 *Ibid.* III. xix. 27 (Oldfather, I, pp. 368,369).

22 "Immo etiam necessitudo et similitudo, quoniam quidem bonus tempore tantum a deo differt, discipulus eius aemulatorque et vera progenies." Seneca, *Moral Essays* I. 5 (ed. J. W. Basore, Vol. I, *L.C.L.*, London: Wm. Heinemann, 1928, pp. 6,7). In regard to man here being called a child or offspring of God, K. Deissner, *Paulus und Seneca*, B.z.F.c.T., 21, 2. Heft, 1917, p. 37, remarks, "an eine lebendige Gemeinschaft der Gotteskinder mit ihrem Vater, an einen persönlichen Verkehr der Menschenseele mit ihrem Gott hat der Philosoph (Seneca) dabei nirgends gedacht."

23 Epictetus, *Discourses* II.xiv. 13 (Oldfather, pp. 308,309).

24 Essentque in corporibus humanis vitam imitati deorum." Cicero, *Tusculan Disputations* I, 72 (ed. J. E. King, *L.C.L.*, London: Wm. Heinemann, 1960, pp. 84,85).

## II. Imitation in the Old Testament

When we step over into the world of the Old Testament, we fail to find the idea of imitation coming to clear and concise expression, at least as it applies to human conduct. In translating the Old Testament writings into Greek the translators found no occasion to use any form of μιμέομαι in their translations of the canonical books. Τύπος is used for images of heathen gods (Amos 5:26) and for the pattern of the tabernacle which God showed to Moses (Exod. 25:40), but never as a pattern, model, or example for human conduct.[25] The absence of these specific terms, however, does not tell the whole story of whether the idea of imitation had any role to play in the Old Testament world.

In the New Testament in Hebrews 11 there is a long song praising the way of faith and the Old Testament heroes who were pre-eminent as men of faith. It begins with Abel, continues through Noah, Abraham, Moses, and finally must make a sweeping summary of the rest: "for the time will fail me if I tell of Gideon, Barak, Samson, Jephthah; of David and Samuel and the prophets" (Heb. 11:32). Whether there was such an attitude in Old Testament Israel toward the great men of her history is not so easily determined, but at least it must be said that there is little expression of it in the Old Testament scriptures. We do not find these outstanding leaders being held up to the people of later times as being exemplary of certain virtues or as being objects for imitation. Perhaps there were certain factors tending to restrain such a development. The Old Testament records the lives and accomplishments of many leading men, men of great daring and valor, leaders accomplishing remarkable military feats, spiritual heroes fearlessly condemning the evil they found arround them. But the spotlight in Scripture is not on what these men were and on what they were accomplishing. It is constantly on God and his actions through men. The source of energy and dynamism in Israel's heroes was the strength of Jehovah that was operative in them. "Heroism in ancient Israel was ... conceived as a direct effluence from Deity acting on the individual human spirit."[26] The great moments of Israel's history were told from father to son, but it was always a "telling to the generation to come the praises of Jehovah, and his strength, and his wondrous works that he hath done" (Ps. 78:4). This phenomenon is illustrated well in regard to Israel's founding fathers, Abraham, Isaac, and Jacob. The many references that are made to them in the Old Testament outside of the account of their lives are almost exclusively in regard to their God, or to the relation which Israel had

---

25 Παράδειγμα is used for a *pattern* of the tabernacle in Exod. 25:8 (LXX) (*cf.* the translation of the same Hebrew word in vs. 40 by τύπος); for various *patterns* for the temple and its furnishings in I Chron. 28:11,12,18,19 (LXX); for a *gazing-stock* in Nah. 3:6; and for *dung* in Jer. 8:2; 9:22; 16:4 (E. Hatch and H. A. Redpath express doubt whether the Greek and Hebrew in these Jeremiah passages represent the same words; see their *Concordance to the Septuagint*, Oxford: Clarendon Press, 1897, *sub* παράδειγμα). Ὑπόδειγμα is found in Ezek. 42:15 (LXX) where the meaning is that the *pattern* or *model* of the house was measured.

26 G. Margoliouth, "*Heroes and Hero-Gods (Hebrew)*," E.R.E., VI, p. 656b.

through them to God by way of the covenant with Abraham. Undoubtedly the way of life exemplified by the patriarchs lost much of its appropriateness as a model life after the Israelites received the law.[27] However, as a model for future generations Moses fares little better than did the patriarchs. Great lawgiver and heroic leader that he was, he does not become a great example to later Old Testament Israel. His name appears in the Old Testament very frequently after his death, but it is usually in connection with the law given through him or the deeds performed by God through him.[28] It is a rare exception to find a reference to his personal conduct or personal relationship to God.[29] Probably the fact of having the minute legal code prescribing the many intricacies of ceremonial procedure, purity, and holiness, as well as more general ethical relationships and standards, tended to de-emphasize individual personal conduct as an example. The pattern for human conduct was in the law, not in the lives of certain outstanding men. Furthermore, the Old Testament pictures the ideal human life not in terms of reaching a certain ethical standard or living on a high moral level, but in terms of a living fellowship with God. Hence it was not Abraham's or Moses' way of life that was all-important to those living later, but Abraham's and Moses' God, with whom there could still be immediate and personal fellowship. Perhaps other reasons can be found in accounting for the lack of emphasis on the example given by Israel's heroes. Whatever explanations can be found do not alter the fact, however. The Old Testament only very seldom recalls the personal conduct of the great men of her history.

The Old Testament shows an awareness of a certain kind of imitation, even though that word was not used to express it. There was recognition of how one's life could be influenced by those living around him and of the tendency to adopt the ways of other people, conforming oneself to their standards and practices. This was precisely the temptation and danger which Israel faced as she stood between Egypt and the promised land: "After the doings of the land of Egypt, wherein ye dwelt, shall ye not do: and after the doings of the land of Canaan, whither I bring you, shall ye not do; neither shall ye walk in their statutes" (Lev. 18:3). The expression "doing after the doings or works" (עשה כמעשה) of others, and especially the expression "going

---

[27] G. von Rad, *Theologie des Alten Testaments*, Band I, München: Chr. Kaiser Verlag, 1957, pp. 176f. He comments further in fn. 15: "Viel Unheil ist bekanntlich durch die verallgemeinerte Auffassung der Erzväter als Vorbilder frommen Wandels vor Gott angerichtet worden. Die Frage, ob und wo die Erzähler auch zur 'Imitatio' anreizen wollen, ist nicht so leicht zu beantworten. In den Erzählungen Gen. 12:1–9; 13; 15:1–6; 22 muss die Gestalt des Ahnherrn doch auch als Vorbild für die Nachfahren verstanden werden. Am deutlichsten ist das in der sicher didaktischen Josephsgeschichte."

[28] "Wenn die Verherrlichung des religiösen Führers als Meister und die sorgfältige Pflege der Erinnerung an ihn im Sinne einer fast religiösen Pflicht im AT keine Stätte gefunden hat, so liegt es also letztlich daran, dass im AT die Selbstenthüllung Gottes als dynamisch und fortschreitend begriffen ist" (K. Rengstorf, μαθητής, *T.W.N.T.*, IV, p. 433, 24–29.

[29] An instance can be found in Ps. 99:6,7, where it is said of Moses, Aaron, and Samuel, "They called upon Jehovah, and he answered them. He spake unto them in the pillar of cloud: They kept his testimonies, and the statute that he gave them."

after, walking after, following" (הלך אחרי) the ways, customs, statutes, ordinances, etc. of others, became familiar and frequent expressions in the Old Testaments writings. These terms have to do with the way one lives, how he acts, what he does, and by what standards and rules he is governed. The Old Testament showed a real consciousness of the fact that every act is basically a religious act; it gives expression to one's religious commitment. Israel thus was not free to do the things the people of Egypt did or the things the people of Canaan were doing; she might not adopt their standards. God immediately proceeds to state the matter positively for Israel: "Mine ordinances shall ye do and my statutes shall ye keep, to walk therein: I am Jehovah thy God" (Lev. 18:4). Israel stood in covenant with Jehovah. Her life was inseparably bound to him. He had outlined the way of life for her in the instructions and law he had given her. He had allowed other nations to go their own ways (Acts 14:16), but Israel's way he had commanded (Deut. 5:33). As Israel stood in the wilderness between Egypt and Canaan she had good reason to become vitally aware of these things. Unfortunately, God had much occasion in the years which followed to complain about the people he had chosen and rescued from Egypt: "Oh that my people would hearken unto me, that Israel would walk in my ways" (Ps. 81:13). Too often Israel took to doing the things which the people around her were doing. She could not resist the impulse to follow them and become like them. She left the ways of her God and walked in the ways of the people around her.

In view of Paul's usage of the terms "way" (ὁδός) and "walk" (περιπατέω) in close connection with the thought of imitating himself,[30] it will be appropriate to pause for a moment to analyse these terms as they are applied to the matter of living and to notice something of their use in the Old Testament.[31] The expressions "walking" and "ways" are both figurative expressions commonly applied to man's life. There are other expressions in common usage today which have the same figure behind them, such as "processes of life," "course of life," and "conduct." These expressions arise from the observation that man's life is not a static thing. There is movement as he lives. In this movement man does not remain passive. He does not vegetate from day to day and from station to station. He takes part in the movement and exerts a measure of influence on both the direction in which his life moves and the rate at which it goes. "Walking" is an apt expression for this phenomenon. It suggests movement, active participation, a responsible determination of the direction in which one is going, orientation to the things around one. In living, man walks.

In the process of walking man produces a *way*. The reality of this is commonly observable. We see it when one walks through newly fallen snow or in the wind-swept sand of the beaches and deserts. The hard-worn paths through the fields and the trails through the woods have been made by many

---

[30] *Cf.* I Cor. 4:16,17; Phil. 3:17; II Thess. 3:6ff.
[31] For a full survey and analysis of ὁδός in the Old Testament (LXX), see W. Michaelis, ὁδός, *T.W.N.T.*, V, pp. 47—56. See also the exposition, "Wandel en weg in de Heilige Schrift," in R. Schippers, *De Gereformeerde Zede*, Kampen: J. H. Kok, 1955, pp. 10—16.

tramping feet. So also metaphorically each act of living is a footstep beating out the path of our life. Our acts of living leave a trail; our walk produces our way. This way is not without significance. The movement of life is not merely onward to ever new and entirely different experiences. Rather it involves much going over and over the same territory. Hence a way once trod is traversed with more ease the following times. As we walk the same way repeatedly, it becomes a well-beaten path, a path which we follow more and more automatically. Like the ruts in a road or the tracks of the railroad the way soon develops a measure of regulative force. Hence, we develop our habits, our customs, our manner, our ways, our way of life.

Our ways are not only of significance for ourselves personally. Man is a social creature. Men live together and walk together. The way that one produces by his walk becomes available for others to traverse with greater facility and confidence. Naturally this is of particular importance to the young and inexperienced. They learn to follow the ways which their fathers and teachers tread. They learn how to live from the experience of those walking ahead of them. A father's way has great significance and influence for his children. He leads his sons in learning the ways of life as he has come to know them. The same holds true for the other leaders among men, the heads of communities, tribes, and nations. The title "leader" already indicates it: the path which he chooses is the way those following him will also walk.

With the awareness that there was in the Old Testament of the fact that every act of life is a religious act, it is not surprising that the expression "way" came to be heavily laden with religious content. A person's way came to be a kind of spiritual description of him. We read that during the days of the judges Israel "played the harlot after other gods," and "turned aside quickly out of the way wherein their fathers walked, obeying the commandments of Jehovah" (Judg. 2:17). Samuel's sons "walked not in his ways, but turned aside after lucre, and took bribes, and perverted justice" (I Sam. 8:3, *cf.* vs. 5). Amon "walked in all the way that his father (Manasseh) walked in, and served the idols that his father served and worshipped them: and he forsook Jehovah, the God of his fathers, and walked not in the way of Jehovah" (II Kings 21:21). Jehoshaphat was influenced by a better example; he "walked in the way of Asa his father, and turned not aside from it, doing that which was right in the eyes of Jehovah" (II Chron. 20:32). Jehoram on the other hand received a curse, the reason for which Elijah explained as follows: "Thou hast not walked in the ways of Jehoshaphat thy father, nor in the ways of Asa king of Judah, but hast walked in the way of the kings of Israel, and hast made Judah and the inhabitants of Jerusalem to play the harlot" (II Chron. 21:12,13). To walk in a person's ways meant to walk so that one's life expressed the same religious commitment that that person had. The person standing at the head of the line was in a position of crucial significance. He was the one who first established the way. The Old Testament records of the kings of Israel and Judah give good attestation to this significance. Repeatedly they make reference to the way of David or the way of Jeroboam. Over and over again later kings are classified as to their walking or not walking in the ways of David, [32] and to their walking in the ways of Jeroboam. [33] The specific difference between the ways of David and those of Jeroboam is stated in the words of Ahijah's prophecy against Jeroboam: "Thou hast not been as my servant David, who kept my commandments, and who followed me with all his heart, to do that only which was right in mine eyes, but hast done evil above all that were before thee, and hast gone and made thee other gods, and molten images, to provoke me to anger, and hast cast me behind thy back" (I Kings 14:8,9). David and Jeroboam established two different religious ways for kings to walk.

There is a silent admission of the insidious influence of Jeroboam's example in the constant recurrence of this phrase "walking in the ways of Jeroboam." Jeroboam set a new course for the kings of Israel; "he made Israel to sin." [34] He marked out the way for the king who would not submit himself to the service of Jehovah. He is the model of an apostate king. David on the other hand is the king with the right religious commitment. He showed how to rule Israel as a servant of Jehovah. As such he established a way and became the example and standard for the kings following him. The constantly recurring reference to his ways shows that there was an awareness among those living after him of the possibility and the duty for kings to learn from him, adopt his ways, and follow the pattern he established of ruling as a faithful servant of God. The Books of the Kings and the Chronicles silently attest the lasting influence of the example of Jeroboam, but they also keep recalling the good example of David. Probably no man in the Old Testament is more often held up as an example to be followed. The expression "walking in the ways of..." indicates a kind of imitation with which the Old Testament people were well acquainted. [35]

A question that naturally presents itself at this point is what does it mean to walk in God's ways. Does this indicate an imitation of God? If walking in David's ways means living the kind of life David did and following David's example of obedience to God, does walking in God's ways mean somehow living a type of life which God lives and perhaps following God's example of obedience to his own laws? The Babylonian Talmud shows that the Rabbis sometimes went in this direction in their understanding of the matter, for there are statements about God's daily study of his own Torah, [36] or his wearing the phylacteries and the fringed garment. [37] God's ways can of course mean the ways God himself acts. [38] The thought then is usually that God's conduct, plans, and deeds differ from men's, are only partially

---

[32] Cf. I Kings 3:14; 9:4; 11:6,33,38; 15:3,5,11; II Kings 14:3; etc.
[33] Cf. I Kings 15:34; 16:2,19,26; 22:52; etc.
[34] I Kings 14:16; 15:26,30,34; 16:19,26; et al.
[35] Josephus understood it thus and spoke of various later kings as being an imitator (μιμητής) of David; e.g., Asa (Antiquities VIII. 315), Jehoshaphat (IX. 44).
[36] Babylonian Talmud: Aboda Zara, 3b.
[37] Babylonian Talmud: Rosh Hashana 17b.
[38] Cf. Michaelis, T.W.N.T., V, p. 55, 11ff., where he cites such examples as Deut. 32:4; Ps. 145(LXX—144):17; Isa. 55:8f.

understood by men, and are not subject to men's critique and judgment. However, when the expression "walking in God's ways" is found, the meaning lies in another direction. God's ways then are the ways that God has prescribed for man. Often there is some specific statement to this effect. We find, for instance: "Ye shall walk in all the way which Jehovah your God hath commanded you" (Deut. 5:33); or again, certain wicked men have drawn Israel aside "out of the way which Jehovah thy God commanded thee to walk in" (Deut. 13:5). "Walking in God's ways" often appears in parallel construction to an expression like "keeping his commandments": "... if thou shalt keep the commandments of Jehovah thy God, and walk in his ways" (Deut. 28:9); "... I commanded thee this day to love Jehovah thy God, to walk in his ways, and to keep his commandments and his statutes and his ordinances" (Deut. 30:16). The same is found in David's charge to Solomon: "Keep the charge of Jehovah thy God, to walk in his ways, to keep his statutes, and his commandments, and his ordinances, and his testimonies, according to that which is written in the law of Moses" (I Kings 2:3). Thus, walking in God's ways is very closely related to keeping his commandments. In many respects the two thoughts are the same.[39]

Nevertheless, the expression "walking in God's ways" has a point peculiar to itself which ought not to be lost from sight. It is heavily laden with associations of fellowship and companionship. Schippers has stated the matter well:

> The ways of God are not to be completely identified with his commands. When God speaks to us about *his* ways, he means *our* walk with him. He has in mind his covenant in which we have the privilege of living with him, and the companionship with him which we enjoy when we love him and keep his commandments. He reserves for himself the right to prescribe the ways in which we are to go and all our activities along the way. Thus we receive our ways from him. Our ways are his ways. They are, however, real ways; there is traffic on them. We do not move forward alone; we go with others and we go with him. *Way* here indicates contact, not in the sense of its bringing us to God, but rather that *God travels along with us as we walk in obedience*. When we are disobedient, we travel alone; at least we have no more than human company. We may be with Jeroboam and Balaam and Cain, but we are traveling without God.[40]

Hence we may conclude that the call to walk in God's ways is not really a call to imitate God's own actions and conduct. It must be admitted that we can not completely escape all thought of imitation in such a context. When friends live together, love each other, and walk together, they tend to adopt each other's ways and grow toward a likeness of each other. Man can not pursue a constant walk with God and remain unaffected by it. The

---

[39] "Der Weg des Herrn ist der dem Menschen vom Herrn gebotene Wandel, ja an vielen Stellen nähert sich der Ausdruck der Bdtg: das (auf den Wandel des Menschen sich beziehende) Gebot des Herrn, ὁδός wird fast synon zu ἐντολή" (Michaelis, *T.W.N.T.*, V, p. 51, 12–16).

[40] Schippers, *Geref. Zede*, p. 13 (my translation).

many perfections of God and the wonders of his conduct will call forth
reactions and responses from man, and some of these will be along the lines
of seeking to compare to and to resemble God. However, the Old Testament
does not seem to have been intent on bringing out this point in its urging
men to walk in the ways of God. The call was not a call to imitation but
to covenantal union and fellowship.

Closely related to the expression "walking in his ways" is the expression
"walking after Jehovah." The Hebrew phrase הלך אחרי, *go after, walk after,
follow*, is the expression corresponding to the Greek ἀκολουθεῖν and ἕπεσθαι,
*to follow*, which also was used in connection with God.[41] We have seen how
these Greek phrases were used to indicate becoming like God and imitating
him. Is the same indicated in the Hebrew expression? The imagery that lies
behind the Hebrew expression is not always the same. Often it is the imagery
of lovers: one goes after or is seduced into following the other (see Prov.
7:21,22); one seeks to give himself away and to become possessed by the
other. Thus Israel went after God in the wilderness as a bride her bridegroom
(Jer. 2:2). Israel, however, also went after other gods; and then the phrase
was expressive of marital unfaithfulness, going whoring, giving oneself into
possession and service of another, and thus falling into apostasy and heathendom.[42] Another quite similar imagery lying behind the expression "going
after" is that of soldiers or subjects following their leader or captain. Here
again one is following the other in order to give service. This imagery can
be seen in Elijah's challenge to the people on Mt. Carmel: "How long go
ye limping between the two sides? if Jehovah be God, follow him; but if Baal,
then follow him" (I Kings 18:21). One might also suspect the possibility of
some cultic meaning lying back of the expression "following God," such as
could have derived from the march through the wilderness with the ark of
God's presence at the head of the procession (Num. 10:33ff.) or from one of
the ritual processions behind the ark to Mt. Zion (*cf.* II Sam. 6; Ps. 24; 132).
No evidence of this can be found, however.[43] Rather the following of Jehovah
spoke of a religious and ethical relationship.[44] It expressed allegiance and
commitment to God and obedience to the commandments which God had
given. It is used in the same way as the expression "walking in God's ways":
"Ye shall walk after Jehovah your God, and fear him and keep his commandments, and obey his voice, and ye shall serve him, and cleave unto him"
(Deut. 13:4). Apparently the constant recurrence of the phrase "following
other gods" resulted in this phrase's becoming so much a fixed expression for

---

41 The Septuagint usually translated it literally with πορεύεσθαι ὀπίσω, although ἀκολουθεῖν
ὀπίσω appears in I Kings 19:20; Hosea 2:5 (Codex Alexandrinus); Isa. 45:14. The latter
expression is not found in classical Greek nor in Josephus, but is found in Matt. 10:38.

42 The expression *is* especially frequent in Deuteronomy, Jeremiah, and Hosea.

43 "Es ist nämlich andererseits unmöglich, den Ausdruck 'Nachfolge Gottes' in Verbindung
mit dem Kulte im A.T. nachzuweisen" (Gulin, *Stud. Orient.*, I, p. 43).

44 "Der I n h a l t der Nachfolge Jahwes ist religiös-ethisch bestimmt. Das können wir am
klarsten bei Elia ersehen. Dieser Gottesmann eifert nicht nur für die religiöse Hingabe an Jahwe,
so dass er den tyrischen Kult am bittersten bekämpft, sondern er vertritt auch die alte Sittlichkeit
des Stammesgottes.... Jahwe folgen bedeutet für ihn, dass man die alte, strenge Religion Moses
mit all ihren Konsequenzen auf sich nimmt" (*Ibid.*, p. 44).

the falling away into heathendom, that a hesitancy developed regarding the use of its counterpart "following Jehovah." [45] At least, "walking in the ways of Jehovah" is a more widely used expression than "walking after (or following) Jehovah." [46] Furthermore, when the Old Testament does speak of "walking after God," the expression does not have the content which the Greek expression "following God" sometimes had, namely, of becoming like God and developing the stature of divinity. In the Old Testament "following" pertained not to the perfections of God's being, but to the revelations and requirements of his word, to his will as he had shown it to man, and to the path of fellowship that he offered in his covenant. The expressions "walking in God's ways," and "walking after God" or "following God" do not have in mind the idea of imitating God. [47]

Tinsley expresses himself quite differently on this matter. He says: "The continuing dominance of the imagery of the 'Way' [in the Old Testament], with its suggestion of movement and advance, meant that for the Hebrew mind the contemplation of God must take not the static form of thinking about the being and perfection of God, but the dynamic form of conforming one's conduct to what he had shown himself to be during the journey to the Promised Land.... The 'imitation of God' was expressed in the imagery of the 'Way'.... The Old Testament expression for the 'imitation of God' is 'to *walk* in the way of the Lord' or 'to *walk* after God'." [48] Tinsley is of the conviction that "Christian spirituality can contain within itself a genuine mysticism which enhances rather than weakens its attachment to a particular historical revelation, and that this mysticism is centred on the idea of the imitation of Christ." [49] He finds the imitation of God to be one of the constants in the religions of the ancient world and states further: "Knowledge of God was held to result in or require a real likeness to him, and religion in some way to render life an imitation of the life of God himself." [50] The unique characteristics of the imitation of God in the Christian tradition is that it was "always dynamically conceived as the imitation of a true life-history, which in the life of the Church, through the action of the Holy Spirit, had a contemporaneous existence with that of the believer." [51] For New Testament times this meant an imitation of the life-history of Jesus Christ; we shall notice this thought further in the progress of our

---

[45] Gulin, *Stud. Orient.*, I, p. 42: "Die sonst zu bemerkende Scheu vor diesem Ausdruck möchte ich dadurch erklären, dass die Redeweise: 'anderen Göttern nachfolgen' als Terminus technicus für den Abfall zum Heidentum einen Schatten auf das 'Nachwandeln' warf, wenn man an Jahwe dachte." *Cf.* also G. Kittel, ἀκολουθέω, *T.W.N.T.*, I, p. 211, 26ff.

[46] Kittel, *T.W.N.T.*, I, p. 211, 28ff.

[47] Gulin, *Stud. Orient.*, I, p. 43, proposed that the imitation idea could be found in the statement that Elisha "went after Elijah" (I Kings 19:21): "Die Nachfolge macht den Schüler dem Lehrer ä h n l i c h, die Göttlichkeit des Lehrers geht dadurch (gleichsam physisch) in den Schüler über, und dies ist der Sinn des Ausdrucks in diesem Falle, zwar dem einzigen im A.T." However, Kittel, *T.W.N.T.*, I, p. 213, 12ff. correctly answers: "Auch diese 'Nachfolge' bedeutet schwerlich etwas anderes als den Ausdruck des Verehrungsverhältnisses. Die Fortsetzung: 'und er bediente ihn' bestätigt das in vollem Masse: der Jünger geht als Diener im ganz eigentlichen Sinn hinter dem Meister her."

[48] E. J. Tinsley, *The Imitation of God in Christ*, London: SCM Press, 1960, p. 35.
[49] *Ibid.*, p. 23.
[50] *Ibid.*, p. 27.
[51] *Ibid.*, p. 29.

study.⁵² Regarding the Old Testament period he says: "The experiences of the Hebrew people during that part of their history which took them from the Red Sea to the Promised Land forced upon them the conviction that this episode was no mere transitory series of occurrences but contained within itself something which would never be outdated. The Lord had shown them that 'religion' was essentially a journey which he invited men to undertake. The revelatory history had not only occurred; it had thrown up images of perennial significance. The way ahead had been indicated by the Lord himself and Israel was committed by the Covenant to 'follow after' him in this 'Way'. This is the form which the 'imitation of God' takes in the Old Testament." ⁵³ Thus, as Tinsley explains: "The historical 'Way of the Lord' was followed by Israel, 'imitated', and known as a present reality through liturgy, social and personal relationships, and in the interior life of the individual believer." ⁵⁴

We have presented these rather extensive citations from Tinsley with a view to illustrating the broad manner in which he conceives of the idea of imitation. His exposition of the profound awareness which the Hebrew had of the *present* reality in his life of past saving events is most valuable and helpful. It may be questioned, however, whether his using the term imitation for this process is equally helpful or even appropriate. When the later Hebrew relived the exodus journey and walked in his own spiritual experience the way that the Lord led his people from Egypt to the promised land, is this best described as imitation? Tinsley in pleading for a genuine Biblical mysticism feels that it is. The matter takes on a slightly different light when applied to the religious experiences which came in connection with the great festival rituals, such as Passover and Tabernacles. Here perhaps there was a kind of imitation. But, even here it does not seem completely appropriate to speak of "the imitation *of* God." In following God in the way he established in the desert and in the Torah, was Israel really engaged in the imitation of God? Surely this can not be understood in any narrower sense of observing God, his being, and his actions, and then becoming like him and doing the same things oneself. This element of religious experience played but a minimal role during Old Testament times. (We shall notice presently that it was not entirely absent.) God did indeed go before Israel in the desert to lead them along the way, but God veiled himself in the pillar of cloud and of fire. He was indeed present among them, but it was the unapproachable presence of Sinai and of the Holy of Holies. His presence with Israel was quite different from Christ's with his disciples. Also God's own involvement in the way from Egypt to the Promised Land was quite different from Christ's involvement in the way from Bethlehem to the Mount of Olives. The form in which God presented himself was hardly such as to call forth imitation. That something of his attributes and his ways could be learned from his dealings with Israel is of course true, and that these things had implications for Israel's conduct is also true. But this matter seems to have been more the by-product of his relations with Israel than the main point. Tinsley's point is well taken that in Israel the contemplation of God took "the dynamic form of conforming one's conduct to what he had shown himself to be during the journey to the Promised Land." ⁵⁵

---

52  See below, pp. 68f.
53  Tinsley, *Imitation*, p. 50.
54  *Ibid.*, p. 51.
55  *Ibid.*, p. 35.

However, the major activity in such a process of conforming was not becoming like God and adopting his ways of acting as one's own, but molding oneself into a proper counterpart as follower, servant, and person in covenant with such a God. The expressions "walking in God's ways" and "following God" express not the imitating of God, but the obeying of him and the enjoying of covenantal fellowship with him. Tinsley's placing all this under the heading of imitation may be of some service in his plea for a proper mysticism. However, such a usage of the term imitation is much broader and looser than that of the New Testament. The service it performs in understanding the background of the New Testament usage is minimal.

We have been discussing the question of whether the idea of imitation of God is to be found in the Old Testament or not. Obviously there is no express statement of it. Neither is it to be found in the expressions "following God" or "walking in his ways." But is it not suggested and implied in certain other passages or expressions found in the Old Testament? There is the matter of the image of God in man, for instance. In the creation account we read that man was made in the image and after the likeness of God (Gen. 1:26,27; 5:1). God's image in man is mentioned again in connection with the command not to shed man's blood (Gen. 9:6). The subject appears less specifically in the great psalm of praise to God concerning the high position he has given man in the creation (Ps. 8:5ff.). The thought which these various passages have in common is their emphasis on the uniqueness of man as God created him, particularly in relation to the animal world.[56] Undoubtedly there are many implications to be found in the fact that man was made in the image of God. Is there the implication that it is incumbent upon man to reflect that image and to be that image? Does this fact not point man to an ethical imperative? The rabbis, the church fathers, and various theologians in all ages have seen this kind of implication here. The New Testament too moves from the thought of being created in God's image to the obligation to imitate him.[57] However, if man's being created in the image of God implied that God is the ultimate pattern for man and that as God's image man ought to measure his conduct in terms of God's and bring it into likeness to God's, then it can only be said that the Old Testament never made this implication specific.[58] The imitation thought, insofar as it lies implicit in the passages on the image of God, remained in the stage of raw material, probably undetected, but at least not clarified and developed.

The thought of the imitation of God also lies very close at hand in certain passages which speak about God's actions or attributes in close connection with man's. For instance, Deut. 10:18f. says, "He (God) doth execute justice for the fatherless and widow, and loveth the sojourner, in giving him food and raiment. Love ye therefore the sojourner; for ye were sojourners in the

---

[56] Sirach 17:3f. speaks of the image in this same context.
[57] See discussion of Eph. 4:25—5:2 and Col. 3:10—13 below, pp. 75ff.
[58] In *Wisdom of Solomon* 3:2 the reference to man's being made in the image of God's eternity is another instance of the usage of the expression to describe man's perfection, but again there is no hint in the context of an ethical imperative deriving from this.

land of Egypt." God loveth the sojourner; love ye therefore the sojourner. This sounds like a clear call to imitate God. Commentators often explain it in such terms.[59] However, it ought also to be noticed that a very specific motive for loving strangers is immediately stated: "for ye were sojourners in the land of Egypt."[60] In speaking about proper treatment of servant classes and foreigners, the Pentateuch on various occasions reminds the Israelites of the days in Egypt when they were in a less favorable social position (see *e.g.*, Exod. 22:21; 23:9; Lev. 19:34; Deut. 5:14f.; 15:15; 24:18). Recalling these days is calculated to remind Israel of how well she can understand the situation of the servants and sojourners and to awaken in her a sympathetic heart. In view of her experience in Egypt she knows "the heart of a sojourner" (Exod. 23:9). Thus she has a special motive for heeding God's commands that they be shown great consideration. Sometimes Israel's obedience to the commands regarding the less privileged classes is further motivated with the reminder that God rescued Israel and brought her out of her bondage and that as their Redeemer and Lord he is issuing commands to them.[61] This kind of motivation is not entirely absent from the verses which follow Deut. 10:19. However, the specific motivation for the command in Deut. 10:19 that Israel is to show love to sojourners is in the addition: "for ye were sojourners in the land of Egypt." While the thought of Israel's imitating God in the matter of loving sojourners seems for the moment to have risen to the surface, this thought is immediately submerged again by the onward movement of the thought. In learning love to sojourners Israel is specifically pointed not to God's attitudes toward sojourners but to her own recent experiences of being a sojourner herself.

In Lev. 19:2 is the command: "Ye shall be holy, for I Jehovah your God am holy." Peter uses this command in connection with the call, "like as he who called you is holy, be ye yourselves also holy" (I Pet. 1:15,16). Hence, he uses it as a call for imitation. The Leviticus command may also lie behind Jesus' words: "Ye therefore shall be perfect, as your heavenly Father is perfect" (Matt. 5:48), in which case it is again in a clear imitation context.[62] In its own context in Leviticus the command presents no direct call to imitation. It presents rather the fundamental condition and requirement for all fellowship and association with a holy God.[63] It does not command

---

59 Driver, *Deut.*, p. 126: "In your attitude towards the dependent foreigner imitate Jehovah..."; J. Ridderbos, *Het Boek Deuteronomium*, K.V. Kampen: J. H. Kok, 1950, p. 152: "Motief hiertoe [the loving of sojourners] is (blijkens het verband), dat ze aldus navolgers Gods zullen zijn, vgl. Ef. 5:1."

60 The "therefore" in "love ye therefore" is not to be stressed. Driver remarks, it is "the enclitic 'therefore' (Hebrew ו), not the emphatic 'therefore' (על כן or לכן)" (*Deut.*, p. 127). It expresses informal inference or consequence (see F. Brown, S. R. Driver, and C. C. Briggs, *A Hebrew and English Lexicon of the Old Testament*, Oxford: Clarendon Press, 1952, *sub* ו, § 4). On the other hand the "for" in "for ye were sojourners" is the causal conjunction כי.

61 *Cf.* Deut. 5:15; 15:15; 24:18, noticing in each case how the reminder of their bondage in Egypt and of God's rescue is followed immediately by a statement to the effect that *therefore* (על־כן) God commands you to do this.

62 See below, p. 73.

63 O. Procksch, ἅγιος, *T.W.N.T.*, I, p. 91, 32f.: "Jahwes Heiligkeit fordert die Heiligkeit des Volkes als Bedingung des Verkehrs."

holiness *like* God's holiness, but holiness *because of* (כי) God's holiness. The laws which follow are no explication or illustration of God's holiness. It is possible that God might serve as an example in regard to some of these areas of holiness; *e.g.*, not doing unrighteousness in judgment (vs. 15), not hating (vs. 17), not taking vengeance (vs. 18), etc. However, for most of the areas God could not be an example or pattern since the matter at issue is foreign to his being; *e.g.*, fearing one's father and mother (vs. 3), offering sacrifice (vs. 5), not reaping the corners of the harvest (vs. 9), lying with a woman (vs. 20), eating blood (vs. 26), etc. One can not entirely escape the matter of imitation in the holiness command, for in commanding Israel's holiness it cites God's holiness. However, the relationship in which the ideas are expressed does not direct attention to Israel's imitating God's holiness, but rather to Israel's recognizing that God's holiness demands her holiness. The laws which follow present the way.

Other texts might be cited where there is possibly some hint at God's being an object for man's imitation. For instance, in I Sam. 20:14 Jonathan says to David: "Thou shalt not only while yet I live show me the lovingkindness of Jehovah, that I die not." Is this the kindness such as God shows, or the kindness imposed by God in obligation of the oath David had made? The same problem is found in II Sam. 9:3 in David's question: "Is there not yet any of the house of Saul, that I may show the kindness of God unto him?" Commentators express differences of opinion on these questions,[64] and it is difficult to decide. It is possible that God was here looked to as an example and pattern of true kindness.

The same can be said for the fourth commandment as it appears in Exod. 20:8–11. After speaking of Israel's duty to work six days and to keep the seventh as a sabbath to Jehovah their God, an explanation and recommendation is added: "For in six days Jehovah made heaven and earth, the sea, and all that in them is, and rested the seventh day: wherefore Jehovah blessed the sabbath day and hallowed it" (vs. 11). Israel is reminded that this pattern which God is commanding them to observe is the pattern which he himself observed in the creation of the world, and that it was from this day of his resting from his creative work that the Sabbath derives its hallowed character. The observation has sometimes been made that we can here see man as an imitator of God.[65] The observation is correct, but to what extent it may be emphasized is debatable. The thrust of the added recommendation is not the appeal, "Be like God in working six days and then resting on the

---

[64] H. P. Smith, *A Critical and Exegetical Commentary on the Books of Samuel*, I.C.C., Edinburgh: T. & T. Clark, 1904, p. 312 says "It is difficult to suppose the meaning to be *kindness such as God shows*. More probably it is the kindness imposed by God in obligation of the oath." N. Glueck, *Das Wort Chesed im alttestamentlichen Sprachgebrauch als menschliche Verhaltungsweise in profaner und religiöser Bedeutung*, (Inaugural-Dissertation), Jena, 1927, p. 15, admits concerning Smith's conclusion: "Diese Deutung ist vielleicht möglich." However, he expresses as his preference "dass David ebensolchen unverbrüchlichen חסד zu erweisen bereit war wie Gott den ihm Nahestehenden, denn der Zug der Pflichttreue, der Unverbrüchlichkeit, wohnt dem Begriffe חסד entschieden bei." So also Tinsley, *Imitation*, p. 60.

[65] Cf. J. Calvin, *Institutes of the Christian Religion* (ed. 1559), Book II, Chapter VIII. 30; W. H. Gispen, *Het Boek Exodus*, K.V., Kampen: J. H. Kok, 1951, Vol. II, p. 70.

seventh"; nor even "Keep the sabbath day holy like God kept the sabbath day holy"; but "Keep the sabbath day holy because God blessed and hallowed it at the very creation of the world." [66] There is no denying that the thought of imitation is to be found here. It may be deduced from what is said. Its role is by no means prominent. Nevertheless the thought does appear momentarily on the scene of Scripture.

We may conclude, however, that the imitation of God is neither one of the clear teachings of the Old Testament nor an integral part of the thinking of the Old Testament people. The raw materials for the idea are present; it seems to be hovering in the background of certain passages; occasionally it springs to the fore momentarily. But even then it is immediately lost in the onrush of other ideas and thoughts before it can be detected, identified, really grasped, and acted upon. The thought did not come to its own in the Old Testament.

Neither is this surprising. One need only remind himself of how highly transcendental a view of God the Old Testament had. God is the Creator of the heavens and the earth, greater than the greatest thing, more powerful than the mightiest. "Behold, the nations are as a drop of a bucket, and are accounted as the small dust of the balance: behold, he taketh up the isles as a very little thing.... All the nations are as nothing before him; they are accounted by him as less than nothing and vanity" (Isa. 40:15,17). "For a thousand years in thy sight are but as yesterday when it is past, and as a watch in the night" (Ps. 90:4). Before such a God man feels very small and powerless. He is only a creature, and that is infinitely different from the Creator God. Abraham is "but dust and ashes" (Gen. 18:27) when he stands before God. There is another side to the matter, of course; man is still a creature of this great God, and a highly favored one with whom God wishes to enter into covenant. And yet, the whole atmosphere of the Old Testament with its highly transcendent God is hardly one in which clear ideas about an imitation of God by man are to be expected. The Roman historian Tacitus described the God of the Jews as not being imitable. [67] By Tacitus' day there were various voices from the Jewish community speaking of the imitation of God. Tacitus, however, has undoubtedly correctly observed the prevailing Jewish opinion of the matter. The Old Testament had revealed a God who is highly transcendent. Hence, in regard to the imitation idea in the Old Testament we may conclude that while it does come to certain limited expression in connection with one person's walking in the ways of another, actually the whole idea plays no vital role in the Old Testament thought.

---

[66] Notice how also for the Deuteronomy version of the command the concluding "therefore"-clause serves to repeat and reinforce the basic statement of the command: "Observe the sabbath day, to keep it holy, as Jehovah thy God commanded thee.... Therefore Jehovah thy God commanded thee to keep the sabbath day" (Deut. 5:12,15).

[67] "... summum illud et aeternum neque imitabile neque interiturum." Tacitus, *Historiarum* V. 5 (ed. H. Goelzer, Paris: Société d'Édition "Les Belles Lettres," 1921. p. 297).

## III. Imitation in the Jewish World

There were changes taking place at the end of the Old Testament period. This can be seen for instance in the interpretations which the rabbinical writings were giving to various Old Testament passages and the comments they were making on them. In the Rabbinic literature the Tannaitic scholar Abba Saul (latter first century A. D.) made the following comment on the holiness command in Lev. 19:2: "It is incumbent upon the family of the King [*i.e.* Israel as God's children] to bear the imprint of the King." [68] In other words he saw the holiness command calling for an imitation of God. This same rabbi interprets Exod. 15:2 quite uniquely. For the clause "This is my God, and I will praise him," Abba Saul writes, "This is my God, and I will be as He." [69] Then he continues: "I will be as He: that is, as he is merciful and gracious, so I will be merciful and forgiving," [70] again reflecting a reasoning from God's conduct to what man ought to do. For the statement in Deut. 1:10, "Ye are this day as the stars of heaven for multitude," the Midrash [71] understands רב not as *multitude* but as *Lord, Master,* and interprets the verse: "Today you are as the stars, but in the coming life you are destined to be as your Lord." The Rabbis also took notice of the Genesis account of man's creation in the image of God. Rabbi Akiba offers a penetrating observation in this regard. He said, "Man has been highly favored: for he was created in the image of God; but it was an even higher favor *to make it known to him* that he was created in the image of God." [72] In other words the fact of our being in the image of God was made known to us to give us the urge to unfold and develop it in our lives, and thus to become imitators of God. The rabbis also found their curiosity being aroused by the fact that Gen. 1:26 had said that man was to be made in God's image and after God's likeness, while the following verse, containing the actual account of the making of man, says only that he was made in God's image. Why was there no mention of the likeness? A haggadistic explanation informs us, "Only in

---

[68] Midrash Sifre on Lev. 19:2. *Cf.* H. J. Schoeps, "Von der Imitatio Dei zur Nachfolge Christi," *Aus Frühchristlicher Zeit,* Tübingen: J. C. B. Mohr (Paul Siebeck), 1950, p. 286.

[69] He has resolved ואנוהו ("I will praise him") into the elements אני והו ("I and he"). This phrase אני והו has been of considerable interest to Jewish scholars. It is proposed that the secret of the tetragrammaton (Jahweh) is to be found in it. Schoeps, *Frühchristl. Zeit*, p. 287, writes: "In dieser Auslegung des Abba Schaul ist ein Geheimnis angerührt worden: das Mysterium des Schem ha-mephorasch, des im Tetragrammaton verborgenen Gottesnamens, der in der Zeit der Mischna nur noch bei einzelnen kultischen Gelegenheiten (Priestersegen, Wasserspende am Sukkothfest) ausgesprochen, später verschluckt und dann mit adonaj umschrieben wurde. Auf Grund je einer Bibel-, Mischna und Talmudnotiz ist zu erschliessen, dass dieser Name אני והו der geheimnisvolle Gottesname gewesen ist oder doch mit ihm in engem Zusammenhang gestanden hat." *Cf.* also G. Klein, *Der älteste christliche Katechismus und die jüdische Propaganda-Literatur,* Berlin: G. Reimer, 1909, p. 48.

[70] Palestinian Talmud: *Peah* 15b. *Cf.* Schoeps, *Frühchristl. Zeit*, p. 287.

[71] Debarim Rabba on Deut. 1:10. *Cf.* M. Buber, "Nachahmung Gottes," *Der Morgen,* I (1925–26), p. 642.

[72] *Pirque Aboth* III. *Cf.* Buber, *Morgen,* I, p. 644.

the image, and not also after the likeness, because the likeness is a matter for man to accomplish." [73]

The rabbis were not satisfied however in speaking of the imitation of God in purely general terms. Some of them sought to say just how God ought to be imitated. Rabbi Chama ben Chanina gave the following explanation:

> What means the text, *Ye shall walk after the Lord your God* [Deut. 13:5]? Is it, then, possible for a human being to walk after the *Shechinah;* for has it not been said, *For the Lord thy God is a devouring fire* [Deut. 4:24]? But [the meaning is] to walk after the attributes of the Holy One, blessed be He. As He clothes the naked, for it is written, *And the Lord God made for Adam and for his wife coats of skin and clothed them* [Gen. 3:21], so do thou also clothe the naked. The Holy One, blessed be He, visited the sick, for it is written, *And the Lord appeared unto him* [Abraham] *by the oaks of Mamre* [Gen. 18:1. The Haggada deduced that the occasion was when Abraham was recovering from his circumcision.], so do thou also visit the sick. The Holy One, blessed be He, comforted mourners, for it is written, *And it came to pass after the death of Abraham, that God blessed Isaac his son* [Gen. 25:11], so do thou also comfort mourners. The Holy One, blessed be He, buried the dead, for it is written, *And He buried him* [Moses] *in the valley* [Deut. 34:6], so do thou also bury the dead. [74]

Hence, for the rabbis the following of God meant to follow his ways; but this did not mean merely the ways which he had commanded. Man must walk in God's own ways, and do what he does. Man must view his attributes and perfections and seek to do the same thing. Man must imitate him. [75]

These passages from rabbinical literature give little help in understanding the passages in the Old Testament to which they apply, since they do not seek to discover and explain the sense of the words in the context in which they appear in the Old Testament. However, these passages do serve to illustrate how the idea of imitating God had taken hold in Jewish thinking.

There was another form in which the matter of imitation came to expression with the development of Rabbinic Judaism. Formal schooling became important for the teaching of the law and the faithful transmission of the sacred traditions. Teachers surrounded themselves with pupils; apt pupils sought to gain admittance to the circles of a suitable teacher. Here, as in Greece, the learning process was viewed as involving much more than acquiring mastery over certain amounts of study material. Rather, it was seen as a kind of

---

[73] Yalqut Reubeni on Gen. 1:27. *Cf.* Buber, *Morgen,* I, p. 644.
[74] Babylonian Talmud: *Sotah* 14a. (trans. A. Cohen, in *The Babylonian Talmud: Seder Nashim VI* [ed. I. Epstein] London: The Soncino Press, 1936 [Sotah] pp. 72,73.)
[75] This explanation by Rabbi Chama has the distinction in incipient form which later Jewish theology made between God's metaphysical and moral attributes. Regarding the imitation of God, K. Kohler, *Jewish Theology Systematically and Historically Considered,* New York: Macmillan, 1918, p. 102, explains: "Moses approached God with two petitions, the one, 'Show me thy ways that I may know thee!' the other, 'Show me, I pray thee, thy glory!' In response to the latter God said, 'No man can see me and live,' but the former petition was granted in that the Lord revealed himself in his moral attributes (Exod. xxxiii. 13–23). These alone can be understood and emulated by man; in regard to the so-called metaphysical attributes, God will ever remain beyond human comprehension and emulation."

apprenticeship in living, where the pupil lived with the master, went with him on all occasions, observed his actions and reactions to all kinds of situations, and learned not only his knowledge but his way of life. The sacred traditions which were to be learned were found in the life and actions of the teacher, as well as in his words. As Gerhardsson observes: "The most mature teachers ... incarnated the perfect tradition from the fathers, from Sinai and from God. That is why their words and deeds were of such interest. The pupil had to absorb all the traditional wisdom with 'eyes, ears and every member' by seeking the company of a Rabbi, by serving him (שימש), following him and imitating him (הלך אחרי), and not only by listening to him. The task of the pupil is therefore not only to hear (שמע) but also to see (ראה)." [76] Thus problems which arose in rabbinic discussions could be settled when some rabbi simply told what he had seen a former authoritative teacher do. [77] Teachers on their part not only taught by use of specific symbolical actions calculated to illustrate some point, but also had to be conscious that their most ordinary actions were being observed, studied, and remembered by their pupils. Sometimes rabbis found it expedient to deviate from some common way of doing things, simply to show that there was freedom in this matter and that the common way must not be considered mandatory and inviolable. [78] Hence, as Gerhardsson has so ably pointed out, the pupil is an imitator; [79] and the teacher is an example. [80]

As for the other Jewish writings of the pre-New Testament and early New Testament times, we have already noted in our survey of μιμέομαι how the thought of imitation has now come to clear expression. The references to the imitation of God are now outright [81] as well as implicit. [82] Also there is a new sense of awareness of the great men of the past and an interest in extolling their virtues. For instance, there is the long passage in *Sirach* (chapters 44—50), which begins thus: "Let us now praise famous men, and our fathers in their generations" (44:1), and then proceeds to do just that. It speaks in glowing terms of their great superiority, perfection, and glory, and of how mightily God used them and how greatly he rewarded them. The passage is interspersed with such utterances as the following concerning the judges: "May their bones revive from where they lie, and may the name

---

[76] B. Gerhardsson, *Memory and Manuscript*, Uppsala: Almquist & Wiksells, 1961, pp. 182,183.
[77] *Cf.* Mishnah: *Sukkah* II. 5; III. 9; Babylonian Talmud: *Berakoth* 24a; 38b.
[78] Tosefta: *Berakoth* I. 6: "Lest the pupils should see it and establish a fixed halakah from your words" (or "action"). Gerhardsson, *Memory*, pp. 186,187, further illustrates how teachers were conscious of their example to their pupils from Tosefta: *Demai* V. 24, and Babylonian Talmud: *Erubin* 93b,94a.
[79] "The alert pupil by studying his teacher's behaviour can learn his wisdom, even on those points on which he does not give verbal instruction. The paths of the Torah are also taught in this way—the way of *imitatio magistri*" (Gerhardsson, *Memory*, pp. 184,185).
[80] "The teacher was, and had to be, conscious of his actions. His behaviour is taken as an example, as teaching. The teacher knows that his pupils will deduce his halakic opinions from his conduct" (Gerhardsson, *Memory*, p. 187).
[81] *Testament of Asher* 4:3; *Letter of Aristeas* 188, 210. 280, 281; Philo, *De Decalogo* 111, *et al.*
[82] *Cf. Sirach* 12:1—7, especially vs. 6; *Wisdom of Solomon* 12:19 and context.

of those who have been honored live again in their sons!" (46:12). *I Maccabees* has a similar, though much less extensive, list (2:51—60), beginning: "Remember the deeds of the fathers." The writer then proceeds to mention a series of famous men and how because of some virtue or virtuous act they came to some high station or received some great reward. Abraham is often cited as an illustration of faith and obedience (see *IV Macc.* 13:12; 15:28; 17:6; *Wisdom* 10:5). Isaac is often held up as the pattern of the willing martyr (see *Judith* 8:26; *Tobit* 4:12; *IV Macc.* 13:12; 17:6). The fathers are also held up in admiration before the heathen.[83] Sometimes there are direct calls to imitate them. We read of the imitation of Joseph,[84] of Moses,[85] of David,[86] and of the forefathers.[87] In *II Maccabees* and especially in *IV Maccabees* the imitation and exemplariness of those who hold fast to the faith at times of persecution become very prominent.

These passages in *II* and *IV Maccabees* present an interesting study in the call to imitation and in the use of various words to express exemplariness. They picture three situations which have remarkable similarities. In each case a person in a position of leadership was on public exhibition before a heathen king who was attempting to get him to commit an idolatrous act. In each case the person chose to suffer the most gruesome kinds of torture and death rather than commit idolatry. In each case the person either saw himself or was seen by others as setting an example for his fellow countrymen of keeping the law and maintaining the faith of the fathers. In *IV Macc.* 13 the seven brothers encouraged each other to imitate Shadrach, Meshach, and Abed-nego, Jewish leaders in Babylon (Dan. 3:12), who accepted the ordeal of the fiery furnace rather than bow down before the golden image. The brothers found this ordeal similar to theirs, and theirs is described in such phrases as " a holy choice of religion" (vs. 8), "die on behalf of the Law" (vs. 9), and "the demonstration of religion" (vs. 10). In *IV Macc.* 9 the eldest of the seven brothers, who is the family head,[88] calls his younger brothers to imitate him in accepting death rather than eating the swine's flesh. The test involves basic religious commitment, since the meat has been consecrated to idols (5:2; *cf. II Macc.* 6:21, where it is called "the

---

[83] *Cf. e.g.*, Josephus' praise of Moses: "Throughout all this he proved the best of generals, the sagest of counsellors, and the most conscientious of guardians. He succeeded in making the whole people dependent upon himself, and having secured their obedience in all things, he did not use his influence for any personal aggrandizement. No; at the very moment when leading men assume absolute and despotic power and accustom their subjects to a life of extreme lawlessness, he on the contrary, having reached that commanding position, considered it incumbent on him to live piously and to provide for his people an abundance of good laws, in the belief that this was the best means of displaying his own virtue and of ensuring the lasting welfare of those who had made him their leader." Josephus, *Against Apion* II. 158, 159 (ed. H. St. J. Thackeray, Vol. I, *L.C.L.*, London: Wm. Heinemann, pp. 354—357). Josephus here is only doing what Hellenistic Jews had been doing now for several centuries. Already in the historical writings of Demetrius (about 200 B.C.) a new attitude toward Old Testament history is apparent. It was being carefully analyzed and interpreted in such a way as to be logically acceptable and morally justifiable. It had to be shown to be worthy of imitation by later generations. See J. L. Koole, *De Joden in de Verstrooiing*, Franeker: T. Wever, 1946, pp. 71,72.

[84] *Testament of Benjamin* 3:1; 4:1.
[85] Philo, *De Vita Mosis* I. 158.
[86] Josephus, *Antiquities* VIII. 315; IX. 44.
[87] Josephus, *Against Apion* II. 205.
[88] That the father is dead is clear from 18:9.

sacrificial meal"). The eldest brother calls them to "fight the sacred and noble fight for religion's sake" (vs. 24). In *IV Macc.* 6 the reference to imitation as such is not found, but in its place is the reference to being an example and model to others. Eleazar, a priest and expert in the law (5:4), [89] refuses to go along with a substitute proposal calculated to present a way out for him, namely, that he simply pretend to eat the swine's flesh rather than actually doing so. He refuses, lest he be "a model (τύπος) of impiety to the young by setting an example (παράδειγμα) for the eating of forbidden food" (6:19). The matter at stake is "to protect our divine Law unto death" (vs. 21), and to "die nobly for piety's sake" (vs. 22). The account of Eleazar's fortitude in *II Maccabees* also speaks of him as an example. Eleazar says: "Therefore, by manfully giving up my life now, I will ... leave to the young a noble example of how to die a good death willingly and nobly for the revered and holy laws" (6:27,28). The account concludes: "So in this way he died, leaving in his death an example of nobility and a memorial of courage, not only to the young but to the great body of his nation" (6:31). In *II Maccabees* the Greek word for example is ὑπόδειγμα rather than τύπος and παράδειγμα as in *IV Maccabees*. *IV Maccabees* also uses this word in the sense of example. In *IV Macc.* 17:23 we read, "For the tyrant Antiochus ... advertised their endurance [namely that of the seven martyred sons and their mother] as a pattern (ὑπόδειγμα) to his own soldiers." Hence in these two books we have a remarkable confluence and interchange of terms expressing exemplariness, where the call to imitation is obviously implicit. [90]

The apocryphal and pseudepigraphical literature speak expressly about imitation. In this they are at one with the rabbinical literature, and in this both groups differ from the Old Testament. [91] How is this development in Jewish thinking to be accounted for? The answer lies immediately at hand. The Jewish world had come into contact with the Greek world. The two worlds penetrated each other from both directions. The Greek world was reaching into the Jewish world; and the Jewish world was also reaching into the Greek world.

After the conquests of Alexander the Great in the fourth century B.C. the

---

89 According to *II Macc.* 6:18: τις τῶν πρωτευόντων γραμματέων.

90 The word ὑπογραμμός is also found in *II Maccabees* (2:28). In I Pet. 2:21 this word is used in the sense of example: "Christ also suffered for you, leaving you an example that ye should follow his steps." However, in *II Macc.* 2:28 it is not used of human conduct but in connection with the condensation of a piece of writing, and means *outline*. In order to complete the survey of the Apocrypha's use of words expressing the idea of personal example, the following two instances may be noted: "Thou didst make them [the men of Sodom] an example (παράδειγμα) to future generations" (*III Macc.* 2:5); and "[Enoch] was an example (ὑπόδειγμα) of repentance to all generations" (*Sirach* 44:16).

91 The Qumran literature is like the Old Testament as far as the matter of imitation and giving or following a personal example is concerned. I have discovered no specific expression of these thoughts in this literature. The expression "walking in the ways of God" is used in the same way as in the Old Testament. The close relation it has to keeping God's laws is seen by the use of such modifiers as "blamelessly" or "which He has commanded" (cf. e.g. 1QS [*Manual of Discipline*] 2:2; 3:9; 8:21; etc.). Also like the Old Testament is such a phrase as "walking in the ways of the godless" (CD [*Damascus or Zadokite Document*] 19:21), where its primary designation is that of the religious commitment, although the idea of imitation is perhaps not entirely foreign to the phrase (see above, pp. 32f.). There is no reference to the image of God in man, nor any use of "likeness" (דמה and related forms) in connection with human conduct (cf. K. G. Kuhn, *Konkordanz zu den Qumrantexten*, Göttingen: Vandenhoeck & Ruprecht, 1960, *s.v.*).

Greek spirit held sway throughout the eastern Mediterranean world. It made its influence felt both through a natural infiltration of the culture of the conquered nations and through various programs of foisting itself on the subject peoples. In Jewry this caused varying reactions. Some were so agreeable and enthusiastic about the new ways that they even submitted to operations to disguise their circumcision. Others were violently and unalterably opposed to all forms of Hellenism. In the Maccabean struggles the strength of the latter reaction becomes apparent. However, in this connection the impossibility of escaping every form of Hellenistic influence also becomes apparent. The accounts which tell us of the immovable faithfulness to the traditions of the fathers by the aged scribe Eleazar and the mother and her seven sons show them giving such attention to the example they are setting and making such an appeal to imitate it that we can only conclude that in their brave fight against Hellenism they have unwittingly adopted a Hellenistic stance. The Hellenistic moralism of Hellenism's most unyielding opponents as pictured in *II* and *IV Maccabees* is an interesting idiosyncrasy.

The impact and influence of Hellenism could not be completely avoided. Neither does that appear to have been the avowed aim and purpose of Jewry in general. The Jewish mind was indeed open to new insights, and was able to work with them and benefit from them, but at the same time it was essentially conservative of the old ways. [92] Contact with Greek thought rarely resulted in its outright adoption. Nevertheless, there was no escaping the effects of it, and even the rabbis were no exception. [93] This new wealth of thought and culture which spread over the Mediterranean world provided the Jewish thinkers with new insights, new expressions, and new ways of thinking.

There were certain elements of Jewry which went much farther than others in absorbing Hellenism. The Greek world had not only moved into contact with the Jewish world, but the Jewish world had also been reaching out into the Greek world. Since the time of the exiles into Assyria and Babylonia the Israelites had become more and more a people dispersed throughout the

---

[92] "Wenn sie aber in Widerstreit mit israelitischer Religion, Sitte und Denkart kamen, wurde der Stoff teils umgearbeitet, teils ausgemerzt, teils ergänzt, teils neu geschaffen. In der Klarheit, mit der dies gesehen und in der Strenge, mit der es durchgeführt wurde, liegt eine der wesentlichsten Leistungen der israelitischen Denker und Schriftsteller. Hinzu kommt, dass auf dem religiösen und moralischen Gebiete Originalität überhaupt nicht hoch geschätzt wird. Im Gegenteil, alle grossen religiösen Geister, auch die originellsten, treten mit dem Anspruch auf, die alte Religion zu verkündigen" (T. Boman, *Das hebräische Denken im Vergleich mit dem Griechischen*, Göttingen, Vandenhoeck & Ruprecht, 1954, pp. 159,160).

[93] "The sharp distinction between a Hellenistic and a Rabbinic Judaism in the New Testament period is being abandoned as it is found that many Hellenistic ideas had crept into, and been consciously taken over by, Rabbinism long before, and that the process, though slowed down, was not halted. Some Jewish scholars take offence at the suggestion of foreign influence. Yet the exclusion of Hellenistic ideas would not prove the Rabbis free from such influence; only they might have adopted the narrow, chauvinistic attitude of some of the surrounding nations, or perhaps have practised *imitation par opposition*. Surely, the greatest were those, who, without sacrificing the essentials of their religion, made use of human achievement regardless of its origin" (D. Daube, *The New Testament and Rabbinic Judaism*, London: The Athlone Press, 1956, p. ix).

Middle Eastern world. Both the banishments by political conquerors and the opportunism of the people themselves in seeking a more favorable lot in life and more favorable circumstances and surroundings worked in the direction of building a Jewish colony in almost every important city in the Middle East. A kind of cosmopolitanism developed among these Jewish people, so that Philo, himself a Jew of the dispersion, could write that while the many Jews living outside of Palestine might look upon Jerusalem and its temple as being their mother city, they nevertheless held the lands in which they lived as being in a real sense their fatherland.[94]

At the same time there developed a sense of mission in these dispersed Jews toward the people among whom they were living.[95] The large body of Jewish literature that was produced during these days was much more than an explanation and a defence of Judaism. It was a recommendation of Judaism to the non-Jewish world. It was propaganda. Men wrote out of a sense of having a revelation from God which must be made known to the world. Paul makes reference to this sense of calling among the Jews when he says of them: "But if thou bearest the name of a Jew, ... and art confident that thou thyself art a guide of the blind, a light of them that are in darkness, a corrector of the foolish, a teacher of babes, having in the law the form of knowledge and of the truth..." (Rom. 2:17,19,20). Hence, on the side of the Jews there was sometimes a real openness to Hellenism, a seeking of points of contact from which reasoning about the Jewish faith could proceed, or a conviction that all the wisdom of the Greeks could finally be shown to be dependent on the revelation of God given in the Old Testament. Hellenistic culture had overflowed the eastern Mediterranean world, and the world of the Jews remained neither impervious nor oblivious to it all.

The extent to which Judaism and Hellenism were being mingled in those days is illustrated most fully in the Alexandrian Jew Philo. Some Jews who were attracted by Hellenism made no attempt to reconcile it with their Judaism, but simply forsook the Judaism in favor of Hellenism. Philo had no such inclinations. He was a Jew through and through, and was intent upon making the revelation from God which was contained in his Old Testament Scriptures known and understood by those living around him. He was also convinced that Greek philosophy was basically at one with the Old Testament and that the Hellenistic world could be brought to recognize the truth of the Old Testament if it were portrayed to them in terms of Greek philosophy. Thus, working as a biblical theologian, beginning with a biblical text, commenting on it, and constantly referring to it and other appropriate biblical passages, he worked out his elaborate explanations and discourses on biblical themes. The end result more often than not turned out to be pure Platonism and Stoicism. In such a man it is not at all surprising to find a Jew purporting to present Judaism and yet using all the typical Greek expressions and ideas. He does so in regard to imitation as the way toward man's goal in life, using

---

[94] *In Flaccum* 46.
[95] Koole, *De Joden*. See especially chapter 2: "De Roeping," pp. 22—27.

such phrases as "likeness to God," [96] "following God," [97] and "imitating God as far as possible." [98] Philo is the pre-eminent example of a Hellenistic Jew.

Koole has pointed out several missteps which the Hellenistic Jews rather generally took in presenting the faith of their fathers to the non-Jewish world around them. [99] The imitation idea as it was coming to expression in Jewish literature had some relation to two of these deviating tendencies. For one thing, the Hellenistic Jew often tended to take the stance of the Greek philosopher and to make his appeal from this position. His Jewish religion turned out to be more of a good philosophy than a living faith. He came offering true knowledge, superior wisdom, correct insight. It was an *Aufklärung;* his religion brought enlightenment. Thus we find him arguing the foolishness of idolatry, the utter ridiculousness of worshipping images, the hygienic values of circumcision, etc. His religion comes closer to being an adequate philosophy for a cultured man than a deep-seated faith which is rooted in a revelation from God and in a personal communion with this God who has revealed himself to him. One detects traces of the same tendency in the interest which had developed in holding God before the world of men, heathen kings included, [100] as an example of conduct worth imitating, or in the interest bestowed on recommending the great men of the past for their virtue. Judaism was presenting itself more as a moral philosophy than as the faith of the fathers.

Another devious tendency which Hellenistic Judaism was developing was to forget that her history as the Old Testament presented it was a history of the course of revelation from God. The Old Testament was no collection of random experiences between this man and God and then that man and God. But Judaism became desperately interested in finding a universal significance in her history and took the questionable course of trying to allegorize a general truth or moralize a nice lesson from each event. The Old Testament was no longer the record of God entering into covenant, speaking in grace, coming in judgment with certain specific men in certain specific historical circumstances. It was a collection of events which, when properly interpreted and understood, could take place in almost anyone's life. The patriarchs, for instance, were hardly living persons any more; rather they were moral figures, models of piety and virtue. As Koole colorfully puts it: "For Philo the whole of sacred history was a kind of Pilgrim's progress to eternity." [101] The new interest among the Jews in the example set by their forefathers could have some bad side effects. They were in danger of losing

---

[96] "Only for souls who regard it as their goal to be conformed to God (πρὸς ... θεὸν ἐξομοίωσιν) ... is it lawful to draw night to Him." *De Opificio Mundi* 144 (Colson and Whitaker, I, pp. 114,115).
[97] "To follow God (τὸ ἔπεσθαι θεῷ) is ... our aim and object." *De Migratione Abrahami* 131 (Colson and Whitaker, IV, pp. 206,207).
[98] "A man should imitate God as much as may be (μιμεῖσθαι θεὸν καθ' ὅσον οἷόν) and leave nothing undone that may promote such assimilation as is possible (τῶν εἰς τὴν ἐνδεχομένην ἐξομοίωσιν)." *De Virtutibus* 168 (Colson and Whitaker, VIII, pp. 266,267).
[99] See Koole, *De Joden,* chap. 7: "De Fouten," pp. 93—101.
[100] Cf. *Letter of Aristeas* 188, 210, 280, 281.
[101] Koole, *De Joden,* p. 97 (my translation).

their Old Testament. It was no longer a record of God's mighty deeds and his glorious revelation; it had become a book of general ethical truths and moral illustrations.

The Jewish world at the dawn of New Testament times was aware of the processes of imitation and the influences of exemplary conduct. However, a person sensitive to the genius of the Old Testament religion could not be overjoyed by much that was being said about these things. Some dangerously moralistic attitudes were developing, and the true faith of the fathers was sometimes going into eclipse. It was not immediately apparent whether the ideas of imitation and personal example could serve a useful purpose in the period of New Testament revelation, or whether they might prove to be harmful influences.

## IV. Imitation in the New Testament World

In the New Testament the center of attention is on Jesus Christ. His central role can also be seen in the whole complex of ideas expressing imitation and personal example. The idea of the imitation of Jesus Christ was a spark which often took hold in Christians of later times, and at some periods of history it has burned with considerable brightness. Sometimes it took on the most rigorous external expression of poverty, humility, and suffering; then again it became a highly internal, mystical, and meditative exercise. In view of the great emphasis which the imitation of Christ has received in the history of the Christian church, it is often rather surprising to note how seldom the New Testament speaks about it directly. Furthermore, the New Testament speaks about other imitation than that of Christ; and this we seldom hear about. In seeking to find the significance of Paul's calling for the imitation of himself, we must have some acquaintance with the other calls to imitation found in the New Testament. Both Jesus and God are held before the New Testament readers as objects of imitation. There is also the call to imitate other men. We shall study the material in this order: the imitation of Christ, of God, and of other men.

### A. *The Imitation of Christ.*

During Jesus' ministry on earth there were people constantly following him. Much of this was a spontaneous enthusiasm for his words and deeds; much of it also was simple curiosity-seeking. But there were some who followed him as a vocation; they had heard his call. Mark's Gospel tells us that one day Jesus saw two men busy with their fishing nets by the sea of Galilee: "And Jesus said unto them, Come ye after me, and I will make you to become fishers of men. And straightway they left the nets, and followed him" (Mark 1:17–18). Here we see the early stages of a movement among men which was to have most far-reaching consequences. Men dropped what they had been doing up to that point, turned their back on the way of life they had known till then, and went along with Jesus. They responded to the call from Jesus: "Follow me." In the gospel accounts the call is heard over and over again. It came to have a very specific meaning and content. Basically it expressed a simple observable fact: Jesus called men to fall in behind him in the procession which he led. Such a scene was common in Old Testament times, where various persons commanding respect travelled about with their retinues following them (cf. Judg. 9:4,49; Jer. 2:2; I Kings 19:20f.). The expression was the standard one to express the relation of the rabbi and his pupils.[102] This use of the term "following" expressed more than just a physical relationship. It was a part of the standard terminology in connection with the educational system common in that day, where pupils left the ordinary relationships and occupations of life, sought admittance to the company of a teacher and committed themselves to living fulltime with the teacher during the period of education. The commitment involved the pupil's time and service, but it went beyond that. The pupil set himself to the task of learning the way of life of the master, and of making that way of life his own. Hence he gave careful heed to all the master knew, was, did, and stood for. The pupil *followed* the master. We read that Jesus chose disciples "that they might be with him" (Mark 3:14). This was not the ordinary procedure by which a rabbi and his pupils came together, for usually the pupils took the initiative and sought to gain admittance to the circle of a rabbi. Nevertheless, in many respects Jesus was forming a company of a teacher and his pupils after the common pattern of the day.[103] The roots of the expression "following Jesus" are probably to be found in this kind of relationship in which he and they lived.

However, "following Jesus," as the New Testament uses the expression, had a much deeper meaning than the common master-pupil relationship. The rigid limits to which the New Testament confines itself in speaking of the metaphorical "following" of a person already suggests how uniquely it viewed the following of Jesus. The New Testament writers present only Jesus as a person to be followed. The uniqueness of Jesus' call to follow becomes fully evident by noting its implications and its results.[104] It was a religious call; in fact, it was the call of the Messiah himself.[105] It was a call to service; to follow meant to serve him personally, both directly (*cf.* Mark 15:41), and indirectly (*cf.* Matt. 25:45). It meant to be directed into the service of those in whose behalf the Messiah had come, to become fishers of men (Mark 1:17),

---

[102] For various examples from Rabbinic literature, see Kittel, *T.W.N.T.*, I, p. 213, 18—28.

[103] For the sense in which Jesus was a rabbi, and for the ways in which he differed from the rabbis of his day, see E. Lohse, ῥαββί, *T.W.N.T.*, VI, pp. 965f. *Cf.* also the differences between Jesus with his pupils and the rabbis with their students with regard to teacher-pupil relationships and the aim of the educational process in T. W. Manson, *The Teaching of Jesus*, 2nd ed., Cambridge: University Press, 1935, pp. 239f.

[104] A full exposition of the subject with a valuable study of the appropriate texts is to be found in E. Schweizer. *Erniedrigung und Erhöhung bei Jesus und seinen Nachfolgern*, Zurich: Zwingli-Verlag, 1955, p. 7ff. See also S. C. W. Duvenage, *Die Navolging van Christus*, Potchefstroom: Pro Rege-Pers Beperk, 1954, pp. 50ff.

[105] See Kittel, *T.W.N.T.*, I, p. 214, 22f.

and later to care for his sheep and lambs (John 21:15ff.). The call to follow was also an act of grace. It went to Levi, the publican, a man living outside the religious circles of God's people in uncleanness and disobedience—a despicable sinner. Levi was obviously no unique exception, for Jesus was often criticized about the company he kept and was dubbed "a friend of publicans and sinners" (Matt. 11:19). Following was a response to the call of grace. And it made one a participant in the program of salvation which he was bringing. It brought entrance to the kingdom of God (Luke 9:61,62), treasure in heaven (Mark 10:17,21), the light of life (John 8:12); it meant being "purchased from among men, to be the first fruits unto God and unto the Lamb" (Rev. 14:4). Following him meant the realization of the hope and promise for which the Israelites had been waiting so long.

Another important aspect of following Jesus was that it involved participation in his lot in life and in his fate. This is already apparent in the incident of the man who pledged himself to follow Jesus wherever he went; Jesus' immediate reply was, "The Son of man hath not where to lay his head" (Luke 9:58 par.). Jesus expressly stated the matter in most straightforward terms: "If any man would come after me, let him deny himself, and take up his cross, and follow me. For whosoever would save his life shall lose it; and whosoever shall lose his life for my sake and the gospel's shall save it" (Mark 8:34,35 par.). In John's Gospel we hear Jesus saying it again: "He that loveth his life loseth it; and he that hateth his life in this world shall keep it unto life eternal. If any man serve me, let him follow me; and where I am, there shall also my servant be" (John 12:25,26).[106] Following Jesus meant a complete fellowship and association with him, living with him and also suffering with him in the adverse reactions that there were to him. We catch a glimpse of the disciples' understanding of this when, in connection with Jesus' warning about the peril of riches, Peter said: "Lo we have left all, and followed thee" (Mark 10:28). They had committed themselves to the way of self-denial, humiliation, poverty, and suffering. However, this situation was being viewed as a temporary one and as the way to a glorious reward, even as Jesus' reply shows when he speaks of the hundredfold reward in this life and eternal life in the world to come (vss. 29,30). The followers of Jesus shared his fate and destiny both as to its humiliation and its final exaltation. The way which he presented was not an entirely unique way. Israel had heard of it before. As Schweizer has shown: "The concept that the righteous individual must pass through the suffering, humiliation, and shame imposed by God in order, finally, to be exalted by him, is widespread in the Judaism of the time. The pathway which Jesus follows and along which he takes his disciples with him is thus, first of all, simply the path which Israel, Israel's

---

[106] It has been my intention in this brief survey of the matter of following as the Gospels present it to deal with the Gospel witness comprehensively, without entering into the matter of possible differences of emphasis and point of view between John's Gospel and the Synoptics. Kittel, *T.W.N.T.*, I, p. 215, finds them "in voller Übereinstimmung." E. Schweizer argues that John "is concerned with the presentation of discipleship as it was experienced in the post-Easter Church" ("Discipleship and Belief in Jesus as Lord from Jesus to the Hellenistic Church," *N.T.S.*, II (1955/56), pp. 91–92; see *Erniedrigung*, pp. 22–28).

prophets and righteous individuals, had ever again to follow."[107] Jesus' call to follow was a calling to living union and fellowship with him in the service of God. It was a call to total commitment to the program of the kingdom of God as he was revealing it.

Kittel is undoubtedly correct when he observes: "Die Aussagen [Matt. 8:19f.; Mark 8:34 par.; John 12:25,26] zeigen deutlich, dass es sich in keiner Weise — wie die spätere kirchliche Deutung annahm — um eine das Vorbild nachahmende imitatio handelt, sondern ausschliesslich um die Lebens- und Leidensgemeinschaft mit dem Messias, die erst an der Gemeinschaft seines Heils entsteht."[108] However, in his article on ἀκολουθέω he has taken no account of Jesus' commands of "Follow me," issued to Peter in the post-resurrection scene in Galilee (John 21:19,22), and of the indication which this passage gives that the "Lebens- und Leidensgemeinschaft mit dem Messias" may lead one into situations that have remarkable similarities to those through which Jesus went. Perhaps Kittel considered these commands about following in John 21 as being purely literal commands to walk behind Jesus or come aside from the group, and thus as not having significance for a *Theologisches Wörterbuch*. The command in vs. 19 does have a literal meaning at least in part, as is clear from the next verse, where Peter looks behind him and sees John following, and asks what his lot and end shall be. However, this can hardly be the only meaning of the words. The elaborate way in which the command is introduced by the gospel writer is hardly appropriate for the mere calling aside for a conference.[109] Furthermore, Peter's asking about what is going to happen to John suggests that Peter understood the command to follow as having something to do with his own end of which Jesus had just spoken. Jesus' answer to the question about John which places the possibility of John's remaining alive over against Peter's following of Christ again brings the matters of following and of Peter's death in closest connection with each other. Also in view of what Jesus had just been saying about the future course of events and the outcome of Peter's life, Jesus' present words about following must have recalled to Peter a former conversation they had had on following. On the night of the last supper Peter had boasted of following Jesus even to death: "Simon Peter saith unto him, Lord, whither goest thou? Jesus answered, Whither I go, thou canst not follow me now; but thou shalt follow afterwards. Peter saith unto him, Lord, why cannot I follow thee even now? I will lay down my life for thee. Jesus answereth, Wilt thou lay down thy life for me? Verily, verily, I say unto thee, The cock shalt not crow, till thou hast denied me thrice" (John 13:36–38). Hence, Jesus' command to Peter to follow him speaks in a particular way about his following Jesus on the path of martyrdom.[110] This is of course no "Vorbild nachahmende imitatio." However, it shows that obedience to the command to follow can lead one on a way that is similar to Christ's not only in generalities and abstractions, and not only in mystical or spiritual resemblances, but also in regard to some very concrete details. As Schweizer

---

107 Schweitzer, *N.T.S.*, II, p. 88; cf. for detailed account, *Erniedrigung*, pp. 35–44.
108 Kittel, *T.W.N.T.*, I, p. 214, 35–39.
109 "Daarvoor zijn de woorden te plechtig" (F. W. Grosheide, *Het Heilig Evangelie volgens Johannes, K.N.T.*, Amsterdam: H. A. van Bottenburg, 1950, Vol. II, p. 564.
110 Cf. C. K. Barrett, *The Gospel according to St. John*, London: S.P.C.K., 1956, p. 487; R. Bultmann, *Das Evangelium des Johannes, K.e.K.N.T.* 11. Aufl., Göttingen: Vandenhoeck & Ruprecht, 1950, p. 553; W. Bauer, *Das Johannesevangelium*, 3. Aufl., *H.N.T.* VI, Tübingen: J. C. B. Mohr (Paul Siebeck), 1933, p. 239.

has put it: "Der Dienst des Jüngers [wird] immer stärker als Zeugendienst geschildert..., der auch den Zeugentod einschliessen kann. Nicht als ob erst darin das ganze 'mit Jesus sein' errungen wäre—als ginge es um die Nachahmung—, wohl aber so, dass man nicht mit Worten Zeuge sein kann, ohne auch handelnd seinen Glauben zu verkörpern, dass der Weg in die Niedrigkeit mit Jesus ein gesegneter Weg ist."[111] Hence the following which begins with a living union with Christ and a total commitment to the program of his kingdom can upon occasion lead to situations and circumstances which most strikingly resemble those which Christ experienced. The command to follow means not to hesitate, not to seek another way, not to desert when the way becomes frightening or distasteful, but to face it and walk it with the same courage and confidence which Christ showed. The matter of imitation is not foreign to such a situation.

The idea of imitation is not to be found in the expression "following Jesus," as such. However, this expression portrays a situation in which imitation not only very likely will develop, but where it must develop. The situation would be most abnormal and unreal if it resulted in no measure of imitation. The whole system of pupils following their teachers and coming into such a close relationship with them was with an eye to making their education broader than the mere learning of certain subject matter. They were to learn a way of life and to learn to be like their teachers. We have seen how much this was a part of the educational process under the rabbis.[112] Jesus had this in mind also in his establishing so close a fellowship with his disciples. Upon occasion we see him becoming specific on this matter in his conversations with his disciples by illustrating his teaching with a reference to himself. For instance in Mark 10:42ff. he says: "Ye know that they who are accounted to rule over the Gentiles lord it over them; and their great ones exercise authority over them. But it is not so among you: but whosoever would be great among you, shall be your minister; and whosoever would be first among you, shall be servant of all. For the Son of man also came not to be ministered unto, but to minister, and to give his life a ransom for many." The implication of these words is not only that he holds himself before them as a model of self-giving and service, but that he finds in himself the true model of greatness. Thus he is not only illustrating some particular virtue, but portraying a whole way of life into which his disciples must be caught up. They must become like him.

In the evening of the last supper we find Jesus speaking still more expressly about his example and the disciples' following of it. To the surprise and consternation of the disciples he took upon himself the menial task of washing their feet. The exchange of thoughts which took place while he was doing this revealed that he saw a deeper meaning in what he was doing than might at first glance be detected. When he was through, he made sure that they had caught the significance of what he had done: "Know ye what I have done to you? Ye call me, Teacher, and Lord: and ye say well; for

---

[111] Schweizer, *Erniedrigung*, p. 145.
[112] See above, pp. 43f.

so I am. If I then, the Lord and the Teacher, have washed your feet, ye also ought to wash one another's feet. For I have given you an example (ὑπόδειγμα), that ye also should do as I have done to you" (John 13:12—15). It was his intention that they should learn a lesson from what he had done and that they should find that his conduct here had given them a pattern and example for their own.

The uniqueness of the pattern and example here held before the disciples is not to be overlooked. It is not only the pupil-teacher relationship which is at work here, but also the servant-Lord relationship, with all the implications which that carried in connection with Jesus. Jesus is not here presenting himself as the supreme teacher portraying the way of ideal ethical conduct so that men may know what constitutes right living and may proceed to do it. The example which he gives is neither in the foot-washing as such, nor is it only in the general attitude of humility, helpfulness, and thoughtfulness which it displays. This incident has larger reaches. It is a summing up of Jesus' whole life of self-giving, and at the same time a kind of preview of the ultimate self-giving which he is about to perform.[113] The climax of Jesus' earthly life was at hand. Judas' heart was already set on betrayal (13:2). Jesus knew that "his hour was come that he should depart out of this world" (vs. 1). His tenderest love embraces the disciples.[114] He performs this symbolic act for them and upon them. When Peter questioned what he was doing, his answer revealed that the meaning lay deeper than what was immediately apparent: "What I do thou knowest not now; but thou shalt understand hereafter" (vs. 7). When Peter objected to Jesus washing his feet, he answered: "If I wash thee not, thou hast no part with me" (vs. 8). The matter of union with Christ was involved here. Apart from Christ's deed there was no participation in the kingdom and no fellowship with Christ. The whole of their following of Jesus was based on the deed here being portrayed to them. The washing of the disciples' feet was a picture of the self-giving and atoning work of Christ, about to be accomplished on the cross.[115] In the giving of himself and the total humbling of himself in their behalf, he became an example to them of how they ought to act toward each other. The "ought" arises from what their Lord has done for them.[116] Jesus does not reason from some ethical ideal or pattern of right conduct which it is incumbent for man to achieve in order to be acceptable to God.

---

113 "Wat thans gebeurt, is niet een bijdrage tot algemene mensenhulp en liefde, geen algemeen-menselijke nederigheid, die ten voorbeeld wordt gesteld, maar wijst hier naar het geheim der *verzoening*" (G. C. Berkouwer, *Geloof en Heiliging*, Kampen: J. H. Kok, 1949, p. 153).

114 Regarding εἰς τέλος in vs. 1, Grosheide says, "[We] moeten verklaren tot aan het natuurlijke einde, tot het hoogtepunt. Er kon of mocht niet meer worden verwacht" (*Johannes*, II, p. 246). So also J. H. Bernard, *A Critical and Exegetical Commentary on the Gospel according to St. John*, I.C.C., Edinburgh: T. & T. Clark, 1928, p. 455: "'He *exhibited His love* for them *to the uttermost*,' i.e. in a remarkable manner."

115 "The act of washing is what the Crucifixion is, at once a divine deed by which men are released from sin and an example which men must imitate" (Barrett, *John*, p. 364).

116 "If I then, the Lord and the Teacher have washed your feet, ye also ought (ὀφείλετε) to wash one another's feet" (John 13:14). One finds the same kind of thought in I John 4:11: "If God so loved us, we also ought (ὀφείλομεν) to love one another."

The relationship between himself and the disciples at this point is not that of the pattern and those who need to be patterned after him. It is not an abstract relationship of one who has lived the perfect human life and one who must still learn to do so. The process of following his example as here called for is not the copying of a model by seeing it, studying it, and then attempting to reproduce it in one's life.[117] Instead, there is a very concrete and personal relationship between the two parties here. There is the Lord and Messiah, who is in living and life-giving fellowship with his followers. His act involves their having a part with him (vs. 8). He has caught them up into a great program of salvation for themselves and the world. He has made them the recipients of great blessedness, and from this derives the obligation upon them. Their new lives in him must now overflow in similar deeds of love and self-giving toward one another. Having their part in him, they must bring this to expression in doing what he does. The process of following his example here means living under the power and influence of what he has done for them and from this, developing a Christlikeness in living with one another.

Jesus returns to the same thought as he continues his conversation with the disciples. After Judas has left the room, Jesus speaks with even greater intimacy with the disciples: "Little children, ... a new commandment I give unto you, that ye love one another; even as I have loved you, that ye also love one another. By this shall all men know that ye are my disciples, if ye have love one to another" (John 13:33—35). Basically the scene is a common rabbinic one. Here is the Rabbi urging his pupils to learn his ways, to be like him, and to let others know whose disciples they are by their likeness to their Teacher.[118] When he speaks of a new commandment, we detect the messianic overtones of Jesus' words. Judaism had been expecting that when the Messiah came he would offer a new interpretation and explanation of the law.[119] The command to love as such was not new, for both the Old Testament (Lev. 19:18) and Jesus himself (Matt. 22:39) had issued such a command. The newness is in the new situation in which the disciples now live, the new ground from which their love springs, and the new moving force with which it must now come to expression. Their love toward each other must be *even as* (καθώς) Christ's love toward them. The immediate reference is to the foot-washing, but this in turn points to Christ's giving himself in death. Hence we see again the penetrating depths of the teaching and action of this new Teacher and Lord. He is calling his disciples to learn from him, but he is doing much more. In his death he is securing the possibility of the love he commands. His love for them is the ground and motive for their love. From the well-spring of his love they will love, and in loving will make his love their pattern and norm. His love is both the

---

[117] *Cf.* Kittel's descriptive phrase, "eine das Vorbild nachahmende imitatio" (*T.W.N.T.*, I, p. 214, 37).

[118] The expression "little children" was commonly used by a rabbi when speaking to his pupils; see H. L. Strack and P. Billerbeck, *Kommentar zum Neuen Testament aus Talmud und Midrasch*, München: C. H. Beck, 1922ff., Vol. II, p. 559.

[119] Strack-Billerbeck, IV, pp. 1–3.

ground and the norm of their love.[120] Imitation of him is to develop, but it is an imitation founded in and springing from the living and life-giving relationship which they have with him.

Hence, we may conclude that Christ expected some kind of imitation to develop from the close fellowship which existed between him and his followers. It was an imitation founded in and flowing forth from his atoning work in their behalf, by which he made them his chosen participants in the kingdom of God. Because there was a living union between them, imitation was forthcoming. Their following of him and the consequent processes of imitation which came into being all were to continue after Jesus went away. Peter's manner of death would be a case of following Christ. Undoubtedly during Jesus' days on earth the disciples understood all these things only very partially and imperfectly. However, they came to clarity on the matter later. As they went out to make disciples of all nations, they were soon preaching to people who had not known Jesus during his earthly days. To these people too they held up Jesus as an example. However, it was not as an example to be followed as a way of salvation. Rather, Jesus' example was held before those who through faith had come into a living fellowship with him and were now participants in his program of salvation. Jesus' example was presented in terms of embracing the Savior's influence over the lives of those who knew him as their Savior. The imitation was rooted in the fellowship and union with Christ and sprang forth from it.[121]

Peter points to Christ as an example in this kind of context. In his first epistle he makes various practical applications of Christianity to the relationships of daily life. In Peter 2:18ff. he addresses his words to servants and speaks about their proper conduct and attitude toward their masters. They must show due submission not only to the kind and considerate masters but also to the perverse ones. If this involves them in suffering innocently when they have done only what is right and good, they must not think this strange nor react in rebellion. Patient submission is the proper reaction; such conduct God views with favor (cf. χάρις, vss. 19,20). To this kind of living they were called, and Christ gave them an example: "For hereunto were ye called: because Christ also suffered for you, leaving you an example (ὑπογραμμὸν), that ye should follow his steps" (I Peter 2:21).

Here once again it is not simply a matter of reproduction or copying of a way that has been shown to them by another. This passage speaks not only about an example shown to them and footsteps to be followed, but about

---

120 Bultmann, *Johannes*, p. 291, fn. 3: "Καθώς hat wie oft bei Joh. nicht einfach vergleichenden, sondern zugleich begründenden Sinn." *Cf.* p. 403. See also the further discussion of this use of καθώς below, pp. 76f.

121 *Cf.* Schweizer, *Erniedrigung*, p. 144: "Es ging stets um das Teilhaben an Jesu Weg im Ganzen, und zwar an *Jesu* Weg, nicht um ein Durchschreiten eines eigenen Weges, der nur jenem ähnlich war. Wo dieser Gedanke aber verschwand, da mussten die moralischen Grundsätze der hellenistischen Popularphilosophie oder der jüdischen Gesetzlichkeit wieder eindringen, oder dann bekam der Gehorsam der Gemeinde einen falschen religiösen Klang, wobei sich beides durchaus verbinden kann."

Christ's having suffered for them (vs. 21), and his having borne their sins on the cross, that they, "having died unto sins, might live unto righteousness; by whose stripes ye were healed" (vs. 24). This much larger and deeper relationship defines the nature of the example-follower relationship. There is much more at work here than the viewing of a pattern and the reproducing of it. The followers have experienced healing. They are now enjoying a health they never before knew. They have had their sins removed from them. They are sheep that have been brought back to the flock and are now cared for by their Shepherd and Guardian (vs. 25). They are in living fellowship with their Shepherd who has suffered for them and brought them to life and safety. Their following of his example is imbedded in this context. His suffering as such is inimitable, for it was death-dealing to sin and the means of healing for his people.[122] But entering into followship with him, his followers enter a fellowship of which this suffering is the basis. Their very life is henceforth founded on his suffering; it is the substratum undergirding them. His suffering is a component part of their lives. Hence, we may conclude that for the Christian the example of Christ's suffering is not simply available to behold and to learn from; it is impressed in his very being. When as a servant he comes under an unscrupulous and unjust master, he continues to do good, and when this brings only further suffering, he bears it patiently, refusing to retaliate, threaten, curse, or fight back. He does this not as the way leading to fellowship with Christ and acceptability with God, but rather as the way issuing from his fellowship with Christ and the acceptability he has with God through him. He does this because he is a sheep in the flock of his Shepherd; he walks in the footsteps of his Shepherd. This is the only path that is open to him. Following Christ's example of suffering then is the bringing to expression of the Christian way which we have experienced in him and seen exemplified in him. The Christian finds the guidelines of Christian conduct in Christ, and learns with gradually increasing skill to trace them in his life.[123]

In the New Testament it is only in the letters of Paul that we ever find the thought of the imitation of Christ literally expressed. In I Cor. 11:1 Paul speaks of himself as an imitator of Christ; and in I Thess. 1:6 he says that the Thessalonian Christians were imitators of the Lord. Since in both these passages the imitation of Christ is found in closest connection with the imitation of Paul, we shall not study them independently now, but await the study of them in direct connection with the imitation of Paul. However, by way of anticipation it may be stated that these two express statements of imitation have to do with the activity by the believer of conforming his life to the way of life Christ showed while on earth. In I Cor. 11:1 the

---

[122] Christ's suffering was ὑπὲρ ὑμῶν (vs. 21). "Das ὑπέρ entzieht den ganzen Vorgang einem wiederholenden Nachahmen" (A. Stumpff, ἴχνος, *T.W.N.T.*, III, p. 407, 22,23).

[123] It is apparent from Clement of Alexandria, *Stromata* V. 8. 49, that ὑπογραμμός had the technical sense of a copy-head in a child's exercise book, a well-formed piece of writing to guide the child in his learning to form the various letters.

reference is to Christ's giving of himself in the interests of others; in I Thess. 1:6 it is to his humbly accepting and enduring the suffering into which the service of God brought him. Believers adopt his ways; they imitate him.

Paul does not speak expressly of Christ being an example. However, there are various passages in Paul where the thought is to be found. [124] Phil. 2:5 is such a passage. In Phil. 2 Paul is exhorting his readers to oneness of mind and purpose and to humility toward each other. He enforces this by directing their thoughts to what Christ was and did: "Have this mind in you, which was also in Christ Jesus" (vs. 5). The specific term "example" is not found here, but in substance Paul here appeals to Christ's example.

This way of understanding and translating Phil. 2:5 has been called into question by various commentators for a variety of reasons. The textual variants in the verse further indicate that already at an early date there was not clarity as to how the text was related to the context and as to precisely what it was saying. The other interpretations which commentators give to the verse usually do not find it speaking of any mind or disposition which is to be found in Jesus. Thus they do not find Jesus being recommended as some kind of an example to the Philippians. Michaelis proposes that the verse means to say the following: "Eine solche Gesinnung, wie ich sie damit von euch gefordert habe, müsst ihr untereinander haben und das um so mehr, als ihr ja doch in der Gemeinschaft mit Christus Jesus steht." [125] Michaelis finds verse 5 serving as a conclusion to the exhortation begun in 2:1. The thought of the following section (vss. 6–11) is not integrally related to the preceding, since it is a hymn or psalm, and "schon diese Beobachtung lässt vermuten, dass der Abschnitt eine gewisse S e l b s t ä n d i g k e i t besitzen wird und dass seine einzelnen Aussagen, so gewichtig und unentbehrlich sie innerhalb des Hymnus sein mögen, nicht alle in der gleichen strengen Beziehung zu 2, 1–5 stehen werden." [126] Dibelius proposes another way of understanding the verse: "Meint es so miteinander, wie (ihr es meint) als Glieder Christi Jesu." [127] Bonnard follows him in this: "Ayez les uns à l'égard des autres les dispositions que l'on a en Jésus-Christ." [128] Bonnard comments on the latter part of the verse: "Cette interprétation a l'avantage de donner aux mots 'en Jésus-Christ' un sens habituel chez Paul. Par cette expression, l'apôtre n'exhorte donc pas les Philippiens à imiter moralement Jésus; il leur rappelle que le Seigneur de l'Eglise s'est abaissé

---

124 Michaelis contests this. He says: "Die Vorbildlichkeit Christi gehört aber jedenfalls nicht zu den geläufigen Gedanken des Apostels Paulus" (*T.W.N.T.*, IV, p. 671, 35,36). Berkouwer comments concerning this statement: "Het is ook alleen uit reactie te verklaren" (*Geloof en Heiliging*, p. 148); and further observes concerning the whole trend of Michaelis' thought in regard to imitation: "Men heeft wel eens uit reactie tegen de onzuivere 'imitatio Christi' de navolging willen vervangen door de gehoorzaamheid.... Maar als men met een zekere nadruk over gehoorzaamheid in plaats van over navolging wil spreken, dan doet men aan de volheid van het N.T. getuigenis te kort en brengt men een wettisch element in de gehoorzaamheid" (pp. 147,148).

125 W. Michaelis, *Der Brief des Paulus an die Philipper*, T.H.N.T. XI, Leipzig: A. Deichert, 1935, p. 33. S. Greijdanus, *De Brief van den Apostel Paulus aan de Gemeente te Philippi*, K.N.T., Amsterdam: H. A. van Bottenburg, 1937, p. 182, remarks concerning such a translation: "Maar dit kan bezwaarlijk iets anders heeten, dan eigene gedachten in Paulus' woorden inwringen, en zoo goed zoo kwaad dat gaat, er mee zoeken te verbinden."

126 Michaelis, *Phil.*, p. 34.

127 M. Dibelius, *An die Philipper*, 3. Aufl., *H.N.T.*, XI, Tübingen: J. C. B. Mohr (Paul Siebeck), 1937, p. 72.

128 P. Bonnard, *L'Épitre de Saint Paul aux Philippiens*, C.d.N.T. X, Neuchatel/Paris: Delachaux & Niestlé S.A., 1950, p. 41.

et humilié pour le salut des hommes et que son élévation démontre que telle est bien la volonté de Dieu pour les membres de son peuple. La volonté expresse de Dieu révélée en Jésus-Christ, c'est la loi et la grâce du service mutuel; Jésus-Christ est ici beaucoup plus qu'un exemple moral, ou que l'expression d'un idéal spirituel; il est le fait historique dans lequel l'Eglise a reçu une fois pour toutes sa loi."[129] One appreciates the emphasis that Jesus ought not to be reduced to a moral example or the expression of a spiritual ideal. However, it may be questioned whether such a tendency necessarily inheres in the translation "[the mind] which was also in Christ Jesus." One hardly catches the full significance of the reference to "Christ Jesus" in this context, when he is seen only as a person depicting a spiritual ideal but without further relationships or significance for those to whom Paul is speaking. "Christ Jesus" is not simply a double proper name used as the common designation of a well-known person. As McCasland has shown in his analysis of the designation "Christ Jesus," "'Christ' was at first an appellative, a verbal adjective, meaning 'the anointed one,' modifying the proper name 'Jesus.'"[130] Greijdanus rightly observes that the use of this double designation here is "om Hem voorstellen naar Zijnen verlossingsarbeid voor ons van Godswege."[131] The thoughts of the Philippians are directed to the attitude, disposition, and conduct of God's anointed One in his great act of self-humiliation not merely as an illustration of an exemplary and ideal way, but as a way in which they themselves were involved and to which they were committed. They were "saints in Christ Jesus" (1:1), and people in whom a good work had been begun (1:5), people to whom "it hath been granted in behalf of Christ, not only to believe on him, but also to suffer in his behalf" (1:29). It is to people living in these relationships to Christ that Paul speaks about Christ's disposition and attitude. It is in view of this relationship to Christ that Paul's appeal has real force. To allow a state of mind, an attitude, or a disposition to reign which is at odds with the one shown by Christ when he gained salvation for mankind was to set oneself apart from Christ. It finally amounted to denial of him. Hence Paul exhorts the Philippians to join in a unity of mind and purpose (2:2) and to live in humility: "each counting other better than himself; not looking each of you to his own things, but each of you also to the things of others" (vss. 3,4). He enforces this by holding up Christ before them: "Have this mind in you, which was also in Christ Jesus."

The objections raised to this exegesis of the verse have to do with such matters as the following: whether in view of the preceding context ἐν ὑμῖν does not have the sense of "among you," "toward each other"; whether ἐν ὑμῖν is not superfluous if the sentence says "have this mind in you," since to "have a certain mind" is already an internal act and the "you" is indicated in the verb φρονεῖτε; whether ἐν Χριστῷ Ἰησοῦ can mean "in his inner being," especially in view of the same expression appearing in 1:1 and 1:26 (*cf.* also 2:1, ἐν Χριστῷ) in a totally different sense; whether τοῦτο can look forward to ὃ καί in view of φρονεῖτε having been twice used in 2:2 and thus directing the thought backwards; what verb is to be supplied in the latter clause of verse 5; whether if Paul had meant to indicate Christ's disposition as exemplary, he would

---

[129] Bonnard, *Phil.*, p. 42.
[130] S. V. McCasland, "Christ Jesus," *J.B.L.* LXV (1946), p. 383. He concludes that, "It is highly improbable ... that 'Christ Jesus' ever achieved the full stature of a double proper name in the early Church" (*loc. cit.*).
[131] Greijdanus, *Phil.*, p. 185.

not have expressed it differently; etc.[132] In view of the fact that these objections have so largely to do with what could and what could not be expressed or understood by the Greek phrases of this verse, it is interesting to note that the extant commentaries from church fathers to whom Greek was still a living language find no difficulty reading the verse as pointing to Christ being an example of humility.[133] Over against the objections which have been raised, there are certain facts which can not be overlooked. This verse forms some kind of link between the preceding exhortation to unity and humility and the succeeding recitation of Christ's act of humbling himself. Also, this verse contains every appearance of being made up of two parallel clauses. The ἐν ὑμῖν and ἐν Χριστῷ Ἰησοῦ, each at the end of their respective clauses, match each other perfectly. So do the τοῦτο and ὃ καί, each at the beginning of their respective clauses. Hence one would expect that the ἐν in both instances would express the same thought, and that the τοῦτο could not only refer backward, but must in some way have ὃ καί in mind.[134] Furthermore, the καί obviously expresses intensification. The translation "Have this mind in you, which was also in Christ Jesus" provides a smooth transition of the thought, and adequately expresses the parallelism of the two clauses and the intensification found in the latter. Hence we find it to be preferred.[135]

In II Corinthians 8 there is a turn of the thought which in many ways resembles that of Philippians 2. Paul is there expressing the hope that in addition to the many things in which the Corinthians already abound, they may also abound in the work of love (χάρις, grace, vss. 6,7) to which he has called them, by showing a liberality in giving for the work of ministering to the saints. In vss. 1–6 he has spoken in glowing terms of the wonderful response there has been in Macedonia. He says that this earnestness shown in Macedonia may serve as a kind of norm by which the sincerity of the Corinthians' love may be measured (vs. 8). And then he adds: "For ye know the grace of our Lord Jesus Christ, that, though he was rich, yet for your sakes he became poor, that ye through his poverty might become rich" (vs. 9).

---

[132] See discussion of this verse in Michaelis, *Phil.*; Dibelius, *Phil.*; Bonnard, *Phil.*

[133] It is true that the text on which they based their comments read φρονείσθω rather than φρονεῖτε, but this would not resolve all the impossibilities or improbabilities of Greek which are supposedly found. Chrysostom begins his homily on this verse thus: "When our Lord Jesus Christ placed a great challenge before his disciples, he always set himself or his Father or the prophets before them as an example (ὑπόδειγμα).... The blessed Paul does the same thing: in exhorting them to humility, he holds Christ before them (τὸν Χριστὸν ἐν μέσῳ παρήγαγε)" (Joannes Chrysostomus, *In Epistolam ad Philippenses Homiliae*, sub 2:5 [ed. Bern. de Montfaucon, Venetiis, 1741, Vol. XI, p. 233]). The comment of Theodore of Mopsuestia on the verse is: "Talia sapite et qualia Christus uidetur sapuisse" (*In Epistolas B. Pauli Commentarii*, sub Phil. 2:5 [ed. H. B. Swete, Cambridge: University Press, 1880, Vol. I, p. 215]. Theodoret comments: "Imitate Him who is Lord of all" (*Interpretatio Epistolae ad Philippenses*, sub Phil. 2:5 [translation of Greek text as given by J. P. Migne, *P.G.*, LXXXII, p. 570]).

[134] The parallelism of the verse decides the matter for C. Spicq, *Agapè*, Analyse des Textes II, Paris: J. Gabalda, 1959, p. 264: "Nous pensons que l'exégèse doit d'abord tenir compte du parallélisme rigoureux des deux propositions et que τοῦτο ἐν ὑμῖν correspond exactement à ὃ ἐν Χριστῷ Ἰησοῦ. Par conséquent on sous-entendra dans la seconde soit ἦν ou mieux ἐστίν, soit φρονεῖ. On évite ainsi des gloses théologiques et l'on supplée dans l'éllipse un verbe que tout le monde peut restituer spontanément."

[135] For a thorough discussion of the exegetical problems of this verse and a defense of the interpretation here adopted, see Greijdanus, *Phil.*, pp. 180–186.

The similarity in thought between this verse and the well-known christological passage in Phil. 2:6ff. is immediately apparent. Does Paul introduce Christ's great act of self-giving into his letter to the Corinthians here in order to hold Christ before them as an example? In this whole passage (vss. 1—15) we detect that Paul is making a play on the words "poverty" and "riches" (*cf.* vss. 2 and 9), and "abundance" and "want" (*cf.* vss. 2, 7, and 14). When Christ's act is put in terms of riches and poverty in this context of an appeal to give liberally for the ministration to the poverty-stricken saints, we quite naturally find thoughts arising about what Christ's great act has to say to us about the actions proper to us. Nevertheless, Grosheide and Pop are undoubtedly correct in pointing out that vs. 9 is not directly calculated to admonish or challenge the Corinthians with Christ's example.[136] Rather, it points to Christ as the source and basis as well as the power which brings the Corinthians to this work of love toward others. They have become spiritually rich through Christ and this carries its implications as to how they ought to act toward others.

However, another and clearer appeal to Christ's example in Paul's writings is found in Romans 15. Paul has been speaking about the differences of opinion which existed as to what it was permitted for a Christian to do. He continues: "Now we that are strong ought to bear the infirmities of the weak, and not to please ourselves. Let each one of us please his neighbor for that which is good, unto edifying. For Christ also pleased not himself" (Rom. 15:1—3a). The specific action of Christ in not pleasing himself is illustrated by the citation of Ps. 69:9 (M.T. vs. 10): "The reproaches of them that reproached thee fell upon me." As the Psalmist in that Old Testament situation, so also Christ felt the sharp opposition of men who were at odds with God. In Christ's case it speaks of his subjecting himself to the unpleasant lot of suffering which was involved in securing our salvation. In the denial of self and the foregoing of his claims, rights, and pleasures which Christ showed during his life of suffering and humiliation and in his death, there is the indication of how Christians are to give themselves in seeking the well-being of their neighbors. The thought of Christ's example remains close at hand as Paul speaks further. In regard to vs. 5 it is difficult to decide whether, when he expresses the wish that they "be of the same mind one with another according to Christ Jesus," this "according to Christ Jesus" is to be understood as "according to the example of Christ Jesus" or "according to the will of Christ Jesus."[137] However, in vs. 7 the thought of Christ's example is again clear: "Wherefore receive ye one another, even as Christ also received you, to the glory of God." Paul finds what Christ has done in receiving us to be an example of what we ought to do for others.[138]

---

[136] F. W. Grosheide, *De Tweede Brief aan de Kerk te Korinthe*, 2e dr., C.N.T., Kampen: J. H. Kok, 1959, p 232f.; F. J. Pop, *Apostolaat in Druk en Vertroosting: De Tweede Brief aan de Corinthiërs* (in *De Prediking van het Nieuwe Testament* VII/2) Nijkerk: G. F. Callenbach, 1953, p. 266f.

[137] See discussion of the similar phrase in Eph. 4:24, below, p. 75.

[138] Paul several times appeals to his readers to do something and then makes reference to Christ, God, or the Lord having done this thing for them (see Rom. 15:7; Eph. 4:32; 5:2; Col.

The attention of the readers of the letter to the Hebrews is also directed to the example Christ had given. These people had been manifesting signs of becoming lax, sluggardly, and less than diligent in maintaining faith, hope, and steadfastness. In urging them on to new diligence, the writer not only points them to the example of their faithful forebears,[139] but also calls their attention to Jesus: "... looking to Jesus, the author and perfecter of our faith.... For consider him that hath endured such gainsaying of sinners against himself, that ye wax not weary, fainting in your souls" (Heb. 12:2a,3). The picture which Jesus presented of steadfastness in the face of suffering and opposition could help the readers in facing their problems. However, Jesus is not presented here merely as an illustration, or as one who has traversed the way before us, and whom we are now to follow. He is the "author and perfecter of our faith" (vs. 2), and in view of what the writer has already stated in such passages as 2:10; 5:9; 6:20, etc., it becomes clear that what Jesus has done goes far beyond illustrating or merely preceding us on the way to salvation. He has brought us into the way and made it possible for us to walk it. Here again the thought of his exemplariness is inseparable from that of his saviorhood. To his saved people who are now themselves faced with anti-Christian opposition, Jesus' manner of facing the opposition against him during his earthly life furnished an example.

Perhaps Paul also has the example of Christ in mind when in II Thess. he makes reference to the patience (steadfastness, ὑπομονήν) of Christ. He writes: "And the Lord direct your hearts into the love of God, and into the patience of Christ" (II Thess. 3:5). Regarding the latter phrase commentators present a variety of interpretations.[140] The matter seems finally to revolve around the possibilities of understanding the endurance as that which Christ gives and inspires in the believer, and that which Christ himself has and which became strikingly evident during his days on earth. Lightfoot has suggested that Paul may not have had one or the other of these interpretations in mind, but both of them. He finds this to be true of the preceding phrase "the love of God," and then continues: "Analogously to this, ἡ ὑπομονὴ τοῦ Χριστοῦ will be best explained not exactly as 'the patience of Christ,' in which the believer participates. Compare the expression in 2 Cor. i. 5 ['the sufferings of Christ abound unto us'], exemplifying the close union of the believer with Christ, [the phrase 'the righteousness of Christ'], and kindred phrases."[141] The conclusion that this phrase carried associations of

---

3:13). The reference to Christ does not merely point to him as an example for their action, but points them as well to the motive and ground of their action. See further discussion of the point below, pp. 76f.

139  Heb. 6:12; and chap. 11. See discussion of these passages below, pp. 81ff.

140  See discussion in Rigaux, *Thess.*, pp. 699,700; J. E. Frame, *A Critical and Exegetical Commentary on the Epistles of St Paul to the Thessalonians*, I.C.C., Edinburgh: T. & T. Clark, 1912, p. 296.

141  J. B. Lightfoot, *Notes on Epistles of St Paul from Unpublished Commentaries*, London: Macmillan, 1904, p. 128. Rigaux, *Thess.*, p. 700, has a similar proposal: "Dans II Cor., I. 5, les souffrances de Paul sont les souffrances du Christ, non seulement parce qu'elle sont supportées pour le Christ, ou à l'imitation des souffrances du Christ lui-même, accomplissant dans les membres de son corps mystique ce qui manque aux souffrances du chef. De meme l'ὑπομονὴ des

the example of steadfastness which was seen in Christ while he was on earth can hardly be avoided. In his first letter to the Thessalonians Paul had called them imitators of the Lord in the way they were responding to the suffering into which their Christian profession had brought them (I Thess. 1:6).[142] Furthermore, it is evident that the early Christians were being pointed to Christ's endurance as an example for themselves. Heb. 12:2,3 shows this. Even clearer is Polycarp's letter to the Philippians: "Let us then be imitators of his [Christ's] endurance (ὑπομονῆς)" (8:2). Christ's example is in the purview of Paul's reference to the believers being directed into the patience of Christ.

One could go on multiplying the number of passages where Christ's example is in the purview of the thought. In II Cor. 10:1 Paul begins his closing exhortation: "Now I Paul myself entreat you by the meekness and gentleness of Christ." As Tinsley comments, "It would appear from this that the 'meekness and gentleness' of the Lord Christ was already a well-known formula in the Christian tradition of which St Paul could remind the Corinthians."[143] Here was an aspect of Christ's life which was exercising a continuing influence in the Christian community. The importance of the example Christ gave in his life as a guide to believers is also apparent in John's first letter. "He that saith he abideth in him ought himself also to walk even as he walked" (I John 2:6). "Hereby know we love, because he laid down his life for us: and we ought to lay down our lives for the brethren" (I John 3:16). Dodd has summed the matter up very well when he writes: "It is clear that from the outset the 'law of Christ' (Gal. 6:2) by which Christians are bound to direct their conduct, was defined in the Church's teaching, not only by the traditional precepts of Jesus, but also by his example.[144]

We have now reviewed some of the passages in the New Testament where the example of Christ is most clearly held up before Christians and the thought is either implicit or explicit that what is seen in Christ is what ought also to be seen in them as people saved by him and united to him. These passages have in effect presented a call to imitation, even though the specific word was not used. Christ was portrayed; and an obligation to action was placed at the feet of the hearers or readers. The result would be either a response of imitation or a resistance and hardening of a defiant heart. An appeal to imitate Christ was a means of furthering the kind of living which ought to be found in Christ's people.

It is well to take note at this point in our study of the fact that in speaking of the call or duty which has come to Christians to imitate Christ, we are surrounded by a vast ocean of closely related material and thought which threatens to engulf us. Stretching out before us is the whole matter

---

fidèles est l'ὑπομονή du Christ, qui se retrouve dans l'endurance accordée et maintenue par lui en chacun d'eux."

[142] See discussion below, p. 122.
[143] *Imitation*, p. 150.
[144] C. H. Dodd, *The Johannine Epistles*, M.N.T.C., London: Hodder & Stoughton, 1946, p. 35.

of how to understand and to express what has happened, is happening, and finally will happen in our being saved by Christ. What does salvation in Christ mean? What was the significance for our salvation of Christ's earthly life? What is the significance for us of the life that Christ now lives as exalted Lord? We feel the encroachments of this ocean at this point primarily because there is no clear shoreline marking off an island which can be given the name "Imitation of Christ." Does every parallelism, likeness, similarity, resemblance, and conformity between Christ and the believer come under the heading "Imitation of Christ"? It can not be denied that these things are closely related. In this connection we shall notice two matters before drawing this section on the imitation of Christ to a close.

First, there is some reason to suspect that the New Testament Christians may have had considerable interest in noting the resemblances between events in Jesus' life and events in the lives of the apostles and others in the early church. Van Unnik speaks of a striking parallelism between the Lord and his apostles in the Book of Acts.[145] This becomes particularly evident by comparing Luke's Gospel with his Book of Acts. Tinsley has presented the matter in some detail both as it applies to apostolic activities in general, and then more specifically to Philip, Stephen, Peter, and Paul.[146] To illustrate the point we quote Tinsley's paragraph on the resemblances in the account of Stephen's death:

> The death of Stephen is narrated in such a way as to constitute a veritable *passio Stephani* having a basic similarity to the *Passio Christi* of St Luke's Gospel. Just as Jesus on trial before the Sanhedrin was sustained by the vision of the triumph of the Son of man in glory (Luke 22.69), so Stephen, full of the Holy Spirit as promised, saw the heavens opened and Jesus standing as Son of man in glory at the right hand of God (Acts 7.55f.). As Jesus prayed for the forgiveness of those who were putting him to death (Luke 23.34), Stephen did the same (Acts 7.60). The final committal of Jesus is found only in St Luke: Πάτερ, εἰς χεῖράς σου παρατίθεμαι τὸ πνεῦμά μου (23.46); and this is echoed by the words of Stephen: Κύριε ᾽Ιησοῦ, δέξαι τὸ πνεῦμά μου (Acts 7.59). Jesus was buried by Joseph of Arimathaea, whom St Luke is careful to describe as a good and righteous man (ἀνὴρ ἀγαθὸς καὶ δίκαιος, Luke 23.50). In Acts this seems to be echoed in the note that devout men (ἄνδρες εὐλαβεῖς) buried Stephen (Acts 8.2). In the Gospel tradition it is Luke alone who mentions the lamentations for Jesus (23.27); these are paralleled by lamentations for Stephen (Acts 8.2).[147]

Taken individually the parallels are not all equally weighty, but they do have a cumulative effect. The phenomenon can be clearly seen, and Tinsley is not without grounds for proposing: "It would seem to be the clear intention of St Luke to stress that the 'Way' of the follower of the Lord Jesus had necessarily to take on the likeness of the 'Way' of the Lord himself."[148] It is

---
145 W. C. van Unnik, "Navolging van Christus," *Christelijke Encyclopedie*, 2e dr., Kampen: J. H. Kok, 1960, Vol. V, p. 149.
146 *Imitation*, pp. 106–112.
147 *Ibid.*, p. 110.
148 *Ibid.*, p. 112.

remarkable, however, that this taking on of the "Way" of the Lord remained utterly natural and genuine in the accounts which Luke gives. Acts has no hint of an artificial imitation or a studied pose. It was simply a living out in the lives and the circumstances of Jesus' followers of the things they had heard and seen and learned from him. Since they lived in the same times and culture as Christ, the external similarities often multiplied. Luke-Acts shows that there was apparently some careful attention given by the early Christians to noting to what extent Christ's life and way was reproducing itself in the men of their day. Undoubtedly the whole situation was most favorable to promoting the influence of Christ's example among the early Christians.

Any difference of opinion on how far the term imitation ought to be applied to this phenomenon is actually more a formal difference of how one chooses to use terms than a material difference of whether or not there is an imitation here. The fact is that the apostles were actively bringing to expression in their lives what they had seen in Christ; they were engaged in imitating him. Paul speaks of imitation in this sense. At the same time many external circumstances converged to increase the correspondences between the early Christians' lives and Christ's. Is it appropriate in this connection to speak of an imitation of Christ?[149] The thought would then be that the lives of the Apostles are copies, reproductions of Christ's life. This had come about in part through their active following of the Lord's ways; at the same time the similarities between their lives and the Lord's had been greatly increased by various accompanying circumstances and events. The parallelism of Luke-Acts suggests that there may have been an interested observing of such a kind of imitation by the early Christians. It is important to notice, however, that when imitation is referred to expressly in the New Testament, whether in noun or verb form, it is an active imitation, an engaging in the activity of imitating, a being an imitator. In this latter sense then (to apply the matter only to the paragraph we have quoted about Stephen), Stephen was an imitator of Christ in his faithful witness, his forgiving love toward his persecutors, and his committal of himself at the point of death to God's care. He was not an imitator in receiving a heavenly vision, in being martyred, buried by devout men, or lamented. In these matters he was at best an imitation, a copy, in a different sense than the term is used in the New Testament.

> Already in the Apostolic Fathers we see the confusion developing between the importance of being an imitator and of being an imitation. Martyrdom was being looked upon as *the* way of imitating Christ.[150] The heart of the matter of being Christ's imitator through faithfully witnessing and humbly giving oneself was not being distinguished from such externalities as standing before kings and judges, being bound in chains or fetters, or being robbed of one's life by cruel forms of torture

---

[149] In such a usage, *imitation* is expressive of the end product (the μίμημα) as distinguished from the agent (μιμητής, *imitator*) or the activity (μίμησις, *imitating*).
[150] See above, p. 15.

and execution. Had this concentration on the externals implied only an emphasis on the fact that in imitating Christ one must be willing to go all the way to martyrdom, there could be little objection. However such was not the case. The martyrdom as such was being viewed as having significance for the Christian life. As Torrance has observed regarding martyrdom in the days of the Apostolic Fathers: "It [the early Church] felt that it was in that way the Christian made saving appropriation of the Cross, rather than by faith. That Ignatius, in many ways the most 'Pauline' of all the Apostolic Fathers, should have laid so much stress on attaining to God through a martyrdom in imitation of Christ, and so failed to see that the death of Christ as an act of salvation can be appropriated by faith alone, is very significant indeed." [151]

It does not seem that we need see more in the parallelisms of Luke and Acts than an attempt by the author and the early Christian community to detect the likenesses between what was happening in and around them and what had happened in and around Christ. Thus, the Christians were emphasizing for themselves and others that Christ really was continuing the work he "began both to do and to teach, until the day in which he was received up" (Acts 1:1,2). What was happening in and around them showed that they were not alone: the Lord was at work (Acts 2:47). [152] Such „imitations" (parallelisms) showed that he was working through them in the same way he had himself worked while among them.

The second matter we must notice before closing our review of the imitation of Christ is the relation of this imitation to the believer's participation in Christ. We have seen how Jesus called men during his days on earth with a call of grace to follow him. This following meant a participation in his lot and destiny of humiliation and suffering, which was to lead presently to a sharing in his glorification and exaltation. With Jesus' death, resurrection, and ascension, the situation was considerably changed. However, this whole history of Jesus' calling men to follow him did not become mere history. It was not looked upon as a record of past events of interest only to those who were engaged in tracing the origin and growth of a certain movement. Neither did it become simply a record of the past, profitable as an example for the church to imitate. It had that element of course, but there was more involved than that. The early church seems immediately to have been aware of this. They collected and composed the gospel records with far more than an historical interest in them. They saw and felt in Jesus' calls to follow a contemporary reference. His words had their validity for the post-Easter church. [153]

---

151 T. F. Torrance, *The Doctrine of Grace in the Apostolic Fathers*, London: Oliver and Boyd, 1948, p. 138.
152 "The mission of the apostles Peter and Paul is presented, as we would ... expect, in a way which reminds us that behind their words and works there is the activity of the Lord himself conforming their lives to the pattern of his own" (Tinsley, *Imitation*, pp. 110,111).
153 In the hymn of Mrs. C. F. Alexander (1852) Christians still sing:
>  Jesus calls us; o'er the tumult
>  Of our life's wild, restless sea,
>  Day by day His sweet voice soundeth,
>  Saying, "Christian, follow Me."

The relationship between Christ and his followers now took on some new aspects, however. It was no longer a literal earthly accompaniment, but a spiritual accompaniment. Nevertheless, Christ's way retained its significance as a way. Christ's followers in walking the road to salvation and glory still had to walk in Christ's train. One important aspect of this travelling the road of Christ occurred immediately upon entering the circle of believers and followers of Christ. He had called them into a living union with himself through faith. This union brought them into the experience and the benefits of Christ's death in their behalf. They were led into the likeness of Christ's death, in that they died to sin; they were led in turn into the likeness of his resurrection, in that they became newly alive in a life of righteousness (Rom. 6:5).[154] Salvation then means coming into a dynamic connection with Christ in which one experiences in one's own life the great redemptive events which were accomplished in Christ's death and resurrection. Other events from Christ's life are also experienced by the believer: he is crucified (Rom. 6:6; Gal. 2:20; 5:24; 6:14); he is buried (Rom. 6:4; Col. 2:12); he is made to sit with him in heavenly places (Eph. 2:6). The believer, in spiritual and mystical union with Christ, participates in the way that Christ has gone and in the benefits which have accrued to Christ and to him from that way. These radical spiritual changes of dying with Christ (Rom. 6:8; Col. 2:20) and being raised with him (Eph. 2:6; Col. 2:12; 3:1) in turn provide the basis on which Christ is formed in a person (Gal. 4:19) and on which a person comes to conformity with Christ (Rom. 8:29; Phil. 3:21). In this process of conformity the way of Christ's life and the example which he gave has an important part to play. At this point it is no longer a matter simply of experiencing benefits which accrue to us in Christ. Here we begin a personal struggle to conform to him, to grow into his likeness, and to adopt his ways of life for our own. In such an activity we refer constantly to the life which he lived on earth and seek constantly to be open to the influence of his example. Here we become imitators of Christ. Paul was speaking of this activity when he spoke of the imitation of Christ (I Cor. 11:1; I Thess. 1:6).

Once again the question arises as to how broadly one ought to apply the term imitation. Obviously the events of Christ's life and the way he walked on earth have established a certain pattern which has significance for his people. The way that Christ has gone in humiliation, humble self-giving, suffering, crucifixion, death, burial, resurrection, ascension, exaltation, glorification lies at the basis of man's whole salvation.[155] But there are various

---

[154] This text has been and still is understood in various ways by commentators and theologians. For a discussion of the alternate proposals and a defense of this understanding of the phrase *likeness of his death*, see H. N. Ridderbos, *Aan de Romeinen*, C.N.T., Kampen: J. H. Kok, 1959, 128,129. *Cf.* also J. Murray, *The Epistle to the Romans*, N.I.C.N.T., London: Marshall, Morgan & Scott, 1960, Vol. I, pp. 218,219.

[155] For a full exposition of this matter see Schweizer, *Erniedrigung*. In essence Tinsley works out the same thing in his *Imitation*. Both Schweizer and Tinsley refuse to become mere exemplarists in their views of the significance of Christ's life and death. They plead that full justice can not be done to the New Testament revelation in terms of a choice between *Christus vor uns* and *Christus für uns*, but only in terms of seeing the truth of both and giving each its due place and emphasis.

aspects of the believer's relation to Christ's way. We have noticed the spiritual and mystical repetition and experiencing of Christ's death and resurrection. This is an accomplished fact; we have died to sin and have been raised to newness of life. We have passed through this part of Christ's way in our following of him. And yet at the same time we continue to be involved in this part of the way. In Colossians we find these thoughts expressed in close sequence: "Ye died with Christ from the rudiments of the world" (2:20); "ye died" (3:3); and then in 3:5 comes, "Put to death therefore your members which are upon earth." The same is true of our resurrection: "If then ye were raised together with Christ, seek the things that are above" (Col. 3:1); thus, we are already resurrected—now we must learn to live as resurrected people. This double truth is found throughout the New Testament: we *are* saved—now we must *become* saved. Is it appropriate to use the term *imitation* for both these phenomena?

Once again the problem is primarily one of semantics. Wingren, writing in German, uses the term *Nachfolge* in speaking both of the spiritual likeness and of the ethical requirement.[156] Tinsley does not hesitate to speak of both matters in terms of *imitation, imitatio,* and *mimesis.*[157] Schweizer confesses that one can legitimately speak of imitation *(Nachahmung)* in connection with the example *(Vorbild)* that can be seen in Jesus' way, but hastens to warn against allowing this matter to get out of focus with the broader matter of the significance of Jesus' way and of following him.[158] Schweizer's warning is appropriate, for the matter of the imitation of Christ has sometimes gotten badly out of focus and out of proportion to the rest of the New Testament revelation. For the sake of clarity it is undoubtedly preferable to use the term imitation only in the way the New Testament uses it, namely, where the believer is active in learning Christ's ways and as a Christian is conforming his life to the example of Christ.

In conclusion we may make certain observations in the light of the foregoing survey of the passages in the New Testament which hold Christ before men and in some way more or less specifically point to him as an example and pattern for their conduct. It is most striking that we always see the same basic pattern, with only slight variations. In John 13 it was self-giving, humility, service; in I Pet. 2 it was suffering, patient endurance of maltreatment; in Phil. 2 it was his attitude of self-giving, humility; in II Cor. 8 again a giving of himself; in Rom. 15 a forsaking of his own pleasure in the interests

---

156 G. Wingren, "Was bedeutet die Nachfolge Christi in Evangelischer Ethik?", *T.L.,* LXXV (1950), pp. 385—392. D. Bonhoeffer, *Nachfolge,* München: Chr. Kaiser Verlag, 1958, also uses the term *Nachfolge* throughout his book. He refers to only one *Nachahmung*-text: Eph. 5:1, the imitation of God; *cf.* p. 224.

157 See throughout his book, *Imitation.*

158 "Man könnte im Weg Jesu das *Vorbild* sehen, das die Gemeinde nachzuahmen hat.... Aber damit wäre die Einzigartigkeit des Weges Jesu verloren—sie muss dann durch andere Aussagen gesichert werden—und damit auch der wirkliche, alte Nachfolgegedanke. Denn um die Nachahmung einzelner Züge, etwa der Ehelosigkeit Jesu, ging es ja nie. Es ging stets um das Teilhaben an Jesu Weg im Ganzen, und zwar an *Jesu* Weg, nicht um ein Durchschreiten eines eigenen Weges, der nur jenem ähnlich war" (Schweizer, *Erniedrigung,* p. 144).

of others; in Heb. 12 and II Thess. 3 it is steadfast endurance; II Cor. 10:1 points to his meekness and gentleness; and I John to his self-giving. To this list may be added Eph. 5:2 where it is again his love and giving himself for us, [159] and Col. 3:13 where it is forgiveness (provided that the reference to "Lord," κύριος, in this text is to be understood of Christ rather than God).[160] The common thread running through all these passages is self-denial, self-giving, losing of self in the interests of others. This was the example of Christ which was constantly being held before young Christians. It is precisely what Christ had called for in his call: "If any man will come after me, let him deny himself, and take up his cross, and follow me" (Matt. 16:24; Mark 8:34; Luke 9:23; *cf.* John 12:25,26). Jesus depicted this kind of life; he looked for it and expected it in his followers; and the apostles diligently urged it upon young Christians.

But these passages also show that this kind of self-giving life in Jesus' followers sprang from deeper roots than merely having come to see him, know him, and adopt his way of life as a good one. Jesus came as a teacher; he came as a good man, even an ideal one; but more basically he came as the Messiah and Savior. The call to follow him was the Messianic call, and to respond to it led to a living and life-giving fellowship with him and a total commitment to the program of his kingdom. Christ's example was applicable to people committed to him. It was urged upon them in view of their being Christians. The example had its part to play where a living union with the Savior existed and where the Holy Spirit was at work in their hearts. Tinsley has stated it well when he writes:

> The life of the Christian disciple as *imitator Christi* is not any kind of yoga of self-endeavour. It is not a process which is initiated and sustained by the Christian believer, as if the *imitatio Christi* were some kind of literal mimicry. It is a process initiated and sustained by the Spirit as Paraclete, and in it he conforms the pattern of the life of believers to that of the Lord so that men may become aware that they are his disciples. The Spirit as Paraclete will guide the disciples along the way which is Christ himself (John 16.13), and bring into their remembrance all the things that he said (John 14.26).[161]

The believer's union with Christ has touched life at its core. It has affected it as to kind, caliber, tenor, basic disposition. The new life that springs from union with Christ naturally finds its pattern in Christ. The pattern becomes known to men in the way he lived during his days on earth. It also becomes known in the total revelation he brought as the Son of God who

---

159 See below, pp. 76f.
160 It is difficult to decide which is meant. The usual use of κύριος is as a designation for Jesus. However, the forgiveness of sins is usually attributed to God. In Col. 1:14 Jesus is the one *in whom* we have forgiveness; in 2:13 God is the one who forgives us. In a passage parallel to Col. 3:13 in Eph. 4:32 we find this full statement of the matter: "even as God also in Christ forgave you." It is not important to our present purposes to come to a decision on the matter.
161 Tinsley, *Imitation*, pp. 130,131.

had left heavenly glory to walk the path of suffering and death for our salvation. Christ is the form to which those who are united with him must learn to conform. Christ's example is a fact and a force to those for whom he has become Savior and Messiah.


B. *The Imitation of God.*

The New Testament also holds God before men as an example for their conduct. In the Sermon on the Mount Jesus took occasion to point to God's manner of conduct and attitude in order to enforce an appeal which he was making. In Matt. 5:43—48 we find Jesus reacting to tendencies to consider the term "neighbor" as applying only to certain classes of men, which then are to be loved, while excluding others, who then could be treated quite differently. Hence, Jesus reissued the command precisely in the terms which others had thought to present an obvious exception: "But I say unto you, Love your enemies, and pray for them that persecute you" (vs. 44). To this he significantly adds, "that ye may be sons of your Father who is in heaven" (vs. 45a). This attitude and conduct of the Father is illustrated with the observation that God makes no distinction between the evil and the good, or the just and the unjust in giving sunshine and rain. Jesus further observes that the practice of loving those that love us is found everywhere among mankind and surely gives no evidence of their being a people in special relationship with God. He issues them a striking challenge and imperative: "Ye therefore shall be perfect, as your heavenly Father is perfect" (vs. 48).

The meaning and implications of this passage are far-reaching indeed and go quite beyond our present concern. However, there are several matters which ought to be noted in connection with this study of imitation. There is the question of how Jesus' command is to be understood when he asks for a perfection like the Father's perfection. Is this the climactic and summary command for the whole series of things he has been speaking of and the various requirements he has laid down? Having spoken about obedience in specific areas of life, does he now summarize by calling for the development of a perfect moral life in all its parts, the life of a perfectly integrated personality? Is this a general and all-comprehending command requiring of us to take God's absolute and complete perfection as the standard for human behavior? [162] If so, then many questions arise as to how man can fulfill

---

162 Heitmann, *Imit. Dei*, pp. 8,9, says the following on Matt. 5:48: "Es ist von Gottes Vollkommenheit schlechthin die Rede wobei natürlich Gottes selbstlose Liebe und Güte besonders gemeint sind, von denen unmittelbar vorher gesprochen wurde.... Der himmlische Vater selbst in seiner vom Menschen nie ganz ergründbaren Vollendung ist also nach Jesu Forderung der Maszstab für das sittliche Handeln der Seinen. Dem himmlischen Vater gleichgestaltet zu werden, darf und muss das Ziel allen Strebens hier auf Erden sein. Ein grösseres Gebot konnte nicht gegeben werden, und hier, gleichsam in den Fundamenten, offerbart sich die wahre Grösse des Christentums." However, if the real greatness of Christianity lies in the greatness of the goal of its ethical struggle (Heitmann uses the expression "die vollkommene ethische Persönlichkeit" in the context), does Christianity not become dangerously similar to the Greek religions of the day? Is their difference only one of degree?

such a requirement, or even whether he can in this life, and if not, what its purpose is, etc. However, it is questionable whether the perfection here referred to is to be abstracted and generalized into an over-all requirement of the ethical life. As du Plessis has cogently argued: "It must be clear that if these words contain an intimation of the innate perfection of God, the imperative to the disciples would be perfectly senseless. By pointing to God as the supreme Example for imitation, Jesus is referring to the way in which He reveals Himself.... The correlative is... not ontological but modal." [163] The command is connected concretely with the love about which Jesus has just been speaking. He has just been criticizing their love that makes its careful distinctions. He implies that this is a very low standard of love. The gentiles and publicans have no trouble living by this standard. But this is not the standard which God has shown. He makes no exception of the evil and unjust in sending rain and sunshine. His love embraces all, and so must theirs. "Ye therefore shall be perfect." The "ye" is said with emphasis (ὑμεῖς), distinguishing them from mankind on the level of gentiles and publicans. The "therefore" (οὖν) draws a conclusion from the fact that they are sons of God. In view of their Father's love being all-embracing, complete, and without exception, their love too must be perfect. The perfection here is the completeness, wholeness, undividedness, universality which their love must show. [164] Jesus presented his hearers with no easy task here, but as children of God and citizens of his kingdom they could be expected to take it seriously and to put it into practice in their lives. God's attitude and action had set the pattern for them.

The point of Jesus' argument here rests on the father-son relationship to which he calls attention in vs. 45. A son resembles his father. This is true not only in respect to stature and appearance, but also in his basic nature, his attitudes, his behavior. Father and son can be expected not only to look alike but also to act alike. In fact, the son is a manifestation and embodiment of his father. [165] On another occasion he said of his hearers: "If ye were Abraham's children, ye would do the works of Abraham.... Ye are of your father the devil, and the lusts of your father it is your will to do" (John

---

[163] P. J. du Plessis, ΤΕΛΕΙΟΣ *The Idea of Perfection in the New Testament*, Kampen: J. H. Kok, 1959, p. 171.

[164] "The singular suitability of *teleios* to render the concept of radical application is shown to advantage here. One who loves friends and hates foes is without *telos*, he is not 'whole'. Love, if perfect, is so profound, radical and consistent that it includes one of the most difficult charges of self-abnegation: to love a personal enemy" (du Plessis, *Perfection*, pp. 170,171). So also R. Bultmann, *Jesus*, Tübingen: J. C. B. Mohr (Paul Siebeck), 1951, p. 103; H. N. Ridderbos, *De Strekking der Bergrede naar Mattheus*, Kampen: J. H. Kok, 1936, p. 143; H. Cremer, *Biblisch-theologisches Wörterbuch der neutestamentlichen Gräzität*, 10. Aufl. (hrsg. von J. Kögel), Gotha: F. A. Perthes, 1915, sub τέλειος, p. 1047; and T. Zahn, *Das Evangelium des Matthäus*, 2. Aufl, K.z.N.T., Leipzig: A. Deichert, 1905, p. 255. The form which the command takes in Luke also indicates that it has to do with the matter of love rather than ethical perfection in general: "Be ye merciful even as your Father is merciful" (6:36).

[165] "With the Hebrews ... the two terms [father and son], and especially 'son', are used when a physical relationship is out of the question, and where the son is so called because he is the representative, the manifestation, the embodiment of him, or of that, of which he is said to be the son. We can talk of a son of peace, or worthlessness (Belial) or of consolation" (W. F. Lofthouse, "Fatherhood and Sonship in the Fourth Gospel," *E.T.*, XLIII [1931/32], p. 443).

8:39,44). In the Sermon on the Mount Jesus has the same reasoning. He strengthens the command to love their enemies with the consideration, "that ye may be sons of your Father who is in heaven" (vs. 45). From what Jesus has already said in his sermon, there can be no doubt that he considers his hearers as already being sons of God and citizens of his kingdom. He is not pointing them to the way of becoming sons, but calling them to be what they already are.[166] They are to bring their sonship to expression in their lives. They must find God to be their Father so really and so closely that his life sets the pattern for theirs and influences theirs. On the basis of such a relationship, behavior which otherwise seems impossible becomes natural and normal.[167] Thus Jesus can command a love that includes even enemies and persecutors. As sons of their heavenly Father, they will do what sons always do: they will form their lives on his pattern. The likeness that is here called for hinges entirely on the father-son relationship.

The similarity between the command to be perfect (vs. 48) and the command in Lev. 19:2: "Ye shall be holy; for I Jehovah your God am holy," has often been observed. Does Jesus have the holiness command in mind when he issues his command? Is he consciously substituting another word for the word "holiness," but adhering so closely to the form of the holiness command that it will surely recall that command to his hearers? One can hardly speak absolutely here, but it is remarkable that even in translation and for people far less at home in the Old Testament than Jesus' hearers or Matthew's original readers, the holiness command of Leviticus keeps coming to mind. On the other hand, it is questionable whether the matter ought to be pressed. Jesus is not rejecting the holiness command nor issuing it in a new form for the New Testament era.[168] It is simply a matter of holiness not being precisely to the point here. Holiness is partially negative, having to do with avoidance of sin and contamination, and in its positive aspect holiness does not fully clarify the matter of breadth and range of love. In the context in which it stands, perfection (τέλειος) makes the matter very clear. However, as we have already noted, Rabbinic Judaism saw in the command of Leviticus 19:2 the expression of the necessity of "the family of the king to bear the imprint of the king."[169] Jesus was using this very line of reasoning here in terms of the heavenly Father and his sons. Hence, it seems likely that Jesus cast

---

166 In ὅπως γένησθε υἱοί the γένησθε need be no more than a substitute for a form of εἰμί (see Bauer, *Wörterbuch, sub* γίνομαι, II). The use of ἔσεσθε in the parallel passage in Luke 6:35 confirms this. *Cf.* also the use of ἔσεσθε in Matt. 5:48 as compared with γίνεσθε in the parallel in Luke 6:36.

167 "Pour faire partie du Royaume de Dieu qui se fonde, il ne suffit pas d'être vertueux au sens philosophique du terme, ni d'obéir aux commandements comme le prescrivait le Judaïsme, mais il faut avoir avec Dieu des relations d'enfant à Père. Seule cette communauté de nature et de vie donne la possibilité d'aimer comme Dieu aime" (Spicq, *Agapè*, Analyse I, p. 27).

168 R. Asting, *Die Heiligkeit im Urchristentum*, Göttingen: Vandenhoeck & Ruprecht, 1930, p. 150, proposes: "An und für sich hätte hier gut ἅγιος für τέλειος stehen können. Aber da ἅγιος in Verbindung mit den Gläubigen schon vom Judentum her ein eschatologischjenseitiges Gepräge erhalten hatte, würde es in einem Ausspruch wie diesem missverständlich wirken können." However, such an explanation is hard to reconcile with the use of the holiness command in I Peter 1:16.

169 See above, p. 42.

his command in the form of the well-known holiness command to help to strengthen the point that the sons ought to bear the imprint of their heavenly Father.[170]

If we can not speak with certainty as to just what part the holiness command of Lev. 19:2 plays in the thoughts on imitation in Matt. 5, the same need not be said for its part in I Peter 1. Here there is a formal citation of the Leviticus passage in substantiation of a command to learn from observing God what is proper for us. Peter begins his epistle with a paragraph about the wonderful thing that has happened to both himself and his readers through the Christian faith that has been born in them. Notwithstanding the difficulties in which they now live, they may look forward to a glorious future. This new faith, hope, and life that is in them can not tolerate the former status quo of their lives, however. As people whose very nature it was to live in obedience to God, they can no longer submit to the rule of the lusts which have until now held sway in their lives (vs. 14). The only appropriate way of life now is the way of holiness. Such is demanded by the character of the One who has called them: "But like the Holy One who called you, be ye yourselves also holy in all manner of living" (vs. 15, according to A.S.V. mg.). He fortifies this with the citation of the command from Leviticus: "Ye shall be holy; for I am holy" (vs. 16). Thus the very law which had formed the basis of the covenantal fellowship between God and Old Testament Israel is now made the norm of the Christian walk of life. Peter lays emphasis immediately, however, on the more intimate relationship which now exists. They call on this holy God, the impartial Judge, as their Father (vs. 17). The idea of their adopting the pattern which is found in God is again in the context of their being his children.

The weaving together of ideas here is noteworthy. As Cremer-Kögel has pointed out, the idea of God's holiness carried with it the idea of his being judge: "D. grundlegende Heilstat Gottes an Israel, d. wunderbare Erlösung aus Ägypten ist geschehen: Gottes Heiligkeit ist ebenso im Gericht über Ägypten, wie in der Israel widerfahrenen Gnade offenbar geworden u. wird sich weiter in d. königl. Regieren Jhwhs, d. Bundesgottes, entfalten.... Diese z w e i s e i t i g e Erscheinung d. Heiligkeit Gottes, in Gericht u. Erlösung, werden wir stets wiederfinden."[171] Hence the holiness command brought God's judgeship to mind. But the holiness command also was closely connected to the thought of parental reverence, since in Leviticus the command to fear father and mother follows immediately upon the command to be holy (cf. Lev. 19:2,3). Peter weaves the two strands together: the holy God, the impartial Judge, is now known to them as their Father.[172] Hence they are to live their lives in

---

[170] To press the similarity of the two commands further than this, so that in view of "holiness" being a general ethical demand, "perfection" is also understood as a general ethical demand, seems to me to be at odds with the context and contrary to the testimony of the parallel passage in Luke.

[171] Cremer-Kögel, Wörterbuch, sub ἅγιος, pp. 46,47.

[172] The prominent position of πατέρα (vs. 17) shows that fatherhood is the main idea, not judgeship. Hence, Selwyn rightly remarks, "The sense cannot be 'if the Father you invoke is the impartial Judge of every man's work,' but conversely 'If you invoke the impartial Judge as Father'" (E. G. Selwyn, The First Epistle of St. Peter, London: Macmillan, 1947, p. 142).

due reverence to him, the more so in view of what he has done for them in Jesus Christ (*cf.* vss. 18ff.).

In Ephesians the imitation of God comes to direct expression. Paul exhorts his readers: "Be ye therefore imitators of God, as beloved children" (5:1). He has been giving various admonitions about the way of life that is appropriate for them now that they have become Christians. This can no longer be the way of life of the Gentiles in its estrangement from God and all its consequent involvement in grievous forms of sin (4:17—19). They are to put away the old man (vs. 22), and to "put on the new man, that is after God, created in righteousness and holiness of truth" (vs. 24, A.S.V. mg.). The implicit reference to the new man's being created in the image of God is noteworthy here as setting the stage for the idea of imitating God.

Paul instructs them to put on the new man τὸν κατὰ θεὸν κτισθέντα. Commentators are not all agreed on what Paul means to say in the phrase κατὰ θεόν. Taken alone, it says merely "according to God," and seems to imply "according to the will of God." [173] However, in this context of the creation of the new man it would seem to mean "like God," "according to his image." In Colossians 3, where Paul's argument and wording are closely similar to this section of Ephesians, Paul says that his readers "have put on the new man, that is being renewed after the image of him that created him (κατ' εἰκόνα τοῦ κτίσαντος αὐτόν)" (vs. 10). In the Genesis account of creation, man is made κατ' εἰκόνα θεοῦ (LXX of Gen. 1:27; 5:1). That κατά does not have to be accompanied by εἰκόνα or some similar word in order to express the idea of likeness or comparability in some fundamental aspect is clear from various examples given by Liddell-Scott, such as, "to marry in one's own rank in life (καθ' ἑαυτόν)," or "none of your sort (κατὰ σέ)." [174] Bauer also gives as a meaning for κατά, "v. d. Gleichheit, d. Ähnlichkeit, d. Beispiel, d. Bild: *entsprechend, gemäss, gleich wie, so wie, ähnlich wie.*" [175] A clear instance of such usage is found in Gal. 4:28: "Now we, brethren, as Isaac was (κατὰ 'Ισαάκ), are children of promise." I Peter 1:15 also is similar: "like as the Holy One who called you (κατὰ τὸν καλέσαντα ὑμᾶς ἅγιον), be ye yourselves also holy." Hence in Eph. 4:24 we understand κατὰ θεόν to express a likeness to God which man possesses in virtue of his new creation.

Paul continues with the theme which he has struck about putting away things characteristic of the old man, suggesting their counterparts which ought to characterize the new man. The sins of the tongue particularly seem to occupy his attention, undoubtedly in view of the expression they give of the basic corruption, ill-will, and enmity characterizing the old man. After speaking of several of them in vss. 25—30, he lists a whole series in one breath

---

[173] E.g., T. K. Abbott, *A Critical and Exegetical Commentary on the Epistles to the Ephesians and to the Colossians,* I.C.C., Edinburgh: T. & T. Clark, 1909, p. 138: "the true interpretation, viz. 'according to the will of God'"; J. A. C. van Leeuwen, *Paulus' Zendbrieven aan Efeze, Colosse, Filémon, en Thessalonika,* K.N.T., Amsterdam: H. A. van Bottenburg, 1926, p. 109: "overeenkomstig Zijn raad en bedoeling"; *cf. N.B.G.:* "die naar (den wil van) God geschapen is."
[174] Liddell-Scott, *Lexicon, sub* κατά, B, IV, 2.
[175] Bauer, *Wörterbuch, sub* κατά, II, 5, b.

and places over against it the conduct which ought to characterize the Christian: "Let all bitterness, and wrath, and anger, and clamor, and railing, be put away from you, with all malice: and be ye kind one to another, tenderhearted, forgiving each other, even as God also in Christ forgave you" (vss. 31,32). Here follows immediately the exhortation: "Be ye therefore imitators of God, as beloved children; and walk in love, even as Christ also loved you, and gave himself up for us, an offering and a sacrifice to God for an odor of a sweet smell" (5:1,2).

How closely the "be ye imitators" is to be connected with the immediately preceding thought "even as God also in Christ forgave you" is not entirely clear. The "therefore" (οὖν) with which he introduces 5:1 does show that the thought springs from the foregoing. However, the connection is not necessarily limited to the immediately preceding sentence, even though this immediately preceding verse is related to the thought of imitation in a particular way. He had previously spoken of the new man's being created "after God" (vs. 24), and this thought too has its relation to imitation. In consideration of the whole context it seems preferrable to think of Eph. 5:1,2 as a separate unit of thought related to the whole preceding argument. Paul's Christian readers must no longer walk as those "alienated from the life of God" (4:18), but rather put on the new man created after God (4:24); they must be imitators of God. [176] This is the broad connection of the thought. On the other hand the summarizing statement about getting rid of malice and learning to forgive each other (4:31,32), and especially the addition, "even as God also in Christ forgave you," paves the way for the outright command: "Be ye therefore imitators of God."

The statement "forgiving each other, even as God also in Christ forgave you" can not be understood as a pure and simple call to imitate God in the matter of forgiving. The statement goes deeper than that. Michaelis quite correctly points out that the reference to God says in effect, "A person who has experienced God's forgiveness can hardly remain unforgiving toward his neighbor." [177] In this connection he calls attention to Jesus' words in the parable of the unforgiving servant: "Shouldest not thou also have had mercy on thy fellowservant, even as I had mercy on thee?" (Matt. 18:33). Here again the mercy which the servant experienced ought to have moved him to show mercy in turn. Thus the addition of the words "even as God also in Christ forgave you" is not primarily calculated to call attention to God as an example in forgiving, but serves to call attention to a specific act of forgiveness of which we were the beneficiaries, and which now serves as the ground and motive for our forgiveness. The argument in 5:2 is to the same effect: "Walk in love even as Christ also loved you and gave himself up for

---

[176] Making a separate paragraph of 5:1,2, as is done by many Bible translations (*e.g.*, A.S.V., R.S.V., N.E.B., N.B.G.) is to be preferred over such divisions as 4:25—5:2 (H. Schlier, *Der Brief an die Epheser*, Dusseldorf: Patmos-Verlag, 1957, pp. 222ff.; P. Ewald, *Die Briefe des Paulus an die Epheser, Kolosser, und Philemon*, K.z.N.T., Leipzig: A. Deichert, 1905, pp. 213ff.) or 4:29—5:2 (C. Masson, *L'Épitre de Saint Paul aux Éphésiens*, C.d.N.T., Neuchatel/Paris: Delachaux & Niestlé, 1953, p. 204f.).

[177] Michaelis, *T.W.N.T.*, IV, p. 674, 7,8.

us." Christ's love for us as it reached its fullest expression in his death for us is the foundation on which our walking in love is based and the soil in which it grows.

However, when due account has been given to the fact that these statements point primarily to the ground and motive for forgiveness and love, it may still be asked whether God's action is in any sense to be viewed as an example and pattern here. The point can probably be seen more clearly by comparing these statements in Ephesians with the somewhat similar statements of Jesus pointing to God as an example. When Jesus said, "Ye shall be perfect, as your heavenly Father is perfect" (Matt. 5:48), and "Be ye merciful, even as your Father is merciful" (Luke 6:36), the fact of God's example is obvious. In both these statements Jesus is speaking about God's attitude toward men in general, including even the publicans and gentiles, the unthankful and the evil. To be comparable in effect to these statements, the Ephesian statements would have to be re-worded in some such fashion as this: "Forgive each other, even as God forgives others," or "Walk in love, even as Christ loved and gave himself for others." But when, as in Ephesians, God's act is performed with specific reference to us, and is an act of such consequence as God's forgiving of us or Christ's loving us even to the point of giving himself in death for us, then the emphasis of the statement shifts. Reference to God's act then becomes more than an illustration of his conduct. It places upon us an urgency and obligation to make a fitting response to what he has done for us in the way we live with others. At the same time it ought to be observed that this new emphasis does not obliterate the fact that in making our fitting response, we are to adopt into our lives the very ways that God has shown toward us. We are to do as he did. This correlation between God's act and our act comes to particularly full expression in the parallel to Eph. 4:32 found in Col. 3:13: "Even as the Lord forgave you, so also do ye" (notice the καθὼς καί ... οὕτως καί). The similarity of conduct in what God has done and what God's people are to do remains an integral part of the thought here. It is at this point that God's action plays its role of example, pattern and norm. Hence, when Paul says to his readers to forgive each other, "even as God also in Christ forgave you," he confronts them with both the ground and motive for their forgiveness and the example and norm of it. If the former takes precedence as far as the immediate impact of the words is concerned, the latter is surely not absent nor to be ignored.[178] Paul proceeds immediately to the direct expression of it: "Be ye therefore imitators of God."

Paul summarizes and further reinforces the individual admonitions he had been giving in the broad command to be imitators of God. He adds significantly "as beloved children." In this he appeals to the same thought

---

[178] When Michaelis says concerning 5:2, "Der Hinweis auf Christus ist vielmehr als ethisches Motiv zu werten, das den Gedanken der Nachahmung eines Vorbildes nicht notwendig einschliesst" (*T.W.N.T.*, IV, p. 674, 15,16) he is right as far as he goes, but he fails to take due account of the fact that the reference to Christ, which serves as ethical motivation of our love, is Christ's *love*, even as in 4:32 the motivation of our forgiveness is God's *forgiveness*. It is this which makes the thought of the imitation of an example difficult to escape entirely.

which Jesus had used when he fortified the command to love one's enemies with the addition, "that ye may be sons of your Father who is in heaven" (Matt. 5:45).[179] The point which both Jesus and Paul are making is that by the very structure of things the offspring are of the same kind as their parents, and that this is not merely a physical fact relating to their bodies but a fact involving their entire being, even their most basic attitudes toward life and toward those around them. Since they are no longer alienated from the life of God (4:18) but are putting on the new man created in the image of God (4:24), they are to be real children of his, sons indeed; they are to be his imitators. Any imitation in the sense of mimicking, aping, artificially and outwardly putting on the appearance of something that is not genuine, real, and heartfelt is entirely foreign to Paul's thought here. This is to be the imitation of beloved children. Never is there more freedom from guile, more openness and naturalness than in the acts of children. At the same time children are born imitators. They have the most acute powers of observation, the most remarkable abilities to reproduce what they observe, and the deepest drives and desires to be like others whom they admire. In a quite unconscious process they form themselves into the likeness of those nearest and dearest to them. Paul shows himself to have been a keen observer of human nature in calling his readers to imitate as *beloved* children, for there is no atmosphere in which the child's imitation so flourishes as that of abundant parental love. The imitation of which Paul here speaks is the imitation of a child nourished in parental love and concentrating on trying to be like his father and mother. When this parent-child relationship is poured full of the content of salvation in Christ and the new relationship between God and his children in Christ, the ramifications of the subject become truly exciting.

> Michaelis sees a quite different import in the words "as beloved children." He explains it thus: "Indem die Leser in ihren Eigenschaft als Gottes geliebte Kinder seine μιμηταί werden sollen, ist der Gedanke der gehorsamen **Befolgung des väterlichen Willens** stark in den Vordergrund gerückt, und es ist zugleich betont, dass die Leser auch als μιμηταί τοῦ θεοῦ nicht aufhören, seine τέκνα zu sein, sondern gerade darin sich als seine τέκνα bewähren. In 5, 1 ist der Abstand, der **zwischen Gott und Mensch** besteht, grundsätzlich festgehalten, und es könnte daher schlechterdings **keine Nachahmung** gemeint sein, durch die man dem Vorbild ähnlich oder gleich zu werden versucht."[180] One does not find ἀγαπητά playing much of a role in the thought thus conceived. Was Paul using it as formally and meaninglessly as modern ecclesiastical language often uses its counterpart "beloved"? But more surprising are the things he finds being expressed in τέκνα. It must be granted that the idea of being a child could in the proper context bring to mind the idea of compliance to a father's wishes, or of a basic difference from the adult. However, what elements are there in the context here to suggest these thoughts, except perhaps the

---

179 No difference can be pressed between Jesus calling them "sons" and Paul calling them "children" in view of Paul's easy interchange of the terms; *cf.* Gal. 4:21f., 28; and Rom. 9:7f.
180 Michaelis, *T.W.N.T.*, IV, p. 674, 20—28.

idea of imitation *as Michaelis conceives it?* Michaelis has found the element of obedience to be strong in the idea of imitation as it comes to the fore in the New Testament.[181] This is a matter which must be further investigated in our study of the various texts. But we fail to find traces of it here in the imitation idea as such; nor do we find it as the real thrust of the reference to imitating as beloved children. Even in the passage from Philo where the imitating is done by obedient (or subject, loyal) children, the imitation is not so much the following of the father's commands as the bringing to expression of the father's nature and characteristics by the children in their lives.[182] The same is the thrust of Jesus' words in Matt. 5:44f. about loving one's enemies that one may be a son of his heavenly Father. In view of the father-son relationship the situation is such that the father's characteristics, attitudes, ways of life both can and may be expected to come to expression in the son. This happens not in the child's obedience to commands but in his conforming to the very essence and structure of being a child. Hence, such comments as the following direct attention to the real point of referring to children in the Ephesian passage: "Τέκνον indicates a community of nature...";[183] "D. Gedanke an d. Art, an d. Bestimmtheit schlägt hier vor";[184] "...des enfants bien-aimés, chez qui on retrouve un trait distinctif du caractère de leur père";[185] and "On sait que les croyants sont fils de Dieu (Rom. VIII, 15–17) et participent sa nature."[186] Over against Michaelis, we would propose that the imitation of beloved children is precisely with an eye to resembling their father, even in view of the fact that the father here happens to be God.

Paul immediately proceeds to specify what he has in mind by calling the readers to be imitators of God. It is in the matter of love that they must become like God: "Be ye therefore imitators of God, as beloved children and walk in love." The second clause is coordinate to the first. As ἀγαπητά children, they are to walk in ἀγάπη. John's well-known words immediately come to mind: "We love, because he first loved us" (I John 4:19). Imitation in many matters develops in the children well-nourished on parental love, and most prominent among these is of course their ability to love and to bring love to expression. Children learn love by being loved. Paul appeals to this well-recognized fact in calling his Christian readers to the fullest expression of their Christian faith. They are God's children and the objects of his love. Thus they can walk in love, and love is to be expected from them. But Paul not only makes clear that he is thinking particularly of the matter of love when he calls them to be God's imitators. He proceeds to indicate God's love in its most specific and striking expression toward us.[187] "Walk in love, even as Christ also loved you, and gave himself for us." As we noted in regard to 4:32, this addition speaks primarily of a ground and

---

[181] Cf. Michaelis, *T.W.N.T.*, IV, p. 675, 1–8.
[182] See above, pp. 10ff.
[183] B. F. Westcott, *Saint Paul's Epistle to the Ephesians*, London: Macmillan, 1906, p. 77.
[184] Cremer-Kögel, *Wörterbuch*, p. 1075.
[185] Masson, *Eph.*, p. 205.
[186] Spicq, *Agapè*, Analyse I, p. 282.
[187] "Dans *Éph.* l'essai de 'définition' est plus net. Après l'évocation de l'idéal: 'imiter Dieu', saint Paul précise 'par la charité', puis finalement 'celle du Christ qui se donne'" (Spicq, *Agapè*, Analyse I, p. 284, fn. 1).

motivation for our love, but it can not be overlooked that Christ's love calls forth a similar response from us. Thus Christ's love serves as an example which we must follow. The combination of thoughts here is indeed fascinating. Paul calls for the imitation of God and in the same breath holds up the example of Christ. He speaks of being like God in love and then points to Christ's act of love on the cross. A clearer indication of the basic oneness of God and Christ for Paul is hardly possible. In effect the call which he issues to his readers here reduces to this: Imitate God by imitating Christ. [188] Through Christ the imitation of God has become real in a way never before known. [189]

It is worthy of note that when the New Testament holds God before Christians as an example to learn from and imitate, it always does so in terms of the father-son relationship existing between God and his people. The example is no philosophical, ethical, or even religious ideal; it is one's own Father. Imitation is seen as proceeding from a personal relationship. In view of an existing union of most fundamental and meaningful proportions, imitation is to be expected and may be urged upon the children. It is self-evident that they will be like their Father in certain basic characteristics. This is the nature of the relationship between them. An appeal to it carries tremendous persuasive power.

C. *The Imitation of Other Men.*

The imitation and example of other men than the Apostle Paul also have a role to play in the New Testament. Old Testament persons have become important on this score. The historical continuity with the Old Testament is apparent throughout the New Testament. Not only is there a constant referring to the authoritative words of the Old Testament; there is a repeated looking to the great personages of the Old Testament to illustrate some point or provide some stimulus and encouragement to the New Testament Christians. Particularly is this true of writings most clearly directed to Jewish readers. To such readers it was especially important to emphasize the fact that Christianity is the true inheritor of the treasures of the Old Testament religion and the true continuation of the faith of the fathers. The appeal then is to learn from the fathers. What they were, Christians are now called to be. The appeal is not to a way on the basis of its moral attractiveness or superiority, but to a way on the basis of its being the way of the service

---

[188] "Die 'Nachahmung Gottes' geschieht in der 'Nachahmung' Christi" (Schlier, *Eph.*, p. 232).

[189] To pursue the subject of the imitation of Christ and of God in the Apostolic Fathers would take us too far afield, for the subject begins a rapid expansion already in these early days. We have already noted briefly the use of μιμέομαι with Christ, God, or the Lord as object (see above, p. 15). For the sake of completeness it may be noticed that there are several instances where God or Christ are specifically referred to as being an example: *I Clem.* 16:17 (re: Christ's humility); *I Clem.* 33:8 (re: the good works of the Lord and Creator); and Ignatius, *To the Philadelphians* 8:2 (re: Christ's endurance of sufferings). In each case the word for example is the word used in the New Testament only in I Peter 2:21: ὑπογραμμός.

of God. It is the way which God's people go and the way they have always gone.[190] It is the way which has proved itself, for it leads God's people finally to their promised end. Hence, in Hebrews 6, after the writer has spoken of the possibilities of falling away and being beyond further spiritual renewal, he says, "But, beloved, we are persuaded better things of you, and things that accompany salvation" (Heb. 6:9). He is persuaded that his readers belong to the class of those that are saved. Thus he proceeds to urge them to follow the ways of saved people. They had made a good beginning in their work and in their love (6:10). Now he urges them to show the same diligence in the matter of perseverance and hope (6:11): "that ye be not sluggish, but imitators of them who through faith and patience inherit the promises" (6:12). He calls the example of Abraham to mind (6:13), and specifically makes his point: "Thus, having patiently endured, he obtained the promise" (6:15). For those standing in the line of salvation, faith and patient endurance was the way (*cf.* διά, vs. 12) to arrival at the promised destination. It was the way that many had walked before them, among others, Abraham. Now the readers, belonging to the same class, and being recipients of the same promises from God, ought to imitate those who have already gone along the way. In this passage in Hebrews the call to imitation was a call to shake off their lethargy and to renew their efforts toward steadfastness and perseverance, so that they like their faithful forefathers would finally come to their promised reward.[191]

The writer of the letter to the Hebrews returns to this subject later and develops the matter of the examples found in the Old Testament in an extended discourse. In the latter part of chap. 10 he has again been warning of the dangers of falling into sin and the hopelessness that resulted for one who had once come to know the truth (10:26ff.). Here too he reminds them of the good beginning which they had made and of the need of steadfastness in order to receive the promise. He confirms this with a passage from Habakkuk concerning the necessity of faithfulness and God's displeasure with those who shrink back. Then he concludes: "But we are not of them that shrink back unto perdition; but of them that have faith unto the saving of the soul" (10:39). His readers belong to the family of the faithful.[192]

Then comes the famous chapter 11 in which the writer presents a long

---

190 We noted above how Jesus' way too was "simply the path which Israel, Israel's prophets and righteous individuals, had ever again to follow." Cf. pp. 52f.

191 There are warning examples also in the context. Heb. 4:11 speaks of the example (ὑπόδειγμα) which Israel presents of falling into destruction as a result of disobedience. This use of ὑπόδειγμα as an example with sinister implications is found also in II Peter 2:6, where Sodom and Gomorrah are called "an example unto those that should live ungodly." Cf. also Papias III, where Judas Iscariot is called "a great example (ὑπόδειγμα) of godlessness." In Jude 7 a thought similar to II Pet. 2:6 regarding the example of Sodom and Gomorrah is expressed with the word δεῖγμα.

192 The genitives ὑποστολῆς and πίστεως express relationship or membership. *Cf.* F. W. Grosheide's edition and reworking of A. T. Robertsons *Beknopte Grammatica op het Grieksche Nieuwe Testament*, Kampen: J. H. Kok, 1912, § 153. 3; also F. Blass and A. Debrunner, *Grammatik des neutestamentlichen Griechisch*, 9. Aufl., Göttingen: Vandenhoeck & Ruprecht, 1954, § 162. 6.

paean of faith. He begins by stating what it is and then proceeds to portray the role it has played in giving hope and steadfastness in the lives of the famous men and women of the Old Testament. He sees the history of God's people as a history in the exercise of faith. The many examples cited illustrate faith in action and constitute a challenge to the Christian community to live in the same way. However, this passage is more than a citing of examples to stimulate the exercise of faith in the readers. There is a presentation of a cosmic program here too. The Christian community constitutes the last act in the great drama of living by faith. It is also the capstone and the climax of this great drama. Apart from the Christian community the whole program remains incomplete: "Apart from us they [the fathers] should not be made perfect" (11:40). It is from this consideration that the writer resumes the exhortation which he had previously been making: "Therefore let us also, seeing we are compassed about with so great a cloud of witnesses, lay aside every weight, and the sin which doth so easily beset us, and let us run with patience the race that is set before us" (12:1). There is indeed an appeal to the example of the fathers in Heb. 11, but the appeal is on a much broader basis than just to learn a lesson from the instances presented and to be encouraged and stimulated by the good example of one's forebears. It is an appeal to be in reality a member of the family of the faithful to which one belongs as a Christian and to fulfill one's role in the divine program as God has brought it to this new and final stage in Christ. [193]

In literary form Heb. 11 has resemblances to the rhetorical technique of the cynico-stoic diatribe. Both the repetition of a single word or idea and the accumulation of a long series of examples from legend and history were characteristic of the diatribe. [194] The style of the diatribe had strongly influenced the style of preaching in the synagogues of the Jewish diaspora. [195] The influence of this rhetorical form is also in evidence in the Hellenistic Jewish literature. [196] Thus it appears that the literary style of Heb. 11 has been influenced by Hellenism, probably by way of Hellenistic Judaism. [197] However the passage does not fall into the Hellenistic moralism which crept into much Hellenistic Jewish literature. The examples of faith are carefully kept in the context of the religious program of God for the world. They form a panorama of the

---

[193] This latter point receives further confirmation when the writer proceeds immediately to direct their attention to Jesus' example, wholly in the context of Jesus' being their Savior. See discussion above, p. 63.

[194] *Cf.* Bultmann, *Paul. Predigt u. Diatribe*, pp. 46ff., 50ff.; L. Sanders, *L'Hellénisme de Saint Clément de Rome et le Paulinisme*, Louvain: Bibliotheca Universitatis, 1943, pp. 2ff., 6ff.

[195] H. Thyen, *Der Stil der jüdisch-hellenistischen Homilie*, Göttingen: Vandenhoeck & Ruprecht, 1955, see I. Kapitel: „Die synagogale Homilie und die kynisch-stoische Diatribe," pp. 40ff.

[196] *Cf.* the accumulating of examples from history in *Sirach* 44–50; *I Macc.* 2:51–60; *IV Macc.* 16:16–23; Philo, *De Virtutibus* 198ff.; *De Praemiis et Poenis* 1ff.; and the constructing of a passage around the idea of wisdom: *Wisdom of Solomon* 10; or of hope: Philo, *De Praemiis et Poenis* 11.

[197] O. Michel, *Der Brief an die Hebraër*, K.e.K.N.T., 11. Aufl., Göttingen: Vandenhoeck & Ruprecht, 1960, pp. 244,245; Thyen, *Jüd.-hell. Homilie*, p. 18; C. Spicq, *L'Épître aux Hébreux*, E.B., Paris: J. Gabalda, 1953, Vol. II, p. 335 (*cf.* Vol. I, pp. 76ff. where he finds especially Philo's influence at work).

way of faith from creation (11:3) to the eschatological fulfillment of all things (11:40). The appeal is not simply to learn from all these examples, but to respond to one's religious calling as a Christian and to assume one's role in the company of all the fathers (12:1—περικείμενον) in the cosmic program of salvation.

The literary form of I Clement is similar to Hebrew 11 and is also to be seen as an adaptation of the form of the cynico-stoic diatribe.[198] Clement seeks in his letter to counteract the sedition and partisanship which were at work in the Corinthian church, and to this end he calls forth hosts of examples to make and support his points. After citing many Old Testament instances of the havoc wrought by jealousy and envy (chap. 4), he proceeds: "But, to cease from the examples (ὑποδειγμάτων) of old time, let us come to those who contended in the days nearest to us; let us take the noble examples (ὑποδείγματα) of our own generation. Through jealousy and envy the greatest and most righteous pillars of the church were persecuted and contended unto death. Let us set before our eyes the good apostles" (I Clem. 5:1–3). Then follow statements about the example of endurance in Peter, Paul ("the greatest example [ὑπογραμμός] of endurance" [5:5]), and other Christian martyrs. Clement cites Enoch, Noah, Abraham, Lot, and Rahab for their examples of obedience, faithfulness, and hospitality. After referring to Christ's example of humility (16:17), Clement makes the plea: "Let us also be imitators of those who went about 'in the skins of goats and sheep,' heralding the coming of Christ; we mean Elijah and Elisha, and moreover Ezekiel, the prophets, and in addition to them the famous men of old. Great fame was given to Abraham, and he was called the Friend of God, and he, fixing his gaze in humility on the Glory of God, says 'But I am dust and ashes'" (17:1,2). He then goes on to point to Job, Moses, and David as examples of humility. In chap. 31 Abraham, Isaac, and Jacob are presented as models of those who have walked in the ways of God. In chap. 33 after recalling that man was created in the image of God, he points to the pattern (ὑπογραμμόν) which God has given us of adorning himself with good works and calls for the following of it (33:7,8). In chap. 55 he gathers examples (ὑποδείγματα) from the heathen of loving self-sacrifice. Near the end of the epistle he summarizes: "It is therefore right that we should respect so many and so great examples (ὑποδείγμασιν), and bow the neck, and take up the position of obedience, so that ceasing from vain sedition we may gain without any fault the goal set before us in truth" (63:1). The sustained effort which Clement makes at pointing men to examples, be they Old Testament, contemporary, divine, or even heathen, and the glowing terms in which he speaks of these exemplary persons arouse the suspicion that Clement may not merely be making use of a cynico-stoic literary form, but that he may be showing traces of a cynico-stoic moralism as well. The suspicion only becomes the stronger upon discovering the deficiencies in Clement's doctrines of Christ and of grace.[199] One can not classify Clement's letter as moralism pure and simple. Nevertheless, it is amazing that the final appeal to this Christian congregation is in terms of the rightness of respecting so many and so

---

[198] Sanders, *L'Hellénism*, pp. 2ff.
[199] See the analysis in Torrance, *Doct. of Grace*, pp. 44—55. He concludes that for Clement "the real object of faith is God alone. Accordingly it is difficult to see any place for Christ in the Christian salvation beyond that of a preacher of the 'grace of repentance'" (p. 46); and "the general meaning of χάρις in this Epistle appears to be that of enabling power granted to those who are worthy" (p. 54). *Cf.* also L. Goppelt, *Christentum und Judentum im ersten und zweiten Jahrhundert*, Gütersloh: C. Bertelsmann, 1954, p. 241, on how the deviating tendencies of Hellenistic Judaism in regard to the Old Testament religion have affected Clement's Christianity.

great examples, rather than of urging a fitting response to the grace of God in Christ.

James in writing to "the twelve tribes which are of the dispersion" (James 1:1) also turns to the Old Testament for examples. "Take, brethren, for an example (ὑπόδειγμα) of suffering and of patience, the prophets who spake in the name of the Lord. Behold, we call them blessed that endured: ye have heard of the patience of Job ..." (5:10,11a). The passage comes in a section where James is appealing, "Be patient, therefore, brethren, until the coming of the Lord" (5:7). To hold the example of the prophets before Jewish Christian readers had a particular appropriateness. In the first place these were persons well known to them, persons related to them, their own national heroes, their own flesh and blood. But more important, these were men who had stood as a small minority or even as a lonely voice speaking for the Lord in the midst of great hostility from their own people. To speak of the prophets to Jewish people brought immediate associations of faithfulness in the face of opposition, and often it brought the association of martyrdom.[200] James' readers lived as a double minority. First they were in the Jewish minority over against the Gentiles all around them. Then they were in the Christian minority over against the whole Jewish community of which they had been a part until their conversion. To call to mind the example of the prophets to people living in such loneliness was to call forth some company for them. God had led the prophets along the way of patient suffering. Job too had traversed the road. It was neither an improbable nor an impossible way for God's servants. In regard to Job they could see how much the kindness and mercy of the Lord was at work in it all. The force of the appeal to example here is to confirm and strengthen them in the way they are called to go as God's servants by bringing them into the company of God's servants of the past.[201]

The author of the epistle to the Hebrews turns not only to the Old Testament in recommending examples of faith. This faith had been in evidence in more recent times also. There had been men who had lived in the midst of his readers, men known to them personally, whose faith furnished them an example. "Remember them that had the rule over you, men that spake unto you the word of God; and considering the issue of their life, imitate their faith" (Heb. 13:7). These men had been preachers of God's word and leaders in the congregation. Through their position and through their work

---

[200] *Cf.* Matt. 5:12; 23:29—39; Mark 12:1ff.; Acts 7:52; Heb. 11:33ff.

[201] It remains an interesting and baffling question why James did not appeal to the example of Jesus' patient suffering here. Perhaps the fact that the oppressed were being encouraged to remain steadfast in awaiting the Lord's coming made the example given by the Lord in a somewhat different situation seem not so appropriate. Grosheide's suggestion also is plausible: "Men heeft aanvankelijk blijkbaar de geschiedenis van Jezus overdacht, zonder alle consequenties daaruit te trekken" (F. W. Grosheide, *De Brief aan de Hebreeën en de Brief van Jakobus*, 2e dr., C.N.T., Kampen, J. H. Kok, 1955, p. 408, fn. 14). At least the proposal by some earlier exegetes to find reference to Christ's example in the words τὸ τέλος κυρίου εἴδετε (vs. 11) can not be sustained. See the convincing answers to the proposal in J. B. Mayor, *The Epistle of St. James*, London: Macmillan, 1892, pp. 152,153, and M. Dibelius, *Der Brief des Jakobus*, K.e.K.N.T., 8. Aufl., Göttingen: Vandenhoeck & Ruprecht, 1956, pp. 227,228.

they had had a formative influence over the readers.[202] Now they were dead. However, this did not bring their influence to an end. The whole event of their dying, the circumstances surrounding it, and their responses and reactions in it and to it furnished one of the most powerful lessons that had ever come from them. While the thought suggests itself that their death may have been a martyr's death, the words do not strictly demand this; it may have been a death from more normal causes.[203] But at least it formed a capstone to the life of faithfulness which they had lived. In their death their faithfulness and steadfastness had become apparent as never before.[204] In view of the evidences and tendencies of sluggishness and lukewarmness found among the readers, they are called to remember what they have seen in these men and to imitate them in their faithfulness. The appeal to become imitators is a call to be Christians indeed, in accordance with the pattern of the Christian way as these leaders had portrayed it.

The New Testament contains one more explicit call to imitation outside of those found in Paul's letters. In III John 11 Gaius is admonished: "Imitate not (μὴ μιμοῦ) that which is evil, but that which is good." The admonition does not point to a specific bad or good example, either from history or in the present. However, the reproachable conduct of Diotrephes has been the subject in the two preceding verses. The general statement about "that which is evil," coming in this context, automatically finds its first application in Diotrephes' conduct. In the same way the general statement about "that which is good" seems to be looking ahead to the mention of Demetrius, the man so well spoken of by all (vs. 12). Hence, while the command to imitate remains general and the imitation and non-imitation of Demetrius and Diotrephes must be arrived at by inference, the whole movement of the thought directs attention to men known to and living among the readers. The imitation here presented then is undoubtedly the following of a pattern of conduct, a way of life known and seen in others around one, a way which may be characterized either as good or as bad. The passage however is too indefinite to supply us with information on the nature and usage of the thought of imitation.

A counterpart to calling people to imitation is the call to leaders to be examples. Here too the remarkable influence which one person's life can

---

202 It is possible that these men were those who first preached the gospel to the readers. The phrase "speaking the word of God" is often used in that way, although it may also simply refer to preaching in the congregation. See E. Riggenbach, *Der Brief an die Hebräer*, K.z.N.T., Leipzig: A. Deichert, 1913, p. 432, fn. 59; Michel, *Heb.*, p. 335, fn. 3. If these men were the original missionaries to the readers, the call to imitation could include the thought of adopting the ways of one's spiritual parents, somewhat in the manner of Paul's appeal in I Cor. 4:16 (see below, p. 144ff.). However, this passage gives no indication of having such a point particularly in mind.

203 *Cf.* Michel, *Heb.*, p. 335; Grosheide, *Heb.*, p. 310; Riggenbach, *Heb.*, pp. 432f.

204 "Die πίστις der ἡγούμενοι, zu deren Nachahmung Hb 13,7 auffordert, ist ... wesentlich als Treue zu verstehen" (R. Bultmann, πιστεύω *et al.*, T.W.N.T., VI, p. 208, 26,27). See also Grosheide, *Heb.*, p. 255: "Geloof is in Hebreeën de kracht om te volharden, het is de menselijke daad, het vermogen om Gods wil te doen, ten einde aldus het beloofde goed te verkrijgen."

have in forming and directing that of another is in evidence. In I Peter 5 there are exhortations for the elders on how they ought to tend the flock of God. Among other things, Peter tells them to do it "neither as lording it over the charge allotted to you, but making yourselves ensamples (τύποι) to the flock" (I Pet. 5:3). The way to be avoided is that of lording it over the people over whom they have been placed. As Foerster has pointed out, there is a strong element of self-centeredness and of being antithetically disposed toward others in the very structure of the word κατακυριεύω, *lord over*, and this is borne out in all the New Testament instances of the word. [205] But this kind of antithetical attitude toward others is strictly at odds with what Jesus had called for from those who would follow him: "Ye know that they who are accounted to rule over the Gentiles lord it over (κατακυριεύουσιν) them; and their great ones exercise authority over them. But it is not so among you: but whosoever would become great among you, shall be your minister; and whosoever would be first among you, shall be servant of all" (Mark 10:42—44). Jesus immediately fortifies this by pointing to himself as example: "For the Son of man also came not to be ministered unto, but to minister, and to give his life a ransom for many" (Mark 10:45). Peter quite likely had these words in mind in his exhortation to the elders. As over against all forms of arrogance, tyranny, domineering, and self-seeking, they are to be examples. The specific nature of their example is not stated, but it can only be an example in Christian living. They are to portray the Christian way of life in the midst of the flock they lead. This example is to be a means for them to tend the flock. Hence, their becoming an example can not merely mean their developing a quality of life which can be viewed with admiration. They must see to it that this example exerts an influence and gives leadership. In tending the flock they must not stand apart or stand above it and drive it, order it, command it. They must come close to the flock, mingle with it, help it, serve it, and lead it by showing it the way. To speak of an example in such a context suggests close personal fellowship in an atmosphere of love, where there can be full and free communication. The example here is entirely dependent on the kind of personal relationship they have to the flock.

The attention of two other leaders in the early Christian congregations is directed to the example they ought to be setting. Timothy had received a difficult assignment from Paul in being placed in Ephesus. There seemed to be some fear that Timothy's youth might work as a handicap to him. Whether this was a fear on Paul's part, indicating that he had some reservations about Timothy's ability to cope with the situation, or whether this was a fear on Timothy's part and gave indication of a naturally timid and hesitant nature is not to be ascertained. But Paul's letter to Timothy is like that of a father to his son, a father who either feels it necessary or else can not resist the urge to prescribe all the smallest details. Perhaps Paul was also writing to strengthen Timothy's hand and voice with the Ephesians,

---

[205] W. Foerster, κατακυριεύω, *T.W.N.T.*, III, p. 1098, 1ff.

since the contents of this letter were surely written for their hearing and benefit as well as for Timothy's. At least Paul leaves no room for doubt, hesitation, or timidity on Timothy's part. He instructs him: "These things command and teach" (I Tim. 4:11). And in immediate connection with this he adds: "Let no man despise thy youth; but be thou an ensample (τύπος) to them that believe, in word, in manner of life, in love, in faith, in purity" (vs. 12). Whatever disadvantages were inherent in Timothy's youthfulness could best be offset and counteracted by the integrity of the example he set. Lock has pointed out that a genitive case is used after "example" here (τύπος ... τῶν πιστῶν) and therefore he proposes, "[It is] not so much 'a model for the faithful to follow' ... as 'a model of what the faithful are' ..., which will make its appeal to all men ... and attract them to complete salvation." [206] Actually the two can not be separated from each other, for a model to Christians is also a model of what Christianity is, and vice versa. However, Paul may have had one aspect of the example more in mind than the other. On the whole it would seem that Paul is thinking more of Timothy's work within the congregation and with the diverse elements, voices, and heresies which were there at work than of the witness he should make outside the congregation before paganism and Judaism in general. It was in this struggle within the congregation that his youth was likely to be despised. At the same time within the congregation there were both the Christian gospel and different doctrines at work (*cf.* I Tim. 1:3ff.). Hence even here Timothy was to be an example for the Christians to follow and at the same time an example of what was the truly Christian way in distinction from various divergent ways which were being recommended. Timothy was to be exemplary both in what he said and in his entire conduct. Particularly his example was to concern itself with displaying love, faith, [207] and purity. Thus in the situation in which he found himself in Ephesus his good example would serve several purposes at the same time—purposes of clarification, attraction, and the calling forth of imitation. He was to command; but his leadership was also to be effected through giving example. His youthfulness only emphasized the indispensability of the latter.

The situation with regard to Titus in Crete is quite similar. He too must face "gainsayers" (Titus 1:9) and men contrary to him (2:8). He too was in danger of being despised (2:15). Paul urges him to pay attention to the example he is setting: "In all things showing thyself an ensample (τύπον) of good works; in thy doctrine showing uncorruptness, gravity, sound speech, that cannot be condemned; that he that is of the contrary part may be ashamed, having no evil thing to say of us" (2:7,8). This instruction to Titus comes as one in a series of "the things which befit the sound doctrine" (2:1), in which things appropriate to elderly men, elderly women, young women,

---

206 W. Lock, *A Critical and Exegetical Commentary on The Pastoral Epistles*, I.C.C., Edinburgh: T. & T. Clark, 1924, p. 52. So also C. Bouma, *De Brieven van den Apostel Paulus aan Timotheus en Titus*, K.N.T., Amsterdam: H. A. van Bottenburg, 1946, p. 165. However, as Lock himself notices, in I Pet. 5:3 τύποι τοῦ ποιμνίου is clearly "example *to* the flock"; so that a distinction between the dative and genitive here can not be rigorously applied.

207 Possibly "fidelity", "trustworthiness"; so Lock, *I Tim.*, p. 52.

and young men are suggested. Reference to Titus' example can be read as an integral part of the command to the young men.[208] However, in view of Titus' special position in the congregation and the fact that the thought leads on immediately to the form and manner of his teaching, his example would seem to apply more broadly than simply to the young men. He is to be an example to the whole Christian community with which he is working. Here again his example of good works and his policy of sound speech will have their impact on those who are opposed to him and are seeking to discredit Christianity (Tit. 2:8). Paul again calls for an example that will make clear, attract, and be productive of imitation in others.

The examples which Timothy and Titus are urged to give again point to a close personal connection which was envisioned between them and the people with whom they were working. Timothy was to give an example in conduct, behavior, way of life (ἀναστροφή). This could become known by others only by associating with him in many situations and on many different occasions. He was also to be an example in love. This suggests the closest and most intimate types of fellowship between him and those with whom he worked. Titus was to be an example of good works in regard to everything (περὶ πάντα). Here once again a rather general contact with him in many phases and aspects of his life is envisioned. The exhortation concerning his teaching seems to suggest a certain amount of personal discussion and debate, and here too the example is to make its impact. The discussions were to be not merely an interchange of religious views or a dueling with the weapons of logic and argumentation, but a meeting of persons, a display of basic attitudes and allegiances, a portrayal of a religious commitment and a life that would leave the opponent with a sense of shame. For Timothy the matter of being an example is placed alongside the exhortations to command and teach (I Tim. 4:11), and for Titus alongside the command to speak (Tit. 2:1) and exhort (2:6). Being an example was an integral part of their giving leadership and it functioned through close and personal contact with people. The Christian way was to be spread not merely by instruction but by the force of contagion through personal contact.

The New Testament holds up men for imitation and as examples. The Old Testament saints sometimes present convincing and compelling illustrations of the way which young Christians must go and must learn. Christianity was no break with the past, and Christians were now called to live as God's servants had always lived. But the Old Testament saints were not the only illustrations presented to the new Christians. The Christians leaders, the elders of I Peter, Timothy, Titus, Demetrius, and many others had a crucial role in the spread of the new gospel and in making clear the way of the service of God which went with it. They performed important service in deepening Christianity's roots and strengthening its grasp in the lives of the believers. They were living specimens of the Christian way as well as instructors

---

[208] *Cf.* the translation of N.E.B.: "Urge the younger men, similarly, to be temperate in all things, and set them a good example yourself" (Titus 2:6,7).

in it. They were the accompanying pictures which added to the reality of the story. Through the living contact which they had with people they were able to show Christianity in addition to telling about it. The Apostle Paul must have been especially conscious of the force and power inherent in personal example. Not only did he call Timothy and Titus to become examples, but he repeatedly called attention to his own example and called for the imitation of it. Here was a resource for spreading the gospel and accelerating its growth in his converts which he was concerned to use to the uttermost.

\* \* \*

In this chapter and throughout our study thus far, we have been on an extended journey through the Greek and Jewish world, gathering and examining evidences of the idea of imitating in the realm of personal conduct and of various closely related ideas. We have found the idea coming to full expression in the Greek world earlier than in the Jewish world. We have also found it coming to outright expression in the Jewish world at the time that the Jewish world had come into closest contact with the Greek world and was being most influenced by it. It is an overstatement to say that the thought of imitation is not to be found in the Old Testament. However, until the centuries immediately preceding Christ's birth, the matter of imitating, being an example, or referring to the example of another played no significant role in the thought life of Israel. We may conclude that in the period between the Old and New Testaments various circumstances combined to bring the thought and matter of imitation into prominence in the Jewish world. There was the spreading over the Jewish world of the Greek culture and its whole world of thought and highly developed language. There was the determination within Jewry after the exile to develop and maintain a purity of religious life, resulting in special attention to the law and the development of the institution of scribes and teachers of the law. This movement evolved finally into the whole rabbinical system with its extreme care to pass things on precisely as received. There was a closer contact between the Jews and the other nations which promoted a sense of national identity. This was accompanied by an effort to portray the great men of Israel's history to the Jews themselves and as recommendations to foreigners. In being a subject people, the Jews faced various and repeated attempts to tamper with their religion and to have other religious practices imposed on them. In this struggle there developed a new kind of religious heroism, which concentrated on remaining steadfast and faithful to one's faith in spite of opposition and even death. All these things served to bring about a consciousness of the importance of imitation and of the influence of personal example.

Then came Jesus calling men to follow him. The far-reaching implications of joining oneself to his band of followers soon became apparent. His call was the Messianic call. The way to salvation, exaltation, and glorification which he presented involved traveling the Messianic way of deepest humiliation, suffering, and self-giving. This was a way which he himself was walking. It was the way of procuring salvation for the world, and as the Messiah and Savior, he accomplished this in his death and resurrection. His call to men was a call to join with him in the way he was going and to participate in the benefits which were accruing to him as the Messiah and Savior. By following him during his earthly days, men were drawn into his way and learned a whole new view of life from the way he portrayed and lived it. After his crucifixion, resurrection, and ascension the literal physical accompaniment gave way to a spiritual accompaniment. By faith and through the Holy Spirit's action in their hearts, men were joined in living union with Christ and became participants in his benefits to them. During his earthly days the following of Christ meant joining him in his ways. Now too a living in union with him as risen and ascended Lord meant taking on his ways and being conformed to him. His way of life during his earthly days retained its significance. He was a pattern to his people and his earthly life was a graphic portrayal for them of the Christian way. Having been called into union with him, Christians became involved in learning to live his kind of life. By observing his pattern, they learned to become more and more like him. Thus, in virtue of having Christ as their Savior, believers became imitators of Christ. The processes of imitation were at work in a new way with eminently great benefit for man. In Christ man now had the pattern, the power, and the desire for imitating a true Servant of God, and thus man could himself become a true servant of God.

In Christ, God's fatherhood also reaches a new stage of meaning and reality. Through Christ we have been adopted as his sons, and through the Holy Spirit in our hearts we have learned his real fatherhood (Gal. 4:5). It is by virtue of this relationship that the New Testament speaks of imitating God. Believers imitate God as a son imitates his father. Their sonship constitutes them God's imitators. God's comprehensive love, his holiness, his forgiveness all determine the form of the sonship into which they have been drawn. These things establish the pattern and the shape of it. The call goes forth to believers to bring this pattern, this form, this quality of life to expression in their lives. Christian imitation of God is no moralistic struggle toward a more virtuous life; neither is it an effort to achieve a divine type of life in place of a human one. It is a realizing of salvation in Christ. It is our taking part in the transformation which the Holy Spirit is working in us as Christ's people. Neither can Christian imitation of God go off into flights of mysticism or pursuits of abstract ideals and absolutes. God has been revealed in Christ. The imitation of God is accomplished in imitating God revealed in Christ.

The New Testament writers were also aware of another imitation which was of service in promoting the believer's conformity to his Savior and his God. Christ was not the only picture of the Christian way; other men pictured it also. Or perhaps it is put more correctly by saying that Christ did not only show his way during the days he walked on earth; he also showed it as he came to live in his followers. Paul said: "It is no longer I that live, but Christ liveth in me" (Gal. 2:20). To follow a Christian in his Christianity was not essentially different from imitating Christ himself. By imitating Christians men were being conformed to Christ. This fact had important implications and usages in the early days of the rapid spread and growth of Christianity. When Jesus' original followers went forth to bring the Christian gospel and way to others, there are indications that they sought and were being encouraged to seek the closest and most vital types of fellowship with men. Their mission was to make Christ known; hence they went out preaching the gospel. But they did not leave it at that. They were aware of the peculiar effectiveness of showing Christ in their personal conduct and example. They went far beyond a mere formal acknowledgement of the fact. They opened up their lives before people. They gave themselves away to people. They cultivated ways of living in close fellowship with people, so that the full impact of their lives—of Christ living in them—might be added to the words they preached and the truths they taught. The Apostle Paul joined in this program of spreading the gospel and preaching Christ. He poured his entire heart, soul, and life into it. His letters give various indications of how intent he was in using the power of his example and the processes of imitation of himself in spreading the gospel and in building Christian lives. This is the matter to which we now turn in our study.

CHAPTER FOUR

# THE IMITATION OF PAUL: EXEGETICAL STUDIES

We have now arrived at the study of the texts which speak of the imitation of Paul. This chapter consists of a series of exegetical studies of the various texts. These studies stand relatively independent of each other, each one entering upon an exegetical examination of the passage and making certain observations on the basis of this examination. The first five sections deal with texts making express statements about the imitation of Paul. They appear in the generally accepted order in which the passages were written, although it is not our purpose to enter upon a discussion of this matter. In connection with the first text, I Thess. 1:6, we shall examine the closely similar text in I Thess. 2:14 about the imitation of the churches of Judea. In the studies of the Corinthian texts we shall take note of some suggestions of imitation elsewhere in the letter. To the study of Phil. 3:17 we shall append a brief examination of Phil. 4:9. The texts from Galatians, the Pastoral Epistles, and Acts do not speak expressly about imitation, but do present closely related material. The three short studies in the Pastoral Epistles will be grouped together in one section. The studies of this chapter appear in the following order:

    I. I Thessalonians 1:6
   II. II Thessalonians 3:7–9
  III. I Corinthians 4:16
  IV. I Corinthians 11:1
   V. Philippians 3:17
  VI. Galatians 4:12
 VII. The Pastoral Epistles
      (I Timothy 1:16; II Timothy 1:13; 3:10)
VIII. Acts 20:35

## I. I Thessalonians 1:6

*And ye became imitators of us, and of the Lord, having received the word in much affliction, with joy of the Holy Spirit.*

In order to understand what Paul is saying when he wrote, "Ye became imitators of us," it is necessary to see the statement in its whole context.

Paul was overjoyed with the good report that Timothy had brought from Thessalonica (I Thess. 3:9). He felt himself living once again (3:8). The weight of a gnawing worry and care had been lifted from him, and he felt exuberantly happy. He was full of praise to the Thessalonian church for their fine Christian witness and work (1:3,8). But he was full of praise and thanksgiving to God above all for bringing about this occasion of joy. Here his thanksgiving literally overflowed, for upon beginning with his customary thanksgiving, [1] his thoughts rushed forward in such a steady stream that in this short letter of five chapters more than half was devoted to telling about his thankfulness (*cf.* 1:2; 2:13; 3:9). He began, and he could not stop.

In his extended thanksgiving Paul did not begin immediately speaking of the good news which had brought him such joy. In fact, he did not get to that until 3:6ff. His beginning thoughts were about how the preaching of the gospel in Thessalonica had resulted in the establishment of a Christian congregation there and about what consequences this had had both in persecution and also for the spread of the gospel. Then later (2:17ff.) his thoughts turned to the great concern he had had about the welfare of the Thessalonian Christians since leaving them, and how anxiously he had tried to return to them. All of this led to the sending of Timothy and to his return with the good news. One can detect from what Paul said in this extended thanksgiving that there were two things in particular which had been troubling him greatly. He had been anxious about what possible effects the continued persecution and affliction might be having on the new Christians. He was also concerned about how his hasty leaving of Thessalonica and his failure to return might have been misconstrued and interpreted in such a way as to bring discredit not only to him but to the gospel which he had brought. Possibly he had heard that such charges were being made by his opponents in Thessalonica. The wandering sophists, the religious quacks, the propagandists of religious cults and strange philosophies were only too well known in those days, as were their immoral practices, their fakery, extortion, greed for personal advantage, glory, and profits. Paul felt it necessary to make a defence against any comparisons with these people and their ways. He did so in a very pointed review of his conduct and methods in bringing the gospel to them (2:1–12). He tells them how happy it had made him when Timothy returned from Thessalonica and could dispel the fear that they might have turned against him. He was greatly encouraged to hear that their memories of him were not unpleasant ones, and that they were longing to see him as much as he was to see them (3:6).

However, the possibility that malicious statements and accusations about

---

[1] Paul begins with thanksgiving or an ascription of praise in all of his letters except Gal., I Tim., and Titus. In this his letters are similar to many other letters of the Greek and Oriental world of his day. The question has been raised whether there was some standard or accepted form for correspondence in those days. (Cf. for discussion and literature on the subject: M. Dibelius, *An die Thessalonicher I–II*, H.N.T., 3. Aufl., Tübingen: J. C. B. Mohr (Paul Siebeck), 1937, pp. 2,3; and Rigaux, *Thess.*, pp. 357,358). Rigaux concludes: "Il ne semble donc pas que Paul ait obéi à une norme stable de l'épistolographie, mais qu'il se soit fait une règle de commencer ses lettres, et sans doute aussi ses discours, par une prière d'action de grâces" (p. 357).

him might be alienating the young Christians in Thessalonica from him and from the gospel was only one aspect of the whole matter which had been causing him such concern. The heart of the matter was the effect the persecutions, afflictions, and pressures might be having on the Thessalonians. How much of a toll were they taking? It was primarily this concern which moved Paul to send Timothy to Thessalonica (3:4,5). Paul recalls to the Thessalonians that, in addition to bringing him information about their faith (3:5), Timothy's mission was "to establish you, and to comfort you concerning your faith; that no man be moved by these afflictions" (3:2,3). The young Thessalonian Christians were being sorely tried.

Commentators are not all agreed that the reference to "these afflictions" in 3:3 is to be understood as including those of the Thessalonians. Some think that Paul is here referring to his own afflictions. [2] Those taking this position object to thinking of "these" in such broad terms as to include the sufferings of the Thessalonians mentioned in 2:14, since, in the words of von Dobschütz: "(2:14 gehört einem ganz andern, in sich geschlossenen Zusammenhang an). Dagegen hat P[aulus] in 2:17ff. immerfort von Bedrängnissen gesprochen, die ihm widerfahren waren. An diese denkt er bei ἐν τ[αῖς] θλ[ίψεσιν] ταύταις, wie die richtig verstandene 1. Person plur. im folgenden beweist." [3] There is no question that the clauses following "these afflictions" serve to explain it; the presence of "for" (vs. 3) and "for verily" (vs. 4) are ample evidence of this. However, the usage of "we" in these following clauses is not necessarily to be understood only as referring to Paul, Silvanus, and Timothy. It may refer to them together with the Thessalonian Christians and Christians in general, as it does later in 4:14 ("For if we believe that Jesus died and rose again"), and 4:17 ("then we that are alive...," or "and so shall we ever be with the Lord"). In 4:15 there is a good illustration of how easily Paul can switch from the one "we" to the other: "For this we [the apostles] say to you by the word of the Lord, that we [the Christians] that are alive... shall in no wise precede them that are asleep." The first person plural in the sense of "we, the Christians," appeared in the form of an adjective already in 1:3 ("our Lord Jesus Christ" and "our God and Father"). [4]

How would the Thessalonians have understood the reference to "these afflictions" when the letter was first read to them? We learn from II Thess. 1:4ff. that the persecutions and afflictions of the Thessalonian converts

---

2 According to E. von Dobschütz, *Die Thessalonicher-Briefe*, K.e.K.N.T., 7. Aufl., Göttingen: Vandenhoeck & Ruprecht, 1909, p. 134, fn. 2, most of the earlier commentators, including Chrysostom, Oecumenius, Theophylact, Ambrosiaster, Pelagius, Erasmus, Calvin, and others, have understood it this way. In more recent times this position has been proposed by von Dobschütz, *loc. cit.*; van Leeuwen, *Thess.*, p. 343; and J. Keulers, *De Brieven van Paulus*, Roermond: J. J. Romen en Zonen, 1953, Vol. I, p. 35. A notable exception among the ancients is to be found in Theodore of Mopsuestia: "ut nemo moueatur in tribulationibus uestris," and again, "ita ut non cedatis tribulationibus uicti" (*Theodori Episcopi Mopsuesteni: In Epistolas B. Pauli Commentarii*, sub I Thess. 3:3 [ed. H. B. Swete, Cambridge: University Press, 1882, Vol. II, p. 17]).

3 Von Dobschütz, *Thess.*, p. 134.

4 G. Milligan, *St. Paul's Epistles to the Thessalonians*, London: Macmillan, 1908, p. xliv, fn. 2, calls attention to the sense of close union between the missionaries and their converts which these letters to the Thessalonians show in "the subtle change from the 2nd to the 1st pers. plur. in I. iii. 2f., iv. 6f., 13f., v. 5, II. i. 11f., by which the missionaries, almost unconsciously, identify themselves with their converts."

were continuing with unrelenting vigor.[5] Is it likely, then, that Paul would have sent Timothy to them to establish and comfort them regarding the afflictions he himself was suffering? The Thessalonians needed comforting regarding their own difficult circumstances. The expression "these afflictions" was undoubtedly a general reference, applying to the afflictions of the Thessalonians first of all, but not excluding the afflictions of the missionaries and of Christians in general.[6]

A further difficulty in discovering exactly what Paul means by "that no man be moved by these afflictions" lies in the verb, σαίνεσθαι. The translation "moved" is typical of the choice which most translators, ancient and modern, have made. A word like *move, disturb,* or *agitate* is what one expects to find here. The commentaries written while Greek was still a living language in the church interpreted the passage in this way. However, many exegetes and Greek scholars of later days have found it hard to justify. The word originally was used of a dog's wagging of his tail, and hence came to mean *fawn upon, flatter.* Many have sought to interpret this passage along these lines, proposing that Paul was afraid that the Thessalonians might allow themselves to be drawn aside, allured, beguiled, cajoled with smooth talk. Morris suggests, "It is likely that, while the Gentiles were persecuting them, the Jews were urging them to abandon the Christian way and accept Judaism, which would immediately free them from their plight."[7] The old interpretation, however, has recently gained new confirmation. A papyrus from Tura near Cairo contains the minutes of a discussion by Origen concerning a certain bishop Heraclides, whose orthodoxy had seemed doubtful to some in the community. In conclusion Origen remarks, "All the questions about the faith which disturbed us (ὅσα ἔσηνεν ἡμᾶς) have been examined."[8] Paul thus was concerned about the possibility of the Thessalonians becoming disturbed and troubled in their afflictions. For this reason he sent Timothy to establish and comfort them (3:2). He was overjoyed when the report came back that they were standing fast in the Lord (3:8).

It is not clear what specific form the afflictions were taking in Thessalonica. Perhaps Paul himself did not know at the time that he sent Timothy. In fact, lack of specific information on this score may have been just what drove his anxiety to the point of being unbearable. He knew how ingenious men could be in their evil schemes. He himself had once been active in devising ways of driving the Christian faith from the face of the earth. Now in more recent years he had had ample experience of how it felt to be on the receiving end. He found an apt phrase to describe the force of afflictions when on another occasion he spoke of being "in deaths oft" (II Cor. 11:23).[9] Afflictions tend to bring one's life into a precarious state. Thus, they place Christians

---

[5] Notice the present tense of ἀνέχεσθε (II Thess. 1:4) and πάσχετε (1:5).

[6] In the same way "hereunto we are appointed" (I Thess. 3:3) and "we are to suffer affliction" (3:4) are general statements applying to all Christians, but here applied primarily to the Thessalonians and the missionaries.

[7] L. Morris, *The Epistles of Paul to the Thessalonians,* T.N.T.C., London: Tyndale Press. 1956, p. 63.

[8] H. Chadwick, "I Thess. 3:3: σαίνεσθαι," *J.T.S.,* I (1950), p. 158. The papyrus text is edited by J. Scherer, *Entretien d'Origène avec Héraclide et les évêques ses collègues sur le Père, le Fils, et l'Âme,* (Publications de la Société Fouad I de Papyrologie: Textes et Documents IX), Cairo: 1949, and the quotation is from p. 140, l. 5.

[9] H. Schlier, Θλῖψις, *T.W.N.T.,* III, p. 147,18,19. *Cf.* the whole of paragraph 2 about "Die gemeinsame Kraft aller θλῖψις ist die in ihr wirksame Todesmacht" (ll. 11ff.).

before a severe temptation (I Thess. 3:5). [10] It becomes a question of whether one will hold to the gospel even at the cost of all earthly well-being and of life itself. Do the promises of God really offer the possibilities of life, so that one can afford to ignore and even despise ordinary earthly possibilities? In the presence of such questions and temptations, Paul wanted to be sure that the Thessalonians were still well aware of what Christianity had to say. This he had made clear to them from the very beginning, and it was sufficient evidence that he had won no converts by flattery or guile (I Thess. 2:3–5). He had declared straightforwardly that "we are appointed" unto sufferings (3:3). They have a definite and vital role to play in the Christian program. [11] In fact, Paul reminds the Thessalonians that he had been able to tell them of their coming afflictions before they became involved in them. It was no afterthought in his preaching, or an attempt to explain unfavorable developments. He had preached it from the start. [12] To become a Christian meant to become involved in suffering. This was the counsel of God. [13]

There is abundant evidence that Paul looked upon becoming involved in suffering as inseparable from being a Christian. This applied not only to himself as an apostle, but to Christians in general. In Phil. 3:10 he is speaking not of his experience as an apostle, but of his experience in becoming a Christian, when he says that he turned his back on his whole former life, "that I may know him [Christ] ... and the fellowship of his sufferings." In the same letter he acknowledged regarding the Philippians: "To you it hath been granted in behalf of Christ, not only to believe on him, but also to suffer in his behalf" (Phil. 1:29). To the Romans he wrote concerning the effects of our being united with Christ, "If so be that we suffer with him, that we may be also glorified with him" (Rom. 8:17). The "if so be" (εἴπερ) expresses a presupposition upon which men are in agreement; it does not express what might happen in case we should be called upon to suffer, but rather it expresses that certain conclusions may be drawn in view of the fact that we are involved in suffering. Paul's preaching as recorded in Acts also gives testimony to the necessity of suffering affliction as Christians. We read that Paul returned to Lystra, Iconium, and Antioch, "confirming the souls of the disciples, exhorting them to continue in the faith, and that through many tribulations we must enter into the kingdom of God" (Acts 14:22). [14]

---

10  Cf. also Rev. 2:10 and I Pet. 4:12ff. Notice also that in the parable of the sower the fate of the seed falling on rocky places is determined, according to Mark 4:17, "when tribulation or persecution ariseth because of the word" — a situation which Luke 8:13 describes as "in the time of temptation."

11  Calvin's comment on this thought is striking: "Nam haec loquutio, i n  h o c  s u m u s  c o n s t i t u t i, tantundem valet ac si dixisset hac lege nos esse Christianos" (J. Calvinus, *Commentarius in Epistolam ad Thessalonicenses I*, sub 3:3 [ed. G. Baum, E. Cunitz, E. Reuss, *Opera Quae Supersunt Omnia*, Brunsvigae: C. A. Schwetschke, Vol. LII, p. 156]); the English translation reads: "For this manner of expression—*we are appointed to it*—is as though he had said, that we are Christians on this condition" (J. Calvin, *Commentaries on the Epistles of Paul the Apostle to the Philippians, Colossians, and Thessalonians*, [trans. Rev. John Pringle, 1851], Grand Rapids, Wm. B. Eerdmans, 1948, p. 266).

12  See below, pp. 114ff., *re* 1:6, "having received the word in much affliction."

13  Notice in 3:4 the word μέλλομεν, *we are to*, "bringing out its Divinely-appointed character" (Milligan, *Thess.*, p. 39); "weist wie das κείμεθα, ohne dass Gott genannt wäre, auf Gottes Ordnung, die sich unausbleiblich vollzieht" (von Dobschütz, *Thess.*, p. 136).

14  Notice the striking parallel between this passage and I Thess. 3:2,3, in both thought and expression (*e.g.* στηρίζω, παρακαλέω, θλῖψις, etc.).

Back of Paul's teaching about the necessity of suffering stood the teaching of Jesus himself on this matter. In John's record of the farewell discourse we hear Jesus stating: "In the world ye have tribulation" (John 16:33). Jesus in this farewell scene was only reiterating a point he had been clarifying for some time. As we have seen earlier in our study, Jesus' calls to follow him did not mean merely to accompany him in his travels and preaching; they meant becoming involved also in his suffering and humiliation. [15] He called men to take up their cross and follow him (Mark 8:34, par.); this was a call to endure scorn, humiliation, and death for his sake and in union with him. [16] These words had had their particular significance during Jesus' earthly days. However, Jesus' followers experienced a new kind of reality in them after Jesus had left them. It was then that they first really faced the stings of scorn and the threats to their lives and well-being which went with being followers of Christ. In this new situation they found Jesus' words about self-denial, cross-bearing, and following him still vitally appropriate and timely. They found themselves bound in a living union with Jesus, and they recognized that this meant not only a union with him as risen and exalted Lord. It meant also a continuing union with him as he had been before his exaltation. It meant a continued walking behind him on the way he had walked, the way of the suffering and humiliated Servant. They continued denying themselves, bearing their crosses, and walking in mystical fellowship with him in his humiliation. [17] The Christian life was thus a life of union with Christ in his suffering. Paul had experienced this deeply himself. He preached it wherever he went. He had preached it also in Thessalonica.

Hence, as Paul was reminiscing in the early part of his first letter to the Thessalonians about how they had accepted Christianity and about what anxiety he had had for them since leaving them, he could be sure that the Thessalonians were aware that becoming a Christian meant entering upon a rough and stormy pathway. He had preached this from the first, and just recently Timothy had been among them re-emphasizing the same thing. But now Paul could write about them with real joy and thanksgiving, for the Thessalonians had come face to face with the afflictions and suffering and they were standing fast. Here was the proof of their Christianity. The word of God had gripped them, and they were Christians indeed. In his extended thanksgiving this same train of thought appears twice (I Thess. 1:2–6 and 2:13–14), running from thanksgiving, to his preaching of the gospel, to the divine working in the hearers, to imitation and suffering. We must now study these passages more closely, with an eye to discovering what Paul is saying by introducing the idea of imitation into them. We shall look at the second passage (2:13–14) first.

\* \* \*

---

[15] See above, pp. 52,53.
[16] J. Kahmann, "Het volgen van Christus door zelfverloochening en kruisdragen, volgens Marc. 8, 34–38 en par.," *T.v.T.*, I (1961), p. 223, concludes: "Het exegetisch onderzoek van deze en verwante teksten heeft aangetoond, dat het kruisopnemen in verband met het volgen van Jezus zowel in de mond van Jezus zelf als in de apostolische prediking als eerste zin heeft gehad: het ondergaan van versmading en dood omwille van en samen met de Meester, dus lots- en lijdensgemeenschap met Hem, en dat ook de zelfverloochening oorspronkelijk in deze samenhang thuishoort."
[17] Cf. Kahmann's discussion of this point, *T.v.T.*, I, pp. 224,225.

Paul had begun his letter with thanksgiving. In 2:1—12 his thoughts have turned to reviewing the type of ministry he had had among them. Apparently he felt it necessary to defend himself concerning certain insinuations and accusations which were circulating about him. With 2:13 Paul returns to the thanksgiving with which he had begun his letter. He was thankful for the way they had received and accepted the gospel which he preached. They had discovered its true nature, namely, that it was the word of God. This word of God in turn had powerfully affected their lives. It was a divine force working in them, [18] bringing them to a whole new set of views, attitudes, and actions. This had become abundantly apparent in their becoming imitators of the Judean churches and suffering for their new faith. Paul reaches the thought of imitation as the summit of his thanksgiving. In it he found the crowning evidence that the Christian gospel had taken hold in their midst.

Such a conclusion as to the place of imitation in this passage finds support in the fact that the thought of imitation is connected to what precedes by γάρ, *for*. Paul speaks of imitation at this point as an explanation, illustration, and confirmation of what he has just said. It is difficult to determine precisely whether the imitation is to be understood as a confirmation of the immediately preceding thought about God's word working in them, or of the broader thought preceding it about their accepting Paul's preaching as God's word. The close connection between imitation and the receiving (δεξάμενοι) of the word in 1:6, may serve as a clue that the thoughts are to be linked here too, and that the matter of imitation is to be seen as a confirmation of their welcoming (ἐδέξασθε) of the gospel as God's word. [19] However that may be, the connective γάρ gives the clue that it is for the purpose of confirmation that Paul brings forth the thought about imitation. [20] It is difficult to see what account Michaelis takes of this connective when he explains the passage to be saying primarily: "euch hat (ohne euer Zutun) dasselbe Schicksal getroffen wie sie, ihr habt das Gleiche leiden müssen wie vorher sie; Paulus will sagen: ihr seid nicht die ersten, denen das widerfahren ist, es ist keine Ausnahme, sondern von jeher die Regel, wie euch das Beispiel der ersten christlichen Gemeinden lehren kann." [21] Michaelis does not explain what brought Paul to speak of these things at this point.

It is important to understand what is the nature of the confirmation expressed in 2:14. Something has happened which shows that Christianity has really established itself among the Thessalonians. What shows this? Is it the fact that persecutions arose and that the Thessalonians became the victims of sufferings and afflictions? When a community reacts in opposition and when the Christians are brought into suffering, is this to be seen as

---

[18] "Le verbe ἐνεργέω ne s'emploie que pour désigner une force divine ou surnaturelle" (Rigaux, *Thess.*, p. 440). (He further supports this conclusion on pp. 668—670.)

[19] Frame finds this latter alternative including the former: "γάρ connects the points of welcome and steadfastness under persecution, and at the same time illustrates and confirms the reality of the indwelling word of God" (*Thess.*, p. 108).

[20] Even a reading of γάρ as some kind of emphatic particle ("in fact," "indeed") does not succeed in disconnecting it from the preceding context; and any reading which does succeed in doing that ignores the clear parallel between this passage and 1:2—6, where the clause on imitation is connected to the preceding by "and" (καί).

[21] Michaelis, *T.W.N.T.*, IV, p. 669, 7—11.

an evidence that the Christian gospel has taken hold? When the pattern of persecution repeated itself in Thessalonica, did this make the Christians there imitators of the Christian churches in Judea? Had the Thessalonians surely become a part of Christ's church because the same things were happening to them at the hands of their neighbors as had happened elsewhere to members of Christ's church? Such a forming of the question looks for an answer in the passive aspects of the verse. Or is it possible to find the confirmation to lie in another direction? Had the Christians in Thessalonica become active in a certain way? Was some activity on their part to be seen as an evidence of the reality of their Christian faith? This latter direction would seem to be suggested by the term *imitators*. The very make-up of the term indicates that it is someone acting, doing, performing. [22] There is a problem here, however, in view of the strong passive accents in the verse. In this context can there be an activity on the part of the Thessalonians, as the term *imitators* would seem to suggest? We shall pursue the matter further by studying more fully the two verbs in this verse and also by examining carefully the point of comparison which Paul expresses.

The verse begins, "For ye, brethren, became imitators...." Already here a passive element can be found, for the verb form is aorist passive, ἐγενήθητε. It might be translated, "you were become," or "you were made to be." The thought which the passive translation would express here is that they had become imitators not through their own activity, but through the activity of another.

> Masson has called attention to the fact that the Vulgate has *facti estis* here, and goes on to remark, "Il est certain que l'agent de ce verbe passif est Dieu." [23] Stanley also remarks about the passive force of the verb, and in connection with its use in 1:6 he says, "The turn of expression indicates that God is the unnamed agent here, which excludes any ordinary kind of conscious imitation." [24] Grammarians, however, are very cautious in asserting the passive sense of the passive forms of deponent verbs. For example, Blass-Debrunner says: "Die spätere Sprache bevorzugt bei den Deponentia den passiven Aorist (wobei eigentliche passivische Bedeutung höchstens möglich ist)." [25] Robertson lists ἐγενήθην among "the chief passive aorists in the N.T. without the passive idea, the so-called 'deponent' passives." [26] Moulton would agree, and says, "The voices were not differentiated with anything like the same sharpness as is inevitable in analytic formations such as we use in English. We have seen how the bulk of the forms were indifferently middle or passive, and how even those which were appropriated to the one voice or the

---

22 See the discussion of this point below, p. 102.
23 C. Masson, *Les deux épitres de saint Paul aux Thessaloniciens*, C.d.N.T., Neuchatel/Paris: Delachaux & Niestlé, 1957, p. 21, fn. 4.
24 D. M. Stanley, "'Become Imitators of Me': The Pauline Conception of Apostolic Tradition," *Biblica*, XL (1959), p. 865. Cf. also W. Bornemann, *Die Thessalonicherbriefe*, K.e.K.N.T., 5./6. Aufl., Göttingen: Vandenhoeck & Ruprecht, 1894, p. 58, where he speaks of "die gottgewirkte und gottgeschenkte Folge der evangelischen Verkündigung" as being indicated by the three aorist passives of γίνομαι that appear in 1:5,6.
25 Blass-Debrunner, *Gram.*, p. 52, § 78.
26 A. T. Robertson, *A Grammar of the Greek New Testament in the Light of Historical Research*, Nashville: Broadman Press, 1934, p. 334.

other are perpetually crossing the frontier."²⁷ Prévot, in his dissertation on this form of the aorist, concludes: "L'aoriste ἐγενήθην, forme neuve, est l'aoriste qui correspond rigoureusement au présent γίγνομαι, avec le sens de 'devenir'. L'aoriste ἐγενόμην, qui prend un sens voisin de 'être', tend à sortir du système de γίγνομαι."²⁸ This would mean that the Thessalonian passages (I Thess. 1:6; 2:14) simply express in the aorist indicative the same thing as Paul is elsewhere saying in the present imperative (μιμηταὶ γίνεσθε: I Cor. 4:16; 11:1; Eph. 5:1; Phil. 3:17), except that he is saying that the Thessalonians already have become imitators, and elsewhere he is asking his readers to become imitators. At any rate, for whatever passive force there is in the verb, the agent is to be found in God or in the working of the divine word. And the working of the divine word in the Thessalonians does not preclude the participation, cooperation, and activity of the Thessalonians themselves in this same direction. In fact, it would seem to imply it. At least, we may observe that the verb ἐγενήθητε does not require that the passage be read as saying, in effect, "You were become imitators by the course of historical events, which brought the same persecutions upon you as the Judean churches suffered."

Paul says that the Thessalonians became imitators of the churches of Judea. His explanation of what he has in mind is as follows: "Ye also suffered the same things of your own countrymen, even as they did of the Jews" (I Thess. 2:14). There is no escaping the passive sound of this statement. It seems to be saying that when the Thessalonians had accepted Christianity, the same thing happened to them as happened to the first Christians in Judea. Their fellow countrymen were offended by their adopting this faith, became antagonistic toward them, and persecuted them, causing them to suffer. Where is there room for imitation on the part of the Thessalonian believers? Or does imitation have a broader meaning and usage than we customarily think?²⁹ Is there activity on the part of the Thessalonians, or are they merely passive?

Πάσχειν ὑπό is a passive construction³⁰ and is found both in classical Greek and elsewhere in the New Testament (cf. Matt. 17:12; Mark 5:26). However, this does not automatically preclude every possibility of Paul's having in mind some kind of activity on the part of the Thessalonians. It is necessary to keep in mind the nature and circumstances of the suffering which the Thessalonians faced. They were not helpless and unwilling victims. Their suffering was not like that from the pain of a disease or the mental anguish over a wayward son, where one is enveloped by circumstances quite beyond his control. The Thessalonians suffered from religious persecution. The very point of such persecution was to threaten the new converts and to exert pressure upon them to give up their new religion out of fear for the consequences. The appeal was to change their ways and thus to escape the suffering. To suffer in such circumstances meant that they had decided to offer resistance to the

---

27 J. H. Moulton, *A Grammar of New Testament Greek*, 2nd ed., Vol. I: *Prolegomena*, Edinburgh: T. & T. Clark, 1906, p. 162.
28 A. Prévot, *L'aoriste grec en -θην*, Paris: 1934, p. 90.
29 Michaelis proposes that this passage "zeigt besonders deutlich, dass der Begriff μιμητής beim Apostel nicht zu eng gefasst werden darf und dass nicht nur eine einzige Bedeutung von μιμέομαι usw in Betracht kommen wird" (*T.W.N.T.*, IV, p. 669, 12—15).
30 Blass-Debrunner, *Gram.*, p. 196, § 315.

community pressures exerted upon them. They had decided to remain steadfast in their chosen way and to endure the suffering. They had made an active choice between the alternatives, and at every moment of the suffering they had to reaffirm their choice. Their suffering involved them in a great deal of activity, for they suffered not as helpless victims, but as Christians fighting the fight of faith. [31]

Πάσχω is found one other time in the Thessalonian letters, and here too the active side of suffering is very much in view. In II Thess. 1:5 Paul speaks of their being "counted worthy of the kingdom of God, for which ye also suffer." That this suffering was no passive affair is apparent from the immediately preceding verse where Paul says he is glorying in them "for your patience [*i.e.* steadfastness, ὑπομονῆς] and faith in all your persecutions and afflictions which ye endure." In Phil. 1:27—30, a passage closely parallel to II Thess. 1:4,5, suffering is again found in a context of real activity on the part of the Christians. This can be seen from the sequence in which Paul places it: standing fast in one spirit (vs. 27), striving for the faith of the gospel (vs. 27), in nothing affrighted by the adversaries (vs. 28), and suffering in behalf of Christ (vs. 29).

It is true that in suffering for their Christian faith the Thessalonians were passive over against their adversaries. They did not actively provoke it, and they did not offer resistance to the measures against them. But this passive submission to suffering was at the same time the product of much inner activity on their part. It took real determination and faith to suffer. They became intensely active. The possibility that this inner determination and activity may have included a more or less conscious imitation of the example given by other Christians is not to be overlooked or immediately ruled out.

The verbs in 2:14 do not bar the way to understanding the Thessalonians as being in some way active in their imitation. These verbs are not that definitely and exclusively passive. But it is another question whether the points of comparison which Paul makes in the second clause leave room for active imitation. He calls attention to the similarity between the Thessalonians and the Judean Christians in regard to the things they suffered and in regard to the source from which the sufferings arose. Can a likeness in these things make them imitators? Is their imitation to be understood as consisting of these things?

The primary comparison is made concerning the things which were suffered: "Ye... suffered the same things... as they" (τὰ αὐτὰ... καθώς). The comparison here receives prominence by being placed at the beginning of the statement: ὅτι τὰ αὐτὰ ἐπάθετε.... There is a

---

[31] It is of particular value in this connection to notice how such early Greek commentators as Chrysostom and Theodore of Mopsuestia understood ἐπάθετε in 2:14, since, as von Dobschütz remarks, "Die Exegese der Antiochener [hat] für uns in bleibenden Wert, weil diesen griechischen Exegeten bei dem Streben nach einer grammatisch=historischen Auslegung ein natürliches Sprachgefühl zu statten kam, das wir uns nur künstlich erwerben können" (*Thess.*, p. 49). That they understood the suffering as involving activity is clear from their comments on the verse. Notice such statements as the following: καὶ 'Ιουδαῖοι πάντα ἠνέσχοντο ὑπομεῖναι (Joannes Chrysostomus, *In Epistolam I. ad Thessalonicenses Homiliae*, sub 2:14 [ed. Bern. de Montfaucon, *Opera omnia quae extant Graece et Latine*, Venetiis: 1741, Vol. XI, p. 442]); [believers] ἤδοντο πανταχοῦ ὡς ἀθλήσαντες (*loc. cit.*); "bene autem eos est adhortatus, commemorans illos qui in Iudaea crediderunt, ut sustineant et ipsi magnanimiter laborent, siquidem non soli contemplatione pietatis patiuntur" (Theodore of Mopsuestia, *Comm.*, sub I Thess. 2:14 [ed. Swete, II, p. 14]).

secondary comparison also expressed, namely, that in both instances the sufferings were brought about by the respective countrymen. There is a problem, however, in understanding these comparisons to be direct explanations of how the Thessalonians had become imitators. Lenski points out the incongruity between these two parts of the statement, when he says, "Paul states it in a striking way when he says that the Thessalonians were 'imitators,' as if *they* copied the Judean Jewish believers in the matter of getting themselves persecuted. One might expect Paul to state it in the opposite way, namely that the Gentile *persecutors* copied the Judean Jewish persecutors." [32] Paul's statement seems better to explain how the Thessalonians had become *imitations* (μιμήματα) than how they had become *imitators* (μιμηταί). Imitators are active in performing imitation. They are the agents of an action, not the results of it. [33] To undergo the same things and from the same relative sources does not make men imitators.

Hence, the second clause of 2:14 with its comparisons between Thessalonica and Judea is not to be understood as a precise and explicit statement of what constituted the Thessalonians as imitators. Rather, it is a description which implicitly suggests how this had come to be. [34] It happened when they were called upon to face the same things as the Judean church and from the same relative sources. To mention the situation immediately called to mind the reaction to the situation. The emphasis in the clause is not to be laid exclusively on "the same things." There is a calculated fulness in expressing the subjects of the sentence: καὶ ὑμεῖς... καὶ αὐτοί, *even you... also they*. The Thessalonians and the Judean Christians stand out prominently in the thought here. Paul says in this verse that the Thessalonians had been faced with the same sufferings as the Judean Christians and in the face of them had shown the same faith, courage, and fortitude as the Judean Christians. In this they were their imitators. [35]

---

32 R. C. H. Lenski, *The Interpretation of St. Paul's Epistles to the Colossians, to the Thessalonians, to Timothy, to Titus and to Philemon*, Columbus: Wartburg Press, 1946, pp. 264,265.

33 The structure of the Greek words indicates this. There does not appear to be any disagreement among Greek grammarians, both classical and New Testament, on the basic ideas expressed in the suffixes which are added to a verbal stem to form the related nouns: -της, the agent; -σις, the abstract action; -μα, the result. Cf. e.g. E. Schwyzer, *Griechische Grammatik*, (*Handbuch der Altertumswissenschaft*, ed. W. Otto), München: C. H. Beck, 1939, Vol. I, pp. 499, 504, 522; R. Kühner, *Ausführliche Grammatik der Griechischen Sprache*, Hannover: Hahnsche Buchhandlung, 1892, Vol. I.2, pp. 270, 272; Blass-Debrunner, *Gram.*, p. 72, § 109; Robertson, *Gram.*, p. 151; J. H. Moulton and W. F. Howard, *Grammar of New Testament Greek*, Vol. II: *Accidence and Word-Formation*, Edinburgh: T. & T. Clark, 1919, p. 365, where μιμητής is listed among the *nomina agentis*. Moulton also remarks that in the Hellenistic period more so than earlier "a differentiation of meanings was observed in the use of the several formations: -σις then expressed the verbal abstract..., -μος generally indicated the state, and -μα the result of the action" (p. 355, note 1). Although μίμημα and μίμησις are not found in the New Testament, there is ample evidence that they were in current usage in the New Testament world. Philo's usage of the words shows the influence of Plato's cosmological system, but Josephus' usage is regular; cf. e.g. *Antiquities* 12:75; *Jewish Wars* 3:111, 123; 7:142; 12:77. Cf. also its usage in the *Sibylline Oracles* 8:116. Polycarp calls the Christian prisoners which the Philippians had welcomed and helped on their way τὰ μιμήματα τῆς ἀληθοῦς ἀγάπης, "the pattern of true love" (*To the Philippians* 1:1).

34 The ὅτι which connects the second clause to the first does not require a more specific or rigid connection than this. Cf. Robertson, *Gram.*, p. 964: "The precise idea conveyed by ὅτι varies greatly"; and Blass-Debrunner, *Gram.*, p. 288, § 456: "Die Subordination ist bei ὅτι... oft recht locker..., so dass man mit 'denn' übersetzen muss." The *N.E.B.* does not attempt to translate it, but makes a sentence break here.

35 Among those who have come to this conclusion in regard to this passage are Rigaux, *Thess.*, p. 441: "L'imitation consiste à supporter avec le même courage que les Judéens les

In our considerations of vs. 2:14 thus far we have been asking whether Paul could have called the Thessalonians imitators as a result of something that had happened to them or whether it was as a result of their own activity. We have concluded that it was the latter. They had stood fast and endured suffering at the hands of their countrymen. In this they were imitators. However, we have not yet come to clarity as to the sense in which Paul is using the word *imitators* here. Has Paul noticed that the Thessalonians were reacting to a similar situation in the same way as the Judean Christians had done, and with this in mind does he apply the term *imitators* to them? In other words, has Paul chosen the term *imitators* to use as a characterization of the phenomenon which he has noticed? Was the connection between the Judean and Thessalonian Christians which could be called *imitation* actually the product of Paul's thinking, a relation seen and expressed by him? [36] Or was there a more factual basis for the use of the term *imitators*? Could the Thessalonians have been aware of the conduct of the Judeans in the face of their sufferings? Is it possible that in a more or less conscious way they had been following their example? Was Paul acknowledging this fact in calling them imitators? [37]

In seeking an answer to such questions, we must first give some thought to whether the Thessalonians could have been aware of what had happened to the Christian churches in Judea. There have been various proposals as to what brings Paul to refer to the persecutions in Judea at this point in his letter. It is striking that in this passage, which follows the thought of the previous thanksgiving (1:2ff.) so closely, there should be such a marked change in the object of imitation. There it was "us and the Lord"; here it is the churches in Judea. Findlay has suggested that Silvanus was from Jerusalem, so that it would be natural that the missionaries would be thinking and speaking often about the churches of that area. [38] Calvin and many others have thought that Paul is conscious of an insinuation by the Jewish opponents in Thessalonica that Christianity was a false religion because God's holy people (the Jews) were constrained to oppose it, and that Paul is

---

persécutions des compatriots"; Frame, *Thess.*, p. 110: "The point of imitation... is obviously not the fact of παθεῖν but the steadfast endurance manifested under persecution"; and von Dobschütz, *Thess.*, p. 109: "πάσχειν ist hier... natürlich nicht nach seiner passiven Seite zu fassen 'leiden mussen'..., sondern durchaus aktiv: 'leidend ausharren' (= ὑπομένειν)."

36 Hippocrates' usage of μιμέομαι in the passage noted above (see pp. 2–3) amounted to this. However, there we noticed that a cosmological relationship undoubtedly underlies the use of the word. And furthermore, such a usage is hardly comparable with this passage, since in Hippocrates it was the verb that was used ("imitate" can mean either "to be an imitator" or "to be an imitation") and here it is the noun of agency.

37 F. C. Baur would have answered, "Of course not!" In fact, Baur found in the very presence of this verse in the letter an evident token that the letter was spurious. He exclaims: "Wie gesucht ist die Vergleichung dieser ebensoher den Juden als den Heiden zur Last fallenden Bedrückungen mit den Christenverfolgungen in Judäa, und wie unangemessen für den Apostel, welcher doch sonst die Judenchristen seinen Heidenchristen nie als Muster vorhält und von jenen Verfolgungen in Judäa nicht reden konnte, ohne an sich selbst, als den Haupttheilnehmer an der einzigen, die hier eigentlich in Betracht kommen kann, zu erinnern" (*Paulus, der Apostel Jesu Christi*, 2. Aufl., Leipzig: Fues's Verlag [L. W. Reisland], 1866, Part II, pp. 96f.).

38 Cf. G. G. Findlay, *The Epistles of Paul the Apostle to the Thessalonians*, C.G.T., Cambridge: University Press, 1904, p. 52.

answering this by pointing out that the Jews have always persecuted the true followers of God.[39] Whatever role such factors may have played in bringing the thought of the churches of Judea to the fore at this point, it is not to be overlooked that these churches continued to hold a central position in early Christianity. They participated in the distinction which pertained primarily to the Jerusalem church: there the apostles were to be found, and from there the gospel had gone forth. Jerusalem was in a real sense the mother-church, with all the significance such a relationship would have in the oriental world in which the church first lived.[40] As Christianity spread, it did not establish new and independent centers of Christianity, but rather new sprouts and branches of the one fellowship whose roots were in Jerusalem.[41] When the gospel came to Samaria, Peter and John were sent from Jerusalem to confirm it (Acts 8:14). With the report that there were believers at Antioch, the church at Jerusalem sent Barnabas to look into the matter (11:22). On various occasions we read of prophets going out from Jerusalem (11:27; 15:22, cf. vs. 32; 21:10). Paul saw Jerusalem as the starting point also of his missionary work (Rom. 15:19). Jerusalem was the center of the growing church, and in her were the roots to be found. When differences of opinion arose in Antioch, the church there sent a delegation to Jerusalem to seek guidance and judgment on the matter (Acts 15:2). Paul was very emphatic about the fact that he had received his apostleship and gospel by direct communication from Jesus Christ and not from man (Gal. 1:1,11). However, this did not prevent his looking upon Jerusalem as having an authority and as setting a standard for Christianity. He went there more than once to confer with the leaders about his gospel and his work (cf. Gal. 1:18ff.; 2:1ff.).

The church in Jerusalem is not to be seen in radical distinction from the churches of Judea, however. What applied in a more concentrated way to the church in the capital city applied also to the churches in the surrounding areas. In the persecution following Stephen's death the Christians of Jerusalem had dispersed (Acts 8:1). Hence, the original Christian converts and probably some of the original followers of Jesus as well (cf. Acts 1:15ff.) were to be found in the churches that sprang up throughout Judea. These churches enjoyed the direct guidance, leadership, and services of the Apostles.[42] They

---

39  Cf. Calvin, I Thess., sub 2:14.
40  Cf. P. A. van Stempvoort, Eenheid en Schisma in de Gemeente van Korinthe volgens I Korinthiërs, Nijkerk: G. F. Callenbach, 1950, pp. 32, 62ff.
41  K. Holl, "Der Kirchenbegriff des Paulus in seinem Verhältnis zu dem der Urgemeinde," in Gesammelte Aufsätze zur Kirchengeschichte, J. C. B. Mohr (Paul Siebeck), 1928, Vol. II, p. 56: "Durch diese über Jerusalem hinaus sich erstreckende Tätigkeit [of such men as Philip in Samaria and later in Caesarea] entstehen nach der Vorstellung der Urgemeinde n i c h t, wie wir es uns unter dem Eindruck der Folgezeit denken, n e u e  s e l b s t ä n d i g e  M i t t e l-p u n k t e, sondern nur A b l e g e r  d e r  e i n e n  G e m e i n d e, die in Jerusalem ihren eigentlichen Sitz hat."
42  This may be gathered by way of implication from Paul's reference to the churches of Judea in Gal. 1:22. In the whole context in Galatians Paul is making the point of his independence of the apostles in receiving his gospel and yet of his recognition and approbation by them. In Gal. 1:18ff. he speaks of his visit and stay in Jerusalem for fifteen days where he saw Peter but none of the other apostles except James, the brother of the Lord. How could this happen?

were still the original Jewish church, the mother-church of Christianity. In them was a standard and established pattern for Christianity. It was a weighty argument indeed when Paul could appeal to their practice in his exhortations of what was proper in the churches established by him.

We find Paul doing this in I Cor. 14:33b—36. He is speaking about whether women ought to be permitted to speak or ought to keep silent in the church meetings. He introduces his exhortation with a pointed reference: "As in all the churches of the saints, let the women keep silence...." The expression "churches of the saints" seems at first sight to be saying to the Corinthians simply that they should follow the practice that is common in all Christian churches. However, in the light of what follows, it appears that Paul has the original Jewish churches in Judea in mind in a special way. We receive the first hint of this in the typically Jewish way in which he supports the argument with "even as the law says" (vs. 34). It becomes clearer when he makes his concluding remark on the whole matter: "What? was it from you that the word of God went forth? or came it unto you alone?" (vs. 36). The implication is that Corinth does not have the privilege of establishing whatever practices she wishes, in view of the fact not only that she has sister-churches alongside her, but especially in view of the fact that there is a mother-church from which her gospel came. This passage gives evidence of an attitude of reverence and respect which was due by the daughter-churches toward the mother-church in the pattern of Christian practice there exhibited. [43]

In view of the central position which the churches of Judea continued to hold in the early Christian church it is particularly interesting that Paul should have referred to the Thessalonians as being imitators of them. However, the question still faces us as to whether the Thessalonians could have been aware of what had happened to the Christian churches in Judea and of their various responses to specific situations. Granted that there was an official relation between Thessalonica and Jerusalem, and that there was the recog-

---

The theory of Paul's remaining in hiding while there can not be harmonized with Acts 9:26ff.: neither does it do justice to the details of the Galatian passage (see S. Greijdanus, *De Brief van den Apostel Paulus aan de Gemeenten in Galatië*, K.N.T., Amsterdam: H. A. van Bottenburg, 1936, p. 112ff.). Apparently the rest of the apostles were away from Jerusalem at this time. And furthermore, they were apparently working in the churches of Judaea. As Machen puts it, "Their presence in the churches of Judea would explain the mention of those churches in Gal. 1:22. Paul is indicating the meagerness of his direct contact with the original apostles. The churches of Judaea would become important in his argument if they were the scene of the apostles' labors" (J. G. Machen, *The Origin of Paul's Religion*, New York, Macmillan, 1928, p. 76, *cf.* also pp. 50—52).

[43] In recent times the exegesis which sees the churches of Judea in the background of this passage has been revived by L. Cerfaux, *La Théologie de l'Église suivant saint Paul*, 2e éd., Paris: Les éditions du Cerf, 1948, p. 104 and elsewhere. Van Stempvoort, *Eenheid*, p. 61ff. has shown that in earlier times it was the position of Calvin, Estius, and Grotius. In connection with the matter of the primacy of the churches of Jerusalem and Judea, van Stempvoort makes a helpful distinction: "Bij de kerkelijke primaatsidee moet men n.l. nauwkeurig onderscheiden tussen een oorsprongs- en een rechtsprimaat. De ekklesia, de christelijke diaspora, heeft een centrum, een uitgangspunt en een concentratiepunt: Jeruzalem. De christenheid is echter niet rechtens en voor altijd gebonden aan de aardse stad: het primaat van Jeruzalem is geen primaat van rechten" (pp. 32,33). He finds I Cor. 14:33b—36 supporting the idea of a primacy of origin as over against any idea of a judicial primacy (p. 62).

nition and respect of a certain kind of primacy in Jerusalem, was the relation extensive enough and personal enough to have led to the possibility of imitation? Is it likely that the Thessalonians themselves either could or would have made any associations and comparisons between their Christian lives and those of the Christians in Judea? Were the events of the first half of the book of Acts known outside of the area where they happened before Acts had been written and circulated? It is one thing to know about the constitution and church order of the mother-church. It is another thing to know her history and her experiences.

There are various indications that what had happened in Judea may have been quite well known in Thessalonica and the other churches established by Paul. We know at least that Paul did not hesitate to speak freely about his earlier persecution of the church (*cf.* Acts 22:4ff.; 26:9ff.; I Cor. 15:9; Gal. 1:13,23; Phil. 3:6; I Tim. 1:13). This in itself was quite a chapter in Judean church history. Then in more recent times he himself had become the victim of persecution from the Jews in Judea. In I Thess. 2:15f. he mentions their persecuting him in the same breath with what they did to the Lord Jesus and the prophets, as though Old Testament history, the history of Jesus' life, and the history of the spread of the gospel and the church were all equally known. From I Thess. 3:4 we know that in his early preaching in Thessalonica he spoke of the necessity of Christians suffering affliction, and it is surely reasonable to suppose that he illustrated this from what had happened elsewhere. We know by way of implication from I Thess. 1:8,9 that Paul was not averse to speaking about his experience in other churches. In II Cor. 8:1ff. he holds up the Macedonian churches in praise before the Corinthian church. It can hardly be unlikely, then, that he held up the exemplary conduct of the Judean Christians before the Thessalonians. The whole matter of the collection for the Christians in Jerusalem (*cf.* Rom. 15:25–27; I Cor. 16:1ff.; II Cor. 8ff.) gives evidence that the other churches were acquainted with the continued suffering and difficulties of their brethren in Judea. The spontaneity and liberality with which the Macedonian churches responded (*cf.* II Cor. 8:1–5) indicates a feeling of living fellowship with the Judean Christians. There is little reason to doubt that the Thessalonians knew quite a bit about how the Judean Christians had suffered from the hands of their countrymen. [44]

In view of these things it is not at all unlikely that the Thessalonians had been imitating the Judean Christians and doing so with a large measure of consciousness and intention. As opposition and persecution began to engulf them and they began to feel the pangs of suffering inflicted upon them for their new faith, what would be more normal than to consider what other Christians had done in like circumstances? Suffering had been the experience of Christians from the very first. Those who had known the Lord personally, who had witnessed his crucifixion and had seen him after his resurrection

---

[44] Stanley, *Biblica*, XL, pp. 868—869, proposes, "It is reasonable to assume that the experiences of these Jewish Christians and their testimony to Christ were included in Paul's version of the kerygma."

had already established a pattern here. The experiencing of suffering was no occasion for weakening and retracting; on the contrary, it was the occasion for joining the Apostles in "rejoicing that they were counted worthy to suffer dishonor for the Name" (Acts 5:41). It was the occasion for praising God and renewing their witness.

In the matter of faithfully continuing in their Christian commitment in spite of all adversity, suffering, and persecution, the Judean Christian community had established the pattern for the Christian church. The corporate life of the Christian community in Judea had taken a recognizable shape, and other younger communities could be referred to it. This pattern which the Judean Christian community set was actually only the latest instance of a pattern which had characterized God's people in all ages. Paul recalls that Jesus himself had faced the antagonism of his fellow-countrymen and finally suffered death at their hands, and that before him the same had been true of the prophets (I Thess. 2:15). Although Paul's words here take the form of a tirade against the Jews, there is more in these words than simply an explosion of wrath against his countrymen. Behind them is the fact of the basic unity of experience of God's people in all ages. As we noted earlier, Jesus' way was basically the way that Israel, Israel's prophets, and righteous individuals had followed ever and again. [45] We also noted how the New Testament letters addressed to Jewish Christians often referred to the example for Christians which could be found in the suffering, steadfastness, faithfulness, and perseverance of the Old Testament saints. [46] Paul undoubtedly held these Old Testament examples before his Gentile Christians. But quite understandably, there was more appeal for Gentiles in the example of their *Christian* forebears. So even as James could appeal to his Jewish Christians: "Take, brethren, for an example of suffering and of patience, the prophets who spake in the name of the Lord" (James 5:10), Paul could appeal to Gentile Christians to take the Christian community in Judea as an example. This the Thessalonians had been doing. In the midst of their own adverse circumstances, they had found help in turning their thoughts to their Judean Christian brethren. They reflected on the fact that sometimes the outcome of a most adverse situation in Judea had been marvellous. God had done great things among the Judean Christians, and now they in Thessalonica were God's servants too. What had happened in Judea could happen in Macedonia. Thus with zeal renewed and resolution strengthened, they turned to walking further the pathway of these Judean Christians. They imitated them. They persisted in the steadfast pursuit of the Christian faith and way in spite of all the sufferings their fellow countrymen inflicted upon them. They remained faithful to their Christian commitment regardless of the consequences, the same as the Judean Christians had done. Paul found in this act of imitation by the Thessalonian Christians a confirmation of the fact that the Word of God was truly doing its work in them and that they were indeed

---

[45] See above, pp. 52,53.
[46] See above, pp. 80—84.

Christians. His Thessalonian Christians, among the very youngest of God's people, were showing the characteristics of God's people of all ages. They were imitating their forebears in standing firm in the face of opposition. Paul could not stop expressing his thankfulness for this.

Michaelis finds this passage to be an evidence of μιμητής used for a simple comparison, where „das ältere Beispiel erscheint 'nachgeahmt', doch liegt keine bewusste Nachahmung vor." [47] He finds this to be an important instance, for it shows that the whole imitation idea in Paul is not to be too narrowly limited or confined to a single meaning. [48] His peculiar interpretation of the passage recommends itself only on the assumption that the Thessalonians had no knowledge of the experiences of the Judean Christians. This is a position, however, which he himself does not insist on. [49] Since we have not been able to accept his interpretation of the passage, we see no reason on the basis of this verse for proposing that the imitation idea in Paul's writings is anything other than the conscious and intentional following of an example seen in others.

\* \* \*

We turn now to our consideration of I Thess. 1:6: "And ye became imitators of us, and of the Lord." In the extended thanksgiving with which Paul begins the first letter to the Thessalonians, the thought of imitation occurs twice. In 1:6 the imitation is "of us and of the Lord"; in 2:14 it is "of the churches of God which are in Judea in Christ Jesus." We have studied this second instance first in order to have that material at hand for our study of the passage on the imitation of Paul.

The similarity of the train of thought which leads to the subject of imitation in these two passages is striking. In both places the thought runs from thanksgiving, to Paul's preaching, to divine working in the hearers, to imitation and suffering. In the second chapter the expression of the thought is more abbreviated and concise. The relationship between the various clauses is more clear. The passage gives the impression that, after having digressed somewhat from the thought with which he began the letter, Paul here (2:13,14) picked up the original thought again and briefly restated it, only to be led off again on a tangent with the mention of the persecution from the Jews. The thanksgiving with which the letter begins, on the other hand, is more elaborate and less closely constructed as to grammar and logic. It gives the impression of being the overflowing of a thankful heart unrestrained by efforts at logical and grammatical precision. The piling of phrase upon phrase and clause upon clause has not left an easy task for commentators as they seek to account for and explain the relationships of the various individual thoughts to each other. The variety of conclusions which the commentators have reached regarding the details of the passage is a bit bewildering. However, the general line of thought is not difficult to detect, especially in view of its

---

[47] Michaelis, *T.W.N.T.*, IV, p. 674, 36,37.
[48] Ibid., p. 669, 11—15.
[49] Ibid., p. 669, 4—5, and fn. 12.

more concise restating in 2:13,14. There the thanksgiving finds its cause in the fact that through Paul's preaching and God's accompanying working the Thessalonians had accepted the gospel and truly become Christians. This fact had become abundantly evident in their imitation of other Christians who had steadfastly held to their faith in the face of persecutions and afflictions. In the first chapter these same elements appear, together with some other thoughts which are interwoven. We shall examine the development of thought here from thanksgiving to imitation.

Paul writes, "We give thanks to God always for you all" (1:2). There follow three participial clauses: (1) making mention... in our prayers, (2) remembering... your work of faith, and (3) knowing... your election. The first participial clause is hardly more than a restatement of the principal clause about thanksgiving, adding only the occasion on which it is done: Paul gave thanks in his prayers. It is in the second participial clause that we come to the heart of the thanksgiving, for in it we are told what has brought it forth. Paul has been impressed with the remarkable response to the coming of the Christian gospel to Thessalonica. He makes no reference to the quantity of the response;[50] his remarks all regard the quality of it. His Thessalonian converts had become active, energetic, and resolute Christians. Their "work of faith and labor of love and patience of hope in our Lord Jesus Christ before our God and Father" (1:3)[51] filled him with thankfulness to God. The mention of God as their Father builds the bridge to the third participial clause. With God as their Father and they as sons of God,[52] they could be addressed as "brethren, beloved of God" (1:4). Paul had come to know their election. Here his thankfulness had reached its ultimate ground. He hastens to add how he had come to this knowledge of their election. It was through what he had seen happen in Thessalonica. The gospel had been so remarkably effective in the lives of his readers. When he had preached

---

[50] It appears from Acts 17:4 that while there were not many Jews that responded to Paul's preaching at Thessalonica, there were a considerable number of "devout Greeks" and "chief women" who became Christians.

[51] Paul gives no precise indication of how the phrases "in our Lord Jesus Christ" and "before our God and Father" are to be understood in relation to the rest of the sentence. Milligan, *Thess.*, p. 7, observes, "The sentence would naturally have finished with ἐλπίδος, but in characteristic fashion St. Paul lengthens it out by the addition of two clauses"; and Rigaux, *Thess.*, p. 367, remarks in regard to the second phrase, "La phrase tire en longueur, comme une phrase parlée, dictée." It seems best in each case to understand the phrase as arising from the most recently expressed thought, rather than finding its connection farther back in the clause. The hope which inspires their steadfastness and joy in the face of persecution and opposition is a very specific hope, a "hope in our Lord Jesus Christ"; cf. I Thess. 4:13,14; 5:8,9; II Thess. 2:16; Col. 1:27; I Tim. 1:1; C. Spicq, *Agapè*, Analyse II, p. 10, fn. 4; W. Hendriksen, *Exposition of I and II Thessalonians*, Grand Rapids: Baker Book House, 1955, p. 47; Frame, *Thess.*, pp. 76,77; Milligan, *loc. cit.; et al.* This hope in Christ reaches out to the time when they must appear "before our God and Father." This will be the fruition of their hope and the day of their salvation (I Thess. 1:10; 3:13; 5:9), as over against the others who will suffer wrath and destruction (I Thess. 1:10; 5:3; II Thess. 1:9); cf. Frame, *loc. cit.*; Milligan, *loc. cit.*

[52] Spicq, *Agapè*, Anal. II, p. 11, points out, "Que Dieu soit désigné comme Père à l'occasion de cette effusion des vertus 'théologales', insinue qu'il ne s'agit pas d'une libéralité quelconque, si généreuse soit-elle, mais d'une relation de Père à enfant, d'un engendrement. Ne serait-ce pas précisément la foi, l'espérance et la charité..., qui caractériseraient la filiation divine?" *Cf.* also *Agapè*, Anal. I, pp. 23ff.

the gospel to them, there had been the communication of far more than human words. The gospel had come to them vibrant with divine power and with the Holy Spirit, and its productivity had been most abundant. The seed of the gospel sown by Paul had sprung to life and blossomed forth in a rich and full harvest.

In regard to the words "not in word only, but also in power, and in the Holy Spirit..." (1:5) commentators express different opinions as to whether they are to be thought of as applying mainly to Paul, or mainly to the Thessalonians. Do they express Paul's subjective experience in preaching the gospel in Thessalonica; or do they express what happened in the experience of the Thessalonians? Perhaps the two can not be totally separated from each other. Grundmann finds both aspects present in Paul's usage of "power" and "spirit" in combination: "Wenn wir daran denken, dass der paulinische Kraftbegriff aus zwei Gesichtspunkten gebildet ist, das πνεῦμα einmal die Weise ausdrückt, in der der erhöhte Herr gegenwärtig ist, und geradezu mit ihm identifiziert wird, zum anderen die Existenzweise der Gläubigen zum Ausdruck bringt, zwei Gesichtspunkte, die ihre Einheit finden in dem mit ἐν πνεύματι synonym gebrauchten ἐν χριστῷ, so wird deutlich, dass in der Verbindung von δύναμις und πνεῦμα die Kraft zum Ausdruck gebracht werden soll, mit der der erhöhte Herr den Seinen gegenwärtig is als πνεῦμα." [53] In these opening verses of I Thess. the attention is mainly upon the Thessalonians themselves, upon their vital Christian lives (1:3), and upon their election (1:4). Hence, in 1:5 where Paul states how he knows their election, it is more to the point to understand Paul as referring to the way the gospel entered into the Thessalonians than to the way that it issued forth from him. [54] It worked in the Thessalonians in power and in the Holy Spirit. Understanding the verse this way makes it parallel to 2:13, which speaks of their finding Paul's gospel not to be the word of men but the Word of God, which also worked in them. The emphasis is not on what it was in Paul, but on what it was in the Thessalonians.

The third term of the series, πληροφορία, harmonizes fully with such an interpretation. The harvest figure lies close at hand in this word. G. H. Whitaker has come to this conclusion in his studies of the word in its verbal form. [55] He states that πληροφορέω "is like εὐφορέω, καρποφορέω, τελεσφορέω and a number of special verbs such as ἐλαιοφορέω, a *nature*-word, denoting the *full-bearing* of soil or tree." [56] (It is interesting to note that in all three synoptic accounts in the inter-

---

[53] W. Grundmann, δύναμαι/δύναμις, T.W.N.T., II, p. 312, 19—26.

[54] In this, I Thess. 1:5 differs from a similar distinction made between words on the one hand and Spirit and power on the other in I Cor. 2:4. There the matter concerns the bringing the gospel to Corinth: "My speech and my preaching were not in persuasive words of wisdom, but in demonstration of the Spirit and of power." His point in this Corinthian passage was that he, in distinction from some others in Corinth, was the one through whom God had worked and that their faith was to be traced to God's power working through him, and not to any words of human wisdom (*cf.* I Cor. 2:5). Hence, by preaching "in demonstration of the Spirit and of power," Paul could be identified as the one in whom the exalted Lord dwelt. This was the point at which Paul proposed to test his antagonists at Corinth: "I will know not the word of them that are puffed up, but the power" (I Cor. 4:19).

[55] G. H. Whitaker, "The Philology of St. Luke's Preface," *The Expositor*, 8th Series, Vol. XX (1920), pp. 262—272; "Notes on the Paper 'The Philology of St. Luke's Preface,'" *ibid.*, pp. 380—384; "Additional Note on 'The Philology of St. Luke's Preface,'" *ibid.*, XXI (1921), pp. 239—240.

[56] *Ibid.*, XX, pp. 262,263.

pretation of the parable of the sower the related word καρποφορέω is used in connection with the seed sown on good ground: "... such as hear the word, and accept it, and bear fruit" [Mark 4:20; cf. Matt. 12:23; Luke 8:15].) Whitaker has shown further that "the verb πληροφορεῖσθαι, literally 'to be put forth in full yield' or 'to put forth a full yield,' denotes not a conviction or assurance of the mind, but the result of such an assurance in life and conduct, the rich fruitfulness for which the conviction prepares the way." [57] In regard to πληροφορία here in I Thess. 1:5, it would seem preferable to understand it in its basic meaning of *fullness, abundance,* [58] rather than its derived meaning of *assurance* (K.J.V., A.S.V.), or *conviction* (R.S.V.), as do most commentators. In the clause in which it stands Paul is giving the evidence for his knowledge of the Thessalonians' election. Thus, Paul is not attempting to explain how he brought the gospel, but rather how it worked among the Thessalonians. It came to them in power and in the Holy spirit and πληροφορία πολλῇ. [59] Since the third term of the series is so intimately linked to the preceding two, it is hardly likely that it would suddenly speak of Paul's experience (his assurance) when the other two had to do with objective realities proving the election of the Thessalonians. [60] The explanation of Rigaux commends itself: "Les trois caractérisent l'évangile et s'opposent à la vanité de la parole. C'est donc le contenu de l'évangile, son efficacité interne qui sont visés. Le choix divin est prouvé par les biens que l'évangile comporte et ceux-ci sont la révélation de la force, de la puissance de Dieu et le don de l'Esprit-Saint. Ceux deux manifestations de l'évangile ont eu lieu 'en grande abondance', en réalisations totales et diverses." [61] He goes on to point out that this is in full agreement with the very essence of Christianity, namely that the gospel is the revelation of the fullness of God's gifts to man. In Tit. 3:6 we read that God poured out the Holy Spirit upon us "richly (πλουσίως), through Jesus Christ our Saviour." In Eph. 5:18 Christians are exhorted to "be filled with the Spirit" (πληροῦσθε ἐν πνεύματι). G. Delling comes to the same conclusion in regard to the use of πληροφορία here: "nicht im blossen Wort, sondern in grosser *Fülle göttlichen Wirkens*... geschah das Ausrichten der Frohbotschaft durch den Apostel. Es ist dann eines der Wörter, mit denen er den übergrossen Reichtum des Tuns Gottes auch im gegenwärtigen Leben der Christenheit sprachlich zu fassen

---

57 *Ibid.,* XXI, p. 239.
58 Vulgate: "plenitudine"; *N.B.G.:* "volheid."
59 The textual reading without ἐν is to be preferred on the basis of weighty manuscript evidence (א B) and as being the more difficult reading in view of the use of ἐν with the two preceding datives of the series.
60 Findlay, *Thess.,* p. 24, and Milligan, *Thess.,* p. 9, cite *I Clement* 42:3, as confirmation of the meaning *assurance*. The passage reads [οἱ ἀπόστολοι] πληροφορηθέντες διὰ τῆς ἀναστάσεως τοῦ κυρίου ἡμῶν Ἰησοῦ Χριστοῦ, ... μετὰ πληροφορίας πνεύματος ἁγίου ἐξῆλθον, εὐαγγελιζόμενοι. The verbal form connected with the resurrection of the Lord seems to set the pattern for the translation of the substantive form linked with the Holy Spirit. Whitaker, *Expositor,* 8th Ser., XX, p. 380, finds his insights regarding this word eminently suited to this passage. He proposes as translation *"either* (Passive) 'put forth as full-fruited branches' (or 'borne as full fruit'), *or* (Middle) 'having attained to full fruit-bearing'... 'with a fulness of fruitbearing' of (i.e. wrought by) the Holy Spirit." Others have not hesitated to translate the noun in the sense of *fullness: cf. e.g.* E. Burton, *The Apostolic Fathers,* Edinburgh: John Grant, 1909, Vol. I, p. 180: "with the fulness of the Holy Spirit"; A. C. Duker and W. C. Van Manen, *De Geschriften der Apostolische Vaders,* Amsterdam: C. L. Brinkman, 1871, Vol. I, p. 206: "in de volheid des Heiligen Geestes"; D. Franses, *De Apostolische Vaders,* Hilversum: N.V. Paul Brand's Uitgevers Bedrijf, 1941, p. 80: "geheel vervuld van den Heiligen Geest."
61 Rigaux, *Thess.,* p. 378.

sucht." [62] It is the abundant results of the coming of the gospel to the lives of the Thessalonian converts that made clear their election.

However, in his happy state of thankfulness Paul was not completely free from all concern for the future of the gospel in Thessalonica and for the spiritual well-being of his readers. He seems to have been disturbed by what the opponents to Christianity might be doing in Thessalonica to blacken his name and thus to bring discredit upon the gospel he brought. [63] Perhaps he had actual knowledge of a campaign against him, and maybe even evidence of its partial effectiveness. At least he suddenly rounds out the thought about how the gospel had come to them by adding, "Even as ye know what manner of men we showed ourselves toward you for your sake." The thought of what they had experienced under his preaching had immediately brought to mind the matter of his personal conduct. The whole working of the gospel at Thessalonica was not to be seen apart from him and the powers which had worked through him. The same divine activity which was the evidence of the election of the Thessalonians was also the credential for him and his companions as ministers of God. Hence, Paul took this occasion to remind the Thessalonians that his conduct in preaching the gospel had been in complete harmony with that gospel and with the divine activity which accompanied it. He had shown no less enthusiasm and devotion than the gospel warranted. In fact, while he was with them he had given himself completely to their benefit and service (δι' ὑμᾶς).

Paul does not pursue the matter of his conduct beyond the mere reference to it at this point. However, he soon returns to this subject. In 2:1–12 he speaks about it very pointedly. We find here the same eagerness to recall certain facts to the Thessalonians: "For yourselves ... know" (vs. 1), "as ye know" (vss. 2, 5, 11), "for ye remember" (vs. 9), "ye are witnesses" (vs. 10). In this paragraph his thought moves once again from the subject of his preaching the gospel (vss. 1–4) to that of his personal conduct (vss. 5–12). He reminds them of how adverse the circumstances had been, having come from the suffering and maltreatment in Philippi only to find himself engulfed in further opposition and conflict in Thessalonica (vs. 2). [64] Nevertheless, as God's ambassador, he had preached the gospel (vs. 4). His allegiance to God had precluded his catering to their desires in an attempt to win them, but it had by no

---

[62] G. Delling, πληροφορία, T.W.N.T., VI, p. 309, 13–16.
[63] See above, p. 93.
[64] Paul's remark in 2:2 about preaching the gospel in Thessalonica "in much conflict" is too slight a reference to give much information. However, it clearly hints that the situation had been none too favorable from the very start. Although the account of Paul's work in Thessalonica according to Acts 17 has no indications of opposition to him before the jealous Jews aroused the crowd to storm Jason's house, still there is a hint to be found in the account of the work at Berea to the fact that Paul had been faced with opposition throughout the Thessalonian stay. Luke says that the Bereans were "more noble than those in Thessalonica, in that they received the word with all readiness of mind" (Acts 17:11). As to the results, in both places there was a considerable number of converts among the Greeks, both men and women (cf. Acts 17:4 and 12). The difference apparently was mainly in regard to the Jews. In Berea "many of them ... believed" (17:12); in Thessalonica "some of them were persuaded" (17:4). Such small indications as "more noble," "readiness of mind," "many believed," placed over against the "some were persuaded" of the account about Thessalonica hint at the difficulties there had been there.

means prevented his deep and earnest commitment to their service and well-being. He enlarges upon this thought particularly, and thus makes his own commentary on the reference in 1:5 that his conduct had been δι' ὑμᾶς, *for your sake*. In vs. 8 he says, "we were well pleased to impart unto you, not the gospel of God only, but also our own souls," and he introduces this thought by likening himself to a mother-nurse cherishing her own children (vs. 7). In vs. 11 the simile has changed to "a father with his own children, exhorting you, and encouraging you, and testifying, to the end that ye should walk worthily of God." He reminds them of how hard he had worked to support himself in order to avoid burdening them (vs. 9). There is a commentary on the οἷοι ἐγενήθημεν ἐν ὑμῖν of 1:5 in 2:10: ὡς ὁσίως καὶ δικαίως καὶ ἀμέμπτως ὑμῖν ... ἐγενήθημεν, "how holily and righteously and unblameably we behaved ourselves toward you." In spite of and in the midst of very adverse circumstances Paul had given himself completely to the furtherance of the gospel and to the service of his hearers. Paul's quick turn of thought in 1:5 about "even as ye know what manner of men we showed ourselves toward you for your sake" apparently intended to arouse these thoughts, at least in their seed form.

Paul's thanksgiving continues to flow forth: "And ye became imitators of us, and of the Lord, having received the word in much affliction, with joy of the Holy Spirit" (1:6). Frame correctly observes, "The sentence is getting to be independent, but ὅτι (vs. 5) is still in control." [65] This does not mean, however, that vs. 6 must be connected directly to ὅτι. Instead, it finds its connection in what has just been expressed, and stands in reciprocal relation to it. Vs. 6 introduces a marked change of subject. Paul had been speaking of things relating to himself: "our gospel" and "the kind of men we were." Now suddenly the subject is *you* (ὑμεῖς), expressed with all emphasis: "and you on your part." The question poses itself as to which of the preceding clauses vs. 6 stands in reciprocal relation. Is the reference to his conduct a parenthetical remark, with vs. 6 picking up the main train of thought again from "in the Holy Spirit, and in much fullness"? If so, Paul would be saying, "Our gospel came to you with a powerful divine working..., and you on your part became imitators of us." Or is vs. 6 related to the immediately preceding clause, so that it is to be read, "You know what kind of men we were while among you for your sake, and you on your part became imitators of us"? The latter would seem to be the more likely, since the idea of imitation flows so naturally from the reference to Paul's conduct. However, it should not be overlooked that the former has marked similarities to the train of thought in 2:13,14: "When ye received from us the word of the message, ... ye accepted it ... as ... the word of God, which also worketh in you that believe. For ye, brethren, became imitators of the churches of God which are in Judaea...." Both passages contain the following sequence of thoughts: the word coming from Paul, the divine working, the imitation. The obvious difference between the two passages is in the persons being imitated: "us and the Lord," as over against "the churches ... in Judaea."

---

[65] Frame, *Thess.*, p. 82.

The first chapter further differs from the second in that the reference to Paul's conduct intervenes before the reference to the imitation, and in that the imitation is not presented as an explicit confirmation of the divine working by being introduced with the conjunction *for*.[66] However, chapter 2 may still give us the clue to the basic relationship of the ideas. Paul's preaching of the gospel was accompanied with divine working and an abundant result. As evidence of this divine working and as expression of the abundant result, Paul could cite the fact that they had become imitators of him. But, as was so typical of Paul's fertile mind, another thought first crowded to the fore, and he interjected a reference to his own conduct. This interjection results in the matter of imitation coming to expression in a slightly different form. He uses the conjunction *and*, instead of *for* (2:14). Thus, he places their imitation of him over against his conduct as they had learned to know him during his stay, rather than specifically stating it as a confirmation and evidence of the divine working which had accompanied his preaching of the gospel. The imitation continues nevertheless to be the evidence of the powerful working of the gospel. The ὅτι of vs. 5 is still in control; Paul is still explaining how he had come to know their election. Their imitation was good evidence.

Paul is not here thinking of a general over-all imitation. He states immediately the imitation which he has in mind. "You became imitators..., having received [67] the word in much affliction, with joy of the Holy Spirit." [68] Paul's adding that they were imitators of the Lord as well as of himself helps to clarify the specific point of imitation which he had in mind. It can not have been the reception and acceptance of the word as such, since in this area no analogy could be found in Christ's life. The specific area of imitation comes to expression rather in the words "in much affliction, with joy of the Holy Spirit." Chrysostom saw the point, when in answer to the question as to how they were imitators of the Lord, he says, "In that he too endured many sufferings, not with vexation, but joyously." [69] The Thessalonians had become involved in this less appealing aspect of Christianity very early in their Christian career. In fact, Paul recalls to them that they accepted the

---

66 See above, p. 98.

67 "Having received" (K.J.V., A.S.V., R.S.V.) is a rather weak statement of the matter. Δέχομαι expresses a willing reception, a welcoming, an acceptance (*cf.* N.B.G.: *aangenomen*). Notice its contrast to παραλαβόντες, *receive*, in 2:13, (where A.S.V., and R.S.V. make the distinction by translating it *accepted*.) W. Grundmann, δέχομαι, *T.W.N.T.*, II, p. 49, 6—9, refers to the distinction between the two words made by Pseudo-Ammonius in his lexicon of synonyms, *De adfinium Vocabulorum Differentia* (c. 100 A.D.) and concludes: "Darnach bringt das Verbum δέχομαι die *Reaktion auf die Aktion von anderer Seite* zum Ausdruck."

68 Grammatically it is possible to read the participial clause merely as an indication of time: "You became imitators after you received the word," or "when you had received the word." This would indicate a general imitation, and would leave the specific areas in which there was imitation entirely unspecified. However, the references to "much affliction" and "the joy of the Holy Spirit" are then without any real purpose in the sentence. They seem a bit too elaborate to be mere concommitants of a time-reference. Quite apparently they give further details about the imitation of which Paul is thinking.

69 πῶς δὲ μιμηταὶ τοῦ κυρίου ἐγένοντο; ὅτι καὶ αὐτὸς πολλὰ παθήματα ὑπέμεινε, καὶ οὐκ ἤλγει, ἀλλ' ἔχαιρεν (Chrysostom, *I Thess. Homil., sub* 1:6, [ed. Bern. de Montfaucon, XI, p. 428]).

word "in the midst of many afflictions." [70] The afflictions were there already at their entrance into Christianity. In becoming followers of the Christian gospel, they accepted the afflictions which went with it. Although we lack the specific details on this matter, it is not too difficult to imagine what the situation had been in Thessalonica. By this time in Paul's missionary labors it was clear what the gospel would bring forth. Faith was not the only response to the gospel. There was also the reaction of hot antagonism, conflict, persecution, and affliction. This fact must have been known in Thessalonica very shortly after the arrival of the missionaries. The pained movements of these men who were still recovering from their public beating in Philippi must have been an early hint to the Thessalonians of the dangerous possibilities in "the way" which these men were holding before them. As soon as the recent events in Philippi had come to light, it would have been clear to anyone in Thessalonica that these men, their message, and their way of life could get one into real trouble. Furthermore, they preached a Christ who had had to suffer (Acts 17:3). Then, they told of the opposition the Christians in Judea had had to face (cf. I Thess. 2:14f.). They soon were in the midst of much conflict also in Thessalonica (2:2). The explosion of hostility that necessitated their hasty departure (Acts 17:5ff., cf. vs. 10) was undoubtedly only the climax to a gradual building up of pressure. Such an outright move against the leaders of this "new way" was an act of desperation on the part of the opponents to Christianity. It revealed the sense of futility and frustration that had developed as it became apparent that reasoning, ridiculing, threatening, and retaliating were failing to stem the growing interest in the new movement. The atmosphere of affliction surrounded the gospel well before the frontal attack against the missionaries. From the very first announcement of the "good news" it could be seen that many were not at all pleased with it, and that they had very strong feelings on the matter. The issues were abundantly clear beforehand. [71] Even to lend an attentive ear to the gospel was to be moving toward dangerous territory. To welcome and accept the word was a crossing of the Rubicon. In so doing, one stepped out into the firing-line of hostile opposition and persecution. Yet, there were people willing to do it; and furthermore, they were doing it with joy. In fact, the quality of their response to the Christian gospel was such that they were soon an example to all the Christians around them (vs. 7). Paul later calls the Corinthians' attention to their example, together with the other Macedonian churches: "how that in much proof of affliction the abundance of their joy and their deep poverty abounded unto the riches of their liberality" (II Cor. 8:2). In their joyful facing and enduring affliction on account of their faith in the word of God, they had become imitators of Paul and of the Lord.

---

70 "ἐν θλίψει = ἐν μέσῳ θλίψεως." Frame, *Thess.*, p. 83.

71 The fact that there was already much affliction by the time the Thessalonians began to respond to the gospel sheds further light on Paul's statement in 3:4, "we told you beforehand (προελέγομεν) that we are to suffer affliction." This was not predictive prophecy to some Thessalonians who had already become Christians as to what lay in their future. Rather, it was a plain and open declaration in his preaching to non-Christians that Christianity brings one into affliction. It had been a part of his message repeatedly (cf. the imperfect tense).

Michaelis agrees that an interpretation such as the foregoing, where the participial clause informs us in what sense the Thessalonians were imitators, and where the emphasis falls on "in much affliction" etc., rather than on "receiving the word," seems at first glance to be the proper understanding of the passage: "so vermutet man zunächst." [72] However, in the light of the following verse he finds it necessary to place a large question mark over his interpretation. Paul continues in vs. 7 by saying, "so that ye became an ensample to all that believe in Macedonia and in Achaia." Obviously, the fact that their imitation resulted in their becoming an example to others draws the point in which they were imitators and the point in which they were an example into very close relationship with each other. Michaelis observes in regard to their being an example, "Ein solcher τύπος wurden die Christen in Thessalonich nun aber offerbar, wie 1,8f zeigt, ganz allgemein dadurch, dass sie gläubig geworden waren und sich zu Gott bekehrt hatten." [73] From this he concludes that in the point of imitation the emphasis must lie after all on the receiving of the word and that the connection of the thoughts must be: "indem die Thessalonicher das Wort annahmen, taten sie, was von ihnen erwartet wurde; denn zu diesem Zweck hatte Paulus im Auftrag des Herrn ihnen das Wort verkündigt." [74] However, this proposal that the example *is* to be found in the very general idea of their having become believers and converts also presents some difficulties. It leaves the reference to the afflictions and the joy of the Holy Spirit in vs. 6 without any real function in the sentence or thought. But more seriously, it fails to take into account certain elements of vs. 7. For one thing, the Thessalonian Christians were an example "to all that believe" (πᾶσιν τοῖς πιστεύουσιν), rather than to inquirers or potential believers; or as von Dobschütz so succinctly puts it: "die Gläubigen (nicht Gläubigwerdenden)." [75] Then again, Paul says, "You (plural: ὑμᾶς) became an example (singular: τύπον [76])"; they were an example corporately and as a church, rather than as individuals coming to faith and conversion. The wording of vs. 7 gives Michaelis no support.

Can Michaelis find support for his proposal in vss. 8—10? He infers that these verses show the example to be in the broad area of becoming believers and converts. Here it is well to begin by noting Frame's introductory comment to these verses, a comment which is typical of many commentators: "The general drift of these verses is clear, but some of the details are obscure." [77] The thought of vss. 8—10 apparently flows forth from the latter part of vs. 7. It must have caused real surprise to the Thessalonian readers to hear that their example was known over so wide a territory as both Macedonia and Achaia. Paul anticipates the possibility of their thinking that he had been speaking about them everywhere he went and with everyone he met. That Paul would not

---

[72] Michaelis, *T.W.N.T.*, IV, p. 672, 35,36.
[73] *Ibid.*, p. 673, 25—27.
[74] *Ibid.*, ll. 33—36.
[75] Von Dobschütz, *Thess.*, p. 73.
[76] While the reading τύπους has considerable manuscript support (ℵ C D^c K L P Ψ, the majority of miniscules, Old Latin g, Harkleian Syriac), the reading τύπον has very weighty evidence (B D*, such important miniscules as 6 33 81 131 424** 1739, the Latin tradition except Old Latin g, the Syriac Peshitta and Palestinian Syriac, the Coptic, Armenian, and Ethiopic traditions, Ephraim and Ambrosiaster). It is of course conceivable that τύπον replaced an original τύπους under the influence of the τύπον used in reference to a plural in II Thess. 3:9 and Phil. 3:17. However, it is much more likely that τύπους replaced an original τύπον under the influence of the plural ὑμᾶς of the same verse.
[77] Frame, *Thess.*, p. 83.

have been averse to doing so is clear from the way he speaks of them later to the Corinthians (*cf.* II Cor. 8:1,2). However, in this case it was not necessary. The matter was already generally known. Others kept mentioning it to him. The news about Thessalonica was spreading fast enough to make it unnecessary for Paul to say anything about them. Thus vss. 8—10 are not added to give further information about the example as such, but rather about the spread of the example.

To what extent the reports referred to in vs. 9 had to do with the circumstances in which the gospel was preached and the manner of the Thessalonians' conversion is not easily determined. They concerned "what manner (ὁποίαν) of entering in we had unto you." The qualitative force of ὁποῖος is not to be overlooked. It may refer merely to the success of Paul's attempt to bring the gospel there (*cf.* 2:1). On the other hand, it may refer to the opposition which Paul faced from the very start (*cf.* 2:2). [78] As for the report of "how ye turned unto God from idols," the πῶς, *how*, may simply be the equivalent of ὅτι, *that*, [79] and may refer only to the fact of their conversion. However, that ἀπαγγέλειν πῶς may have a strong emphasis on the manner in which the event occurred and not only on the fact of it is abundantly clear from Luke 8:36 (*cf.* the parallel passage in Mark 5:16). [80] If there is an emphasis on manner here in vs. 9, then there is probably a similar phenomenon in the phrase "your faith to God-ward" (vs. 8b). Thus Paul may be referring to their faith in its content and quality and as the effect of conversion as being the thing which had become generally known, [81] rather than to the mere fact that their reception of the word and conversion had become generally known. [82] There is at least the possibility of reading vss. 8—10 with considerable emphasis on the manner of their conversion and the quality of their faith. However, this matter is not clear. Neither does it need to be pressed. Vss. 8—10 are not speaking of this specific matter. Thus, in view of the details of vs. 7 and the general thrust of vss. 8—10, Michaelis' objection to the interpretation

---

78 Cf. Chrysostom's explanation of "what manner of entering in" etc.: ὅτι κινδύνων ἔγεμεν, ὅτι θανάτων μυρίων (*I Thess. Homil.*, sub 1:9, [ed. Bern. de Montfaucon, XI, p. 433], *i.e.*, "we were surrounded with dangers and countless deaths." G. Wohlenberg, *Der erste und zweite Thessalonicherbrief*, K.z.N.T., Leipzig: A. Deichert, 1903, p. 36, concludes regarding the clause: "so werden wir ... an die mit jenem Eingang verbundenen Schwierigkeiten und Verfolgungen zu denken haben."

79 Both Blass-Debrunner, *Gram.*, p. 245, § 396, and Robertson, *Gram.*, p. 1032, cite I Thess. 1:9 as an illustration of this usage of πῶς.

80 Findlay, *Thess.*, p. 28, and Wohlenberg, *Thess.*, p. 36, read the clause in this way.

81 The Greek commentators of the early church understood ἡ πίστις ὑμῶν ἡ πρὸς τὸν θεὸν in this way. Notice the following comments they offer on it: Theodore of Mopsuestia, I Thess., sub 1:8, [ed. Swete, II, p. 6]: πάντες ἔγνωσαν ὅσα ὑπὲρ τῆς πίστεως ἐπάθετε, καὶ πάντες ὑμῶν τὸ βέβαιον θαυμάζουσιν τῆς πίστεως, ὥστε καὶ προτροπὴν ἑτέροις γενέσθαι τὰ ὑμέτερα, *i.e.* "They all know how much you have suffered for your faith and they all marvel at the steadfastness of your faith, so that these things concerning you have also become an encouragement to others"; Theodoret of Cyrrhus, *Interpretatio Epistolae ad Thessalonicensis primae*, sub 1:8, [ed. J.-P. Migne, *P.G.*, LXXXII, p. 632]: τούτων ἡ περὶ τὰ θεῖα προθυμία πολυθρύλλητος γενομένη πολλοὺς εἰς ζῆλον τῆς εὐσεβείας ἐκίνησεν, *i.e.* "Their earnestness in sacred matters having become generally known moved many to a zeal for piety"; and Chrysostom, *I Thess. Homil.*, sub 1:8, [ed. Bern. de Montfaucon, XI, p. 433]: τῆς ὑμετέρας ἀνδρείας ἡ φήμη, *i.e.* "the report of your manliness [had gone forth]." In more recent times the phrase has also been read this way by Findlay, *Thess.*, p. 26: "The *effect*, rather than the mere fact of the conversion of the Thessalonians, made the Good News 'ring out from' them."

82 *Cf.* Rigaux, *Thess.*, p. 386: "leur foi, c'est-à-dire, comme 9 et 10 vont l'expliquer, leur réception des apôtres et leur conversion, est connue et louée par tous"; and p. 387: "πίστις est la même chose que le δεξάμενοι τὸν λόγον du verset 6."

which he himself admits at first glance seems to be the proper one can not be sustained.

We have postponed until now the consideration of the persons which were imitated, since it seemed best to attempt first to come to some clarity as to the specific point in which the imitation lay. Paul says that the Thessalonians had become imitators "of us." Who is the *us*? Is it Paul, Silvanus, and Timothy, the three who had addressed the congregation in the salutation of the letter (1:1)? Does he mean that they had become imitators of "the three of us"? Or is the *us* a term for himself, either himself to the exclusion of the other two, or at least himself primarily?

Paul's use of *we, us,* and *our* in his epistles has called forth considerable discussion. [83] In none of Paul's epistles is the plural more consistently used than in these two letters to the Thessalonians. The first person singular appears in them only five times: I Thess. 2:18; 3:5; 5:27; II Thess. 2:5; 3:17. Grammatically there is no objection to understanding the plural as expressing the singular. This had become acceptable usage in later Greek and can be found in ordinary correspondence of Paul's day. [84] However, in the Thessalonian letters it is hardly the most natural reading to understand *we* as meaning simply *I, Paul*. That Paul was the actual author of the letters is clear from the places where the singular is used, especially in I Thess. 2:18 and II Thess. 3:17, where he calls himself by name. But both letters begin, "Paul, and Silvanus, and Timothy, unto the church of the Thessalonians.... We give thanks...." The *we* takes on even more of its normal plural meaning when compared with several of Paul's other letters which are addressed from several persons but turn immediately to the use of *I* in the substance of the letter. [85] *We* in Thessalonians can hardly be interpreted as leaving Silvanus and Timothy completely out of the picture. Does this mean, however, that Paul uses *we* in these letters because he has in mind that he is speaking also for Silvanus and Timothy? [86] Rigaux, in studying the first person plurals in the Thessalonian letters, has classified them in three groups: those referring to (a) Paul together with his readers or with Christians in general; (b) Paul, Silvanus, and Timothy, the three missionaries; and (c) Paul, where it is hard to say whether he has others in mind together with himself or not. In regard to these latter, doubtful cases, Rigaux finds that the accent of the passages is on the individual, and that their style is adapted to Paul. [87] He concludes that when Paul chooses to speak

---

83 For a summary of the discussion until 1900, *cf.* K. Dick, *Der Schriftstellerische Plural bei Paulus*, Halle a. S: Max Niemeyer, 1900, pp. 4—14. Dick's very thorough study of the subject, however, did not put an end to the discussion. *Cf.* Rigaux, *Thess.*, p. 77f., fn. 6, for a bibliography of the discussion since Dick's monograph.

84 *Cf.* Dick's chapter, "Das Zeugnis späteren Gräcität für den schriftstellerischen Plural," *Plural*, pp. 15—32; and for further confirmation from the papyri, G. Milligan, *Thess.*, pp. 131,132. Moulton, *Gram.*, I, pp. 86,87, comments, "It would seem that the question must be passed on from the grammarian to the exegete; for our grammatical material gives us not the slightest evidence of any distinction between the two numbers in writing."

85 I Cor. 1:4; Gal. 1:6; Phil. 1:3; Philemon 4.

86 Milligan, *Thess.*, p. 132, speaks of "a closer and more continuous joint-authorship than was always the case at other times," and Findlay, *Thess.*, p. xl, sees Paul as "conscious of expressing and seeking to express the mind of his companions, and more particularly of Silas, throughout."

87 Rigaux, *Thess.*, pp. 78,79.

in terms of *we* even in these instances, one can detect his resolute intention to make of the apostolic witness a group witness and a group work. He submerges himself in the group and prefers to disappear in the group. His use of *we* might best be described as the plural of apostolic witness.[88] Von Dobschütz also observes that while Silas and Timothy may have been in mind, they have no prerogatives whatever.[89] Hence, when in the beginning of the first letter we come upon such expressions as "our gospel" (1:5), "what manner of men we showed ourselves toward you" (1:5), and "ye became imitators of us" (1:6), we are not confronted with something other than Paul himself, or with Paul and two others completely on a par with him. It is simply the Apostle Paul, here speaking of himself in terms of the team which he led and with which he found himself completely united in bringing the apostolic witness to the Thessalonians. The Thessalonians had become imitators "of us," *i.e.* of the missionaries who had brought the gospel to them, but particularly of Paul himself, the leader and dominating figure.

When Paul referred to the Thessalonians as imitators of himself and his companions in their undergoing affliction with joy, it must have aroused some vivid recollections to the first readers. The full impact of this is lost to those who did not know him and did not live through the situation. The only real information we have on what happened at Thessalonica is Luke's mention in Acts 17:5ff. of the crowd that had been aroused by jealous Jews and sought to lay their hands on Paul and Silas, so that it became expedient to send Paul and Silas away immediately (17:10). This was undoubtedly only the culmination of a situation which had been growing increasingly adverse. At least, the Thessalonians had seen and known Paul in the midst of his afflictions. How much they knew about Paul's experiences elsewhere is difficult to say. That they knew about the public beating, imprisonment in Philippi, and the attempt by the officials to get them out of the city without further notice is clear from I Thess. 2:2 (*cf.* Acts 16:19ff.). There is the implication in I Thess. 2:15,16 that they knew about the suffering Paul had endured at the hands of the Jews. They must also have known about the activities of the Thessalonian Jews against Paul in Berea (Acts 17:13), and possibly something of the mocking at Athens and the further troubles at Corinth. That this is only a small fraction of the instances about which they might have known is clear from the book of Acts. That Acts too is only a partial record of Paul's labors and the attending difficulties is clear from

---

[88] "Les premières personnes de nos lettres sont commandées par une intention bien particulière. Paul se retire du groupe apostolique pour insister sur ses volontés ou ses actions personelles.... Le sens des 'nous' est plus subtil. Il n'y a pas un seul pluriel qui ne puisse être véritable. Dans les cas ... où l'on pourrait douter, tant le ton est individuel et le style propre à Paul, on ne lira qu'une accentuation plus nette de cette volonté apostolique, qui présente le message chrétien comme l'oeuvre du groupe tout entier. La fonction, l'oeuvre, la prédication communes priment sur l'individu. Tout entier à l'évangile, Paul préfère disparaître dans le groupe. C'est pourquoi, quand il envoie une lettre, il y joint ceux qui ont oeuvré avec lui.... On pourra penser ... à un pluriel d'apostolat et de témoignage" (*Ibid.*, p. 79).

[89] "Man wird also dem Gefühl, das Paulus dies 'Wir' in die Feder diktierte, am ehesten gerecht werden, wenn man zunächst immer nur an ihn selber denkt, daneben bald an diese, bald an jene Kategorie, mit der er sich solidarisch fühlt. Die 'Mitverfasser' kommen dabei höchstens mit in Betracht, haben aber gar keine Prärogative" (von Dobschütz, *Thess.*, p. 68).

such characterizations as Paul gives of his life in I Cor. 4:11ff.; II Cor. 4:7ff.; 6:4ff.; and especially in the summary Paul makes of his apostolic labors and sufferings in II Cor. 11:23ff. Who ever lived in more constant affliction for the sake of the gospel! And yet, Paul's letters show that in the midst of all this suffering and affliction there was a deep rejoicing filling all his life; *cf.* such statements as Rom. 5:3; 12:12; II Cor. 6:10; 7:4; 13:9; Col. 1:24; etc. Luke presents the same picture of Paul, persecuted and driven out of the city (Acts 13:50), and yet "filled with joy and with the Holy Spirit" (13:52). Paul was a picture of Christian joy in the communities where he traveled. This joy which could express itself even in the midst of suffering was an anomaly which the non-Christian world found totally baffling. It was a Christian possession and stemmed from salvation in Christ. The Christian's union with his Lord, possession of his Spirit, and participation in his kingdom all called forth this eschatological reality.[90] The Christian became supremely happy, serenely at peace, and filled with the greatest hopes for the future. His participation in salvation was reflected in the joy that filled his life in spite of and even in the midst of adversity and suffering. Possession of the Holy Spirit brightened his whole life, and nothing could succeed in darkening it. The Thessalonians had seen this in Paul. They had learned what kind of men he and his companions were and what were the inner resources which accounted for their type of life. They had listened to the preaching of these men and heard its "good tidings of great joy." They had also heard about Jesus' words that "in the world ye have tribulation" (John 16:33). They had responded to the gospel, receiving it willingly, "in much affliction with joy of the Holy Spirit." In this they had adopted the Christian way of life which they had not only heard but seen portrayed to them. "Ye became imitators of us."

Paul adds that they had become imitators also of the Lord. The structure of the Greek sentence with the verb intervening before "and of the Lord" suggests that this was a thought added to the former one, rather than an integral part of it: καὶ ὑμεῖς μιμηταὶ ἡμῶν ἐγενήθητε καὶ τοῦ κυρίου. The matter has called forth a variety of proposals and explanations.

> Stanley finds Paul calling them imitators of the Lord "only as a kind of afterthought."[91] Others have proposed that it is in the nature of a self-correction, like that found in I Cor. 15:10: "I labored more abundantly than they all: yet not I, but the grace of God which was in me." Various reasons for such a correcting of himself have been found, such as, a sudden sense of humility and reserve in the face of so high a position as being an example,[92] a desire to be seen as bearers of Christ,[93] a

---

[90] H. Preisker, *Das Ethos des Urchristentums*, Gütersloh: C. Bertelsmann, 1949, p. 134, fn. 1, defines joy and cites the Biblical evidence as follows: "Es [χαρά] ist die innere seelische Zuversicht mitten im Leid auf Grund endzeitlicher Erfahrung u. Hoffnung; vgl. Mt 5,12; Lk 6,23; 10,20; Mt 25,23; 28,8; Lk 10,17; Joh 15,11; 16,20.24; Apg 13,52; Röm 14,17; 15,13; 2 Kor 1,24; Gal 5,22; Phil 1,18; 1,25; 1 Thess 1,6; Hebr 12,2; Jak 1,2; 1 Petr 1,8; 1 Joh 1,4; 2 Joh 12."

[91] Stanley, *Biblica* XL, p. 866.

[92] Von Dobschütz, *Thess.*, p. 72; E. Eidem, "Imitatio Pauli," *Teoligiska Studier Tillägnade Erik Stave*, Uppsala: Almquist & Wiksells, 1922, p. 75.

[93] Dibelius, *Thess.*, p. 5.

profound sense of being "in Christ," so that they could speak of themselves and Christ in the same breath without self-consciousness. [94] Some have been struck by the remarkable order which places Christ in second place, and have commented upon this being the historical order for learning imitation. [95] Several have appealed to I Cor. 11:1, making some observation about the imitation of Paul being dependent on the fact that Paul himself was an imitator of Christ. [96] Calvin saw a parallel in another passage, namely Exod. 14:31, where it says that the people "believed in Jehovah, and in his servant Moses." Calvin comments that it is not as though Paul and Moses had anything different from God, but their names are added because God had worked powerfully through them, as his ministers and instruments. [97] Thus, Calvin's explanation of the addition "and of the Lord" is that it served to indicate the power and authority behind Paul. Such is also the view of Hadorn: "es ist... der Regressus auf den Autor: die Gemeinde, Paulus, der Herr"; and he sees in this a polemic bent on establishing the fact that Paul's Christianity was indeed the Christianity of Christ. [98] None of these proposals, however, appears to be either highly objectionable or strongly appealing. Michaelis' judgment commends itself as well as any: "Die Koordination, in der Paulus und der Herr hier genannt werden, hebt nicht auf, dass καὶ τοῦ κυρίου als Steigerung empfunden werden muss, sei es, dass es sich um eine Art Selbstkorrektur handelt..., sei es, dass die der Gemeinde gewährte Anerkennung vertieft und erweitert werden soll." [99] The argument which can be raised against the addition being a self-correction is that there are other occasions where Paul directly calls for the imitation of himself and makes no attempt at correction (cf. II Thess. 3:7—9; I Cor. 4:16; Phil. 3:17). Thus the alternative explanation seems preferable. Paul had in fact been an example to them; they had in fact become imitators of him. There is no attempt to de-emphasize or detract from this relationship between the Thessalonians and Paul. But one could pursue the matter further. The roots of their Christian conduct spread broader and deeper than the area of influence which the missionaries had exerted over them. They had been influenced by the example of the Lord himself. [100] Their conduct was an imitation also of him. [101]

---

94 W. Neil, *The Epistle of Paul to the Thessalonians*, M.N.T.C., London: Hodder & Stoughton, 1950, pp. 18,19.
95 Cf. e.g. L. Morris, *The First and Second Epistles to the Thessalonians*, N.I.C.N.T., Grand Rapids: Wm. B. Eerdmans, 1959, p. 58; Neil, *Thess.*, p. 18; Lenski, *Thess.*, p. 228.
96 Cf. Rigaux, *Thess.*, p. 381; Keulers, *Brieven v. Paulus*, I, p. 25; K. Staab and J. Freundorfer, *Die Thessalonicherbriefe, die Gefangenschaftsbriefe und die Pastoralbriefe*, Regensburg: Fr. Pustet, 1950, p. 15; E. G. Gulin, *Die Freude im Neuen Testament*, 1. Teil: *Jesus, Urgemeinde, Paulus*, Helsinki, 1932, p. 236. While this thought may be true, the words of this passage do not directly say this. The Thessalonians could only have understood it thus if it recalled to them one of Paul's specific teachings during his mission among them. It becomes clear from II Thess. 3:6,7 that Paul had spoken specifically about the imitation of himself to the Thessalonians; see below, pp. 136f. It is not unlikely that he spoke about the imitation of Christ and about his personal imitation of him.
97 Calvin, *I Thess.*, sub 1:6.
98 W. Hadorn, *Die Abfassung der Thessalonicherbriefe in der Zeit der dritten Missionsreise des Paulus*, Gütersloh: C. Bertelsmann, 1919, p. 39.
99 Michaelis, T.W.N.T., IV, p. 672, 30—34.
100 Cf. the version of I Thess. 1:6 which Ambrosiaster uses in his commentary: "Et vos imitatores nostri facti estis, et ipsius Domini" ("Commentaria in XIII Epistolas Beati Pauli," *Ad Opera Sancti Ambrosii, Appendix*, [ed. J.-P. Migne, P.L., XVII, p. 467]); and the Latin commentary of Theodore of Mopsuestia on I Thess. 1:6: "in pressuris non solum imitare apostolos uidentur, sed et ipsum Dominum" (ed. Swete, II, p. 5).
101 Frame's translation (*Thess.*, p. 82) "and above all of the Lord" seems to depreciate Paul's example more than is necessary.

The imitation has to do with the suffering of afflictions. Hence the reference here is to Jesus in his earthly life of suffering. He had taught in a most striking manner that the afflictions and hardships which would come to those following him were an occasion for great rejoicing (*cf.* Matt. 5:11,12; Luke 6:22,23). The picture of his life had been no less striking than his teaching. While the gospels seldom speak expressly about his rejoicing, [102] they show him as one completely possessed of joy, willingly giving of himself, and living in calm confidence and sure triumph even in the midst of the most adverse circumstances. At his last supper with his disciples, in the face of his own death, he could speak about not drinking the fruit of the vine anymore, "until that day when I drink it new in the kingdom of God" (Mark 14:25, par.). He viewed the dreadful things which were about to happen as being no threat or hindrance whatsoever to the coming of the kingdom. When the disciples had all fled in fear, Jesus could still stand before the high priest and the whole Jewish council and say, "Ye shall see the Son of Man sitting at the right hand of Power, and coming with the clouds of heaven" (Mark 14:62, par.). His confidence remained to the end, and he died commending his spirit into the hands of his Father (Luke 23:46). He met his afflictions and sufferings in the spirit of utter triumph. It was a striking picture for his followers later to contemplate.

It ought not to be overlooked that Paul calls the Thessalonians imitators of *the Lord* (κυρίου). Since the imitation has reference to Jesus in his earthly life of suffering, we might have expected the use of the name *Jesus* or the title *the Christ* instead of *the Lord*. [103] Paul does occasionally use the term *Lord* to apply to Jesus as he lived here on earth. [104] However, its regular usage by the time of Paul was "as a brief and comprehensive description of Jesus as the Divine Lord, risen, glorified, and exalted." [105] As Phil. 2:6–11 shows, the name *Lord* was given to him as God's answer (διό, vs. 9) to the whole process of his voluntary humiliation, suffering, and death. Milligan has nicely stated the significance of the addition "and of the Lord," when he describes it as "pointing not merely to the supreme pattern to be copied, but to the living power in which alone this 'imitation' could be accomplished,

---

102 There is a notable instance in Luke 10:21: "He rejoiced in the Holy Spirit." Plummer remarks, "Nowhere else is anything of the kind recorded of Christ" (A. Plummer, *A Critical and Exegetical Commentary on the Gospel according to S. Luke*, 5th ed., I.C.C., Edinburgh, T. & T. Clark, 1922, p. 281). There follow Jesus' words about hiding things from the wise and understanding and revealing them to babes. This saying is found in a quite different context in Matthew (11:25–27). It is not possible to speak with certainty about the historical situation calling forth these words. However, the saying bears such obvious marks of the struggle with the Jewish religious leaders that we can detect something of the atmosphere of affliction in which this rejoicing took place.

103 The reading χριστοῦ does appear in two late miniscules (39 [11th cent.] and 10 [13th cent.]), possibly under the influence of I Cor. 11:1. A much earlier alternate reading is found in θεοῦ, appearing in Codex Alexandrinus and in some manuscripts of the Sahidic version. (For the latter, *cf.* J. L. Koole, *Studien zum koptischen Bibeltext*, [*Beihefte zur Z.N.W.* 17], Berlin: Alfred Töpelmann, 1936, pp. 33, 82, 100.) The only explanation that suggests itself for either of these alternate readings is that of attempting to clarify the ambiguous κυρίου. The same thing is found elsewhere; see *e.g.*, Col. 3:13.

104 G. Quell and W. Foerster, κύριος, *T.W.N.T.*, III, p. 1092, 7ff.

105 Milligan, *Thess.*, p. 138. Cf. Quell-Foerster, *T.W.N.T.*, III, pp. 1087–1090.

and man's highest end successfully reached." [106] Paul's own example of joyous bearing of affliction for the sake of the gospel was of great significance to the Thessalonians. Their personal contact with him had made his example vivid and powerful. But the example of the Lord involved breadths and depths and heights far beyond Paul's. It was the example of a man who had not only faced suffering and death triumphantly, but who had also overcome death itself and had been crowned with everlasting life. He had now reached the destiny for which man was made. The Thessalonians had become imitators of that Lord in the sufferings which they were facing, and they could do so with joy, because they had become sharers in his victory. They had taken up the imitation of him with a steadfastness of hope in this Lord Jesus Christ (*cf.* 1:3). Here was again proof of their salvation and of their election.

The question arises again as to whether this imitation was conscious and intentional or not. The question remains impossible of definite answer. The only thing we learn from Paul's words is that the influence of what Jesus had done and been in the midst of his sufferings could be detected in their lives. They were showing a resemblance to him, and his resemblance was not mere coincidence. By their own confession, he held an influential place in their lives. He was their Savior and their Lord. They knew him, loved him, and worshipped him. Naturally the pattern of his conduct while on earth was held in high esteem. When faced with similar situations, consciously or unconsciously, the Thessalonian converts became imitators of him.

\* \* \*

Certain observations can be made on the basis of our study of I Thess. 1:6 and its allied text, I Thess. 2 : 14. Among the passages where Paul speaks expressly of the imitation, these two texts are unique. Paul elsewhere urges the importance of imitating him, and several times he makes of it an appeal and a call to action. Here he acknowledges it as an accomplished fact: "You became imitators." It was an element in the whole complex of facts which he had learned in regard to the Christian church at Thessalonica and which had made him so supremely happy and so abundantly thankful. Twice over he acknowledges the fact in the long expression of thanksgiving that flows forth from his pen in his letter to the Thessalonian church.

The fact that the Thessalonians had become imitators was an extremely important part in the whole complex of facts that made him thankful. The imitation was the open proof of their Christianity. In I Thess. 1:6 he cites the imitation as an evidence of the Thessalonians' election and as an instance of the fullness with which the gospel had come to them. In I Thess. 2:14 the imitation is seen in essentially the same way, namely, as a confirmation of their true acceptance of the word and of God's having worked in them. Paul rejoiced with thanksgiving to God when he could detect imitation, for then it was apparent that the gospel had taken root and sprung to life.

The proof of election and of divine working in the lives of the Thessalonians

---

[106] Milligan, *loc. cit.*

was not in the act of imitation as such. This would seem to be self-evident. The imitation that Paul found so significant can not be divorced from the content in which the imitation consisted. In other words, it was not a formal and a general relationship that Paul found so worthy of note, but a material and specific one. According to I Thess. 2:14 there was cause for thanksgiving in the fact that the Thessalonians were standing firm in their faith in the face of the suffering and persecution directed against them because of their commitment to Christ. According to I Thess. 1:6 the cause for thanksgiving is essentially the same, except that now one more element comes to expression. They had not only committed themselves to Christ with full knowledge of the suffering it would involve; they had faced the suffering with a deep sense of joy. Such events were incontestable proof of election and salvation.

In giving due account to the importance of the content of the imitation, however, the significance of the fact of imitation as such must not be overlooked. The full matter has not been stated when we say that the Thessalonian Christians endured suffering. They endured suffering in imitation of Paul, the Lord, and the Judean churches. It is not that the element of imitation somehow added to the virtue or importance of the suffering. The element of imitation rather points to the means by which they came to accept the suffering and endure it with steadfastness and joy. They adopted the stance of a resolute facing and bearing of sufferings as though such a stance were the most natural thing in the world. And for them as Christians, it actually was the most natural thing in the world, for they were living in imitation of Paul, the Lord, and the Judean churches.

We have noticed how the suffering of the Thessalonian Christians could really be an imitation of others. As an imitation it was in no sense artificial or put on; it was no less genuine for being an imitation. It was an imitation in the deep and basic sense of the word; it was a bringing to expression in their own lives of what they had seen and detected outside of themselves. [107] It was a capturing of something they had witnessed around them and making it a part of themselves. Paul had made them aware of the way of life that involved humiliation, suffering, non-retaliation, steadfast faithfulness to God and his Christ, and patient endurance of opposition and adversity. Christ had portrayed it, preached it, and called men to it in his call to follow him. Paul had made this eminently clear in Thessalonica in his presentation of Christ's teaching, Christ's call, and Christ's portrayal of these things. Paul had also shown this way portrayed in the early Christians and churches in Judea. And finally, he had been a most graphic and living portrayal of this way himself. This was the Christian way as Christ, the Judean churches and Paul portrayed and lived it. When the Thessalonians became Christians, this is the Christianity they knew, and this is the Christianity they adopted. They began walking the Christian way; they brought to expression in their lives the Christianity that had been pictured to them. They imitated those who were their Christian elders and parents.

---

[107] See above, pp. 1—8.

The power of the example of Paul, Christ, and the Judean churches over the Thessalonians is not to be traced to some intrinsic appeal in the example or in the way presented. Imitation was not the result of moral appeal or the compulsion of moral superiority. The Thessalonians' imitation was no case of moralism. It was rather a case of natural and normal growth and development in view of their situation. Their becoming Christians was effected through a divine working (I Thess. 2:14). It happened when the gospel worked in them in power, in the Holy Spirit, and in much fullness (I Thess. 1:5). They became united to Christ, participants in his salvation, and members of his family. There is a homogeneity in Christianity in virtue of all members sharing their life and union in Christ. Thus, one group of Christians could establish a pattern for others. We have noticed how the Judean churches by reason of their primacy of origin established a pattern for other Christian churches that sprang from them and came after them. The term "mother-church" has its appropriateness here, even though Paul did not use it. The daughter in Thessalonica adopted the pattern of life which her mother in Judea had established. It was not the morality, goodness, and virtue of the Judean Christian way that moved the Thessalonians to adopt their way. Rather, the Thessalonian babe learned what the Christian way of life was from her elders in Judea, and she began imitating them.

The same relation existed between the Thessalonians and Paul, and on this Paul was more specific. He saw himself as a nursing mother, lovingly caring for her children (I Thess. 2:7), and as a father, guiding and encouraging them (I Thess. 2:11). Paul viewed himself as the spiritual parent of the Thessalonian Christians. He mentioned their imitation of him in the same breath with recalling how completely he had acted in their behalf ("for your sake," I Thess. 1:5) while among them. This close relationship of love and parental devotion had resulted in imitation. The children were bringing the Christianity of their father to expression.

In I Thess. 1:6 the imitation of Christ is placed alongside of that of Paul. There is obviously an intensification of the example in Christ, although as we have seen, this makes the imitation of Paul none the less vital or real. In regard to the imitation of Christ, this verse is the earliest record of the term that we now possess. There is no way of knowing whether Paul coined the term or not. It must be admitted at least that it fits most appropriately and beautifully into the context in which Paul has placed it. The Thessalonians in their joyful acceptance and bearing of sufferings had become imitators of Christ. They were bringing to expression in their lives the very way that he had portrayed so beautifully and walked so perfectly.

It has long been a puzzle how to account for the change in terminology from the gospels' speaking of following Jesus to Paul's speaking of imitating him. Kahmann has recently suggested a bridge.[108] The following of Jesus which continued to have particular import after his earthly life was the following of his way of humiliation, suffering, self-denial, and cross-bearing.

---

108 Kahmann, *T.v.T.*, I, p. 224.

On this score there was a kind of mystical reaching back to the time before his death and continuing in living fellowship with him as he then walked. In regard to this same living in the way of humiliation, suffering, self-denial, and cross-bearing, we find Paul speaking in terms of imitation. The change of viewpoint is but slight. The tendency had been to think of Christians as joining in Christ's way of suffering by mystically continuing to walk with him during his earthly days. Paul proposes that Christians look to Christ in his earthly days, study his way, and then, in virtue of their being united to Christ, bring Christ and his way to expression in their lives by imitation. To combine the ideas of cross-bearing and imitating in place of cross-bearing and following is but a slight adaptation of the old thought to the new situation. The adaptation might very well have originated with Paul, since among New Testament writers the use of the word imitation is almost limited to him. Also in view of Paul's never having enjoyed the privilege of walking with Christ during his earthly days, perhaps it is more likely that he would propose a substitute term for following. The bridge between following Jesus and imitating him may well be, as Kahmann suggests, the continuing fact of the Christian's being involved in sufferings for Christ's sake. [109]

## II. II Thessalonians 3:7—9

*For yourselves know how ye ought to imitate us: for we behaved not ourselves disorderly among you; neither did we eat bread for nought at any man's hand, but in labor and travail, working night and day, that we might not burden any of you: not because we have not the right, but to make ourselves an ensample unto you, that ye should imitate us.*

The high praise which Paul had for the Thessalonian church in his first epistle to them did not mean that there were no problems in the congregation. Neither were these problems simply the kind that arose from ignorance or misunderstanding. There were traces of insubordination, willful disobedience, and rebellion among the brethren in Thessalonica. In addressing himself to this matter in the second letter, Paul again refers to the Thessalonians' imitation of him. This time his words do not have a complimentary and joyful tone. Now he is not speaking happily about what they have done. Rather he is admonishing them and pleading with them about what they ought to do. Imitation now is not an observable fact, but a call to activity.

In his second letter to the Thessalonians Paul calls the congregation to take decisive steps toward rectifying an unwholesome situation that existed there. Some of the group were "walking disorderly" (περιπατεῖν ἀτάκτως, II Thess. 3:6,11). He had spoken of the matter also in the first letter. There

---

[109] "Misschien kan men zeggen, dat de lijn van het evangelische 'volgen' naar het paulinische 'navolgen' loopt via de idee van het lijden om Christus' wil" (Kahmann, *T.v.T.*, I, p. 224).

he called them to "admonish the disorderly" (I Thess. 5:14) and appealed to them all that they exercise more diligence in living calmly, that they tend to their own affairs, and that they work with their hands (I Thess. 4:11). These latter counsels he repeats in effect in the second letter, this time directing them specifically to the disorderly persons: "Now them that are such [*i.e.* the disorderly, *cf.* vs. 11] we command and exhort in the Lord Jesus Christ, that with quietness they work, and eat their own bread" (II Thess. 3:12). However, the command of the first letter to admonish the disorderly has changed in the second letter to a command to separate from them (3:6) and to have no further company with them (3:14). Paul had clearly taught from the beginning of his contact with the Thessalonians that the Christian way of life included a duty to work (*cf.* I Thess. 4:11; II Thess. 3:10).[110] This instruction had been disregarded. Furthermore, the admonitions of the first letter had apparently gone unheeded. The situation now called for the more drastic steps of withdrawal and separation. In addition to the problems which the disorderly were causing within the church fellowship, they were having an adverse effect on the church's witness to others. Their conduct was unbecoming in view of the impressions that were being made on non-Christians (*cf.* I Thess. 4:11,12). The command to withdraw from the disorderly persons thus becomes doubly appropriate, since such a withdrawal would make it clear both within the church and without that such disorderly conduct was at odds with Christian profession.[111]

The exact nature of the disorderliness is not clear. The most obvious fact about the whole situation is that some were not working (II Thess. 3:11). Possibly this had reduced them to poverty so that they were dependent upon others providing them the necessities of life. Or possibly for some reason they considered that they had a right to receive support from others. At least Paul's command that they eat *their own* (ἑαυτῶν) bread (3:12) implies that they were living off others. His comment that he had not eaten bread for nought at any man's hand, but rather had worked hard in order not to burden them (3:8), points in the same direction. Furthermore, these people who were not working had apparently not become inactive, but had rather become involved in a frenzy of activity. Paul calls them busybodies (περιεργαζομένους, 3:12); he charges them to tend to their own business (πράσσειν τὰ ἴδια, I Thess. 4:11); and he counsels them to calmness (ἡσυχάζειν, I Thess. 4:11; ἡσυχίας, II Thess. 3:12). The further details of the situation, however, are not so easily determined.

The disorderliness in Thessalonica has often been seen as connected with

---

110 The παρηγγείλαμεν (I Thess. 4:11) and παρηγγέλλομεν (II.3:10) echo the παραγγελίας of I.4:2: "... ye received of us how ye ought to walk and to please God.... For ye know what charge (παραγγελίας) we gave you through the Lord Jesus" (4:1,2). Hence the command to work formed a part of the regular preaching and instruction of Paul to the Thessalonians, probably, as van Leeuwen, *Thess.*, p. 450, remarks, "om een averechtsche opvatting van de vrijheid, die in Christus is, af te snijden en te voorkomen." At least the command gives no indication that Paul could detect the beginnings of the disorderliness already during his stay in Thessalonica.

111 *Cf.* D. van Swigchem, *Het Missionar Karakter van de Christelijke Gemeente volgens de Brieven van Paulus en Petrus*, Kampen: J. H. Kok, 1955, p. 116.

the eschatological interests and problems of that congregation. Some kind of connection does indeed appear quite likely, for the two matters lie in such close proximity to each other in both letters. In the first letter Paul proceeds from his exhortation to work (4:11,12) to his instruction about the resurrection of the dead and the return of the Lord (4:13—5:11); and then he returns to further exhortations, including the one to admonish the disorderly (5:14). In the second letter the matter of the disorderliness (3:6ff.) follows closely upon the section concerning the eschatological events pertaining to the day of the Lord (2:1—12). However, in spite of the close proximity in which he places these two matters, the connectives which lead from the one to the other do not indicate what the nature of the relationship was, or even that there was one. It can be established only by inference.

Many have found the disorderliness related to an excitement over the imminent return of the Lord. [112] They propose that probably some of the Thessalonians lost all incentive to keep on with the ordinary daily routines in view of the near end of the world, according to their expectations. Prayer, spiritual reflection, and religious discussion may suddenly have become matters worthy of full-time pursuit by them. Constant religious discussion could easily have degenerated into great speculation about eschatological matters and may have resulted in much confusion and doubt. Possibly the excited brethren had become very zealous in alerting the whole community to what was about to happen and in pleading with them to flee from the wrath to come. Von Dobschütz presses further for details of the situation, taking a cue from the ancient writers' use of ἡσυχάζειν and πράσσειν τὰ ἴδια to describe the retiring from civic affairs and the pursuit of reflective study in the quiet of private life. [113] On the basis of this usage of the words he suggests that the Thessalonians may not only have been out in the public places making propaganda for Christianity and warning men of Christ's return, but even mingling in public affairs with a view to promoting Christian eschatological interests. Hence the command to be quiet (ἡσυχάζειν) and to do their own business (πράσσειν τὰ ἴδια) would have been to the point. Frame has pointed out the weakness of this proposal: "The Thessalonians are not philosophers but working people, and the context (περὶ τῆς φιλαδελφίας [I Thess. 4:9]) points to church rather than to public affairs." [114] However, in disagreeing

---

112 Cf. von Dobschütz, Thess., p. 182: "Danach ist es die gespannte Enderwartung, welche Christen zu diesem unordentlichen Lebenswandel verführt, d. h. dazu statt dem regelmässigen Broterwerb nachzugehen, sich im Vertrauen auf die baldige Umgestaltung aller Verhältnisse um die irdischen Dinge nicht zu bekümmern, und dafür viel von Gott und seinen bevorstehenden Machttaten zu reden, auch wohl mit solchen eschatologischen Spekulationen in die Öffentlichkeit sich vorzuwagen und hier eine geschäftige Propaganda zu treiben." W. Lütgert, *Die Vollkommenen im Philipperbrief und Die Enthusiasten in Thessalonich*, (B.z.F.c.T., 13,6), Gütersloh: C. Bertelsmann, 1909, p. 72, calls this type of explanation the traditional one and mentions as proponents of it Neander, Baur, Holtzmann, Weiss, Weizsäcker. Since Lütgert's time the tradition has continued; cf. Milligan, Thess., p. 154; Frame, Thess., p. 160; Van Leeuwen, Thess., p. 286, cf. p. 450; Lenski, Thess., p. 322; Neil, Thess., p. 87; Hendriksen, Thess., p. 105; Masson, Thess., p. 52; Morris, Thess., (N.I.C.), p. 251; et al.

113 Von Dobschütz, Thess., pp. 179,180; cf. the usages in Plato, *The Republic*, VI, 496D; IV, 433A; and Dio Cassius, 60,27.

114 Frame, Thess., p. 161.

with von Dobschütz over whether the disturbance from the disorderly persons was limited to the church or extended to the public in general, Frame sees no difficulty in the main thrust of the proposal. For him the exhortations to quietness are a reflection of "the excitement created in the minds of some by the expectation that the day of the Lord was at hand." [115]

This very popular and traditional explanation of the state of affairs at Thessalonica calls for further scrutiny. Obviously the exhortations to quietness reflect a state of unquietness, excitement, and maybe even fanaticism among some of the Thessalonians. The excitement and the eschatological problems and concerns are probably not unrelated. However, on what basis are we to conclude that the disorderliness stems from an expectation of the imminent return of Christ? Paul does not make this connection, and what he does say about eschatological matters provides a very meagre basis for inferring it. In the first letter immediately following the exhortations to quietness, tending their own business, and working with their hands (4:11), he turns to giving instruction "concerning them that fall asleep" (4:13ff.). The instruction is no attempt at explaining or giving reasons for the foregoing exhortations. It is simply a new section and another subject. [116] It is an eschatological matter on which Paul gives further information, but the atmosphere in which the matter was viewed in Thessalonica was surely not one of excitement. Rather, it was sorrow over death and a fear that the dead would be at some kind of disadvantage over against those who survived until the Lord's coming. While the section may reflect that there was a hope and expectation among the Thessalonians to live until the Lord's return, there is no indication here of their excitement over the immediate nearness of it. Paul proceeds from this matter to another eschatological matter, namely, that "concerning the times and the seasons" (5:1ff.). Here his tone changes from that of instructing to that of admonishing. One detects here not an atmosphere of excitement over the imminency of the Lord's return, but rather a tendency toward unconcern, inattentiveness, and negligence. The call is to avoid going to sleep or falling into a drunken stupor; "let us watch and be sober" (5:6). Where in the first letter do we find indications of such an excitement over the return of Christ that men would be inclined to lay aside all earthly concerns and give themselves completely to spiritual concerns while they were waiting?

Is there evidence for such excitement in the second letter? It is customary to find it in II Thess. 2:2: "to the end that ye be not quickly shaken from your mind, or yet be troubled, . . . as that the day of the Lord is just at hand." This translation (A.S.V. [117]) of the latter clause is hardly a true rendering of the Greek: ὡς ὅτι ἐνέστηκεν ἡ ἡμέρα τοῦ κυρίου; it is more a commentary than a translation. [118] The R.S.V. is a definite improvement:

---

115 *Loc. cit.*
116 "In loser Verknüpfung bringt Paulus ein neues Stück, das seines bedarf, vor" (von Dobschütz, *Thess.*, p. 184). So also Frame, *Thess.*, p. 163.
117 The *K.J.V.* amounts to the same thing: "as that the day of Christ is at hand."
118 "'Ἐνέστηκεν, est la . . . ; c'est la seule traduction valable. Traduire: imminent est un commentaire" (Rigaux, *Thess.*, p. 653).

"to the effect that the day of the Lord has come," as is also the N.E.B.: "alleging that the Day of the Lord is already here." Frame correctly explains, "ἐνέστηκεν means not 'is coming' (ἔρχεται, I.5:2), not 'is at hand' (ἤγγικεν, Rom. 13:12), not 'is near' (ἐγγύς ἐστιν, Phil. 4:5), but 'has come,' 'is on hand,' 'is present.'" [119] The inclination by both translators and commentators to make "is present" to mean "is at hand" probably comes "from the supposed necessity of the case rather than from any grammatical compulsion." [120] As von Dobschütz has noted, it is inconceivable that the Thessalonians in the midst of all their persecutions and afflictions (cf. II Thess. 1:4) should even have been open to the suggestion that the day of the Lord was already there in any real sense of the word, that is, as a day of judgment and of salvation. [121] On the other hand, if the imminency of the Lord's return is what is causing the unrest in Thessalonica, and if Paul wished to set their minds at rest over this possibility of the immediate return of Christ, we must conclude that Paul expressed himself most ineptly here. Paul's answer to the confusion that existed over the day of the Lord dispels no illusions about its being close at hand. He says only that it will not come until the falling away come and the man of lawlessness has been revealed (2:3). However, he adds that there is a mystery of lawlessness already working, though under restraint (2:7). When the restraint is removed, the lawless one will come, whom Jesus shall slay (2:7,8). There are no time indications whatever for these matters. Only the sequence of the events is revealed. He says nothing about the falling away, the removal of the restrainer, the coming of the lawless one, and the coming of the Lord not happening in the immediate future. In fact, he informs them that the processes are already at work; the program is in process. The further instruction which Paul offered shed no light on how near at hand or how far off these events were; but it left the general impression of considerable imminency. [122] Hence, Paul could hardly have been intent on dispelling that idea. What Paul's words did show clearly, however, was that the day of the Lord was not already there. Paul had told them earlier about certain things which must precede its arrival (2:5). He now reminds them of these things: "... except the falling away come first" (2:3); "... until he be taken out of the way" (2:7); "and then ..." (2:8). The idea of the day of the Lord being already present is clearly dispelled. Thus it appears that whatever confusion and excitement there may have been in Thessalonica over what was being said about the day of the Lord (II Thess. 2:2) was not because some were urging its imminency, but because the idea was abroad that it was already there.

---

119 Frame, *Thess.*, p. 248. Bauer, *Wörterbuch*, sub ἐνίστημι, agrees. Frame, *Thess.*, p. 249, calls attention to an "exhaustive note" by John Lillie, *Epistles of Paul to the Thessalonians, Translated from the Greek, with Notes*, 1856, in defence of the translation "is present," and in rejection of all attempts to understand it as "almost, but not quite, here."
120 Lillie, as quoted by Frame, *Thess.*, p. 249.
121 Von Dobschütz, *Thess.*, p. 267.
122 *Cf.* R. Schippers, *Mythologie en Eschatologie in 2 Thessalonicenzen 2:1–17*, Assen: G. F. Hummelen, 1961, pp. 5–15. He finds Paul intent on saying: "De parousie is geen perfectum, maar futurum. Dat is waar, maar het is daarom nog niet een verre toekomst. Het is nabij en bijna present. In de voortekenen als zijn aanloop is het reeds aanwezig" (p. 10).

Von Dobschütz has openly admitted that seeing the disorderliness in Thessalonica as stemming from an excitement over the near end of the world is a view that must be accepted more by way of default than because of specific indications.[123] There are, however, other possibilities of explaining the phenomenon of the disorderly persons. Spicq makes only the briefest reference to the possibility that the disorderliness may have stemmed from eschatological concerns. Rather, he finds it significant that in I Thess. 5:14 the disorderly are placed alongside the fainthearted (ὀλιγοψύχους) and the weak (ἀσθενῶν). He sees in this the suggestion that the disorderliness was a basic character deficiency more than some specific kind of infraction. According to him some of the Thessalonians simply were not inclined to a well-regulated and orderly way of life.[124] Rigaux, on the other hand, sees more the hint of a tendency to excitement and excess that accompanies all revolutions and new movements.[125] Even von Dobschütz had an interesting alternate suggestion, which to him seemed not to merit further pursuit. He first observed how unlikely it was in view of their persecutions that the Thessalonians might have thought that the day of the Lord had already arrived. To this he adds the qualification: unless the early Christian idea of the day of the Lord were somehow being reinterpreted in a Gnostic sense, like the false teachers pictured in II Timothy were doing with the resurrection: "men who concerning the truth have erred, saying that the resurrection is past already" (II Tim. 2:18).[126] In the same year that von Dobschütz published his commentary, Lütgert

---

123 "Wenn dies Verhalten einzelner in Thessalonich doch einen religiösen Grund gehabt haben muss, so wüsste ich nicht, worin anders er bestanden haben soll" (von Dobschütz, *Thess.*, p. 183).

124 C. Spicq, "Les Thessaloniciens 'inquiets' étaient-ils des paresseux?" *S.T.*, X (1956), p. 11: "Il s'agit d'une 'faiblesse' de conscience, d'une 'pusillanimité' d'âme, d'une disposition à s'affranchir des règles communes. Nous y verrions, par conséquent, sinon des esprits faux — qui concluent, géométriquement, de la proximité de la parousie à l'inutilité de tout labeur —, du moins des instables, comme les Galates ἀνόητοι, qui ne peuvent s'immobiliser sous le joug d'une discipline. Toujours en marge de la règle, ils manquent de cette σωφροσύνη indispensable au salut (I Tim. 2:15) et troublent la vie commune. Que ce soit par négligence ou insubordination, ils vivent dans un désordre constant...." *Cf.* also Findlay, *Thess.*, p. 203: "The call to enter the kingdom of God and seek its glory brought men of a naturally idle or restless disposition under temptation upon this score. To such natures the rumours current about the Day of the Lord ... would appeal with particular force."

125 Rigaux, *Thess.*, p. 521: "On penserait plutôt à une excitation provenant tout d'abord de la nouveauté elle-même du mouvement chrétien. Toute révolution, même religieuse, connaît des dangers de trouble, de susceptibilité et d'intransigeance. Il suffit que l'un ou l'autre esprit, sans responsabilité, se croie plus malin que ses voisins pour qu'une surenchère se fasse jour et que, sous prétexte de zèle, on mette le trouble dans la communauté. On comprend ainsi le passage de la φιλαδελφία à ἡσυχάζειν." Elsewhere he adds in regard to the eschatological aspect of the matter: "Il est curieux que le passage ne porte aucune trace de l'attente eschatologique pourtant si prononcée partout ailleurs. Mais dans une assemblée, les abus se tiennent par la main, et ceux qui s'occupent de tout en refusant de faire quelque chose, auront été probablement les premières victimes, sinon les agents, de la fausse attente du Seigneur" (p. 74).

126 "Nach alttestamentlicher und urchristlicher Auffassung gehört zu dem Herrntag ein solches Mass äusserlich wahrnehmbarer, tiefeingreifender, weltumgestaltender Wundervorgänge, dass kein Christ jener Zeit das 'er ist da' aussprechen konnte im Sinne des 'wir leben bereits in ihm', es sei denn, er habe den urchristlichen Begriff gnostisch umgedeutet, wie es etwa die in den Pastoralbriefen bekämpften Irrlehrer mit der 'Auferstehung' taten II Tim. 2:18" (von Dobschütz, *Thess.*, p. 267).

took issue with him for not following the lines of this alternate suggestion.[127] Lütgert found numerous reasons for proposing that there were nascent forms of Gnosticism present in the Thessalonian church, as well as in Philippi and Corinth and in the false teachers pictured in the Pastoral Letters.[128] He did not propose that Gnosticism as a specific religious teaching was being circulated in the early Christian congregations, but rather that a new form of religious expression which he called fanaticism (Schwärmerei) was developing. Thus the way was being paved for a full grown Gnosticism which would cause the church much trouble in later years.[129] Recently Schmithals has been reviving some of Lütgert's insights in his own studies of the nature of the opponents and false teaching which Paul seems to be combatting in many of his letters.[130] He is persuaded that Gnosticism in a Jewish-Christian form was being propagated in many places where Paul had been preaching the gospel and that the erroneous ideas which Paul was combatting in many of his letters are to be traced to this source.[131]

It appears, thus, that an idleness and excitement stemming from an expectation of Christ's imminent return may not be nearly so self-evident as has sometimes been assumed. The eschatological confusions in Thessalonica were complex, and the various hints which can be gathered from what Paul says about them give much credibility to the proposal that the teachings of Gnosticism had been at work in the Thessalonian congregation.[132] The warnings about libertinism (I Thess. 4:1–8) and about maintaining a proper

---

[127] Lütgert, *Phil. u. Thess.*, pp. 83f.

[128] Besides his studies concerning Philippi and Thessalonica (*op. cit.*), see also his *Freiheitspredigt und Schwärmgeister in Korinth*, (B.z.G.c.T., 12, 3), Gütersloh: C. Bertelsmann, 1908; and *Die Irrlehrer der Pastoralbriefe*, (B.z.F.c.T., 13, 3), Gütersloh: C. Bertelsmann, 1909.

[129] Lütgert, *Phil. u. Thess.*, p. 101.

[130] W. Schmithals, *Die Gnosis in Korinth*, Göttingen: Vandenhoeck & Ruprecht, 1956; "Die Häretiker in Galatien," Z.N.W., XLVII (1956), pp. 25–67; "Die Irrlehrer des Philipperbriefes," Z.T.K., LIV (1957), pp. 297–341; "Die Irrlehrer von Rm. 16:17–20," S.T., XIII (1959), pp. 1–19.

[131] W. Schmithals, "Zur Abfassung und ältesten Sammlung der paulinischen Hauptbriefe," Z.N.W., LI, p. 229: "Ich... habe in einer Reihe von Untersuchungen den Nachweis zu erbringen versucht, dass Paulus sich in seinen während der 3. sogenannten Missionsreise verfassten Briefen mit missionierenden Vertretern einer ausgeprägten Gnosis judischer bzw. judenchristlicher Observanz auseinandersetzt." Concerning the Thessalonian letters, he says, "I, II Thess sind... zu einer Zeit geschrieben in der die Auseinandersetzung mit den korinthischen Irrlehrern schon recht weit vorgeschritten war. Das stimmt mit der Tatsache überein, dass die Thessalonicherbriefe nicht mehr mit einer akuter Bedrohung der Gemeinde zu Thessalonich rechnen. Die Irrlehrer sind weitergezogen, ihre Anhänger haben in der Gemeinde keinen grossen Einfluss gewinnen können" (pp. 232,233). His substantiation of this must await the publication of the study "Die historische Situation der Thessalonicherbriefe," which will be soon forthcoming (*cf.* p. 229, fn. 10). Our present interest is not to enter into discussion of these matters, but simply to notice that new insights are being opened as to the possible nature of the troublesome situation in Thessalonica. E. Schweizer, while showing a general agreement with Schmithals on the character and details of the heretical movement troubling Paul's churches (see Schweizer's description of the movement quoted below, p. 173, fn. 243), doubts whether it can properly be called Gnosticism (Cf. "Die Kirche als Leib Christi in den paulinischen Antilegomena," T.L., LXXXVI [1961], p. 252, fn. 48).

[132] For instance, in connection with the day of the Lord being already here (II Thess. 2:2), and the relation of this teaching to that of the resurrection having already happened (II Tim. 2:18), Schmithals in his studies of Phil. 3:12–14 (Z.T.K., LIV, pp. 322–325) and I Cor. 4:7ff. (*Gnos. Kor.* pp. 146–148) gathers a great deal of evidence for his assertion, "... nichts passt besser zu den Gnostikern der frühen Zeit als ein übersteigertes Vollendungsbewusstsein" (Z.T.K., LIV, p. 322).

respect for the Spirit with a discernment between what is good and what is evil in this regard (I Thess. 5:19–22) can be seen as pointing in the same direction. The excitement of the disorderly brethren may very well have involved a grasping for positions of superiority and an assuming to give instruction and inspiration to the rest. [133] In short, there is much to recommend the view that some of the Thessalonians had been infected with devious ideas about what constitutes true spirituality and a really mature Christian way. [134] They had become enthusiasts and fanatics in spiritual matters, laying aside their ordinary earning of a living, and were devoting themselves to prophesying, edifying their fellow Christians, and ministering to the spiritual needs which, according to them, were being neglected. For this they expected to receive support from the congregation. Paul found this whole development very much at odds with the instruction and the example which he had set. He terms it "walking disorderly" (3:6,11).

This problem of disorderliness had an utterly simple solution. Let the disorderly persons resume gainful employment. In a very practical way this would tend to solve whatever problems might be arising from their fanaticism, their meddlesomeness, and their need of support. However, Paul's instruction goes much deeper than the level of the practical maxim, "Idleness is the Devil's workshop." This whole matter concerned the fundamental Christian way; "the tradition which they [135] received of us" (vs. 6) was being disregarded. The disorderly brethren were failing to observe a divine imperative. There is a note of sternness in what Paul here has to say.

The idea of a divine imperative comes to clear expression in δεῖ (vs. 7): "For yourselves know how ye ought. . . ." In classical Greek the word often expressed the necessities which were implicit in a mechanistic view of the world. Biblical Greek adapted the word to express the necessities which were implicit in the will of a sovereign and personal God. [136] Jesus stood under a divine necessity (δεῖ) (cf. Luke 2:49; 4:43; 9:22; 13:33; 24:7; etc.). So also did the disciples, the apostles, and the early Christians (cf. Luke 12:12; Acts 9:6,16; 14:22; 23:11; etc.). In the present instance the δεῖ is again expressive of the divine will that calls for definite response. [137] Paul's reference to the tradition (τὴν παράδοσιν,

---

133 In I Tim. 2:12 "being in quietness" (εἶναι ἐν ἡσυχίᾳ) is placed over against teaching (διδάσκειν) and domineering (αὐθεντεῖν).

134 One is reminded immediately of I Cor. 12–14, where Paul gives instruction concerning spiritual gifts (περὶ δὲ τῶν πνευματικῶν). "If any man thinketh himself to be a prophet, or spiritual, let him take knowledge of the things which I write unto you, that they are the commandment of the Lord" (I Cor. 14:37). Spicq, S.T., X, p. 13, has also called attention to the parallel choice of words in the concluding statement of this section about spiritual gifts: "But let all things be done decently (εὐσχημόνως) and in order (κατὰ τάξιν)" (I Cor. 14:40), and the Thessalonian problem of the disorderly (ἄτακτοι), who ought to walk becomingly (εὐσχημόνως) (I Thess. 4:12).

135 The problem of whether the text reads "they received" or "you received" is an interesting and difficult one from the textual standpoint. However, from the standpoint of the meaning of the passage the variations are not highly important, since in either case Paul is directing the reader's attention to the original proclamation which he had made.

136 W. Grundmann, δεῖ, δέον ἐστί, T.W.N.T., II, p. 22, 20ff.

137 Ibid., p. 25, 21–27: "Im Zusammenhang mit der Beschreibung des Willens Gottes, wie er sich auf das Verhalten des Menschen richtet und wie er im Gesetz wie im Handeln Jesu entsprechend

vs. 6) also indicates how radical he found this departure of the disorderly brethren to be. The tradition was the essential Christian way. It came to expression not only in the central message of salvation, the gospel, but also in the application of this message to various practical situations in the life of the believer. [138] It is this aspect which is in view here, as the sequence "walketh disorderly and not after the tradition" suggests. [139] Rigaux has pointed out that the use of the definite article, *the* tradition, suggests not so much some particular command about working, but rather a whole set of commands, a sort of norm, maybe even a kind of catechism which was normally known and accepted and which the apostles would not have neglected requiring of their new converts. [140] An appeal to the tradition came as an appeal with great authority and called for subjection in obedience. [141] Hence, as Michaelis has noted, the context into which the thought of imitation is introduced is full of an atmosphere of authoritativeness and imperative. [142]

Paul solemnly issues a command in the name of the Lord Jesus Christ that the Thessalonians are to withdraw from the ones who are walking disorderly and not according to the tradition. He proceeds immediately to give an explanation and justification for so radical an action: "for yourselves know how ye ought...." The right way is a matter of common knowledge to them. There is an unexpected turn of the thought, however, when he completes the thought about what ought to happen with *to imitate us*. We would have expected something about how it was necessary to follow the tradition, [143]

---

dem von ihm erkannten Willen Gottes deutlich wird (... vgl allgemein als Ausdruck einer im Willen Gottes begründeten Notwendigkeit R 12,3; 1 Th 4,1; 2 Th 3,7; 1 Tm 3,2.7; 3,7 uö), steht das δεῖ als Ausdruck d e s Willens Gottes, der ein b e s t i m m t e s B e t e n verlangt."

138 H. Ridderbos, *Heilsgeschiedenis en Heilige Schrift van het Nieuwe Testament*, Kampen: J. H. Kok N.V., 1955, p. 41; O. Cullmann, *La Tradition*, Neuchatel/Paris: Delachaux & Niestlé, 1953, pp. 16,17, where he describes the latter aspect of the tradition as "de règles morales qui, à la façon de la 'halacha', se rapportent à la vie des fidèles."

139 In fact, here undoubtedly is the essence of the disorderliness. Those not working were at odds with God's will and his express commands. "Wer nicht arbeitet, sich gegen Gottes heilige Ordnung vergeht. Dementsprechend bezeichnet denn auch Paulus den Müssiggänger als einen ἀνὴρ ἄτακτος" (A. Juncker, *Die Ethik des Apostels Paulus*, 2. Hälfte: *Die konkrete Ethik*, Halle a. S.: Max Niemeyer, 1919, p. 158. So also Spicq, S.T., X, pp. 11—12: "Ils sont ἄτακτοι précisément parce qu'ils refusent de se soumettre au principe d'ordre, à la règle de vie que constituent les enseignements et prescriptions pratiques transmis par saint Paul. La παράδοσις, ici évoquée, correspond exactement aux γεγραμμένα ou προγεγραμμένα des inscriptions et des papyrus."

140 Rigaux, *Thess.*, p. 705.

141 Ridderbos, *Heilsgeschiedenis*, pp. 45,46: "De traditie, waarvan het Nieuwe Testament spreekt, ... is niet anders dan de autoritatieve verkondiging, die aan de apostelen als de getuigen van Christus en als het fundament der kerk is toevertrouwd en die zij als een kostbaar pand, in nauwkeurige overeenstemming met hun opdracht hebben over te dragen.... Daarom wordt deze overlevering ook telkens de *leer* genoemd, waaraan men zich in gehoorzaamheid moet onderwerpen, Rom. 6:17." *Cf.* also R. Bultmann, *Theologie des Neuen Testaments*, 3. Aufl. Tübingen: J. C. B. Mohr (Paul Siebeck), 1958, p. 451: "Der Begriff des Apostels als des vom auferstandenen Herrn entsandten Verkündigers ist also primär bestimmt durch den G e d a n k e n  d e r A u t o r i s i e r u n g; sein Wort ist das vom Herrn legitimierte. Allmählich gewinnt daneben der T r a d i t i o n s - G e d a n k e das Übergewicht, der freilich zu Beginn auch nicht fehlte (1 Kr 15, 3. 14f.)."

142 Michaelis, *T.W.N.T.*, IV, p. 669, 29ff. We can not agree, however, with the conclusion which Michaelis draws from this fact; see below, p. 138, fn. 151.

143 Keulers, *Brieven v. Paulus I*, p. 84, suggests "hoe gij u volgens mijn overlevering te gedragen hebt."

or how they ought to walk orderly as over against those walking disorderly (3:6). In fact, Lightfoot proposes that "how ye ought to imitate us" is an abridgment of expression and thought for "how ye ought to walk, so as to imitate us"; [144] thus it would be analogous to "as ye received of us how ye ought to walk and to please God" (I Thess. 4:1). It would seem that the question may legitimately be raised whether Paul wished the imitation of himself to be understood as a really necessary thing, an ordinance on a par with the rest of those making up the tradition, a matter which is properly the object of δεῖ. Paul's words, taken literally, can be made to say that, of course. However, is this really the import of the words? Is it not more likely that there has been an abridgment of the thought here, or a sudden change in the direction of the thought with the introduction of the idea of imitation? Right at the point of fullest authoritativeness (in the utterance of the δεῖ), Paul shifts to the approach of persuasion. With the words of command on the verge of crossing his lips, he suddenly changes his tone to an appeal and a plea. He maintains a unique balance of apostolic authority and fatherly, brotherly love. [145] That which is a divine imperative has been presented to them earlier with the magnetic attraction of a powerful personal example. Paul here continues to make this same kind of appeal.

The imitation which Paul has in mind receives further clarification in the description of his own conduct which follows. [146] It consisted particularly in two things, his industriousness and his determination not to be a burden to his hearers. He had worked hard, "in labor and travail"; and long, "night and day." He was intent upon caring for his own needs and avoiding any possibility of being burdensome to the people to whom he was bringing the gospel. After leaving Thessalonica, he apparently followed the same policy among the Corinthians and with the same intent (cf. II Cor. 11:9; 12:13). It was strictly a voluntary policy on his part, for to both the Thessalonians and the Corinthians he firmly insisted that he had a right to look to them for support (I Thess. 3:9; I Cor. 9:18). In writing to the Corinthians he emphasized the mission concern that led him to adopt such a policy: "We bear all things, that we may cause no hindrance to the gospel of Christ" (I Cor. 9:12); and "that, when I preach the gospel, I may make the gospel without charge" (I Cor. 9:18). He would not allow the effect of his gospel to be blunted by the appearance of its being personally profitable for him to preach. To

---

144 Lightfoot, Notes on Epistles, p. 130. Lightfoot's proposal has been quoted with approval by many commentators; cf. e.g., Frame, Thess., p. 301; Rigaux, Thess., p. 706; Morris, Thess., (N.I.C.N.T.), p. 252.

145 Notice the same combination in the preceding verse (3:6): "We command you, brethren," where he continues the brotherly tone of the command by basing its authority not on himself but on Christ. Frame, Thess., p. 297, says of this whole section (vss. 6–15), Paul's "attitude throughout is not that of an apostle exercising his apostolic authority but that of a brother appealing to brothers in the name of a common authority, the Lord Jesus Christ."

146 Here again the specific import of the ὅτι which provides the bridge between the imitation idea and what follows is difficult to determine. Cf. above, p. 102 re I Thess. 2:14. Robertson, Gram., p. 964, says, "In 2 Th. 3:7f. exegesis alone can determine the nature of ὅτι." Perhaps an indefinite for is the best translation that can be given. The R.S.V. and N.E.B. simply punctuate with a semicolon and colon respectively, and leave the ὅτι untranslated.

the Thessalonians he emphasized another aspect of this policy. It was his purpose and intent to make the fullest possible use of his example. Thus, by foregoing his right, he heightened the impact of his example and the powers it exerted toward bringing about imitation. He thus gave a clear picture of self-sacrificing industry, a picture which had many ramifications regarding selfless devotion to God, the spread of the gospel, and the well-being of one's fellow man.

The statement "in labor and travail, working night and day, that we might not burden any of you" (II Thess. 3:8) is an almost exact verbal repetition of I Thess. 2:9: "For ye remember, brethren, our labor and travail: working night and day, that we might not burden any of you." The context of this latter statement discloses the extent to which Paul had entered into close personal relationships with the Thessalonians in bringing them the gospel. Notice in the immediately preceding context how he likens himself to the nurse cherishing her own children (I Thess. 2:7), "affectionately desirous of you, ... well pleased to impart unto you ... our own souls, because ye were become very dear to us" (I Thess. 2:8). Following the statement about his working so as not to burden them, he speaks about "how we dealt with each one of you, as a father with his own children, exhorting you, and encouraging you, and testifying, to the end that ye should walk worthily of God (I Thess. 2:11). Paul found his relationships with the Thessalonians to be just those which would most naturally lead to imitation, those of a mother and father. One sees here an evidence of the conscious purpose with which he lived and worked of using the power of personal example in influencing the lives of those with whom he worked.

Paul's statement "to make ourselves an ensample unto you, that ye should imitate us" (II Thess. 3:9) may sound a bit tautological.[147] However, by rounding out his statement with the addition of "that ye should imitate us," he returns to the thought with which he began. They knew how they ought to imitate him, for he had worked hard and unselfishly precisely with an eye to their learning to imitate him. It had been his avowed intention to call forth an imitation from them.

The indications of a resolute and deliberate conduct on Paul's part ought not to be overlooked. The two purpose clauses, ἵνα ... δῶμεν and εἰς τὸ μιμεῖσθαι, show this clearly. In addition, the particular idiom which Paul chooses, ἑαυτοὺς τύπον δῶμεν, further emphasizes the fact. Frame finds in δῶμεν ὑμῖν the likely intention "to emphasize the self-sacrifice involved in this waiving of his rights, an emphasis which is conspicuous in a similar connection in the first epistle (2:8 μεταδοῦναι ... τὰς ἑαυτῶν ψυχάς)."[148] In view of this latter comparison one can not entirely avoid the force of Frame's observation that there may be an emphasis on the self-sacrifice here. However, due account ought to be taken of the fact that δῶμεν here has a double accusative. The same construction is found in Eph. 4:11 and 1:22. It is a construction found

---

[147] Von Dobschütz, *Thess.*, p. 312: "... die fast tautologischen Sätze."
[148] Frame, *Thess.*, p. 304.

in the Septuagint in translation of נתן with a double accusative, where the meaning is *to make, constitute, appoint*: cf. Exod. 7:1; Num. 11:29; Isa. 55:4; etc.[149] The double accusative ἑαυτοὺς τύπον suggests that Paul has the same meaning in mind here. Hence, he had made himself an example; he had constituted himself in that position and determined to play that role. The idiom gives evidence of the determination and deliberateness with which he worked.

This passage also expressly states the relation between τύπος and μιμέομαι. A τύπος has the purpose of being imitated. In the first letter another aspect of the relationship was shown. There it was seen that when one had become an imitator of someone's good example, this resulted in his becoming an example to others (I Thess. 1:6,7). A τύπος draws others to itself by way of calling forth imitation; and when the imitation has been accomplished, new τύποι have been created. Here is a kind of spontaneous growth within the realm of Christianity.

The fact that Paul worked so hard at being an example does not mean that it was imitation as such or imitation in itself that he looked for in his hearers. He sought to impart the Christian way. As Christians they ought to be industrious and self-giving, and he had sought to impress that upon them and to win from them a like response by means of his personal example. Naturally, he also gave them specific instruction and direct commands in regard to proper Christian conduct. He reminds the Thessalonians of this in II Thess. 3:10: "For even when we were with you, this we commanded you...." He then proceeds to issue a direct command to those behaving disorderly: "Now them that are such we command and exhort in the Lord Jesus Christ, that with quietness they work, and eat their own bread" (vs. 12). But the striking feature of his present dealing with the problem of disorderliness is that when he comes to speak about what ought to be, he first appeals to his example and calls for them to imitate him, and only later turns to the matter of the specific instruction and direct commands. This passage brings out in sharpest relief the high importance which Paul placed on his example and on using it as a stimulation to imitate him.[150] He found imitation to be a means of bringing people into obedience to the divine will. The "oughts" of their lives could be fulfilled by their becoming like him and by their adopting his ways and attitudes. He recognized the strange power of attraction which inheres in close personal relationships. He pressed this power into the

---

[149] L. Koehler and W. Baumgartner, *Lexicon in Veteris Testamenti Libros*, Leiden: E. J. Brill, 1953, *sub* נתן, 13: "נתן c. 2 ac. jmd zu etw. machen." Some have called its use in the New Testament a Hebraism. Van Leeuwen, in commenting on Eph. 4:11, says, "διδόναι in dezen zin is meer Semietisch dan Grieksch" (*Efeze*, p. 98). Liddell-Scott, *Lexicon*, *sub* δίδωμι, illustrate the usage exclusively from Biblical Greek. However, J. H. Moulton and G. Milligan, *The Vocabulary of the Greek Testament*, London: Hodder & Stoughton, 1952, *sub* δίδωμι, cite its usage in the papyri and conclude that it is not to be considered a Hebraism.

[150] Eidem, *Stud. Tillägnade E. Stave*, p. 74, remarks about how in spite of the constant use of the first person plural pronoun the whole picture presented by this passage seems so individual. He also calls attention to Acts 20:34, where Paul reminds the Ephesian elders: "Ye yourselves know that these hands ministered unto my necessities, and to them that were with me." Here is further confirmation of the judgment which was earlier expressed that the plurals point primarily to Paul, rather than to Paul, Silas, and Timothy (see above, pp. 118f.).

service of God as one more means of becoming "all things to all men, that I may by all means save some" (I Cor. 9:22). [151]

\* \* \*

Several observations have been made in the course of the exegesis of this section. They do not at this point call for further discussion, but simply for summarizing statement. The specific area of imitation and example in view in this passage is Paul's industriousness and self-giving. This example is especially appropriate for the disorderly brethren, but Paul holds it up for the instruction and guidance of the whole congregation. It is an example which he had given with the deliberate intention of calling forth imitation. His policy of providing for his own support was a policy pursued for a variety of reasons. Here the full emphasis falls on the purpose of supplying a striking example of the Christian's obligation to work, to be no burden to others, and to give himself totally for the benefit of others. He had given this example not simply hoping that it might be followed. He had given it with the expectation that it would be followed. He had so acted with the deliberate purpose of leading them by way of imitation into the Christian way. His example was no indifferent matter, to be followed or disregarded as each Christian saw fit. Paul ranked his example alongside his teaching and instruction. In fact, it constituted a part of his teaching and instruction. In it he was delivering the Christian tradition to Thessalonica.

This passage significantly reveals what importance Paul attached to his example and to the imitation of him. In the face of a constantly degenerating situation he was forced to expose the conduct of some in Thessalonica as a radical departure from the Christian tradition. He made his point first and foremost by calling attention to the fact that they were out of harmony with the example he had given them and that they had failed to imitate him. He also makes some reference to his specific instructions and commands in regard to work. However, this comes in the nature of a secondary charge, substantiating and confirming his previous complaint (cf. γάρ, 3:10). Paul's primary complaint here is not that there has been disobedience in Thessalonica. It is that there has been a failure to imitate him, a failure to grasp the Christian tradition mediated by his personal example. With great personal anguish

---

[151] Hence, we are not able to agree fully with Michaelis' statement: "Dass mit τύπος weniger das Muster, das nachgebildet, als das V o r b i l d, das b e f o l g t werden soll, gemeint ist, und dass infolgedessen μιμεῖσθαι die Anerkennung einer Autorität einschliesst, ergibt sich aus der Parallelität zu der 3, 6 genannten παράδοσις, die ebenfalls b e f o l g t sein will" (T.W.N.T., IV, p. 669, 26—30). The element of authority is surely very prominent in the context, and παράδοσις is one of its clearest expressions. However, as we have already noted (above p. 135 and especially fn. 145), Paul maintains a careful balance of authoritativeness and fatherly, brotherly love. He will not stand over the Thessalonians without also standing among them and drawing them along with him. Τύπος and μιμεῖσθαι reveal more the character of moral persuasion than authoritativeness and disclose a non-authoritarian means which Paul was using of leading people into obedience to the divine will.

Paul the father is facing the possibility that some whom he had counted as his children are not his children after all, in view of their total lack of resemblance to him. He prescribes radical measures regarding them. Nevertheless, he closes with the admonition that they not be looked upon as enemies but admonished as brothers (3:15). He secretly hopes that the imitation may still develop. He does not hesitate to issue direct commands concerning their conduct. However, at the same time he continues to urge his own personal example.

### III. I Corinthians 4:16

*I beseech you therefore, be ye imitators of me.*

The situation in the church in Corinth was far from wholesome in the first years following Paul's mission there. The letters of Paul's correspondence with this congregation which have been preserved for us reflect the serious state of affairs in that congregation. Paul was able to give thanks to God for the Corinthians (I Cor. 1:4), but his thanksgiving did not betray the overflowing joy with which he had been able to thank God when he wrote his first letter to the Thessalonian church. His thanksgiving is directed to God for the grace which God had shown in enriching the Corinthians in Jesus Christ, but the enrichment of which he can speak is mostly in terms of an intellectual response; he makes no mention of any reactions of love, joy, humility, and service. In fact, Paul directs his letter to this very matter immediately: "Now I beseech you, brethren, through the name of our Lord Jesus Christ, that ye all speak the same thing, and that there be no divisions among you; but that ye be perfected together in the same mind and in the same judgment. For it hath been signified unto me concerning you, my brethren, by them that are of the household of Chloe, that there are contentions among you" (1:10,11). The Corinthian church was being torn by disunity, wrangling, and dissension.

What Paul writes to the Corinthians in these first chapters reflects something of the disturbed and confused situation there. Something was at work in the congregation causing considerable division and strife. For one thing, a great interest had developed regarding the wisdom of the Christian gospel and the wisdom of the words with which it was being presented. Paul is not happy about this development. He finds it dangerous. He has no doubts about there being a wisdom in the gospel as he had preached it. However, it was no ordinary wisdom. In fact, by many standards it was likely to be judged as pure foolishness. Nevertheless, his message of Christ crucified was indeed the power of God and the wisdom of God (1:24). If some found this message foolishness and others found it a stumbling block, this need surprise no one. The wisdom of God was to be discovered only along spiritual lines. And here was precisely the problem in Corinth. The strife and party spirit in which they lived gave ample evidence of how little their lives had been captivated by true spirituality. Rather, a basic carnality was incapacitating them from discerning spiritual things.[152]

The basic carnality in the lives of the Corinthians and their interest in devious types and manifestations of wisdom had affected their attitudes toward the men who had given spiritual leadership among them. It had led them to apply the wrong standards in evaluating them. It had helped them lose all sense of the real unity they had as Christians. Moffatt describes the matter well when he says: "Such differences of opinion and taste, treating apostles and teachers as though they were rival lecturers on moral philosophy or even popular actors on the stage, took men's attention off the common Lord, roused undue pride in human leaders and preachers, set Christians at loggerheads, and ignored the fact that all the different capacities of prominent men were so many varieties and organs of the one life which God himself provided for his Church in Jesus Christ."[153] Paul was dismayed at the way he and Apollos were being pitted against each other in Corinth. He points out how unwarranted such activity was, since both men were simply teachers endeavoring to be faithful to the stewardship in which Christ had placed them. In most respects the work of the two could not be compared with each other, for each had his own capacities, and each had served in different phases of the life of the Corinthian church. A steward must finally be judged on the basis of faithfulness, but even here human estimates are not particularly valid; only God knows all the details (cf. 4:1—5). Against the background of these thoughts Paul proceeds to make his appeal to the Corinthians to change their ways. His appeal reaches its peak when he implores: "I beseech you therefore, be ye imitators of me" (4:16).

Paul begins his personal application of what he was written thus far regarding the Corinthian disunity with the statement, "Now these things, brethren, I have in a figure transferred to myself and Apollos for your sakes; that in us ye might learn not to go beyond the things which are written; that no one of you be puffed up for the one against the other" (4:6). The things which he had been writing about himself and Apollos had been said with the purpose "that in us ye might learn . . . ." There was a lesson for the Corinthians in Paul's words about himself and Apollos.

The exact nature of this lesson is not so easily determined. There are several matters in this verse which are not entirely clear to us later readers and about which commentators have engaged in considerable discussion and speculation. For one thing, the import of Paul's saying that he had transferred

---

[152] The recent insight as to the possibility that opponents of Paul had been propagating gnostic views in the Corinthian congregation offers new possibilities in the understanding and interpreting of these early chapters in I Corinthians. E. Dinkler, "Korintherbriefe," R.G.G.3, Vol. IV, p. 19, comments as follows about I Cor. 1—4:21: "In der Polemik verwendet Paulus die Begriffe σοφία, γνῶσις, μυρία u.a. dialektisch, nimmt den Mythos auf (2,6—9) und vergeschichtlicht ihn doch wieder, spricht von erlesenen geistbegabten Christen als τέλειοι (2,6) und ist gleichwohl der Meinung, dass jeder Christ den Geist und deshalb keiner einen Vorrang habe. Die exegetischen und sachlichen Schwierigkeiten liegen also in der Aufnahme einer gnostischen Rede- und Denkweise, die sodann von Paulus in der Linie seiner Verkündigung interpretiert wird." Cf. for a more detailed exposition: W. Schmithals, Die Gnosis in Korinth.

[153] Moffatt, I Cor., p. 8.

these things in a figure (μετεσχημάτισα) to himself and Apollos is not immediately clear.[154]

Many of the Greek and Latin commentators from Chrysostom's time through the Middle Ages and early Reformation times proposed that this verse indicates that the controversial situation in Corinth did not really center around Paul, Apollos, Cephas, and Christ at all, but that Paul had substituted these names in order not to mention the real sources of controversy and trouble. Such a proposal does indeed spring naturally from μετεσχημάτισα, for, as Lightfoot has described the word, "We find from both Greek and Latin writers that σχῆμα (schema) was used at this time especially (and almost exclusively) to imply a rhetorical artifice, by which, either from fear or respect or some other motive, the speaker veiled the allusion to individuals under an allegory or a feigned name or in any other way."[155] However, to read these first chapters of I Corinthians totally in terms of feigned names does not fit with the figure of Paul's planting and Apollos' watering (3:5–9), or with Paul's laying the foundation upon which others are building (3:10). Such figures can only apply to the person of Paul. Furthermore, "these things" (ταῦτα), which Paul says he has transferred in a figure to himself and Apollos, follows immediately upon a section where he has been speaking most really about his own person. Hence, the whole usage he makes of the names of himself, Apollos, Cephas, and Christ can not be figurative and feigned. It is also noteworthy that the persons to whom he says he has transferred these things in a figure are himself and Apollos. In discussing persons and work and relationships, he has in fact spoken concretely only about himself and Apollos. Paul speaks no further about Cephas than to mention his name (1:12; 3:22), and as for persons presently or recently in Corinth, the reference does not go beyond the very vague and indefinite "anyone" (τις) (cf. 3:12,14,17,18). Hence, it is a fact that what Paul has said about the whole situation he has said specifically only in terms of himself and Apollos.

In saying that he has transferred these things in a figure to himself and Apollos, Paul probably means to point out to the Corinthians that what he has written is a veiled allusion from which they must learn. In effect, what Paul has done is to restrain himself extremely in speaking about the unwholesome situation in Corinth. He has spoken about it only in regard to himself and a man most closely associated with himself. Thus, in discussing the situation he was using the names of those whom the Corinthians had involved in their controversies, but who were themselves not responsible for these controversies. Also in speaking about himself and his associate Apollos, he could illustrate most pointedly and personally how much the present reactions in Corinth were at odds with the way he and Apollos viewed themselves, their work, and each other. They were ministers (3:5; 4:1), fellow-workers of God (3:9), stewards (4:1); there was no jealousy nor rivalry between them

---

[154] Allo, I Cor., p. 71, calls μετασχηματίζω "un des mots embarrassants du vocabulaire paulinien." The R.S.V. has translated it: "I have applied all this to myself and Apollos." Héring, I Cor., p. 35, fn. 1, rejects such a translation absolutely: "... 'j'ai appliqué', ce qui n'est nullement le sens du verbe." The N.E.B. resorts to a very vague translation: "Into this general picture ... I have brought Apollos and myself."
[155] Lightfoot, Notes on Epist., p. 199.

(*cf.* 3:6,8—10; 16:12). The Corinthians would do well to pay careful heed to these things he has said about himself and Apollos and to learn the lessons which needed broad application in Corinth. There were people in Corinth sowing the seeds of discord and stoking the fires of rivalry. There were also people in Corinth ever so ready to receive and nurse such seed or to have such a fire fanned in them. Paul had tempered his words and had avoided speaking directly about those most at fault. He had written about the matter only in terms of himself and Apollos. But from this the appropriate lessons could be learned.

Paul says that he has written these things "that in us ye might learn not to go beyond the things which are written." The significance of the phrase "not to go beyond the things which are written" is most elusive and probably can not be recaptured with certainty by us who are so far removed from the original Corinthian readers.[156] There are almost as many explanations and proposals concerning it as there are commentators.[157]

The phrase "the things which are written" (ἃ γέγραπται) immediately brings to mind the common terminology for the Old Testament scriptures.[158] At the same time, it looks very much as if Paul is quoting a common saying when he writes "not beyond the things that are written."[159] Could this have been a catchword from Paul's preaching, or a common saying among Christians; or might it have been a rabbinical saying? There is the further possibility that it was a slogan current in the common speech of the day, either in the city of Corinth or throughout the Hellenistic world. In this latter case it would, of course, not be referring to the Old Testament.[160] Such a possibility can not be discounted. However, there are evidences that in Corinth there was an enamorment with a philosophical approach to the gospel and a reckless drunken sense of being free and having attained to highest bliss (*cf.* 4:8ff.), both of which would have made it far from superfluous for Paul to make an appeal to be bound by God's revelation in Scripture. On

---

[156] *Cf.* such comments on the phrase as the following: "... whose meaning lies beyond recovery" (Moffatt, *I Cor.*, p. 46); "Voll verstehen können wir die Stelle nicht" (Lietzmann, *I Kor.*, p. 19); "De zin, die volgt, is nauwelijks te verstaan" (A. van Veldhuizen, *Paulus' Brieven aan de Korinthiërs*, T.U., Groningen: J. B. Wolters, 1917, p. 77).

[157] For a summary of the various interpretations which have been given to the phrase and the objections which can be made against them, see P. Wallis, "Ein neuer Auslegungsversuch der Stelle I. Kor. 4, 6," *T.L.* LXXV (1950), pp. 506,507.

[158] K. L. Schmidt has recently argued for understanding the passage in the sense of giving proper heed to the Old Testament in his article "Nicht über das hinaus, was geschrieben steht! (I. Kor. 4, 6)," in *In Memoriam Ernst Lohmeyer*, hrsg. von W. Schmauch, Stuttgart: Evangelisches Verlagswerk, 1951, pp. 101—109. Grosheide states the matter too dogmatically when he writes: "Γέγραπται wordt steeds gebruikt van geschreven zijn in het Oude Testament en moet daarom ook hier zo worden genomen" (*I Kor.*, p. 124).

[159] Both the elliptical form without any verb and the article τό introducing it suggest this.

[160] C. Spicq, *Épitres aux Corinthiens*, in *La Sainte Bible*, Paris: Letouzey et Ané, 1948, Vol. XI, Pt. 2, p. 199, suggests that it is a proverbial call for moderation, analogous to the French proverb, "Ne pas être plus royaliste que le roi." An American expression along the same lines would be "not to go overboard on the matter." *Cf.* N.E.B.: "learn to 'keep within the rules', as they say." The solution of Wallis, T.L. LXXV, pp. 507f., is somewhat similar. By placing a comma between μὴ ὑπέρ and ἃ γέγραπται, he proposes that the whole verse should be understood as follows: "Dies, Brüder, habe ich in bezug auf mich und Apollos gesagt, damit unser Beispiel euch das 'nicht zu viel' lehre, und ihr habt es hiermit schwarz auf weiss, damit nicht einer vor dem andern mit seinem 'Einzigen' gross tut!" (p. 508).

the other hand, it must be admitted that if this is the import of the phrase, it is not immediately clear how the things that Paul has said about himself and Apollos constitute a lesson in not going beyond the Scriptures. It could be so only in the most general sense of their being God's fellow-workers, his servants and stewards, seeking to be faithful to the charge given them. To obtain a lesson in faithful submission to God's word, the Corinthians would have had to draw much upon their recollections of Paul and Apollos and would have had to go far beyond what Paul has here written to them. Furthermore, Paul shows by what he proceeds immediately to say that his real intent in this passage is not to speak on the normativity of Scripture, but to strike at the haughtiness, the pride, the egotistic self-sufficiency, and the consequent contentiousness of the Corinthians. We leave the exact meaning of the phrase "not to go beyond the things which are written" in abeyance, observing simply that it somehow helped to make this latter point.

Of more importance to our present purpose than trying to detect the exact significance of not going beyond the things that are written is the fact that Paul points out that he has been desirous that they learn (μάθητε) something from what he had written and that that lesson was to be learned "in us." Clearly, the Corinthians are being referred to the example of Paul and Apollos.[161] Paul had been intent on recalling to the Corinthians what he and Apollos had been. A clear and unperverted recollection of himself and Apollos would in itself be a lesson to them. He views his example as helping to convey to the Corinthians certain things he wishes them to learn. Already here we have a hint at the direction in which Paul's thought is going, and it is hardly surprising that after a few sentences we hear him calling for the imitation of himself.

Paul says he has written thus far and presented them with a lesson in Apollos and himself with this purpose in mind: "that no one of you be puffed up for the one against the other." With these words Paul has brought himself to state openly the heart of their trouble. He had hinted at it in mentioning their contentions (1:11), their jealousy and strife (3:3), their glorying in men (3:21), their judging (4:3), etc. Now he has stated it openly. He has been intent on counteracting their being puffed up, their being "inflated with pride," as the *New English Bible* puts it. Paul uses the same expression a few verses later: "Now some are puffed up, as though I were not coming to you. But I will come to you shortly, if the Lord will; and I will know, not the word of them that are puffed up, but the power" (4:18,19). Paul was aware of a self-assertiveness, a vanity, a cocksureness, a completely warped sense of self-importance that had taken hold of some of the Corinthians. It was his desire to correct this spirit through his letter and through Timothy's visit. However, if these means remained ineffective, he was determined to use stronger measures to explode it when he came in person. Its strength was in its ability to spout words; but Paul was confident that there was an "Achilles' heel" at the point of power. They were not able to produce

---

[161] Rengstorf, *T.W.N.T.*, IV, p. 411, 11,12. *Cf.* N.B.G.: "opdat gij uit ons (voorbeeld) zoudt leren."

Christians; Christian lives were not forthcoming; there was no growing in grace under their influence; the Corinthians were not learning the basic Christian duty of love. Behind the great impression that these persons were always bent on making on those around them by their barrage of words, there was only sterility. They were puffed up to great size, but the substance of it all was only air. And yet, while they remained intact in their swollen vanity and pride, they could cause such havoc in the Christian congregation. In fact, that is what had been happening. Their sense of self-importance was leading them to express themselves most positively and categorically, to take most definite positions and to hold intransigently to them, and to line up behind certain persons who were heralded as paragons of virtue and angels of light, while denouncing others as utter scoundrels and the devil incarnate. Paul had sought to write things that would counteract this being "puffed up for the one against the other" (4:6).

Personal and contentious pride was tearing the Corinthian congregation to shreds. When Paul had finally brought himself to state this openly to them, a flood of pent-up feelings broke forth. In an impassioned outburst of sarcasm and irony, he compared their idle thoughts about life as a Christian with the experiences which he had been having (4:7–13). They see the Christian life in terms of being filled, being rich, reigning, being wise and strong, having glory. [162] His lot has been to live as one doomed to death, a spectacle to the world, a fool, weak, in dishonor, hungry, thirsty, naked, buffeted, treated as the filth of the world and the offscouring of all things. [163] The inconsistency between the two is extreme, and any conscientious Corinthian Christian, having heard the letter to this point, must already have been squirming in uneasiness. But Paul was not yet through. He had one more deep thrust to make in their consciences. Against the background of all he has hinted at and said about their contentious, jealous, strife-ridden, and devisive conduct, he reminds them of his own conduct: "We toil, working with our own hands: being reviled, we bless; being persecuted, we endure; being defamed, we entreat" (4:12,13a). The inconsistency between their lives and his is total.

Paul's exasperation with the Corinthians, however, stemmed from his love for them. They must not misunderstand his sharp words to them. The sharpness had arisen from the very peculiar pain he himself felt over the devious ways in which the Corinthians were going. These are his children, his own beloved children (4:14). He is the father that has brought them into the world of life in Christ (4:15). Their present conduct has caused him all of the anxiety and grief and sickness of heart that any loving father feels over an errant child. It is this which has caused the outburst which he just

---

[162] This characterization of the views present in the Corinthian congregation gives one of the clearest hints that the troubles there are to be traced to the work of teachers spreading gnostic doctrines in their midst. *Cf.* Schmithals, *Gnos. Kor.*, pp. 146f.

[163] Tinsley, *Imit.*, p. 152, has pointed out the "interesting echoes in this passage of the influence of the 'parable' of the Sheep and the Goats on the early Christian conception of the life of the apostle." *Cf.* the hungering, thirsting, being naked, being sick (weak: ἀσθενής) in Matt. 25:35f. and I Cor. 4:10f.

uttered. His only intention was to do what every good father does; he was admonishing his children in love.[164]

Paul often uses the figure of a parent-child relationship in speaking of himself and his converts. Timothy, Titus, and Onesimus are spoken of as "my child" (I Tim. 1:18; II Tim. 2:1; Philem. 10; cf. Phil. 2:22); "my true child" (I Tim. 1:2; Tit. 1:4); or "my beloved child" (I Cor. 4:17; II Tim. 1:2). He addresses the Corinthians, the Galatians, and the Thessalonians as his children (I Cor. 4:14; II Cor. 6:13; Gal. 4:19; I Thess. 2:7,11; cf. II Cor. 12:14). He sees himself as having begotten them (I Cor. 4:15; Philem. 10), or as being in travail for them (Gal. 4:19). Sometimes he takes the stance of a father, performing fatherly duties (I Cor. 4:14,15—admonishing; I Thess. 2:11—exhorting, encouraging, and testifying) or receiving fatherly honor (Phil. 2:22—being served); sometimes that of a mother (I Thess. 2:7—as a nurse cherishing her own children; cf. I Cor. 3:2—feeding them with milk). The figure is by no means unique to Paul. Jesus addressed his disciples as children (Mark 10:24; John 13:33); John's first letter has the constantly recurring refrain of "my little children" (I John 2:1,12,28; etc.); and Peter speaks of Mark as "his son" (I Pet. 5:13). The application of the father-son relationship to that of teachers and their pupils was both of long standing and general in the ancient world.[165] Paul's usage, however, is best accounted for in terms of the world immediately at hand to him. Rabbinic Judaism had the saying: "He who teaches the son of his neighbor the Torah, Scripture ascribes it to him as if he had begotten him."[166] In fact, the thoughts run so parallel, that when Paul substitutes for the Torah the gospel as the means by which the new life was awakened, he must be suspected of Christianizing a Jewish figure of speech.[167]

Paul pauses for a moment to reinforce this thought of his fatherhood on the Corinthians. They have apparently been losing sight of this fact, and he wishes not only to remind them of it, but to draw an important consequence from it. A child can have but one father. The child may be placed in the care of ever so many different people; these people may have ever so many different roles to play in his life; they may be worthy of ever so much respect; and they may make ever so many unique contributions to his life.

---

164 The father's role toward his children is often presented as that of an admonisher (νουθετέω/ νουθεσία) in the literature of the day: e.g., Eph. 6:4: "Ye fathers, provoke not your children to wrath: but nurture them in the chastening and admonition of the Lord"; Wisdom 11:10: "For thou didst test them as a father does in warning"; Psalms of Solomon 13:8: "For he [God] will admonish the righteous as a beloved son: and his chastening is as a man chasteneth his firstborn" (trans. H. E. Ryle and M. R. James, Cambridge: University Press, 1891). Cf. further Josephus, Antiquities III. 311; Testament of Reuben 3:8; Plato, Republic VIII. 560a.

165 L. Dürr shows that it can be found at least as far back as the 19th and 20th dynasties of Egypt (about 1300–1100 B.C.) and that it is also to be found at a relatively early date among the Assyrians and Babylonians. See his "Heilige Vaterschaft im antiken Orient," in Heilige Überlieferung. Ausschnitte aus der Geschichte des Mönchtums und des Heiligen Kultes ... Ildefons Herwegen dargeboten (= Beiträge zur Geschichte des Alten Mönchtums und des Benediktinerordens. Supplementband) Münster, Aschendorff, 1938, pp. 6ff. See also his review of this usage in the Old Testament (pp. 9ff.).

166 Babylonian Talmud: Sanhedrin 19b (trans. J. Shachter in The Babylonian Talmud: Seder Nezikin V [ed. Epstein], London: Soncino Press, 1935, p. 102); the same in Sanhedrin 99b. See Strack-Billerbeck, III, p. 339, on I Cor. 4:14, note 1; and III, p. 340 on I Cor. 4:15, note c.

167 G. Schrenk, πατήρ, T.W.N.T., V, p. 1007, 16ff. Cf. also F. Büchsel and K. H. Rengstorf, γεννάω, T.W.N.T., I, p. 664, 22ff.; p. 666, 21ff.

But none of them will ever do what his father has done: none of them can ever beget him. That has happened once for all, and with it the basic shape of his life was determined. He is the offspring of this one father and he will always remain so. The Corinthians had been born into the world of Jesus Christ through the gospel, and Paul was the begetter. They lived in a father-son relationship to Paul, and to him alone. [168]

From this vantage point (cf. οὖν) Paul makes his great plea to the Corinthians: "I beseech you therefore, be ye imitators of me" (4:16). As my children, be what children ought to be: be my imitators. As children begotten (4:15), beloved (4:14), fed (3:2), taught (4:6), admonished (4:14) by me, reflect the kind of life you have come to know in your father.

The question arises as to what imitation Paul has in mind. In what does he wish to be imitated? Is it a general over-all imitation of his life, or does he have some specific thing in mind? In the light of the preceding context where he has shown himself to be so distressed about their pride and their contentious self-assertiveness, it would seem that his thought must be particularly centered on the humility and the giving of himself for others that can be seen in his life. He toils, he blesses, he endures, he entreats (4:12,13). These things reveal an attitude toward life quite different from theirs. The call to imitation appears to be directed particularly to this matter. However, such an understanding of this passage has been vigorously contested on the basis of what Paul says in the next verse. Hence, we must go on to an examination of this verse before drawing our conclusions as to the meaning and intent of imitation in this passage.

Paul says, "For this cause have I sent unto you Timothy, who is my beloved and faithful child in the Lord, who shall put you in remembrance of my ways which are in Christ, even as I teach everywhere in every church" (4:17). Until we come to the last clause "even as I teach...," the thought seems to continue in the same direction we have thus far been going. Timothy had been sent with an eye to the service he can perform in bringing forth this imitation. Timothy has much in common with the Corinthians, for he, like them, is one of Paul's beloved children in Christ. But Paul can also call him a faithful child, trustworthy, reliable, and true to the form of his father. Thus, he is the better qualified for his mission to the Corinthians, since in reminding them of Paul's ways he will not merely have to try to describe Paul to them, but will himself be a living representation of Paul in their midst. He can show Paul to them.

The decision to send Timothy did not come at the same time as the decision to write this letter. Timothy had already left Ephesus on his journey into Macedonia (cf. Acts 19:22), and from there he was apparently to go to Corinth. [169] In view of this fact, Weiss has proposed that Timothy's mission

---

[168] It ought not to be overlooked that the sentence is so constructed that the two pronouns, I-you, are found next to each other: ... ἐγὼ ὑμᾶς ἐγέννησα.

[169] Cf. the aorist ἔπεμψα, I sent. It is unlikely that this is an epistolary aorist, for that would suggest that Timothy is to bring the epistle with him. But, as I Cor. 16:10 shows, this is not the case. Also, if Timothy were with Paul at the time of the writing of this epistle, one would expect

to Corinth was to remind them of Paul's ways only in the broad and general sense. He assumes that the situation revealed by those from Chloe's household could not yet have been known to Paul when he sent Timothy on his mission. Hence, he could not have had in mind Timothy's reminding them of humility in particular.[170] The assumption, however, that the reports from Chloe's household were not known at the time of the sending of Timothy is wholly gratuitous. It seems more likely that just these reports had occasioned the decision to send Timothy to Corinth in connection with his Macedonian trip. Then, after Timothy's departure a letter was received from Corinth asking for information on specific questions (7:1; cf. 7:25; 8:1; 12:1; 16:1). Also a delegation came from Corinth and served as a further source of information about the whole situation (16:17). In view of these latter developments Paul decided to write this letter. Thus, in effect his letter throughout these first chapters deals with the same matter for which he had sent Timothy to Corinth. Timothy's instructions to bring them to remembrance of Paul's ways arose from the same situation as Paul's call to them in his letter to be his imitators. Timothy would remind them of Paul's humility, his self-surrender, his toiling, blessing, enduring, entreating; and as a faithful son of Paul, they would find in Timothy himself a reminder of these ways of Paul.

The whole train of thought to this point makes Paul's reference to "my ways which are in Christ" sound like he means his personal conduct, *i.e.* the way in which faith in Christ had taken hold in his life and was coming to expression in the various situations in which he found himself. Can "my ways which are in Christ" mean the Christian way of life as you saw it in me? One would suppose this to be almost self-evident. However, Paul proceeds to add a clause which has caused interpreters and commentators to hesitate, backtrack, reinterpret, and reconsider the whole passage which seemed to be so clear up to this point. Paul says: "... my ways which are in Christ, even as I teach everywhere in every church." It suddenly becomes apparent that the ways of which he has just spoken constitute a part of his teaching. Can we now still think that he is referring to his personal conduct? Could he call his personal ways a part of his teaching? This matter must be investigated before we can draw our conclusions as to what Paul means by his call to imitation.

Heinrici has sought to alleviate the difficulty of conceiving of personal ways as being a part of the teaching by making the "even as" refer back to "put you in remembrance." In this way he understands Paul to say that Timothy's manner of putting them in remembrance will be the same as the manner in which Paul does his teaching no matter where he is. The "even as" clause refers to "die ganze Charaktereigentümlichkeit, mit welcher Paulus als Lehrer zu Werke ging."[171] Formally this is possible, but it

---

to have his name mentioned in the salutation, as in II Cor. 1:1; or at least one would expect that greetings would be sent from him in view of his not arriving in Corinth until sometime after the epistle.

170 J. Weiss, *Der erste Korintherbrief*, K.e.K.N.T., 9. Aufl. Göttingen: Vandenhoeck & Ruprecht, 1910, p. 119.

171 G. Heinrici, *Kritisch exegetisches Handbuch über den ersten Brief an die Korinther*, K.e.K.N.T., 7. Aufl., Göttingen: Vandenhoeck & Ruprecht, 1888, p. 135.

hardly appeals as being the natural construction of the sentence. It is appropriate to notice, nevertheless, that the καθώς clause is not integrally related to the thought of the sentence as Paul has thus far stated it. Rather it is an additional thought interjected at the end. Furthermore, this thought, which has suddenly occurred to Paul and which he inserts at this point, is not calculated to emphasize the fact of his having been engaged in teaching. Rather, he is intent upon making clear to the Corinthians that they are no unique instance among the churches he has served. The ways he has made known to them are the ways he has made known "everywhere in every church"—the redundancy of the phrase helps to emphasize the point. The Corinthians are no exception, and they can not be permitted to think that they are an exception. Repeatedly in his letter he interjects this thought about the general pattern that applies throughout the Christian church (cf. 7:17; 11:16; 14:33,36). In view of the point which the καθώς clause is calculated to make, the fact that Paul refers to his teaching is a subsidiary matter, not the primary one. At the same time there is no escaping the fact that he has spoken of teaching in connection with the ways to which he has just referred. In an indirect way we learn that he viewed these ways as being included in his teaching.

Paul's intent at this point in his letter is to appeal to the Corinthians to bring their lives into conformity with Christianity as he had presented it to them. To accomplish this he had sent Timothy to remind them of certain ways which he teaches in all his churches. To speak of the teaching of ways in a context of how one ought to live in view of his religious commitment brings recollections of Old Testament terminology. God's people walk in God's ways (Deut. 10:12); the Gentiles walk in the way of the nations (Jer. 10:2). As we have noticed earlier, [172] to walk in God's ways is to walk in fellowship and communion with God. We walk in God's ways when we live according to the commands he has given us, applying them to the various situations in which we find ourselves in life. Ways are the experiences of living through which we go. They are God's ways when they are lived in accordance with the will of God, in obedience to his command, and thus are walked in covenantal fellowship with him. However, the ways having to do with the service of God were not always designated by his name. They could also be identified in terms of the people keeping them. Thus we hear God making certain promises to the nations around Israel, "if they will diligently learn the ways of my people" (Jer. 12:16). The frequent reference to David's ways is only another way of expressing God's ways as they were lived by an obedient king. [173] The same terminology also described the other religious allegiances. There was the way of the nations (Jer. 10:2). Jeroboam's ways were the ways of a king apostate from God. [174] The Old Testament used the term *way* or *ways* to designate the religious affiliation and commitment which the course and events of one's life expressed.

The writers of the Old Testament found that a person came to adopt a certain way through its being taught or its being learned. They used several

---

[172] See above, p. 34.
[173] See above, p. 33.
[174] Ibid.

words all expressing the general idea of teaching, showing, guiding, instructing. [175] It is of particular interest for our present study that the word *teach* (διδάσκειν, למד) was one of the most common terms. God teaches his ways to man (Ps. 25:9). When a man has learned God's ways, he may, in turn, be a teacher of them (Ps. 51:13). The terminology continues into the New Testament times, for Jesus was recognized as teaching the way of God (Mark 12:14 par.). Furthermore, the ways of Baal were taught to Israel, and sometimes Israel learned the way of the nations (Jer. 9:14; 10:2; 12:16). Rengstorf has called attention to the fact that διδάσκειν, as the Septuagint uses it, addresses itself not merely to the understanding, but primarily to the will. It lays its claim to the whole man, not just to certain aspects of him. [176] Through being taught, a person becomes completely involved. One suspects that the teaching process here referred to must be thought of in fairly broad terms.

The totality of involvement and the comprehensiveness of the concept of teaching can be seen in such a passage as Jer. 12:16: "And it will come to pass, if they [the other nations] will diligently learn [M.T.: למד ילמדו, LXX: μαθόντες μάθωσιν] the ways of my people, to swear by my name, As Jehovah liveth; even as they taught [M.T.: למדו, LXX: ἐδίδαξαν] my people to swear by Baal; then they shall be built up in the midst of my people." The learning and teaching here have to do with bringing people into a religious commitment which affects their whole status. [177] They become Jehovah worshippers or they become Baal worshippers, in each case with all the far-reaching implications of such a religious commitment. As for the nations teaching Israel to serve Baal, Rengstorf says: "Das Erscheinen von διδάσκειν stellt fest, dass es sich einerseits um eine organisierte, systematisch betriebene Lösung Israels von seinem angestammten Gott handelte, dass aber andererseits dies Unternehmen auch von Erfolg gekrönt war." [178] The picture of the teaching here goes far beyond any academic exercise of giving instruction in rules, principles, and practices. It suggests the totality of influences which were active and of pressures which were brought to bear to get Israel to leave the service of Jehovah and join in the service of Baal. It is the comprehensive process by which the Gentiles led Israel away from her God.

In classical Greek also the idea of teacher and teaching were sometimes used in a broad and not too technical sense. Interestingly enough, we find traces of such a usage in a passage which also speaks of imitation. To the charge that Socrates was corrupting the youth, Xenophon answers: "On the contrary, he cured these vices [impiety, crime, etc.] in many, by putting into them a desire for goodness, and by giving them confidence that self-discipline would make them gentlemen. To be sure he never professed to teach this (καίτοι γε οὐδεπώποτε ὑπέσχετο διδάσκαλοι εἶναι τούτου); but by letting his own light shine, he led his disciples to

---

[175] *E.g.*, M.T.: למד, ידע, ירה, נגד; LXX: διδάσκειν, δεικνύειν, γνωρίζειν, ἀναγγέλλειν, συμβιβάζειν, νομοθετεῖν. See Michaelis, *T.W.N.T.*, V, p. 53, 28ff.
[176] K. Rengstorf, διδάσκω, *T.W.N.T.*, II, p. 139, 48ff.
[177] The swearing by the name of Jehovah or Baal is to be seen as an act of central religious significance, a kind of confession of faith, symbolic of the total service of the respective deity. See G. Ch. Aalders, *De Profeet Jeremia*, K.V., Kampen: J. H. Kok, 1953, Vol. I, p. 153.
[178] Rengstorf, *T.W.N.T.*, II, p. 140, 1–4.

hope that they through imitation of him would attain to such excellence."[179] Thus, Xenophon's answer is that, although Socrates did not profess to be a teacher of virtue, in actual fact he did accomplish the teaching of virtue. A more striking illustration of the usage is found in Xenophon's account of Antipho's accosting Socrates for his poor example: "Now the professors (διδάσκαλοι) of other subjects try to make their pupils copy their teachers (μιμητὰς ἑαυτῶν): if you too intend to make your companions do that, you must consider yourself a professor (διδάσκαλος) of unhappiness."[180] In effect this says that by leading pupils to imitate oneself, one is engaged in teaching them. Another instance of how mere fellowship was conceived of as possibly resulting in teaching and learning is found when Xenophon writes: "The society of honest men is a training in virtue, but the society of the bad is virtue's undoing. As one of the poets says: 'From the good shalt thou learn (διδάξεαι) good things.'"[181] Such instances show that the Greeks too were not inclined to limit teaching and learning merely to academic exercises and formal instruction but sometimes used the words to describe the total influence of one person upon another.

The thought suggests itself then that, when Paul speaks about the teaching of his ways, he may have in mind the comprehensive process by which he sought to lead the Corinthians to the Christian faith and into a way of life appropriate to such an allegiance. At least, it would seem that in view of the breadth which the idea of teaching could have in classical Greek and in view of the comprehensive process which the Old Testament expression "teaching a way" could have, the limits of its meaning in Paul's letter ought not to be too narrowly conceived.[182]

In making an appeal to the Corinthians to recall the ways they have been taught, one expects a reference to their being taught Christ's ways or the Christian way. In effect, what Paul has said is not really different from that, for he speaks of "my ways which are in Christ." Paul has no aversion to referring to himself when we would have expected him to refer to Christ. In Rom. 2:16 he speaks of "my gospel," and in I Thess. 1:5 he calls it "our gospel." Why does he say "my ways which are in Christ," instead of simply "Christ's ways"? This particular terminology is undoubtedly determined by what Paul has just said. "Be ye imitators of me.... [Timothy] shall put you in remembrance of my ways." The call to imitation leads Paul to make reference to his ways. But he leaves no room for the thought that he is being

---

[179] *Memorabilia* I. 2:2,3 (Marchant, pp. 12—15).
[180] *Ibid.*, I. 6:3 (Marchant, pp. 68,69).
[181] *Ibid.*, I. 2:20 (Marchant, pp. 20,21). In regard to the original reading in the poet Theognis of the line here cited, there is a textual problem as to whether μαθήσεαι or διδάξεαι is correct. J. Carrière places the former in his text and notes that it is found thus in Musonius, Clement of Alexandria, and Stobaeus' version of Xenophon, while the latter is found in Plato (Meno 95d), Xenophon, and Hermogenes. See Théognis, *Poèmes Élégiaques* (ed. J. Carrière, Paris: Société d'Édition "Les Belle Lettres," 1948, re l. 35). The matter is of no further concern to our present pursuit than to notice that Xenophon's form of the quotation was one that was current in his day and illustrates an accepted usage of διδάσκω.
[182] It is remarkable that Rengstorf in his article on διδάσκω and related words in *T.W.N.T.*, II, pp. 138—168, makes no reference to the usage of the word here in I Cor. 4:17, especially in view of his making at least some reference to every other appearance of the word in Paul's writings. Cremer-Kögel, *Wörterbuch*, pp. 292—295, also makes no mention of the usage of the word in I Cor. 4:17.

arbitrary here, for he adds immediately the clarification that these ways are ways in Christ. They are the ways he has come to know and walk since becoming a Christian. They are the Christian life as he now lives it wherever he goes. Paul refers to his ways in broadest terms, but in view of the situation in Corinth he obviously has in mind especially his ways of humility, selfgiving, toiling, blessing, enduring, entreating. These ways he had shown them; he had lived them in their presence. He had laid out a way, a path, a road for them. His footsteps have marked it. He had undoubtedly talked about his ways as a Christian and discussed them thoroughly with his hearers and his converts, for they were indeed radical to the non-Christian mind. These ways—the Christian walk of life, the way Paul walks in the fellowship and service of his Lord Jesus Christ—he teaches everywhere. He teaches Christianity, like the Gentile nations taught Israel the service of Baal, and like the Gentile nations might learn the ways of God's people from God's people. [183] Words were important; instruction was a *sine qua non;* but the totality of the contact was included in the process of teaching. Paul saw himself teaching Christianity with everything he said, everything he did, and everything he was. Hence, he could speak of what he had taught in the ways he had lived and conducted himself in the Corinthian community and in every other place.

Michaelis says regarding I Cor. 4:17: "Der καθώς-Satz [zeigt], dass nicht an die persönliche Lebensführung des Apostels gedacht werden darf, denn diese bildete nicht den Inhalt seines διδάσκειν." [184] Others have come to the same conclusion. [185] Such a conclusion has led to a variety of proposals as to what Paul meant by his ways. They are described as "allgemeiner 'Grundsätze'"; [186] "'règle de foi' commune"; [187] "les principes moraux". [188] Sometimes the ways are compared to the *halacha* or *halachoth* of the rabbis. [189] It has also been proposed that evidence is to be found here of an early form of catechism. [190] Stendahl finds these "ways" of Paul a possible stage in the development from the School of Jesus to the "rather elaborate School of

---

183 The implication of Jer. 12:16 is that the ways of God's people were to be learned from God's people; there is no hint at any other source for the knowledge. Furthermore, the promise is: "then shall they be built up in the midst of my people."
184 Michaelis, *T.W.N.T.*, V, p. 91, 36ff. *Cf.* also *T.W.N.T.*, IV, p. 670, 28ff.
185 Particularly Weiss has wrestled with the problem: "Wenn wir nicht den Satz καθώς etc. läsen, würden wir ohne Zweifel verstehen: meine Wege, die ich wandle in der Gemeinschaft des Herrn Jesu." But he finally concludes: "Aber all diese Betrachtungen, die sich immer wieder aufdrängen, werden verboten durch den Schlusssatz, der uns zwingt, wohl oder übel die ὁδοί des Paulus als seine Lehren zu fassen" (*I Kor.*, pp. 119,120). *Cf.* also O. Michel, μιμνήσκομαι, *T.W.N.T.*, IV, p. 681, fn. 12; Lietzmann, *I Kor.*, p. 22; Bachmann, *I Kor.*, p. 206.
186 Lietzmann, *I Kor.*, p. 22.
187 Allo, *I Cor.*, p. 78.
188 Héring, *I Cor.*, p. 38.
189 Moffatt, *I Cor.*, p. 51; Héring, *I Cor.*, p. 38; Lietzmann, *I Kor.*, p. 22; W. Bousset, *Der Erste Brief an die Korinther*, in *Die Schriften des Neuen Testaments*, 2. Aufl., Göttingen, Vandenhoeck & Ruprecht, 1908, Bd. 2, p. 89. However, in the 3. Aufl., 1917, Bd. 2, p. 93, Bousset rejects the idea that the rabbinic idea of a *halacha* helps explain Paul's saying "my ways"; his concluding statement is: "Wie also Paulus dazu kommt, seine Lehren (Grundsätze) als Wege zu bezeichnen, ist noch nicht aufgeklärt."
190 See Michaelis, *T.W.N.T.*, V, p. 93, fn. 170 for a partial bibliography on the subject.

Matthew." [191] Gerhardsson suggests the possibility that "these 'ways' consisted of extensive summaries of the Apostle's *didache*, his τύπος διδαχῆς (Rom. 6.17), divided up into various tractates, and dealing with other than strictly ethical questions." [192] Michaelis reasons from the close connection between God's ways and his commands in the Old Testament, and lays heavy emphasis on the authoritativeness and imperative which he finds expressed here: "μιμηταί des Paulus werden, das heisst hier ganz klar: seinen ὁδοί nachgehen, seine διδαχή, soweit sie Gebotscharakter trägt, annehmen, seine Gebote befolgen." [193] However, it must be said of all these proposals that they are at odds with the context and with the way one naturally understands Paul's ways until he centers his attention on the mention of teaching here. In the context Paul has not been speaking about the formal instruction he had given the Corinthians, but about himself, his conduct, his way of living the Christian life. That Paul could have had these things in mind when he spoke of what he taught everywhere would not be contrary either to Old Testament or to classical Greek usage. Furthermore, Paul has just explained that he had written as he had about himself and Apollos that "in us ye might learn" (4:6). Their personal example could teach the Corinthians. The objections which have been raised to considering Paul's ways (4:17) as his personal conduct and his way of living the Christian life arise from conceiving of the teaching process in too narrow and too formal terms. Paul saw himself as teaching in the personal example which he set. Paul's ways are his personal conduct, the ways he lived as a Christian, the imitation of the Christian way of life which he set. [194]

\* \* \*

This passage from Paul's letter to the Corinthians enables us to make several observations regarding the imitation of Paul. First, it is striking how much confidence he displayed in this means of promoting Christian living. The situation in the Corinthian church was serious. The deviations from elementary Christian ways were radical. His own good name was being defamed, and the same was happening to other eminent Christian leaders. It is surprising that in such a situation he does not speak with crystal clarity: here exactly is the Christian way; these ways of yours can not be tolerated for the following reasons ... etc. It is surprising that he has no specific orders to issue to them and no solemn injunctions to place upon them. He does not

---

191   K. Stendahl, *The School of St. Matthew*, Uppsala: Almquist & Wiksells, 1954, p. 34.
192   Gerhardsson, *Memory*, pp. 304,305.
193   Michaelis, *T.W.N.T.*, IV, p. 670, 33—35. Quite typically, Michaelis finds in the figure of the father and son which Paul uses in this context, "dass die Frage des Gehorsams im Mittelpunkt steht" (p. 670, fn. 15). See discussion above, pp. 78—79, concerning this particular significance of the father-son relationship as Michaelis conceives it.
194   Among those understanding the passage thus are Grosheide, *I Kor.*, p. 135; H. Riesenfeld, "La voie de charité," *S.T.*, I, pp. 155,156; A. Schlatter, *Paulus Der Bote Jesu*, 2. Aufl., Stuttgart: Calwer Verlag, 1956, pp. 164,165; Juncker, *Ethik*, Vol. II, pp. 103,104. Cf. *N.E.B*.: "[Timothy] will remind you of the way of life in Christ which I follow." Schippers, *Geref. Zede*, p. 15, has pointed out the particular significance of Paul's speaking of his ways: "Tegen de achtergrond van wat wij in het Oude Testament vonden [concerning "walk" and "way"], mag worden gezegd, dat de apostel, door het christelijk leven *zijn wegen* te noemen, zijn wegen in Christus, wel te verstaan, ruimte toont voor het positiveren van de geboden Gods in het concrete leven. Hij heeft de christelijke zedevorming op gang gebracht."

approach them with a solemn "Thus saith the Lord." Rather, he approaches them as Paul, their friend, their servant, and their father. He seeks to motivate a change in them by an appeal to their personal attachment to him. He sets aside any impulse to command them with apostolic authority. He is determined to exploit to the fullest extent the way of gentleness and love (*cf.* 4:20). He is confident that there is still a personal tie between them, and he makes his appeal to them on the basis of this personal tie. As beloved children of your father, be my imitators.

In this passage we find the idea of imitation expressly derived from the relationship of father and child in which Paul found himself and his readers to stand. He is making no appeal to himself as a paragon of virtue. This is no moralistic appeal to a high and beautiful example, or one that would inspire them with great feelings of nobility and righteousness. The call to imitation is the call of a father to his children to walk in his ways and to become like him. In calling the children to do this, he is seeking to stimulate a process which ought to be taking place naturally. Children, by virtue of the fact that they have had their origin in their parents, are stamped with certain characteristics of their parents from the very beginning. Furthermore, they are born into an exceedingly close relationship of dependency on their parents and from them learn their elementary and most basic ways of life. Much of this learning process makes no appeal to careful reasoning, but is by way of simple observation or by being shown and then doing for oneself. By imitation the child grows in his likeness to his parents. He catches and adopts something of the essence of his parents. The closer the relationship of parent and child, the more the similarities develop. And this closeness of the relationship is largely determined by the factor of love. Hence, it is not insignificant that Paul refers to the Corinthians as beloved children. In the measure that he and they had really lived in love toward each other, in this measure he could now hope for imitation.

He had been a father to them in Christ: "in Christ I begat you through the gospel" (4:15). Hence his fatherhood had to do with the matter of living in Christ. It was Paul's "ways which are in Christ" (4:17) in which he was looking for imitation. He had been with them at their birth into Christianity and during those first tender months when they were learning the Christian way of life. Under his guidance the basic pattern of their Christian lives had been set. In him they had learned to see and know what Christianity was as it came to expression in the affairs of one's everyday life. They had learned to imitate his ways as Christians. Hence, although Paul makes his appeal on the basis of personal attachment, his appeal is neither arbitrary nor self-centered. This was the extent to which he had lost his own life in the service of Christ. An appeal to follow him was simply an appeal to be a Christian and to live as a Christian. He was busy personally mediating Christianity.

It was Paul's intention that people should learn Christianity through contact with him. He was conscious of the magnetic force of close personal relationships. He was intent upon capturing this force in the service of his Lord.

It was his avowed purpose to make use of the processes of imitation in building Christian lives. He found the processes of imitation to be an essential part of his whole program of furthering the gospel. Christianity did not take hold in the lives of people merely by their being instructed and being told. An important element in the communication of Christianity is that which was shown unobtrusively in the lives of those bringing the gospel. Paul's ways communicated Christianity. People "caught the idea" of Christianity from being with him and observing him. His ways and way of life and commonest little reaction in an everyday situation were matters of considerable importance. He viewed them as being a part of his whole work of teaching. By bringing about an imitation of his ways, he was engaged in teaching.

The imitation of Paul was to take place along the entire front of life. When he appeals to the Corinthians to be imitators of himself, basically he appeals to them to renew their efforts and recapture their original keenness and vigor in the entire matter of Christian living. However, in view of the specific situation of strife and contentiousness about which Paul had just been writing, we must judge that the thrust of his appeal to imitation in this passage is directed primarily to this matter. He had shown them the Christian way of humility and self-giving. He reminds them again of some of the things that had been happening to him and of the ways he had been going as a Christian. In essence they added up to a refusal to retaliate to the unkind and harsh treatment he was receiving on every hand, and in place of retaliation, to submit, to engage in hard work, to bless, and to show kindness, good will, and friendliness. [195] The Christian way was the way of humility and of giving oneself in love to others. The Corinthians had not been going this way. Paul calls them back to it: "Be ye imitators of me."

## IV. I Corinthians 11:1

*Be ye imitators of me, even as I also am of Christ.*

In I Corinthians Paul issues the call a second time to imitate him. The second instance is in precisely the same words as the first, except for the addition of the clause about Paul's being an imitator of Christ. The call to imitation comes once again as an appeal with which he closes the discussion of a matter. This second call to imitation is surely to be heard with some echoes of the first still in mind. [196]

---

[195] For παρακαλέω (4:13) in the sense of "gute Worte geben", see O. Schmitz and G. Stählin, παρακαλέω, *T.W.N.T.*, V, p. 794, fn. 172; Bauer, *Wörterbuch*, s.v., 5.

[196] "Wenn im gleichen 1 K später 11, 1 genau dieselbe Wendung wiederkehrt: μιμηταί μου γίνεσθε, so wird sie nicht ohne Zusammenhang mit 4, 16 zu verstehen sein" (Michaelis, *T.W.N.T.*, IV, p. 670, 37—39). Even for those who have proposed that the present I Corinthians is a collection and interweaving of several individual letters, the two passages on imitation (4:16 and 11:1) are often found as parts of the same letter. *Cf.* the proposals of Schmithals, *Gnos. Kor.*, p. 17; Héring, *I Cor.*, p. 11. On the other hand, J. Weiss, *Das Urchristentum*, Göttingen: Vandenhoeck & Ruprecht, 1917, p. 271, finds the passages respectively in the third

In writing to the Corinthians Paul turns at the beginning of the seventh chapter to discussing the questions raised by the letter he had received from Corinth (*cf.* I Cor. 7:1). In I Cor. 7 he speaks about problems relating to marriage and celibacy. Then he proceeds to a broader discussion of the problems which had arisen in connection with the eating of food which had been sacrificed to idols. The discussion runs from I Cor. 8 through I Cor. 10, and concludes with the call to imitation in 11:1.

Paul found that the problem which had arisen in Corinth and about which the Corinthians had inquired could be solved only by giving due consideration to two important Christian principles. On the one hand, the Christian enjoys freedom; and on the other hand, he is bound to act in love. The Corinthians must learn to find a way that does justice to both of these principles. Paul discusses the matter in these terms. He begins by acknowledging that as Christians we all know that the idol represents a non-entity. Thus, as far as the food sacrificed to it is concerned, the matter is one of indifference, and the Christian is free to eat it. However, this does not mean that he will take up the practice of eating it. There are brethren of his who are living in weakness and fear and who have scruples against such eating. The way of Christian love demands that every man avoid being a stumbling block to his brethren. The Christian is free, but his freedom is not the motivating and guiding force of his life. He is motivated and guided by love. In effect, then, the point that Paul makes in I Cor. 8 is that for the sake of love the Christian willingly foregoes the exercise of various rights, powers, and privileges which are his by reason of his freedom in Christ.

Paul then proceeds to speak about how he has applied this matter of foregoing one's rights to his own life and calling as an apostle (I Cor. 9). He points out that as an apostle he has rights in various matters, among them the right to receive support from those to whom he preaches the gospel. Nevertheless, lest this should somehow act as a hindrance in the furtherance of the gospel, he has adopted the practice of foregoing this right. He has determined that he will make use of no right which might interfere in the bringing of salvation to others (9:22). And he adds immediately a corollary thought to this. He maintains a rigorous attitude for his own sake too. He is bent on the salvation of others, but he is also bent on becoming a participator in salvation himself (9:23). He finds possibilities of a dreadful outcome in allowing the matter of rights, liberties, and privileges to be the regulative force in his life. He has placed himself under a self-imposed bondage, "lest by any means, after that I have preached to others, I myself should be rejected" (9:27). When Paul tells of the rights he has foregone for the gospel's sake, one can hardly escape the implication that in comparison it becomes a pretty small matter if it may be appropriate for some of the Corinthians to forego certain foods out of love for their weaker brethren. Paul has not

---

and the second letters, which, he proposes, were written within a very short time of each other and may even have been sent simultaneously. D. Völter, after severely paring away much of the present I Corinthians as spurious, still finds the two imitation passages to be a part of the original letter (*cf. Paulus und seine Briefe*, Strassburg: Heitz & Mündel, 1905, p. 73).

spoken specifically about furnishing them an example in this matter of foregoing one's rights. Nevertheless, his turning so abruptly to his own conduct in illustration and application of the principle he has just expounded hardly permits one to escape the thought that he wished to suggest himself as an example.

As Eidem has pointed out, [197] these sudden and easy shifts by Paul from speaking about others to speaking about himself often suggest the implication that he is an example for them. Such a sudden turn of the thought is made in the verses immediately preceding chapter 9: "And thus, sinning against the brethren, and wounding their conscience when it is weak, ye sin against Christ. Wherefore, if meat causeth my brother to stumble, I will eat no flesh for evermore, that I cause not my brother to stumble" (8:12,13). A similar turn is found in 9:24—26: "Even so run; that ye may attain. And every man that striveth in the games exerciseth self-control in all things.... I therefore so run, as not uncertainly." Such small indications reveal that the thought of his example is more than just a momentary one, in mind only when Paul makes a specific appeal for imitation. The thought of his example underlies much of the thought in what he writes between the first call for imitation (4:16) and the second (11:1).

At this point it is perhaps appropriate to notice that Paul makes an appeal to his example also in I Cor. 7 in connection with the question of marriage. Here his indication of his example comes accompanied with statements carefully qualifying it: "Yet I would that all men were even as I myself. Howbeit each man hath his own gift from God, one after this manner, and another after that. But I say to the unmarried and to widows, It is good for them if they abide even as I. But if they have not continency, let them marry" (7:7—9). He has a wish, a preference, and a longing that in regard to the matters of marriage everyone could be like him. However, the qualifying statements show that he is aware of how disastrous it would be to create the impression that the unmarried state is the right one for people who have not been given the gift of continency. He is also realistic enough to realize that not all people enjoy this gift as he does. What he longs for is the continency in men to enable them to remain unmarried. He sees in this a real boon for the furtherance of the gospel (7:32—35), especially in view of the troubled times in which they were living (7:26). The force of the reference to Paul's example here is not to recommend the unmarried state as such, but to recommend the value of the gift of continency and to suggest the increased opportunities of service which may become possible through it. Marriage is not to be despised. But men do well to seek the best gifts (I Cor. 12:31). The gift of continency is a gift to be highly prized. "I would that all men were even as I myself" (7:7).

In the latter part of I Cor. 9 Paul explained that the rigor with which he had determined to forego his rights had not only the well-being of others in mind. He found a rigorous stance necessary also to his own well-being. There was the possibility that he could preach to others, and himself be rejected (9:27). This dreadful possibility of presuming upon one's past and upon one's privileges to his own disaster could be well illustrated from Israel's

---

[197] Eidem, *Stud. Tillägnade E. Stave*, p. 70.

history in the wilderness. Paul proceeds to remind the Corinthians of this and to warn them about it (10:1—13). This illustration and the warnings accompanying it pave the way to make one aspect of this whole problem of eating food sacrificed to idols very clear to the Corinthians. The Christian was not free to participate in heathen sacrifices and sacrificial feasts. In so doing he was involving himself in the heinous act of worshipping other gods and demons (10:14—22).

In 10:23 Paul returns to the subject as he had first begun to develop it in the eighth chapter. This paragraph forms his concluding judgments on the matter of sacrificed food. He re-emphasizes the fact of the Christian's freedom, but he makes it clear in just as emphatic a way that this is not the starting point for the Christian's action. The place to begin is with the command of love: "Let no man seek his own good, but each his neighbor's good" (10:24). In regard to the food which one could buy or which one might be served at the home of a friend, there need be no concern about whether it had previously been sacrificed to an idol or not. However, where there was some indication that the eating of it might be misunderstood by another to the injuring of his conscience, the Christian would abstain. This abstinence in no way endangered one's liberty; it simply showed his concern for the well-being of the other. Thus, Paul comes to his conclusion of the matter in which he issues a series of counsels of most comprehensive scope: "Whether therefore ye eat, or drink, or whatsoever ye do, do all to the glory of God. Give no occasion of stumbling, either to Jews, or to Greeks, or to the church of God: even as I also please all men in all things, not seeking mine own profit, but the profit of the many, that they may be saved. Be ye imitators of me, even as I also am of Christ" (10:31—11:1).

Doing all things to the glory of God is a broad requirement. Taken alone it is abstract and unspecific. But when it is placed in the context in which it was issued, there is specific content immediately at hand to be poured into it. As Moffatt puts it: "God is glorified as his Church displays such considerate love on the part of the strong for the weak (Rom. xiv. 13f., xv. 6), and this applies to the very details of ordinary life, where one can help or hurt another's soul." [198] On the other hand, Paul by no means wishes to be understood as speaking only in regard to the present situation of the strong and the weak in the church at Corinth. The instance at hand must be only one specific application of a rule that has universal scope. Where there is love and honor for God, people will be sensitive not only to the needs of the weaker brethren, but to the needs of all their fellow men, whether Jew, Greek, or fellow member of the church (10:32). This means being an occasion of stumbling for no one. Here is the test for exercising their Christian freedom. They are to act to the glory of God as this becomes concrete in the spiritual well-being of their fellow men. Paul illustrates and fortifies his point by referring to his own conduct: "even as I also please all men in all things." And that such a policy could have nothing to do with

---

[198] Moffatt, *I Cor.*, p. 144.

desires on Paul's part to be popular and well-liked is clear when he adds immediately that he is not in search of his own profit, but of theirs, that they may be saved. The key to Paul's conduct is the salvation of his fellow men. He had stated this same thing in fuller form in the discussion he had just presented (*cf.* 9:19ff.). There too he had concluded: "I am become all things to all men, that I may by all means save some" (9:22). Paul had given himself wholly to the salvation of his fellow men. To the Corinthians he calls: "Be ye imitators of me."

> We may notice in this paragraph (10:23—11:1) that Paul has been gradually working up to this specific call for imitation of his conduct. He begins in general terms: "Let no man seek his own good" (10:24). Soon he is speaking to them in the second person—"if someone bid you" (10:27); "if someone say to you" (10:28). But suddenly in 10:29 he has switched to the first person: "why is my liberty judged"; "if I partake"; "why am I evil spoken of." He has stepped right into the midst of the Corinthian circle, as it were, in order to make his point in person and to illustrate it by pointing to himself. In 10:32—33 he becomes still more specific in pressing the matter of himself as an example. To the command "Give no occasion of stumbling," he adds, "even as I also please all men." The command receives specific illustration in himself. Then, after speaking about himself in terms suggesting himself as an illustration and example, Paul clinches his point with the call to action as straightforward and incisive as Jesus' "Go and do thou likewise" after the parable of the good Samaritan (Luke 10:37). Paul calls, "Be ye imitators of me."

The point of imitation here is eminently clear. It is the development of such an attitude and such a conduct toward other men that one is always promoting their salvation. The salvation of others must take precedence over the pursuit of one's own desires or the exercise of one's own rights. It is a call to give oneself for the sake of the gospel. Paul has indicated how far he is willing to go. He will forego enjoying certain foods and drinks (9:4); marriage (9:5); his right to an income from his apostolic labors (9:6—22); he will become all things to all men and will do all things for the gospel's sake (9:22,23). In this kind of conduct the Corinthians are to follow him, showing the same pattern and shape in their lives.

To the call for imitation of himself Paul adds, "even as I also am of Christ." It is not surprising that Christ's example should come to Paul's mind when he has been thinking about a person's giving himself in behalf of the salvation of others. The thought of Christ's self-giving had occurred to Paul earlier while writing this passage to the Corinthians about the problem of eating food offered to idols. He cautioned the "strong" about the injury they could do to a weaker brother "for whose sake Christ died" (I Cor. 8:11). It is noteworthy that in writing to the church at Rome about a similar situation of differences of opinion between the "strong" and the "weak" about the matter of foods, Paul points his readers to Christ's example of not pleasing himself (*cf.* Rom. 15:1—7). [199] The train of thought is found again in Philip-

---

[199] The similarities between Rom. 15:1—7 and our present passage in 1 Cor. are striking. Notice such things as the similarity of the problem ("strong" and "weak" in the matter of food);

pians. Paul writes them: "Be of the same mind, ... not looking each of you to his own things, but each of you also to the things of others" (Phil. 2:2,4); then he proceeds immediately to point them to Christ's example (Phil. 2:5—11). [200] It is fully in harmony with Pauline thinking and writing that he should bring the matter of Christ's example into the discussion here in I Corinthians.

The question has been raised whether Paul is really referring to the example of Christ as he was known in his life on earth. Dibelius has observed: "Dem Apostel steht also nicht der Mensch, sondern der vom Himmel gekommene Gottessohn vor Augen, nicht der Geschichtsverlauf, sondern der Mythus, in dem das geschichtliche Leben Jesu nur eine Periode bildet; die zur 'Nachahmung' empfohlenen Eigenschaften sind nicht die Tugenden einer menschlichen, sondern die Qualitäten einer göttlichen Person." [201] Over against such a conception of how the imitation of Christ is to be understood, Dodd quite correctly observed: "These passages [I Cor. 11:1 and I Thess. 1:6] exclude the idea that Paul is referring to an ideal Messianic figure and not to the Jesus of history, for Christ is an object of imitation in the same sense as Paul himself is." [202] It is questionable whether it is helpful to an understanding of this passage to attempt to distinguish in regard to Christ between the historical man and the pre-existent Son of God. It is impossible to ascertain to what extent Paul is thinking here of the self-giving which was apparent in Jesus' way of life on earth and to what extent he is thinking of the total humbling of the pre-existent Son of God to the death on the cross for our salvation. Sevenster sensibly proposes: "Waarschijnlijk heeft men de levensopenbaring van den Heer als een geheel gezien en daarom geen duidelijk onderscheid gemaakt." [203]

It is another question as to how much Paul really knew of the details of Jesus' life and teaching while on earth. How specific could Paul's imitation of Christ be? We have noted earlier how the matter of following Jesus involved one in sharing his way of life and its consequences, both as to humiliation and suffering and as to exaltation. [204] There are various indications in Paul's letters of how much he found himself caught up in such a way of life through his commitment to Christ. He mentions to the Philippians about his gaining Christ, knowing him, "and the power of his resurrection, and the fellowship of his sufferings, becoming conformed unto his death" (Phil. 3:10). To the Romans he writes about being "joint-heirs with Christ, if so be that we suffer with him, that we may also be glorified with him" (Rom. 8:17b). When in writing to the Corinthians Paul refers to his imitation of Christ in the context of how

---

the matter of edifying (Rom. 15:2; I Cor. 10:23); pleasing one's neighbor rather than oneself (Rom. 15:2,3; I Cor. 10:33); acting to the glory of God (Rom. 15:7; I Cor. 10:31); referring the readers to an example (cf. καθὼς καὶ ὁ χριστός Rom. 15:17; καθὼς κἀγώ I Cor. 10:33, 11:1). Michaelis acknowledges the relation between the passages (T.W.N.T., IV, p. 671, 20—21), but remarks. "Nicht einmal R 15, 1—3 wird die Vorbildlichkeit Christi bzw die Pflicht, seinem Vorbild zu folgen, mit deutlichen Worten ausgesprochen" (ll. 36—38). However, the cumulative force of Rom. 15:3,5,7 does not leave the matter particularly unclear. See discussion of passage above, p. 62.
200 See discussion above, pp. 59—61.
201 M. Dibelius, "Nachfolge Christi im N.T.," R.G.G.2, IV, p. 395.
202 C. H. Dodd, *History and the Gospel*, London: Nisbet, 1938, p. 65, fn. 6.
203 G. Sevenster, *De Christologie van het Nieuwe Testament*, Amsterdam: Holland Uitgeversmaatschappij, 1946, pp. 296f., fn. 3.
204 See above, pp. 52f.

one ought to forego his own pleasures and rights and give himself for the benefit of others, did he have in mind any particular scene, or words, or teaching from Christ's life on this matter? There are some of Jesus' words to his disciples which come to mind immediately: "Whosoever would become great among you, shall be your minister; and whosoever would be first among you, shall be a servant of all. For the Son of man also came not to be ministered unto, but to minister, and to give his life a ransom for many" (Mark 10:43–45, par.). In these words Jesus was not only telling the disciples how they should live, but also illustrating it and grounding it in his own conduct (*cf.* Mark 10:45: γάρ, *for*). Could Paul's imitation of Christ have been influenced by such instruction as this from Christ? Wilckens doubts that Paul was acquainted with the details of Jesus' life and teaching as contained in the synoptic tradition. [205] Haenchen, however, finds Wilckens view highly improbable in view of Paul's close connection with the congregation at Antioch. He points out that this congregation had been established by Christian refugees from Jerusalem only a few years previous to Paul's coming there, and that these Christians had surely come to Antioch well informed on Jesus' life and teaching as that was known in Jerusalem. [206] There appears to be little reason to question that Paul's thoughts about Jesus' life and example were formed by the same tradition which we presently possess in the Synoptic Gospels. Paul knew Jesus Christ, the Son of man, who was minister to all and servant of all and who gave himself completely in behalf of men. This Christ Paul was bringing to expression in his imitation.

The way in which Paul makes his reference to Christ's example is not what we would have expected. He does not refer the Corinthians directly to the example of Christ, but rather says: "Be ye imitators of me, even as I also am of Christ." What is the significance to the whole argument which Paul has been making when he adds in a final breath "even as I also am of Christ"? The phrase has brought forth a variety of explanations and observations, not all of them particularly to the point nor equally helpful in discovering the original intent and meaning of the words.

Hadorn heard echoes of a party strife in Corinth, and thought that Paul's making clear that he was an imitator of Christ was an attempt to counteract the Corinthians' preference for Peter because he had been a companion of Christ. [207] Eidem proposes that in thinking of himself as an example of self-giving, the far greater example of another occured to him, and he makes reference to it as a kind of correction or improvement of what he had just said, as he does in I Cor. 15:10 on another subject. [208] Others have also commented on how effectively this addition

---

[205] "Das Überlieferungsgut, das Paulus empfangen und seinen Gemeinden weitergegeben hat, ist auf kerygmatische, liturgische und paränetische Stoffe beschränkt; es fehlt dagegen bei Paulus fast durchweg die Masse der synoptischen Jesusüberlieferung" (U. Wilckens, *Die Missionsreden der Apostelgeschichte*, Neukirchen: Neukirchener Verlag, 1961, pp. 197,198).

[206] E. Haenchen, *Die Apostelgeschichte*, K.e.K.N.T., 13. Aufl., Göttingen: Vandenhoeck & Ruprecht, 1961, p. 687. H. Schürmann has pointed out the likelihood that Jesus' utterances on following him had been gathered into a collection of sayings already before Jesus' death and resurrection; *cf.* "Die vorösterlichen Anfänge der Logientradition," in *Der historische Jesus und der kerygmatische Christus*, hrsg. von H. Ristow und K. Mattiae, Berlin: Evangelische Verlagsanstalt, 1961, p. 368.

[207] Hadorn, *Abfassung Thess.briefe*, p. 39.

[208] Eidem, *Stud. Tillägnade E. Stave*, p. 75. *Cf.* the similar explanation for the addition "and of the Lord" in I Thess. 1:6; see above, p. 120.

dispels any suspicions that Paul might be showing evidence of pride, arrogance, or presumption in all his talk about himself. [209]

Some have found the reference to Paul's imitation of Christ to serve as a guide to the Corinthians on how they ought to imitate Christ. [210] Such an observation may be proposed as a legitimate deduction from the words which Paul has here used, and as such it undoubtedly has its place in commentaries on I Cor. 11:1. However, it is hardly likely that Paul had such a thought in mind when he wrote these words. After having built up to the climactic calling of men to imitate himself in his life of self-giving, would Paul suddenly have added some thought about this being the proper extent or the real way in which Christ was to be imitated? The thought about just how Christ ought or ought not to be imitated is something entirely new to the context and foreign to the whole train of thought. To make observations on this matter on the basis of Paul's words here is to find light in Paul for a problem which undoubtedly never occurred to him. At any rate it is hardly likely that Paul added the statement "even as I also am of Christ" in order to alert his readers to find in him the proper (in distinction from the improper) imitation of Christ.

We must be careful in our seeking to discover the original intent of the words "even as I also am of Christ" not to be misled into over-emphasizing them. In the history of the church the imitation of Christ has become both a very important matter and a very controversial one. Hence, it is not surprising that commentators and interpreters center much attention on this phrase and seek to derive its very last implication from it. However, for Paul it was the last short subordinate thought at the close of a long discourse he had been giving. He had examined the problem of the food offered to idols and the attending problems in the Corinthian congregation. He had presented specific regulations and also general guiding principles. He had finally brought his discussion to a conclusion by presenting the basic guidelines of doing all things to the glory of God and to the salvation of one's neighbor. He had illustrated this by calling attention to his own conduct. He had made this illustration still more emphatic by turning it into a straightforward and climactic call for action: "Be ye imitators of me." Here was the point toward which he had been moving. Here was the call that must be left ringing in their ears. His final clause about his imitation of Christ must not be read as looking at some new aspect of the whole question or as adding some new material for consideration. It is rather a final stroke of the pen to accentuate the thought of the imitation of Paul. [211]

---

209 See e.g., Allo, I Cor., pp. 251,252; Robertson-Plummer, I Cor., p. 225.
210 Notice such statements as the following: "The Corinthians are to take him as an illustration of what is essential in the character of the Lord" (Moffatt, I Cor., pp. 145,146); "[Paul] urges others to follow him in so far as he follows Christ" (W. D. Davies, Paul and Rabbinic Judaism, London: S.P.C.K., 1948, p. 147); "De apostel toont in eigen leven, wat Christus van Zijn dienstknechten vraagt.... De Schrift wekt niet op om Christus na te volgen ... zonder meer" (Grosheide, I Kor., p. 286).
211 Grosheide, I Kor., p. 286, observes: "Dat hij den Korinthiërs vragen kan hem na te volgen is alleen, omdat de apostel zichzelf een navolger van Christus weet. Dat is het nieuwe, waardoor 11:1 geen herhaling van 10:33 is." The observation is formally correct. However, it does not help toward an understanding of this passage if it means to imply that Paul has added 11:1 with the specific intention of introducing the subject of the imitation of Christ into the

In proposing that the general function of the clause "even as I also am of Christ" is to emphasize and accentuate the thought of the imitation of Paul, we are still faced with the question of how these words serve to do this. Here is a matter about which it is difficult to speak with precision. Calvin has proposed that one function of this addition is in order that Paul may show that he, like any good teacher, is not asking them to do something which he himself does not practice.[212] Calvin, thus, finds the clause to be at least partially explained as Paul's pointing to his example even in the matter of being an imitator. While such an interpretation has certain considerations to recommend it, it hardly seems to be the most natural interpretation in view of the total thought of the passage. It is hardly likely that Paul would end with a thought about the act of imitation as such, after he had argued so intently for an imitation with a certain content. Such would make a very anticlimactic and ineffective conclusion.

Understanding the clause "even as I also am of Christ" as furnishing an example of imitation to stimulate the Corinthians' imitation does seem to be the most natural interpretation of καθὼς κἀγώ. These words were used in just this way in the preceding verse, where Paul illustrated the point of not being a stumbling block by saying: "even as I also please all men in all things." Hence, the two verses would thus be understood as being constructed along parallel lines: each made up of a command, with a καθὼς κἀγώ-clause of illustration. Furthermore, within 11:1, as within 10:33, when Paul speaks of what he *also* (καί) does, it seems to be placing his conduct alongside what he is asking from the Corinthians and illustrating the similarity. The use of καθώς in introducing a clause of illustration and example had also been prominent earlier in the chapter. In connection with the warning illustrations and examples from Old Testament history there are a series of four commands of things not to do, each illustrated by an "even-as" (καθώς) clause speaking of Israel's conduct (*cf.* 10:6,7,8,9 [213]). Καθὼς καί is used elsewhere in Paul's writings for pointing out similar actions which serve as examples (*cf.* Rom. 15:7; Eph. 4:32; 5:2; Col. 3:13). A similar sentence by Ignatius would seem to point in the same direction. Ignatius writes: "Be imitators of Jesus Christ, as was he also of his Father (ὡς καὶ αὐτὸς τοῦ πατρὸς αὐτοῦ)" (*To the Philadelphians* 7:12). This exhortation is found simply in a list of exhortations without further context or explanation. Its form is so similar to Paul's that one is inclined to see a reminiscence of I Cor. 11:1 in his words. One could perhaps raise the question whether the additional clause about Jesus' being an imitator of God is anything more than pious phraseology. If so, it would seem to be added with a view to the thought that since Christ himself was an imitator, this should stimulate the Philadelphians' becoming imitators of him. Hence, it is in harmony with similar clauses found elsewhere to understand Paul's thought about his imitation of Christ as furnishing an example and illustration. The

---

whole matter he had been discussing before bringing it to a close. The real subject matter of 11:1 is the imitation of Paul, and Paul's reference to his imitation of Christ is subordinate and subservient to that thought.

212 "Nihil praescribit aliis quod non prior observaverit.... Nam sicut boni doctoris est, nihil verbo praecipere nisi quod opere praestare sit paratus" (Calvin, *I Cor.*, sub 11:1 [Baum, Cunitz, and Reuss, XLIX, p. 472]).

213 In 10:10 καθώς is attested to only by manuscripts of less weight; the testimony of P46Bא for καθάπερ would seem to be conclusive.

thought would be: "Be my imitators; and as for the matter of imitation, here too I have been an example to you in my imitation of Christ. Be an imitator like I am an imitator. Let my imitation stimulate your imitation."

However, in spite of the naturalness with which καθώς κἀγώ seems to lead to this interpretation, the interpretation as a totality does not really recommend itself as being the most natural or likely. It has Paul finishing his discussion of the problems surrounding the matter of foods sacrificed to idols with thoughts about the matter of imitation as such. The whole development of his argument has been toward an appeal to imitate him in the matter of his conduct toward the weaker brother and toward all men. Is it likely that he would conclude the subject with a parting flourish about imitating him as an imitator? Furthermore, the argument gets pretty complicated and a bit overwrought when thus understood. It would say that the Corinthians are to do all to the glory of God and to the benefit of their neighbor; in this Paul has given them an example; hence, let them be imitators of Paul; here too Paul has given them an example. It is not necessary to insist that καθώς καί determines the interpretation of the clause which it introduces. The meaning of καθώς is not that rigidly specific.[214] It is true that καθώς καί in the preceding verse (10:33) indicates a correlation which serves as illustration and example. However, we have noticed in other instances where the idea of example is present that the thought of the passage could convey an idea deeper and broader than example alone.[215] Furthermore, the καί need not receive special emphasis, as though Paul wishes to point out something that he *also* is doing. The usage of καθώς followed immediately by καί appears to have been somewhat of a mannerism with Paul.[216] Nor does the use of ἐγώ direct any special attention or emphasis toward Paul; the ἐγώ is necessary to the clause in view of the ellipsis of the verb, and it appears in contracted form.[217] Neither does the pattern in the previous context (10:6-9) of using καθώς in citing examples carry over to this present instance. In 10:1-11 there are clear evidences of Paul's use of rhetorical devices of repetition,[218] but there is no evidence that he has continued this rhetorical manner down to the present verse. Understanding Paul's reference to his imitation of Christ as furnishing the Corinthians with an example of imitation to stimulate their own imitation is a possible interpretation of the passage, but it recommends itself finally only in the absence of something better.

It is probably more correct to explain the added clause "even as I also am of Christ" along the lines of giving a ground for the action for which

---

214 Robertson, *Gram.*, p. 968, lists in addition to its expression of correlation, its use in a causal sense, as a temporal signification, in indirect questions, and to indicate epexegesis.

215 See above, p. 62, fn. 138, and pp. 76-77, where the καθώς-clauses are found to express ground and motive as well as example and norm.

216 In the 86 instances in which Paul uses καθώς, 25 have a καί immediately following. In the non-Pauline New Testament writings there are 94 instances of καθώς, only 5 of which are followed immediately by καί. Thus, the combination is found in 30% of the Pauline usage, as against 5.3% outside of Paul.

217 B. F. Westcott and F. J. A. Hort, *The New Testament in the Original Greek*, London: Macmillan, 1907, Vol. II, p. 152, says: "καί often coalesces with ἐγώ... but there are many exceptions, and especially where there is distinct coordination of ἐγώ with another pronoun or a substantive. There is much division of evidence." Apparently then κἀγώ tends to be less specific than καί ἐγώ.

218 *Cf.* the fivefold repetition of "all" (πάντες) in 10:1-5, with the concluding statement about God's not being pleased with most of them; and the repetition of the formula μηδέ-καθώς in 10:6-11.

Paul has called. The Corinthians are to be imitators of him in view of the fact that he is an imitator of Christ. His imitation of Christ makes their imitation of him particularly important. However, one must hasten to warn against placing undue emphasis on the thought of Paul's giving a ground for their action. The clause καθὼς κἀγὼ Χριστοῦ is both a highly contracted and severely elliptical statement. When the A.S.V. makes the translation "even as I also am of Christ," it catches all the elements of the clause, but its expression of them becomes a bit too explicit and emphatic. The translation of the R.S.V. "as I am of Christ," is better in making clear the shortness of the thrust with which the thought is expressed. The clause serves as the parting flourish with which the preceding discussion is concluded. It is not at all Paul's intention at this point to reason with the Corinthians about the justifiability and the grounds for calling them to imitate him. In connection with his earlier call for imitation in 4:16 he had made it clear why he was looking for imitation from them. He had fathered them in the gospel; they were his children in Christ. We have noticed that since this earlier call he has kept referring to his conduct and example in discussing the various questions before him. With the repetition of an express call to imitation in 11:1, the same situation prevails as previously, and the call arises from the same relationship which he holds to them. He is their father and they are his children in Christ. There is no thought of his substituting for the thought of his being their father the thought of his being an imitator of Christ, as though this time his calling for their imitation is on the basis of the latter relationship. He is indeed an imitator of Christ. He has brought Christ and Christ's ways to living expression in his life. His life now bears the mold of Christianity. His ways are the ways of Christ. When at this point in his letter Paul makes reference to his imitation of Christ, he does so simply as a swift and brief characterization of himself as their father. He had fathered them *in Christ*. It is his Christianity, then, that can stimulate and motivate the Corinthians in imitating him. His portrayal of Christ and Christianity makes their imitation of him all-important. As Paul's children in Christ they are to follow him, since his ways are the Christian way. Paul says in effect: "Be ye imitators of me—my way is Christ's!" The mere mention of this latter thought would surely dispel the last remnants of resistance, hesitancy, and sluggishness on their part.

By understanding Paul's words about his imitation of Christ so generally as to find them simply pointing to the Christian character of his life and way, there is no reason for concluding that the idea of the imitation of Christ was either not current in Paul's thinking, or that it was a very broad, nebulous, obscure, and vapid idea with him. It in no sense lacked currency, substance, or content. The very fact that Paul could refer to it so fleetingly reveals how much it possessed him. This passing reference at the same time reveals how well-acquainted the Corinthians were with the thought and how immediately it aroused a host of associations for them. Hence, although this passage in its context is not intent on explicating the concept of the imitation of Christ as such, it does show how vitally this concept functioned in the early church. Paul had learned from Christ this kind of life of giving oneself totally for the well-being of others. Through imitation he had brought Christ's life and his ways to living expression in his own life. The Thessalonians had done the same in regard to the joyful endurance of suffering for the sake of the gospel (I Thess. 1:6). Other congregations were urged to learn other things from Christ and to bring them to expression in their lives. [219] It would appear that in the early church there was much attention bestowed on capturing Christ's life and ways and bringing these to personal expression in individual Christian lives.

The importance of Christ's life and of the imitation of it has always been felt by the church, although with varying degrees in different ages and under different circumstances. In view of the importance of the idea of the imitation of Christ, it appears the more remarkable to us later readers that Paul should have placed so much stress on the imitation of himself. This passage invites the attempt to determine Paul's conception of the relation of the two. Stanley proposes: "There is an essentially hierarchical structure in this Pauline conception of 'imitation,' which shows how important he considers his function of transmitting the apostolic faith to others. His own mediatorial role is highly necessary. He is not merely a mouthpiece through which the Gospel is handed on mechanically to other men. Not only what he says, but how he says it, as well as what he is, have a part to play in the Christian formation of those he evangelizes.... The Corinthian community is not called upon to imitate Christ directly, but to imitate Paul in whom they possess a concrete realization of the imitation of Christ." [220] With the general thrust of Stanley's remarks we can express much agreement. However, one wonders how rigidly Stanley wishes to press this matter of a hierarchical structure and a mediate imitation, and what conclusions he might wish to derive from these for the post-apostolic age. [221] At least it must be noted that the imitation of Paul and of Christ appear side by side in I Thess. 1:6: "Ye became imitators of us and of the Lord." There is no indication here that Paul thought of this particular instance of imitation of the Lord as being by way of the imitation of him. There are no other passages in the New Testament writings which speak expressly about the imitation of Christ. However, in the various passages where the thought in effect is found, the appeal to the example of Christ comes as an appeal to the reader to appropriate Christ directly. Interestingly enough, in the letter to the Philippians there is an appeal to Christ's example without any hint that Paul had represented such conduct to them (*cf.* Phil. 2:5ff.); and then very shortly thereafter there is the call to imitate Paul without any hint that this is a direct representation of Christ's conduct (*cf.* Phil. 3:17).

---

219 See above, pp. 54—64, and the summary, p. 69—70.
220 Stanley, *Biblica*, XL, p. 874.
221 For instance, it is not immediately apparent what implications Stanley sees when he says, "By insisting upon this necessarily mediated *imitatio Christi*, Paul is simply witnessing to the necessity of apostolic tradition in the life of the church" (*loc. cit.*). One could wish that he had explained himself further on this point.

There seems to be some latitude in thinking of the imitation of Christ and the imitation of Paul in direct connection with each other and in thinking of them in independence of each other.

There is little evidence that Paul saw two radically different things in the imitation of himself and the imitation of Christ. In his cultivation of Christian conduct in his spiritual offspring he seems to find both ideas serving the same purpose. Sometimes he appeals for the one, sometimes for the other. The two ideas differ of course in that they direct attention to two different persons. However, even this distinction is not entirely rigid. In Paul there is a kind of fusion. In imitating him one is imitating an imitator of Christ. Thus, in imitating Paul one is not only bringing Paul and his ways to expression, but is taking a step in the direction of bringing Christ himself to personal expression. In I Cor. 11:1 we see how closely these two matters are linked together. Paul urges the imitation of himself, but he stimulates this with the consideration of his imitation of Christ.

Stanley's observation about the important role of the one bringing the gospel in the Christian formation of those he evangelized is a point well made. It perhaps serves no real purpose to try to evaluate the appropriateness of his statement that there is "an essentially hierarchical structure in the Pauline conception of 'imitation.'" Such would likely be merely a struggle over terms. There does seem to be real appropriateness, however, in thinking of Paul's concept of imitation according to the structure of family relationships. This is the context in which Paul repeatedly places the thought of imitation. It appears where a father has begotten children and is exercising a formative influence over them. Through imitation and the other processes of learning and growth the child matures to be what the father is. When this has occurred, the child will forever bear the mold of the father's formation, but at the same time he will be a mature individual in his own right and with his own direct relationships. In conceiving of a structure in the Pauline concept of imitation, it is undoubtedly helpful to keep in mind the distinction between the immature and the mature state of the child. The Corinthians were still very immature in their Christianity; they had much to learn and showed room for much development. In nurturing them, Paul, their father, points them to his conduct, and to the fact that such conduct is a true imitation of Christ. They must grow up to be like him and must also learn the mature imitation of Christ as he experienced it. The Thessalonians, on the other hand, had in a certain instance shown real Christian maturity. They had joyfully undergone suffering for the gospel's sake. They were imitators both of Paul, their father, and of Jesus Christ, their Lord. Their father's imitation of Christ was now being experienced in a real personal way by them. It had come to them by way of Paul, but they were now experiencing the reality of a mature, direct, and living contact with Christ. They were sharing Christ's life with him in the point at issue. The aim of the nurturing process by Paul was to bring his children to a living and personal imitating of Christ in their own right. Toward this goal he found the imitation of himself a natural stepping stone and a helpful means.

Michaelis once again rejects the thought that imitation here can mean becoming like someone by following his example: "Jedenfalls ist in 11, 1 nicht von Vorbildern die Rede, denen man nacheifern soll, geschweige denn von Vorbildern, denen man durch Nachahmung ähnlich oder gleich werden soll, sondern von Autoritäten, deren Befehl und Mahnung man nachkommen soll." [222] He admits that the preceding context and particularly the preceding verse might lead one to read 11:1 in the sense of following Paul's example. However, he dogmatically asserts: "Unter dem Eindruck von 4, 16 jedoch ergibt sich, dass diese Deutung nicht ausreichen dürfte. μιμηταί μου γίνεσθε, das muss heissen; lasst es euch gesagt sein, nehmt's euch zu Herzen und haltet euch daran, s e i d f o l g s a m !" [223] If, however, as we have proposed, 4:16 is to be understood as a call by Paul to the Corinthians to imitate his conduct and bring it to expression in their lives, [224] this argument of Michaelis fails completely. In fact, his proposal that 11:1 can not be understood in isolation from 4:16 [225] only makes the case against his own exegesis the stronger. Michaelis' main argumentation, however, is directed against the clause "even as I also am of Christ." If the command "Be ye imitators of me" is to be understood as following an example, then the added clause must mean that Paul sees himself as following Christ's example. Such a proposal is laden with difficulties, according to Michaelis. For one thing, why are the Corinthians not pointed to Christ's example directly? An answer to this objection, however, lies immediately at hand in the observations we have just made concerning the relation of the imitation of Paul and of Christ. One can not interject an antithesis between the imitation of Paul and the imitation of Christ. It was Paul's wise tactic to nurture his spiritual offspring through an imitation of himself as their father into a full-fledged imitation of Christ. He had been at work in this in his previous argument, and, as we have seen, the final outright call to imitate him is the climax of his whole discussion. The preceding argument would have had to be somewhat differently constructed to end with a direct call to imitate Christ. Michaelis finds it striking that the sense in which Christ is an example is not specifically stated. But surely this point is sufficiently clear from 10:33—the more so, when we recall Paul's description of Christ in Rom. 15:3 as not pleasing himself. There is no need of finding the road blocked to all comparison between Paul and Christ because of the infinite difference between their respective roles of bringing salvation to men. The point is that they both acted not according to their own pleasure and desire, but for the eternal well-being of others. This was the kind of Christian life that the Corinthians needed to learn. Michaelis further objects that if 11:1 is to be understood as pointing to the example of Christ, then the thought so fleetingly expressed is totally out of proportion to the breadth with which Paul has been discussing the various aspects of the problem and its solution ever since 8:1. However, we have come to the conclusion that it was not Paul's purpose to refer to the imitation of Christ as a constituent part of his whole argument. In fact, it was not his purpose to become engaged in the subject of the imitation of Christ at all. He only made the fleeting reference to it to accentuate and underline the thought toward which he had been moving for some time, namely, the direct call to the imitation of himself. The additional clause about his imitation

---

[222] Michaelis, *T.W.N.T.*, IV, p. 672, 26—29.
[223] *Ibid.*, p. 671, 6—9.
[224] See above, p. 151 f.
[225] Michaelis, *T.W.N.T.*, IV, p. 670, 37—39.

of Christ served only to throw into boldest relief the basic Christianity of his ways. Michaelis adds one further consideration: a writer makes such brief and passing references only to matters which are very much part and parcel of his thinking; but "die Vorbildlichkeit Christi gehört aber jedenfalls nicht zu den geläufigen Gedanken des Apostels Paulus." [226] This is indeed a bold assertion and one which our study has not verified. [227] We have found the very opposite to be true, namely, that Paul can make such passing reference to his imitation of Christ precisely because this thought was so much a part of his thinking and of that of his converts. Michaelis' own explanation of the passage is along the lines he has proposed throughout his article. Here he prints it in his most emphatic type: "d e r μιμητής j e m a n d e s  s e i n  b e d e u t e t:  s i c h  n a c h  d e m  G e b o t  j e m a n d e s  r i c h t e n,  j e m a n d e m  g e h o r s a m  s e i n." [228] Such an understanding of imitation he derives entirely from his interpretation of 4:16 and other imitation passages. In proposing it here, he had to be content with showing that, in view of the difficulties which the following of an example presented, this idea of obedience to authority could be harmonized with the context, and that the idea was to be found elsewhere in I Corinthians. His interpretation of the meaning of imitation never sounds more artifical or manufactured than when applied to this passage.

\* \* \*

In this passage we have again seen Paul coming to the outright call for the imitation of himself as the climax and close of an extended discussion. The discussion concerned proper Christian conduct, and in the course of the discussion Paul several times made reference to his own conduct in illustration of his point. In the verses immediately preceding 11:1 he carefully builds up to a call for outright action, a straightforward call to become his imitators. The point of imitation is the giving oneself for the sake of the gospel and for the sake of the salvation of one's fellowmen. To develop such a quality of life would amply solve such problems as had arisen in Corinth between the "strong" and the "weak" brethren over the matter of eating meat sacrificed to idols.

The unique feature of this text on imitation is Paul's additional statement about his imitation of Christ. We have concluded that this statement was added not to speak expressly about the subject of the imitation of Christ, but rather to accentuate the propriety and necessity of the Corinthians' imitation of Paul. It served to emphasize the basic Christianity of Paul's ways. We noticed also how the fleeting nature of this reference to the imitation of Christ gives evidence of how current and how important this thought was to Paul and how well-known it was to his readers. Finally, we sought to detect something of the relation which Paul saw between the imitation of himself and the imitation of Christ. In view of the fact that the Corinthians are spiritual children of Paul, the pattern of their father's life is of vital importance in helping to form the pattern of their lives. During the days

---

[226] *Ibid.*, p. 671, 35—36.
[227] See above, pp. 58—64; 69—70; and p. 158, fn. 199.
[228] Michaelis, *T.W.N.T.*, IV, p. 672, 3—5.

of their Christian immaturity the pattern of their father remains particularly important. As they grow toward maturity they will become Christians who continue to bear the stamp of their father's pattern on their lives. However, at the same time they will be reaching the mature stage of a direct imitation of Christ, a bringing Christ and his ways to expression in their lives as a result of their own knowledge of and fellowship with him. This is the aim of Paul in promoting the imitation of himself. Imitation of him is a means of nurturing and guiding the young Christian life. It is leading young Christians into conformity to Christ. His call to the Corinthians is to become imitators of him, even as he is of Christ. He hopes someday to be able to announce the happy fact about them that he once was able to announce about the Thessalonians: "Ye became imitators of us and of the Lord" (I Thess. 1:6).

## V. Philippians 3:17

*Brethren, be ye imitators together of me, and mark them that so walk even as ye have us for an ensample.*

The call to imitate Paul is found also in the letter to the Philippians. In the context both before and after this call Paul is warning about false teachers and devious ideas and ways that are being propagated in Philippi and are making their influence felt among the Christians. Over against such tendencies he points to the Christian way as he had taught and showed it to them. In this connection he both calls for imitation and points to the fact that they had an example in him.

In his letters to the Thessalonians and the Corinthians Paul had recalled the fact that his readers were his spiritual offspring; he had fathered them in the gospel. In such a context he speaks about their imitation of him. In his letter to the Philippians he does not expressly point to this kind of relationship between himself and them. However, his letter reveals a most intimate and personal relationship between Paul and the Philippian church. McNeile speaks of the letter to the Philippians as the "affectionate letter to St Paul's best loved converts." [229] As Plummer puts it, Paul's letter is "the natural outpouring of a very affectionate, cheerful, and grateful, but somewhat anxious and sensitive friend and teacher, to the disciples who (as he knows) admire and love him, but are in need of both encouragement and warnings." [230] The close fellowship and union he felt between the Philippian

---

229 A. H. McNeile, *An Introduction to the Study of the New Testament* (revised by C. S. C. Williams), Oxford: Clarendon Press, 1953, p. 178.
230 A. Plummer, *A Commentary on St. Paul's Epistle to the Philippians*, London: Robert Scott, 1919, p. xvii. *Cf.* also such characterizations as the following: "Es ist ein bekanntes Urteil, dass der Phil. tiefer als alle anderen paulinischen Briefe von der herzlichen Wärme persönlicher Verbundenheit getragen ist. Keine Gemeinde stand Paulus je so nahe wie diese, keine gab ihm je so reichlichen Anlass zu uneingeschränktem Lob und Dank" (E. Lohmeyer, *Die Briefe an die Philipper, an die Kolosser und an Philemon*, K.e.K.N.T., 8. Aufl. Göttingen: Vandenhoeck & Ruprecht, 1930, p. 4); "Cette lettre n'a rien de dogmatique; elle ne prétend

Christians and himself is subtly evident in his frequent use of words prefixed by συν- (*with,* = the English prefix *com-*) in referring to matters involving both himself and them. [231] Bonnard has pointed out that this communion is one that goes deeper than simply having like sentiments and personal affinities; they are united in a common faith and above all in the common struggle to further the apostolic mission. [232] The union between Paul and the Philippians had continued strong and living long after Paul's original preaching of the gospel in Philippi had had to be abruptly discontinued (*cf.* Acts 16:39f.). In view of their union to him the appeal for them to be his imitators comes as a most natural thought in the course of the epistle.

After beginning his letter with the customary salutation and thanksgiving, and after mentioning his thoughts of and prayers for his readers, Paul turns to writing about various matters of personal interest (Phil. 1:12ff.). In the latter part of the first chapter he tells them of the confidence which he has that in spite of all his present miseries, setbacks, and imprisonment he will still be seeing them again (1:25,26). This thought leads him to admonish them to walk worthy of the gospel and to stand fast in the face of the opposition which they are experiencing (1:27–30). He points out that "to you it hath been granted in the behalf of Christ, not only to believe on him, but also to suffer in his behalf: having the same conflict which ye saw in me, and now hear to be in me" (1:29,30). The stage, thus, has already been set for his later call for imitation. They have seen his conflicts as a Christian; they are now experiencing the same kind of conflicts; and they have continued to hold him and his work in highest regard (*cf.* 1:5). In view of these things, it could surprise no one to find the stamp and pattern of his life still very much in evidence in Philippi.

In the second chapter there is further exhortation and counsel for the Philippians, as well as further information on personal matters concerning himself, Timothy, and Epaphroditus. Then, in the third chapter there is a striking change of mood. Paul turns to writing about a matter that obviously disturbed him greatly. He suddenly warns: "Beware of the dogs, beware of the evil workers, beware of the concision" (3:2). This latter term is a carefully chosen one, with an eye to making a play on words. Paul distinguishes those whom he labels as "the concision" (κατατομή) from those who can properly claim the title of "the circumcision" (περιτομή). He says: "For we are the circumcision, who worship by the Spirit of God, and glory in Christ Jesus, and have no confidence in the flesh" (3:3). This assertion in turn leads Paul to remark about how no man really had more grounds than he to stand

---

éclairer aucun problème de foi. Elle est plutôt un entretien coeur à coeur où l'Apôtre prisonnier met ses chers enfants au courant de ce qu'il devient, leur fait part de ses sentiments intimes et les remercie de leur sollicitude à son égard" (P. Benoit, *Les Épîtres de saint Paul aux Philippiens, et al.,* in *La Sainte Bible,* Paris: Éditions du Cerf, 1949, p. 17f).

231 *Cf.* συναθλεῖν (1:27; 4:3); συνεργός (2:25; 4:3); συστρατιώτης (2:25); συγκοινωνεῖν (4:14); συγκοινωνός (1:7); συγχαίρειν (2:17,18); σύζυγος (4:3). Whether συμμιμητής (3:17) ought to be included in this list will be considered presently.

232 Bonnard, *Phil.,* p. 53, fn. 7. He adds, "C'est une communion qui englobe tout le combat apostolique de l'apôtre et non seulement ses sommets, ou ses détresses."

confidently before God in his own right and on the basis of the kind of life he had lived. However, he had come to see the utter folly of such a confidence. He had turned his back on all these things and had turned to Christ, gaining the righteousness there is in Christ through faith. One detects in the emphatic language that Paul is here using an awareness on his part of some tendencies toward a Judaistic type of confidence before God that were either threatening or already at work in Philippi. His efforts to make clear his own rejection of a confidence in himself and his own deeds is not simply a dispassionate explanation of an important experience in his life. He is reacting to a threat posed by some "evil workers."

In 3:7ff. Paul makes a beautiful statement of what he finds Christianity to be, in distinction from any system where righteousness is attained by personal merit and an obedience to laws. He describes his Christian life in terms of vigorous activity and struggle, and states as his aim the hope of attaining to the resurrection of the dead (3:11). This, however, leads him to make a counter-assertion: "Not that I have already obtained, or am already made perfect" (3:12). He now continues by emphasizing how hard he is working to arrive at the goal of the Christian calling. It appears that Paul is here reacting against some perfectionist tendencies either threatening or already at work in Philippi.

Presently Paul calls the Philippians to imitate him. After this call he continues: "For many walk, of whom I told you often, and now tell you even weeping, that they are the enemies of the cross of Christ: whose end is perdition, whose god is the belly, and whose glory is in their shame, who mind earthly things" (3:18,19). It sounds like Paul sees another danger threatening the Philippian Christians, the danger of libertinism.

Hence, in close succession to each other we find Paul alerting the Philippians to the dangers of Judaistic legalism, of perfectionism, and of libertinism. What is happening in Philippi? From where are all the seeds of error coming? It is impossible to speak with definiteness about the situation, for the necessary information is not available. However, it is not unlikely that these various deviating tendencies are to be traced to a common source. It may be that there were teachers propagating Gnostic teachings and Gnostic interpretations of Christianity among the Philippian Christians.

It has been common among expositors to find Paul warning against the Judaisers in 3:2ff. In regard to 3:12ff., until recently the tendency has been more to seeing Paul's warding off possible misunderstandings and misinterpretations of the doctrine of righteousness by faith in Christ, than to seeing his reacting against some wrong teaching already present and being propagated in Philippi. It is in regard to the group which Paul calls "enemies of the cross of Christ" (3:18) that expositors have expressed the most widely varied opinions. During much of the history of interpreting this letter it was common to see here the same persons as were described in vs. 2, namely, false teachers of Judaistic tendencies.[233] The reference has also been seen as applying to the hea-

---

[233] A. H. Franke, *Handbuch über die Briefe an die Philipper, Kolosser, und Philemon*, K.e.K.N.T., 5. Aufl. Göttingen: Vandenhoeck & Ruprecht, 1886, p. 206, lists the following as

then. [234] Another proposal was that these were Christians who weakened in the face of opposition or were unable to sustain the reproach that accompanied faith in the cross. [235] Vincent, writing at the end of the nineteenth century found: "The majority of modern commentators [understand the reference as applying to] antinomian Libertines of Epicurean tendencies: nominal Christians of immoral life." [236] Ewald, writing in the early years of the twentieth century, agrees that this was the common view of the day. [237] However, Ewald ably presented the arguments for understanding vss. 18ff. as referring to the same Judaistic opponents as in vss. 2ff. [238] In more recent commentaries this latter solution has often been proposed. [239] Hence, it may be observed that for decades commentators have been proposing and counterproposing to each other whether these "enemies of the cross of Christ" are legalistic Judaisers or antinomian libertines. Recently a new insight has opened interesting perspectives for the whole chapter. Dibelius comments in regard to Paul's speaking of "as many as are perfect (τέλειοι)" (vs. 15): "Es scheint, als sei τέλειος in der Gemeinde oder ihrem Umkreis ein Schlagwort gewesen — und das ist dort, wo man die Terminologie der Gnosis verstand, von vornherein wahrscheinlich." [240] Heinzelmann proposes that vss. 18ff. are to be seen as "einen Angriff auf Christen..., die in falsch verstandener Geistlichkeit das Recht des Sinnengenusses als etwas Ungefährliches zugestehen. In Korinth gab es solche (vgl. 1. Kor. 6,12ff., auch Röm. 16,17ff.)." [241] Schmithals has worked out an exegesis of the entire chapter in terms of Paul's reacting against a Jewish-Christian Gnosticism which was at

---

interpreting vss. 18ff. in terms of Judaisers: Theodoret, Luther, Erasmus, Estius, Calovius, a Lapide, Wolf, Heinrichs, Rheinwald, Matthies, Schinz, Hilgenfeld, Holsten, and Schmidt.

234 M. R. Vincent, *A Critical and Exegetical Commentary on the Epistles to the Philippians and to Philemon*, I.C.C., Edinburgh: T. & T. Clark, 1897, p. 116, lists Weiss and Rilliet in support of this position.

235 "Unbeständige Elemente der Gemeinde haben sich unter dem Druck der Verfolgung von ihr und ihrem Glauben getrennt; sie sind zu 'Feinden des Kreuzes Christi' geworden. Es sind also, um es mit einem technischen Wort späterer Verfolgungszeiten zu sagen, *lapsi*" (Lohmeyer, *Phil.*, p. 153). Calvin knew about a somewhat similar interpretation in his day: "Alii... [interpretantur], quod crucem fugerent, nec se vellent periculis obiicere pro Christo" (*Phil. sub* 3:18 [Baum, Cunitz, and Reuss, LII, p. 55]). For arguments against Lohmeyer's proposal, see Bonnard, *Phil.*, p. 71.

236 Vincent, *Phil.*, p. 116. He lists *(loc. cit.)* the following as proposing it: Lightfoot, Meyer, Klöpper, DeWette, Ellicott, Alford, Beet. The list could be extended. Cf. e.g., Franke, *Phil.*, pp. 206ff.; E. Haupt, *Die Gefangenschaftsbriefe*, K.e.K.N.T., 7./8. Aufl., Göttingen: Vandenhoeck & Ruprecht, 1902, pp. 148ff.; Plummer, *Phil.*, pp. 82f.; M. Meinertz and F. Tillmann, *Die Gefangenschaftsbriefe des Heiligen Paulus*, (in *Die Heilige Schrift des Neuen Testaments)*, Bonn: Peter Hanstein, 1931, pp. 155ff.; Michaelis, *Phil.*, pp. 61f.; Dibelius, *Phil.*, p. 93; F. W. Beare, *The Epistle to the Philippians*, B.N.T.C., Londen: Adam and Charles Black, 1959, pp. 133f.

237 P. Ewald, *Der Brief des Paulus an die Philipper*, K.z.N.T., 1./2. Aufl., Leipzig: A. Deicherts, 1908, p. 183: "Doch hält man es in der neueren Zeit zumeist für ausgeschlossen, weil die folgende Beschreibung ganz im Gegenteil zu dem gesetzlichen Wesen der Judaisten vielmehr einen auf heidnischen Ursprung zurückweisenden Libertinismus erkennen lasse." In the third edition of Ewald's commentary, which was reworked by G. Wohlenberg (Leipzig: A. Deicherts, 1923), the sentence remained the same (see p. 198).

238 *Phil.*, (1./2. Aufl.), pp. 183ff.; (3. Aufl.), pp. 198ff.

239 Greijdanus, *Phil.*, pp. 296, 298ff.; R. C. H. Lenski, *The Interpretation of St. Paul's Epistles to the Galatians, to the Ephesians, and to the Philippians*, Columbus (Ohio): Wartburg Press, 1946, pp. 857ff.; K. Barth, *Erklärung des Philipperbriefes*, 5. Aufl., Zollikon=Zürich: Evangelischer Verlag, 1947, pp. 110f.; Bonnard, *Phil.*, p. 71; J. J. Müller, *The Epistles of Paul to the Philippians and to Philemon*, N.I.C.N.T., Grand Rapids: Wm. B. Eerdmans, 1955, pp. 130ff. Cf. also Eidem, *Stud. Tillägnade E. Stave*, p. 81.

240 Dibelius, *Phil.*, p. 92.

241 G. Heinzelmann, *Der Brief an die Philipper*, N.T.D., 7./8. Aufl., Göttingen: Vandenhoeck & Ruprecht, 1956, p. 103.

work in the Philippian congregation and making its influence felt there. [242] It seems quite likely that Paul's reactions against Judaistic tendencies, against perfectionist tendencies, and against libertinistic tendencies were all called forth from the same source. [243] There were teachers propagating Gnostic interpretations of the Christian gospel in Philippi. Paul found it necessary to repudiate their teachings in the strongest possible terms.

When Paul stated as his aim the attainment of the resurrection from the dead, he hastened immediately to add, "Not that I... am already made perfect (τετελείωμαι)" (vs. 12). As Lightfoot has noted, "St Paul is not contrasting his own estimate of himself with other people's estimate of him, but his estimate of himself with others' estimate of themselves. He is in fact protesting against the false security." [244] Probably Paul was reacting against a Gnostic proposal that the fulness and very pinnacle of blessedness can presently be experienced and enjoyed by those who have been saved. [245] That there could be those in the New Testament Church who looked upon themselves as having reached the consummation of blessedness is clear from Paul's biting remarks in I Cor. 4:8: "Already are ye filled, already ye are become rich, ye have come to reign without us." Schmithals has amply illustrated from Gnostic and anti-Gnostic literature how much such a teaching was a part of the Gnostic system. [246] Paul repudiates the thought of present perfection in no uncertain terms and points out that the Christian life is a constant struggle onward, a pressing forward toward the goal. He illustrates

---

242 Schmithals, *Z.T.K.*, LIV, pp. 297–341. *Cf.* the same characterization of the false teaching present in Philippi by H. Köster, "Häretiker im Urchristentum," *R.G.G.*3, III, p. 19; and G. Bornkamm, "Paulus," *R.G.G.*3, V, p. 173.

243 Schweizer, *T.L.*, LXXXVI, p. 252, gives the following characterization and account of the movement against which Paul was reacting in various of his letters: "Die erste Zeit nach Ostern war durch einen überbordenden Enthusiasmus gekennzeichnet, der vor allem im palästinensisch-syrischen Raum auftrat. Die Erhöhung Jesu zum himmlischen Thron und die Gegenwart des Geistes mit all seinen Wunderphänomenen, scheinen den Anbruch der Heilzeit, die wiedergewonnene himmlische Herrlichkeit zu garantieren. Die Gegner, mit denen sich Paulus immer wieder auseinandersetzt, und die eine vermutlich viel einheitlichere Bewegung darstellen, als man oft meinte, mögen hierin wurzeln. Ihr jüdischer Charakter, eine gewisse Gesetzlichkeit und ein sich seiner Herkunft Rühmen ist typisch für sie. Zugleich betonen sie aber den Besitz des Geistes (im Sinne des Enthusiastisch-Ekstatischen) und der Weisheit (im Sinne der Erkenntnis verborgener Geheimnisse). Das gibt ihnen ihren schwärmerischen Charakter. Christus ist für sie vor allem der Offenbarer himmlischer Geheimnisse, neuer Erkenntnisse, unerhörter Weisheit, wie es auch andere Offenbarergestalten sind. In ihren Geisterfahrungen leben sie schon im 'Himmel'." The mixing of Jewish and heathen religious elements in the false teaching troubling the churches is apparent also from the letter to the Colossians. H. N. Ridderbos, *Aan de Kolossenzen*, C.N.T., Kampen: J. H. Kok, 1960, p. 106, describes the false teaching at work in Colossae as follows: "Hoewel het beeld van de dwaalleer te Kolosse in vele opzichten voor ons zeer wazig blijft, zal men in deze haeresie toch wel een vermenging mogen zien van Joodse en heidens-syncretistische religiositeit, waarin (Joods-)wettische, en (heidens-)speculatieve elementen met elkaar vermengd waren."

244 J. B. Lightfoot, *Saint Paul's Epistle to the Philippians*, London: Macmillan, 1890, p. 152.

245 Schmithals describes the Gnostic use of τέλειος as follows: "Das Kennzeichen des gnostischen τέλειος ist gerade nicht, *irgend etwas* erlangt zu haben, sondern *alles*, die *unaussprechliche* Seligkeit, über die hinaus es nichts mehr zu erlangen gibt. Er hat das Ziel schlechthin erreicht.... Es wird gesprochen von 'reich sein', 'zur Herrschaft gelangt sein', 'vollendet sein', 'vollkommen sein', 'in das Pleroma eingegangen sein','satt sein', 'in der Höhe sein', 'frei sein', 'zur Ruhe gekommen sein', 'Gott geworden sein' usw." (*Z.T.K.*, LIV, pp. 323–24).

246 *Ibid.*, pp. 322ff.

this point by continuing to speak of his personal experiences and his personal views on these matters, even as he has been doing since vs. 4. *He* was the one who might have found grounds for confidence in the flesh; but *he* had rejected all this for Christ and the salvation through faith in him. So in the same vein he continues: *he* has not yet attained perfection, but *he* is pressing on. In vs. 15 he suddenly admonishes: "Let us therefore be thus minded." In effect this is a call to imitate him. The Philippians are to take care to adopt the same view of the Christian life, rejecting confidence in their own merits, looking to Christ in faith, continuing in their awareness of their imperfection, and struggling onward toward the goal. They are to view these things as Paul views them.

When Paul appeals, "Let us be thus minded," the question arises to whom he is directing his appeal. There might be some reason for directing such an appeal to the whole membership of the Philippian church. Perhaps Paul wished to alert the entire congregation to a danger he saw in the world around them. He might thus be seeking to fortify them against it. However, in view of the form of address which he uses, it appears that he has some specific group in Philippi primarily in mind. He says, "As many as are perfect, let us be thus minded." [247] Is Paul perhaps making an appeal to some of the Philippian Christians who have become too attentive or maybe even a bit enamoured with the teaching of the men whom Paul calls "the dogs," "evil workers," "concision," and "enemies of the cross"? It was a custom of the Gnostics to identify themselves as "the perfect ones"; the term had become a slogan for them. [248] It appears that some of the Philippians were quite taken with the idea. Paul is thus applying the term to them with a bit of irony.

> Schmithals proposes: Dass diese τέλειοι eine schismatische Gruppe innerhalb der Gemeinde bilden, zeigt deutlich das ὅσοι οὖν τέλειοι, das nicht die ganze Gemeinde meint, aber — ein für Paulus unvollziehbarer Gedanke — natürlich auch nicht einen geistlich besonders ausgezeichneten Kreis in der Gemeinde meinen kann. Es muss sich um eine Gruppe handeln, die sich selbst als eine Schar von Vollkommenen innerhalb der Gemeinde separiert, nämlich um genau die Gruppe, von der Paulus sich in V. 13 bewusst absetzt, weil er eben noch nicht vollkommen ist und sein darf. Weil der V. 13 mit Sicherheit eine Gruppe von τέλειοι erschliessen lässt, *gegen* die Paulus sich wendet, kann der Apostel zu Beginn von V. 15 nur in paradoxer Rücksicht auf sie positiv von τέλειοι sprechen: Lasst uns die Vollkommenheit in dem demütigen Bekenntnis

---

[247] Ὅσοι οὖν τέλειοι, τοῦτο φρονῶμεν. To translate this: "Let us therefore, as many as are perfect, be thus minded," puts a slightly different slant on the verse. The "us" and the "perfect ones" are not necessarily so closely connected as to be equated. As Schmithals has pointed out: "Vielmehr dürfte das ὅσοι οὖν τέλειοι auf eine Fortsetzung in der 2. Pers. Plur. angelegt sein (wie V. 15b): τοῦτο φρονῆτε. Paulus benutzt dann freilich im Nachsatz, um sich mit den so Denkenden dialektisch zusammenzuschliessen, die 1. Pers. Plur., die man aber nicht ohne weiteres auch für das ὅσοι unterstellen darf: Also: 'Wer (von euch) auch immer 'vollkommen' ist: deises wollen wir bedenken (die wir eben dadurch unsere Vollkommenheit beweisen)!" (Schmithals, Z.T.K., LIV, p. 325, fn. 3).

[248] "Die τέλειοι sind gnostische Pneumatiker, die durch die Gnosis und in ihren Ekstasen zur Vollendung ihrer eschatologischen Existenz gelangen. In ihren Kreisen ist der Begriff τέλειος mit den verwandten Worten als term. techn. verbreitet" (*Ibid.*, p. 326).

unserer Unvollkommenheit suchen." [249] Whether the whole matter has gone as far as a schismatic group within the congregation, a group which has set itself apart from the rest ("separiert"), may be questioned. It does not seem that we need go further than to find in Paul's reference to ὅσοι τέλειοι a term of "reproachful irony" [250] directed toward all who were showing an openness to Gnostic teachings. It is particularly to these that Paul makes his appeal to be likeminded with him. [251]

It has been common among commentators to interpret Paul's reference to τέλειοι as designating a Christian perfection properly so-called, in distinction from the kind of perfection Paul had found it necessary to repudiate in vs. 12. [252] One can not raise serious objections to this view from the standpoint of grammar, word usage, or theology. However, the passage has remained unclear in many of its details and has called forth what Du Plessis has well described as "a truly bewildering mass of interpretations." [253] The proposal that Paul's reference to the τέλειοι is called forth by the Gnostic use of the term as a slogan opens the way for new insights on some of the puzzles of the passage. It also suggests more of a unity of thought and purpose for Phil. 3 than had formerly been seen. Throughout the chapter Paul is at work counteracting the influence of false teachings all stemming from the same source.

Paul has another thought which he attaches immediately to the appeal to be likeminded with him: "And if in anything ye are otherwise minded, this also shall God reveal unto you" (vs. 15b). The precise import of this remark is difficult to determine. However, the proposal that Paul is not speaking to the Philippian congregation in general, but has in mind primarily those who had been showing devious views about the state of their attainment, makes room for a new view also of this remark. Schmithals proposes that Paul's remark about things being revealed may have been called forth by the Gnostic interest in revelations. [254] Perhaps he wished to remind "the perfect ones" that it was not only Gnostic teachers who could speak of revelation. He too knew about revelations (*cf.* especially I Cor. 2:10 and Gal. 1:12,16); and he was confident of further revelations for Christians (Eph. 1:17). Paul refuses the Gnostic teachers the privilege of a monopoly on divine revelations. He is confident that God both can and will reveal to the Philippians the reality of the Christian struggle as he has outlined it.

Whatever the import of the remark about differing opinions and receiving revelations from God, Paul at least leaves no doubt as to the import of his whole previous argument. With vs. 16 he breaks off his discussion of the

---

249   *Ibid.*, p. 325.
250   Lightfoot's phrase; see, *Phil.*, p. 153.
251   It is interesting that here the appeal is to adopt his mind (φρονῶμεν). In the previous chapter in regard to their factiousness and vaingloryíng, Paul had called the Philippians to adopt Christ's mind (φρονεῖτε, 2:5). On the one hand it is likemindedness to himself; on the other hand it is likemindedness to Christ. Here is another indication of how easily Paul can interchange or place side by side the likeness to Christ and the likeness to himself (*cf.* I Thess. 1:6; I Cor. 11:1).
252   For a recent defence of this view of the passage, see Du Plessis, *Perfection*, pp. 194ff. *Cf.* also Preisker, *Ethos*, pp. 130ff.
253   Du Plessis, *Perfection*, p. 197.
254   Schmithals, *Z.T.K.*, LIV, pp. 327ff.

matter and underlines the point of it all: [255] "Only, whereunto we have attained, by that same rule let us walk." As Christians, his readers had "gained Christ," "were found in him," and had "the righteousness which is from God by faith" (*cf.* vss. 8,9). Paul calls for a way of life and for thoughts and attitudes which are consistent with their Christian profession. Salvation in Christ calls for a certain kind of life. Paul issues his call in broad general terms. Once again he includes himself: "Whereunto *we* have attained ... let *us* walk." The call goes forth as a general one to all in Philippi who profess Christianity. Nevertheless, Paul undoubtedly still had "the perfect ones" in mind in a special way. They had been showing signs of wandering from the Christian way as he had presented it. They, in particular, must realize that Christian profession calls for Christian living.

To this call for Christian living Paul immediately adds the call to imitate him. The one leads him to the other. The call to walk in the Christian way leads to the call to walk in the way he had showed them: "Brethren, be ye imitators together of me, and mark them that so walk even as ye have us for an ensample" (vs. 17). Paul is not here calling their attention directly to himself simply in order to give them a concrete illustration of the things about which he has been speaking. In fact, his speaking in the first person throughout the chapter thus far has had a deeper purpose than simply to make these matters as personal as possible. There are tones of great urgency and deep feeling underlying his words. This becomes the more clear with the next statement: "For many walk, of whom I told you often, and now tell you even weeping, that they are the enemies of the cross of Christ" (vs. 18). He is aware that his influence and example are not the only ones operating on the Christians in Philippi. He finds this other influence a sinister one; it leads Christians away from their heavenly calling and citizenship and sets their minds on earthly things (vss. 19,20). The Christians need strength and stamina in standing their ground against it and in remaining steadfast in the Lord. In seeking to strengthen them and to counteract the other influences, he has not engaged in an abstract presentation of the Christian teaching and the Christian way over against the teaching and way he opposes. He presented Christianity in terms of himself, what he had been through, what he had found it to be, and what he was now striving to do. He presents the Christian life in terms of the way he lives and what the Philippians have seen him to be. He seeks to exploit to the fullest his personal involvement in Christianity. But all of this is more than a personal illustration. He is intent upon pressing to the fullest extent his personal relation to the Philippian Christians and their relation and attachment to him. He seeks to draw with all the powers of attraction that the personal relationships between them will afford. The depth of feeling and emotion he had for them is evident from his appeal: "Wherefore, my brethren beloved and longed for, my joy and crown, so stand fast in the Lord, my beloved" (4:1). He wants the

---

[255] Such is the significance of Paul's usage of the conjunction πλήν with which the verse begins. *Cf.* Blass-Debrunner, *Gram.*, p. 282, § 449.2.

Philippians to feel this emotion and to allow it to arouse their feelings toward him. There are enemies of the cross abroad and their ways are devious and dangerous. The situation calls for much more than simply a picture of what Christianity is. Paul is making the most of the personal relationship between himself and the Philippians. He is attempting to draw them and secure them in his way, the Christian way. He summons with all the magnetic and attracting forces available to him. He calls them to walk consistent with the Christianity to which they have attained. To this he adds the appeal: "Be ye imitators of me!"

The call to imitation is directed to the whole Philippian congregation. His addition of the appellation "brethren" indicates this. Such at least is the significance of the term "brethren" both in the preceding context (cf. 3:13) and in the succeeding context (cf. 4:1). He is speaking to the entire congregation. Nevertheless, it is once again hard to avoid the thought that Paul still has "the perfect ones" in mind in a special way. This is suggested not only by the previous context. Paul has also chosen a very unusual form of the word "imitator" in his appeal here. He calls the Philippians to be συμμιμηταί, literally: "co-imitators." It is a subtle way of urging them one and all to join in a united imitation of him.

Paul's use of the word συμμιμητής has called forth much discussion. Some have judged the prefix συν- to be without significance and have ignored it as simple redundance and tautology.[256] However, the fact that Paul twice made his appeal to imitation to the Corinthians in exactly the same words with the exception of the prefix συν- causes one to suspect that he chose the word συμμιμητής intentionally and with some purpose in mind. The word, however, is a rare one. Plato once used it in its verbal form in the sense of one person's joining another in this one's imitation of a third.[257] Such a meaning has also been found in Paul's words. The suggestion has been made that Paul means to say: "Be fellow imitators with me of someone else, i.e., Christ."[258] Although the grammar of the clause permits such a meaning, it is hardly likely that Paul would have left the object of imitation completely to inference. Furthermore, the rest of the sentence makes it clear that Paul has his own example in mind.

It has been more common to understand the clause, "Be imitators with others (συν-) who imitate me."[259] The question immediately arises as to the identity of these "others." On this question opinions have been divergent. It has often been suggested that Paul means that they should join the churches or the Christians in other places in imitating him.[260]

---

256 Franke, *Phil.*, p. 202, lists J. H. Heinrichs as proposing this, and refers also to the interpretations of von Hofman and C. Holsten. Also Michaelis, *T.W.N.T.*, IV, p. 669, fn. 13, finds this the probable explanation. It is interesting that, when Chrysostom gives the text in his homily on this section, he writes simply μιμηταί (cf. *In Epistolam ad Philippenses, Homilia* XII [ed. Bern. de Montfaucon, Vol. XI, p. 293]).Also the Vulgate made no attempt to translate it: "Imitatores mei estote, fratres."

257 *Politicus* 274d.

258 This interpretation was proposed and argued by W. F. M'Michael, "Be Ye Followers of me," *E.T.*, V, p. 287. J. A. Bengel had proposed the same thing earlier, cf. his *Gnomon, sub* Phil. 3:17.

259 Franke, *Phil.*, p. 203 lists among those so interpreting the clause Estius, Erasmus, Vatablus, a Lapide, Wiesinger, B. Weiss, Ellicott, Schmidt, and others. Franke himself defends

This is possible, although there is little evidence that faithfulness in imitating Paul in other churches was generally so superior to that of the Philippian congregation that it could form the basis of a special appeal to the Philippians. Furthermore, in the next clause Paul calls the attention of his readers to some people in their immediate environment who are following the example Paul set and whom they ought to heed closely. Here it is not Christians elsewhere, but Christians in Philippi. Joüon has proposed that these "others" indicated by συν- are Paul's associates in the work of the ministry, such as Timothy, Epaphroditus, and others known to the Philippians.[261] It has been more common to see Paul's associates in the apostolic work indicated in the "us" of the latter part of the verse. While it is possible that they are also indicated in the συν-, such a proposal makes the sentence even more complicated and cryptic than it already is. The thought arises as to whether Paul's call to imitation here might be an appeal to "the perfect ones" to become imitators with the others, namely, with the Philippians who have remained consistent to the Pauline teaching and ways. It is possible to read all the matters since Paul's addressing "as many as are perfect" (vs. 15) as being addressed specifically to this group. However, when Paul inserts in his call for imitation the appellation "brethren" (vs. 17), he shows that he has in mind the entire Philippian congregation rather than a certain group within it.[262] If Paul's words are to be understood in the sense of "Be ye imitators with others who imitate me," then we must conclude that it is not apparent with whom the Philippians are to join in their imitation.

There are, however, other ways of understanding the prefix συν-. Perhaps the significance of the prefix is too subtle to admit of simple translation. Ewald has proposed: "Übrigens kann man hier, wenn man will, doch eine Art Steigerung in dem συν- sehen.... Nicht nur, dass sie Nachahmer des Ap werden, sondern dass sie durch Nachahmung sich mit ihm zusammenschliessen sollen, ist sein Wunsch und seine Bitte, die durch das φρονῶμεν zuvor nur erst angedeutet war."[263] This suggestion has a measure of plausibility. When so understood, the μιμητής prefixed by συν- conforms to Paul's frequent practice in this letter of prefixing a συν- to a word in order to emphasize the fellowship and union he feels between himself and the Philippians.[264] It is possible, however, that Paul is emphasizing another unity in his use of the prefix συν-. Perhaps it is not so much the union between himself and the Philippians that he has in mind as the union of the Philippians among themselves. Paul had taken note that some of the Philippians are "otherwise minded" (vs. 15).[265] There are other indications in his letter of the need of more unity among the Philippians: cf. 1:27; 2:1–4; 4:2. Perhaps Paul is here summoning them to a unity of effort, "omnes uno consenso et una

---

this interpretation (loc. cit.); in more recent times P. Joüon, "Notes philologiques sur quelques versets de l'épître aux Philippiens," R.S.R., XXIII, pp. 307f.

260 E.g. Franke, Phil., p. 203; B. Weiss, Das Neue Testament nach Luthers berichtigter Übersetzung mit fortlaufender Erläuterung versehen, 2. Aufl., Leipzig: J. C. Hinrichs, 1907, Vol. II, p. 440.

261 Joüon, R.S.R., XXIII, p. 307f.

262 Lohmeyer, who saw vss. 15f. directed particularly to a separate group, observed also that the presence of "brethren" in vs. 17 indicated that the whole congregation was here again being addressed (see Phil., pp. 148, 151).

263 Ewald, Phil.3, p. 198, fn. 2.

264 See above, p. 170.

265 The εἰ followed by an indicative in vs. 15b indicates the real situation; cf. Gal. 5:15. If only the possibility of such a situation were being expressed, ἐάν with the subjunctive would be used. Cf. Greijdanus, Phil., p. 295.

mente," as Calvin strikingly put it.[266] This is an interpretation which has found quite general acceptance among commentators,[267] even though Ewald dubs it "ganz sprachwidrig."[268]

When it comes finally to deciding precisely what Paul meant by prefixing the συν- to μιμητής, one wonders if there is not the temptation of becoming more precise than Paul meant to be. May Paul not have chosen intentionally to express himself a bit ambiguously? Could there not be varying nuances for the various brethren in the presence of this συν-? Basically it was a subtle call to unity. Such a call applied to all. It was important that everyone do his part in promoting unity of effort and action. However, for the deviating ones it was a special call to join with the more faithful ones in their imitation. At the same time the more faithful brethren were called by it to be helpful in regard to the deviating ones. They must so live and act as to encourage a more consistent and total imitation from those who were taking too many liberties in doctrine and life. In so far as the συν- carried any overtones of an intensified fellowship with Paul, one can only imagine that Paul used it with the more enthusiasm. The addition of συν- was an attempt to multiply the effectiveness of his call. He wished them all together to join in the imitation of him.

In connection with his call to the Philippians to be his imitators, Paul calls their attention also to the example they have in him: "Ye have us for an example" (vs. 17c). One is immediately struck by the slight change he has now made. The thought has expanded from "the imitation of *me*" to "the example in *us*." Between these two expressions Paul has expressed another thought. The Philippians are to give particular notice to the conduct of certain men. These three thoughts flow from Paul's pen in rapid succession to each other. One could wish that he had expressed himself more carefully and fully at this point, and in language less open to several interpretations. Just what Paul has in mind at each point in this verse is not immediately evident. The lack of clarity arises in part from the structure of the sentence. This too admits of two different constructions. The clause about Paul's example can be viewed as giving a reason for imitating him, or it can be viewed as describing the manner in which certain people live. The latter interpretation would seem to be preferable.

Phil. 3:17 is composed of three clauses: (a) "Be ye imitators together of me, brethren"; (b) "and mark them that so walk"; and (c) "even as ye have us for an example." It has been proposed that clause (c) serves to give a reason for the two things Paul has just called the Philippians to do.[269] The sense would thus be: "Imitate me, and mark those who

---

266 Calvin, *Phil.*, *sub* 3:16 (Baum, Cunitz, and Reuss, Vol. XXX, p. 54).

267 Among the older commentators, Franke, *Phil.*, p. 203, lists Beza, Grotius, Matthies, Hoelemann, van Hengel. In more recent times this been the interpretation of Lightfoot, *Phil.*, p. 152; Vincent, *Phil.*, p. 116; Plummer, *Phil.*, p. 81; Michael, *Phil.*, p. 168; Lohmeyer, *Phil.*, p. 151; Bonnard, *Phil.*, p. 71; Müller, *Phil.*, p. 128; *et al.*

268 Ewald, *Phil.*3, p. 198. Michael takes the other extreme: "This interpretation is the only meaning that is not open to some evident objection" (J. H. Michael, *The Epistle of Paul to the Philippians*, M.N.T.C., London: Hodder & Stoughton, 1928, p. 168).

269 Franke, *Phil.*, p. 204, adopts this interpretation, and lists Meyer, Wiesinger, and B. Weiss as others who have adopted it. Haupt, *Phil.*, p. 151, follows the same course. Beare, while not

walk in imitation of me, since you have an example in us (them and me)." Such an interpretation is grammatically permissible, for οὕτω often refers to what has just been mentioned,[270] and καθώς can have a causal meaning.[271] This interpretation sees Paul directing the Philippians' attention to himself and to everyone who is an imitator of him. It proposes in effect that every imitator of him thereby becomes an example to his fellow Christians. On the basis of such an understanding of the text and in view of Paul's use of συμμιμηταί, Lenski finds an interesting situation existent in Philippi. He says: "In Philippi there were many who walked so as to serve as an example together with Paul. All these imitate each other and are to keep on doing this, Paul himself being one of them. They are not to be imitated merely by those who are not yet fit to be imitated. They are not to serve as dummy models. Themselves active imitators, their very imitating is to be imitated, by each one of themselves as well as by all others. The Philippians have a most intensive and stimulating model."[272] One might also find in clauses (b) and (c) an appeal directed particularly to "the perfect ones" to take for their example all the Philippian brethren who had remained more faithful to Paul. However, it remains open to question whether we have really caught the point of Paul's words when we understand him to say that every imitator of himself thereby becomes an example to the rest.[273]

It is also possible to read clauses (b) and (c) as standing in correlation to each other. Clause (c) would then express the manner implied in the οὕτω of clause (b). The sense of the passage would be: "Mark those that walk in the way that our example has set for you." Such an understanding of Paul's words gives the combination of οὕτω and καθώς its normal and natural function, namely, that of expressing correlation. Admittedly, καθώς may have a causal meaning, as just noted. However, in the instances which Robertson[274] and Blass-Debrunner[275] cite of such a usage, there are no correlative words in the near context. Here only one word intervenes between οὕτω and καθώς, and that is the verb which οὕτω modifies. Furthermore, Blass-Debrunner proposes that καθώς may have a causal sense when used "als satzeinleitende Konjunktion,"[276] a position which it surely does not hold here. The presence of οὕτω in clause (b) presents a major obstacle to reading καθώς in a causal sense. Perhaps such a reading is conceivable, but it remains artificial. It would probably never have occurred to interpreters, were it not for the other exegetical difficulties in this verse.

When clauses (b) and (c) are read correlatively, the subject of clause (c) offers difficulty. Paul says, "Mark them that so walk even as ye have us for an ensample." We would have expected him to say, "Mark them that so walk even as *they* have us for an ensample." The correlation would then come to fuller expression. The subjects would be the same: „They walk even as *they* have...." Their walk would correspond to their possession of the example. And yet, this can hardly have been precisely the point Paul was trying to make. Is it not obvious that whatever

---

analyzing the relation of the clauses in his commentary, shows by his interpretation that he reads the sentence in this way; cf. Phil., p. 135.

270 Cf. Bauer, Wörterbuch, sub οὕτω, 1. 6.
271 Blass-Debrunner, Gram., p. 285, § 453, 2; Robertson, Gram., p. 968.
272 Lenski, Phil., pp. 856, 857.
273 While Paul might not have repudiated such a thought categorically, the question is whether such a meaning is to be read from his words here.
274 Robertson, Gram., p. 968; cf. p. 963.
275 Blass-Debrunner, Gram., p. 285, § 453, 2.
276 Loc. cit.

correspondence Paul might wish to express here would be not between *their walk* and *their possession* of his example, but between *their walk* and *his example,* or between *their walk* and *his walk?* Hence, even with a change of subject, Paul's phraseology would still be a bit awkward. The awkwardness of the clause is not confined to the unexpected use of the second person pronoun instead of the third person pronoun. Instead, the awkwardness inheres in the whole way Paul has expressed himself here.

It need surprise no one to find awkwardness in Paul's phraseology. Paul has never been acclaimed for a consistently smooth and grammatically coherent method of expressing himself. The exegete is often faced with the challenge of detecting Paul's meaning in his awkward phraseology. In this passage the difficulties arising from the phraseology must not be overly emphasized. Neither is it necessary to resort to unusual interpretations of words in an attempt to find a smoother flow of the thought. The basic thought that Paul wishes to express here is sufficiently clear in spite of any awkwardness in phraseology. The Philippians have been given an example of Christian conduct. They presently possess that example. It serves as a pattern for them. They are to pay careful attention to those that walk according to this pattern. They are to beware of the dogs and evil workers (vs. 2), but they are to give close heed to those walking according to the Christian pattern. [277] Paul is intent upon emphasizing the distinction between those walking according to the pattern he has given and some others who walk quite differently. He makes this contrast specific in what he writes here: "Mark them that so walk even as ye have us for an ensample. For many walk, of whom I told you often, and now tell you even weeping, that they are the enemies of the cross of Christ: whose end is perdition, whose god is the belly, and whose glory is in their shame, who mind earthly things" (vss. 17b–19). The Philippians are to ward off the influence of certain men, and to concentrate on being influenced by those walking according to the Pauline pattern. Clause (c) describes the manner in which the men spoken of in clause (b) are walking.

Paul gives another command immediately after the one to imitate him: "Mark them that so walk even as ye have us for an ensample." Whom does he have in mind specifically in his expression "them that so walk"? The expression as such is general and can be understood as meaning Paul and everyone who walks according to Paul's example, both in Philippi and everywhere else. When so understood, it would include all Christians of the Pauline stamp. [278] However, since the Philippians are directed to pay attention to these people, the expression must certainly have in mind those who are in Philippi, or at least those who are present in Philippi from time to time. Furthermore, "the ones that so walk" are contrasted not to members of a general populace who manifest the lack of moral restraint, but to certain teachers, missionaries, and leaders giving the wrong kind of leadership. Hence, it would seem that Paul is not thinking of every member of the congregation

---

277 The σκοπεῖτε of vs. 17 stands in contrast to the βλέπετε of vs. 2.
278 *Cf.* Bonnard, *Phil.*, p. 70: "... l'apôtre entouré de ses collaborateurs (cf. 1 Th. 1. 6) et de tous ceux qui lui sont fidèles." Michaelis, *Phil.*, p. 61, would understand it still more broadly: "... irgendwelche anderen (auswärtigen) Christen, die, weil sie wie er um einen rechten Christenwandel sich mühen, ihm gleichen."

when he directs attention to "them that so walk," but rather to those giving the right kind of leadership to the congregation. They are to take note of the conduct of their elders, pastors, and teachers. This exhortation to the congregation to give heed to the walk of their leaders forms a kind of counterpart to the exhortations which the New Testament writers upon occasion directed to various leaders to be examples to their congregations. [279] The exhortation here also resembles the one in the letter to the Hebrews, where the readers are urged: "Remember them who had the rule over you, ... and considering the issue of their life, imitate their faith" (Heb. 13:7). [280] Here in his letter to the Philippians, Paul sees the faithful walk of the leaders as a hopeful counteractive to the influence of the false teachers. The conduct of these leaders, in so far as it conforms to his example, is placed on a par with his example. In effect, the Philippians are directed to become imitators also of the leaders in their midst, the ones who are following the Pauline pattern.

We may now seek to answer the question as to whom Paul has in mind in the "us" in his statement, "even as ye have us for an example." It would be wholly within the range of usage in his day for him to mean by the first person plural simply himself. [281] Such an interpretation might seem more likely in view of Paul's not giving the slightest hint as to what other persons are to be included here. [282] However, Paul's speaking of "me" in the first part of the sentence all but rules out the possibility that he uses "us" in the sense of "me" in the latter part of the sentence. There can be little doubt that Paul wishes to include others with himself in speaking of the Philippians' having "us" for an example. Apparently, then, Paul is speaking of himself and those associated with him in his missionary travels and work. In first bringing the gospel to Macedonia, he was accompanied by Silas and Timothy (cf. Acts 16:6ff.; especially 16:19; 17:14; 18:5). In this letter Timothy is associated with him in the salutation (1:1), and the Philippians are informed that Paul intends to send Timothy to Philippi shortly to minister further to them (2:23). Paul and his associates form a team, and collectively they supply a pattern (cf. singular, τύπον). A Christian tradition had been initiated in Philippi through the work of Paul and his associates. Paul is now calling upon the Philippians to notice the leaders in their midst who conduct themselves in conformity to the Christian pattern furnished by the apostolic team.

The question remains why Paul switched from "me" to "us." It has been proposed upon occasion that the "me" sounded too egotistical to him after he

---

[279] Cf. I Tim. 4:12; Titus 2:7; I Peter 5:3. See discussion of these texts above, pp. 85ff.
[280] Also here the exhortation comes where there is the danger of the readers being carried away by diverse and strange teachings; cf. Heb. 13:9.
[281] See above, p. 118.
[282] The use of the first person plural in the context gives no help. In 3:3 the "we" is generally understood to mean "we, Christians." (A dissenting voice is to be found, however, in T. Zahn, *Einleitung in das Neue Testament*, 3. Aufl., Leipzig: A. Deichert, 1905, p. 383, § 7, who proposes it means Paul and Timothy.) In 3:15f. the "we" is in the form of an exhortation to the readers to whom he is speaking. In 3:20f. it has all Christians in mind. Hence, in all these instances the first person plural includes the Philippians. That can hardly be the case in 3:17, where the Philippians are designated by the second person plural.

had used it, so that he changed it to "us" in the latter part of the sentence.²⁸³ While this is a possible explanation, his unmodified usage of "me" twice over in calling the Corinthians to imitate him (*cf.* I Cor. 4:16; 11:1) hardly supports the idea. The thought occurs that possibly the matter of being an example is a broader and less specific matter than that of being the source of imitation, so that being an example can apply to the whole apostolic team, while the object of imitation can only be applied to Paul. However, here too, the evidence will not permit such a conclusion. The calls to imitation in the letters to the Thessalonians (I Thess. 1:6; II Thess. 3:7ff.) are against it. There the call is to the imitation of "us," and the "us," while applying primarily to Paul, the dominant figure of the team, can not entirely exclude Silvanus and Timothy, Paul's associates.²⁸⁴

It does not seem that it is necessary to seek too far to account for the shift of the pronoun from singular to plural. The singular pronoun flows naturally from what Paul has been saying. He has been speaking about his own personal experiences, his own personal faith, and his own struggles in Christian living. It is only natural that his call for imitation should come as a call to imitate himself. However, the pattern is not limited to Paul. This too is important for the Philippians to keep in mind. They are faced with false teachers in their midst. The Christian walk was not merely one man's peculiarities, but the consistent pattern of Paul and his associates, seen both when they were all together, and when only various of the associates revisited Philippi.²⁸⁵ Hence, this Christian pattern had been held before them more than once. It had been stamped on their minds repeatedly and under various circumstances by Paul and his associates. There were presently leaders in Philippi who were themselves conforming to this Christian pattern. Paul directs his readers attention to them. In the face of false teachers and devious tendencies in Philippi, Paul is intent on appealing to the Christian pattern on as broad a base as possible. He says in effect: "You know the example all of us showed you. Take notice of those who are walking in this way, but beware of the others."

In what does Paul seek the imitation of himself by the Philippians? In what does the example of which he speaks consist? This passage in the letter to the Philippians probably contains the broadest and most general call to imitation that we find in Paul's letters. It is a call to be like Paul in distinction from those who are termed "dogs," "evil workers," "the concision," and "enemies of the cross of Christ." If we knew more specifically who these were, what they were teaching, and how they were living, we would have a clearer idea of the details of the imitation for which Paul here calls. The general idea of the imitation, however, is sufficently clear. The example he has in mind has in large measure been portrayed in the things he said about himself in the preceding verses. The Philippians must avoid the temptation

---

283 *Cf.* Lightfoot, *Phil.*, p. 152; Plummer, *Phil.*, p. 81.
284 See above, pp. 118f.
285 Silas and Timothy undoubtedly visited Philippi before coming from Macedonia to meet Paul in Corinth; *cf.* Acts 18:5.

and danger of seeking and finding any confidence in their ability to stand before God on the basis of what they are in themselves and on the basis of their manner of life and their deeds. They must follow Paul's example of writing off completely everything that has seemed to be an asset in their account with God, in order to gain the one asset of real value, Jesus Christ, and the righteousness that comes through faith in him. They must be like Paul in accepting the consequences of being joined to Christ. Salvation in Christ could not be described only in terms of experiencing the power of his resurrection; it also involved one in the more somber, the more humiliating, and the more difficult experiences of sharing his sufferings and learning conformity to his death. Some had completely failed to notice this cardinal aspect of Christianity. They were teaching a way of life quite contrary to this, and to Paul's great grief and sorrow he finds it necessary to expose them for what they are: enemies of the cross of Christ. Imitation of Paul meant also throwing off all complacency and every notion that one's present state of Christian life was either the ultimate or the best possible. The Philippians must imitate Paul in his strenuous efforts to make further progress toward a goal not yet attained. Others were setting a pattern of absorption in the pursuits and pleasures of this earth. Paul and his companions had set a pattern of absorption in the pursuit of a higher and heavenly goal. The pattern, as far as it pertains to Paul's own activity, has a strong imprint of negative elements: he counts all things to be loss, he must suffer, he must be conformed to death, he lacks perfection, he must forget. The positive item in the pattern is not found in Paul and his activity, but in Christ and his benefits. Thus, as Barth has suggested, Paul can call for the imitation of himself without any trace of self-exaltation. [286] In a word, the example lies in the total and continuing humiliation of self in favor of gaining Christ and the goal in him.

What is the significance of the call to imitation and the calling attention to the example in this passage? The example which we have just noted is not one to arouse an enthusiastic urge in the hearts of men to emulate it. Paul and his associates do not present such a winsome picture of the real and the full life for man that others are attracted to become like them. Paul can not point to an inherent worth in his conduct and recommend this to others. The whole matter of imitation here has nothing to do with a personal exemplariness as this is commonly understood. When Michaelis rejects such an understanding of the matter, we can agree with him wholeheartedly. [287] On the other hand, Michaelis' own understanding of the significance of this call for imitation is not beyond dispute. He proposes that imitation here

---

[286] "Was an i h m, Paulus wahrzunehmen ist in christlicher Beziehung, das ist ja eben nicht etwas Positives, dessen e r sich rühmen könnte, sondern C h r i s t u s, d. h. aber die Spuren der δύναμις τῆς ἀναστάσεως αὐτοῦ (der "Kraft seiner Auferstehung"), die Gemeinschaft seiner Leiden, ein L o c h sozusagen, ein Mangel, ein Defekt: er ist n i c h t heilig, n i c h t gerecht, n i c h t volkommmen, alles um Christi willen n i c h t. Diesen τύπος (dieses "Vorbild") darf er ihnen wirklich ohne Selbstüberhebung zur Nachahmung empfehlen" (Barth, *Phil.*, p. 110).

[287] Michaelis, *T.W.N.T.*, IV, p. 670, 11.

really has to do with obedience to apostolic authority. He says concerning the command to be imitators of Paul: "To be sure, this means: Walk as I do!, but at the same time and primarily it means: Acknowledge my authority, do as I tell you, be obedient! Thus it is an imitation not in the sense of reproducing an example, but as an expression of obedience."[288] The question may be posed whether such an understanding of the matter has really caught the import of the command.

Paul's apostleship was indeed an important factor in his whole relationship to the Philippians. He was Christ's apostle, and this gave authenticity to the message which he proclaimed and the way of Christian life that he showed. There can be no doubt that his apostleship clothed him with great authority. However, was the matter of authority an element of particular prominence at this point in his letter?[289] Is Paul at this moment intent on urging *obedience* on the Philippians? Paul's tone in his previous argument has not been authoritarian, at least, not toward his readers. Rather, he has repeatedly placed himself alongside of them, as one of them in their midst, and spoken about matters applying to them all in common, himself included. He affirms, "We, you and I as Christians, are the circumcision" (3:3). When he speaks to "the perfect ones," we might have expected his words to take a stronger form. However, even here he expresses himself in an exhortation in which he joins himself directly to them: "Let us be thus minded" (3:15). Once again, immediately preceding his call to imitation, he expresses himself in words directed equally to himself and his readers; he says in effect: "Let us all walk consistent with the Christianity we profess" (3:16). Immediately after the call to imitation we find him reduced to tears in telling them about certain disturbing developments (3:18), and he goes on to speak of "our" Christian citizenship and the things awaiting "us" Christians (3:20,21). He concludes the subject with his tenderly emotional appeal to remain steadfast (4:1). His stance throughout is one of common ground with them; he stands in the midst of them in close fellowship and union with them. Such a stance need not detract in the least from the fact of his apostolic authority or from the Philippians' recognition of it. But such a stance does not make the element of authority a prominent factor in the relationship. The relationship

---

288 *Ibid.*, ll. 19–23 (my translation). The following is Michaelis' complete statement of the matter in his own words: "Die Sonderstellung, die Paulus immerhin einnimmt, wird mit seiner apostolischen Autorität zusammenhängen (auch die οὕτω περιπατοῦντες stehen aber vielleicht in der Missionsarbeit, ebenso die 3, 18f bekämpften Christen). Darum wird auch hier der Begriff der Nachahmung (mag die Aufforderung an 3, 16 anknüpfen oder nur das Folgende einleiten) mehr enthalten als das Bestreben, ein Vorbild, das vorgelebt wird, als Muster zu nehmen und nachzubilden: obschon der Wandel des Apostels solchen vorbildlichen Charakter trägt (diese Voraussetzung macht er offenbar, sicher ohne Ruhmredigkeit, in klarer Erkenntnis, wie gefährdet auch diese seine Vorbildlichkeit ist; vgl 1 K 9, 27), geht es doch nicht um seine Person und ihre 'Vollkommenheit' (Phil 3, 12ff), sondern um die A u t o r i t ä t, die ihm verliehen worden ist und von der aus er für seine Verkündigung Gehör und im Zusammenhang damit auch für seinen Wandel Nachahmung beansprucht. συμμιμηταί μου γίνεσθε, das heisst gewiss: wandelt so wie ich!, aber es heisst zugleich und es heisst zuerst: anerkennt meine Autorität, befolgt, was ich euch sage, seid gehorsam! 'Nachahmung' also nicht als Wiederholung des Vorbilds, sondern als A u s d r u c k d e s G e h o r s a m s" (*ibid.*, ll. 7–23).

289 *Cf.* Michaelis' statement: "Es heisst *zuerst:* anerkennt meine Autorität, ... seid gehorsam" (*ibid.*, ll. 20,21 [my italics]).

toward the Philippians that Paul is here emphasizing is not that of the apostle with authority to command, as compared to the Philippians, whose position is simply to follow in obedience. In calling for imitation he is not directly calling for obedience.

Paul's stance here is like that of a father in the midst of the children he loves so dearly. Here too the matter of authority is not foreign to the relationship. But it is not necessarily consciously present in all their activities together; neither are all the activities and conversations between parent and child with an eye to urging and maintaining the point of parental authority. Paul here is the father who is seeking to lead, guide, direct, and draw his children into the ways of his own life as a Christian. He is seeking the perfection of his own image as a Christian in them. In more colloquial terms, he is seeking to bring up his children to be good Christians. He is seeking to bring about an imitation of himself and a following of his example. The processes here at work are more subtle than a direct urging of his authority and a pressing for obedience to his commands. Obedience is no indifferent matter, of course. But the obedience will be an accomplished fact, if the imitation can be secured. Paul's aim is to cultivate in his readers a living experience of the Christian way as he knows it. Hence, he calls them to be his imitators.

The imitation of which Paul here speaks is not to be thought of as a mere reproduction or formal copying. A formal copying by the Philippians of what they have observed in Paul would be far removed from what Paul is here seeking. Mere repetition of his ways would be no counteractive to the dangers and threats facing the Philippian congregation. They are faced with false teachers and must cope with the detrimental influence of their teachings and way of life. Paul is not worried that the Philippians might begin to take up a formal copying of the ways of the false teachers. The danger is that they will begin to *live* in that way. Paul counteracts by calling for imitation. It is no formal, mindless, mechanical activity, unworthy of the dignity of a human being. It is an experience in living. As we saw in the first chapter, the Greeks knew of a much loftier kind of imitation than slavish reproduction. Basically, imitation was the activity of bringing things into expression, representation, and realization through one's own capacities and abilities. It could be a creative experience and an activity of real value. [290] Furthermore, it was one of the most important processes of living and of growth. Children have always been imitators of their parents and teachers, and adults have always tended to imitate their leaders. This phenomenon is not simply an indication of obedience; it points to a process whereby the content of the lives and ways of the one is absorbed and brought to living expression in the other. Paul makes an appeal here to this phenomenon and capacity in man. Man is an imitator. "Be then imitators *of me*," says Paul; "Bring to expression in your lives the Christianity and the Christian way you see portrayed in me."

---

[290] See above, p. 2, and especially pp. 5ff.

Michaelis' characterization of imitation as an expression of obedience does not strike directly at the import of the concept. Obedience is expressive of a formal relation between Paul and the Philippians. Paul, in calling for imitation, is concerned with a material relation between them. The content of Christianity as he knows it and as he displays it must come to expression in the Philippians. He is pointing to this content in himself as pattern or example and calling them to bring it to expression in their lives. Imitation is not bringing obedience to expression, but bringing the content of the pattern and example to expression. Imitation here means a personal living like Paul lives. This, in distinction from Michaelis's interpretation, is the primary idea being expressed.

\* \* \*

Paul makes one more reference to the matter of his example in the letter to the Philippians. Both the context and the words are most general. Paul precedes the reference with a direction to the Philippians to think about "whatsoever things are true, ... honorable, ... just, ... pure, ... lovely, ... of good report; if there be any virtue, and if there be any praise" (4:8). Then he says: "The things which ye both learned and received and heard and saw in me, these things do" (4:9). Although there is no specific word for "example" or "imitation," the thought is abundantly clear in the reference to what was heard and seen in Paul.

Michael has pointed out: "The first pair of these four verbs refer to the definite Christian instruction which the Philippians had received from the Apostle; the second pair to the example he had set them."[291] The Philippians knew Paul through his preaching, but they knew him also through their personal living, working, and fellowshipping with him. This latter was important for them. They were to do the things learned from his example as well as the things learned from more direct instruction and commands. Bonnard remarks that Paul is not presenting himself as a great example to be followed, but as an authorized representative of the teaching of the church.[292] This antithesis is, however, not wholly valid. It applies only when one thinks of "a great example" in a moralistic sense. Paul's words here indicate that Paul (as authorized teacher of Christianity) saw himself engaged in his teaching function not only in his formal acts of giving instruction, but also in the example he set in all of his life and conduct among men. Paul leaves it to the good judgment of his readers not to misunderstand and wrongly apply his very general and comprehensive command. Obviously there were limits to their doing what they had seen Paul do. Nevertheless, this statement indicates the breadth of scope in which Paul conceived of himself as being an example to his converts. In effect his whole life constituted an example to be followed.

\* \* \*

---

[291] Michael, *Phil.*, p. 206.
[292] Bonnard, *Phil.*, p. 77.

Paul's call to the Philippians to imitate him does not reveal new aspects of the concept of imitation which we have not noted before. In this letter he does not speak specifically about his readers' being his children, or about his having fathered them. However, the whole letter shows the close personal relationship that exists between them. Paul finds this personal bond between them especially important in view of the present situation in their midst. The Philippians are coming in contact with false representations of Christian doctrine and the Christian way of life. He reminds the Philippians of what true Christianity is by presenting his own Christian experiences, beliefs, and attitudes. The accent is strongly on a total and continuing humiliation of self in favor of gaining Christ and the goal in him. This is basic Christianity, and the appeal is to imitate Paul in this. The Philippians must mold their Christian beliefs and life according to this pattern. Paul had shown it to them; the united witness of the apostolic team had portrayed the same pattern; and it was to be found in their midst in their leaders who had developed according to the Pauline form. Imitation is a call to bring to personal expression the Christianity which Paul had portrayed to them. It is a means by which Paul seeks to lead the Philippians to mature and steadfast Christian faith and life.

## VI. Galatians 4:12

*I beseech you, brethren, become as I am, for I also am become as ye are.*

It is evident from Paul's letter to the Galatians that somebody was working havoc in the Christian congregations there. Paul manifests complete astonishment that the whole situation there could have degenerated so radically and so swiftly. He expresses himself in caustic terms, anathematizing those who are preaching the new kind of gospel, and calling the Galatians foolish (N.E.B.: "stupid") and bewitched (Gal. 3:1). Paul's severity and sharpness reveal how deeply disturbed he was by the whole development in Galatia. This was not the type of thing that he could face dispassionately; these were his own little children (4:19), and he grievously feared for their salvation (4:11).

The precise details of the false teaching which was troubling the Galatian churches can not be discovered. It is obvious from what Paul writes in the first two chapters that his apostleship was being called into question. There was also a concerted attempt to wean the Galatians away from their allegiance to Paul and his teaching (*cf.* 4:17). The heart of the matter, however, concerned the adopting of a form of legalism. The Galatians had acquired a desire to be under the law (4:21; 5:4). There was an insistence on the necessity of circumcision (6:12; *cf.* 5:2—12) and an observance of days, months, seasons, and years (4:10). Paul's letter, from the third chapter to the end, deals with the matter of the law and the kind of life which freedom from the law ought to call forth in the Christian.

It has long been common to identify the propagators of these erroneous teachings as "Judaisers," with the assumption, either implied or expressed, that they represented a type of Christianity which insisted on the necessity of keeping at least part of the Jewish law. The origin of the movement has usually been traced to Jerusalem, and often to "the pillars": James, Peter, and John (*cf.* Gal. 2:9). However, the whole heretical movement may have been much more complex than this. Schmithals has recently pointed out many difficulties with the traditional "Judaiser" interpretation. [293] He proposes that Paul's opponents were propagating a Jewish-Christian form of Gnosticism. [294] Others too are speaking in broader and more general terms about the matter, as is clear from the following characterizations: "Ihr Judaismus [erscheint] doch ganz im Gewand zeitgemässer orientalisch-synkretistischer Religiosität"; [295] "Man wird ... mit einer sektiererischen judenchristlichen Bewegung zu rechnen haben, die gnostisch gefärbt, aber doch in der Hauptsache gesetzlich bestimmt war"; [296] "... ein heterodoxes Judenchristentum mit 'gnost.' Tendenzen.... Das Judenchristentum der späteren sog. Kerinthianer, Elkesaiten, u. Ebioniten steht dem v. Paulus bekämpften nahe." [297] It is not necessary to our present purpose to pursue this matter further. Whatever the details of the error may have been, the heart of the matter, as Paul saw it, was the involvement in legalism.

In the midst of his discussion of the law, its place and function in history, the bondage to which it subjected those who were under it, and the inferiority of such a condition, Paul suddenly turns away from further arguing for the moment. He had just remarked about how the Galatians had turned to observing days, months, seasons, and years (4:10). This caused him to exclaim that he fears for them lest his work for them has been in vain. [298] He turns to them in a most tender and personal way and appeals, "I beseech you, brethren, become as I am, for I also am become as ye are" (4:12). He then proceeds immediately to recall his visit to Galatia. How enthusiastically they had received him in spite of his poor health (4:13–15). But now there are those who are trying to drive a wedge between them. In tenderest love he embraces them: "My little children, of whom I am again in travail until Christ be formed in you" (4:19); but he drops the sentence unfinished and goes on to exclaim: "But I could wish to be present with you now, and to change my tone; for I am perplexed about you" (4:20). Paul is nearly beside himself with anguish over what has happened in Galatia. His thoughts no longer entirely cohere as he pours out his heart to them.

The question arises whether, when Paul appeals, "Become as I am," he

---

293 Schmithals, *Z.N.W.*, XLVII, pp. 25–67.
294 *Ibid.*, p. 66.
295 Köster, *R.G.G.*³, III, p. 18.
296 G. Stählin, "Galaterbrief," *R.G.G.*³, II, p. 1188.
297 H. Schlier, "Galaterbrief," *L.T.K.*², IV, pp. 487–488.
298 "The ὑμᾶς following φοβοῦμαι in the sense of *I fear for you*, or, *have fears in respect of you*, is unusual. Still, that is unmistakably the meaning" (H. N. Ridderbos, *The Epistle of Paul to the Churches of Galatia, N.I.C.N.T.*, Grand Rapids: Wm. B. Eerdmans, 1953, p. 162, fn. 9). So also H. Schlier, *Der Brief an die Galater*, K.e.K.N.T., 10. Aufl., Göttingen: Vandenhoeck & Ruprecht, 1949, p. 146; M.-J. Lagrange, *St Paul: Épître aux Galates*, E.B., Paris: J. Gabalda, 1926, p. 109; F. Sieffert, *Handbuch über den Brief an die Galater*, K.e.K.N.T., 7. Aufl., Göttingen: Vandenhoeck & Ruprecht, 1886, p. 262; *et al.*

is in effect calling the Galatians to imitate him. The passage has been generally understood in this way, and, it would seem, quite rightly so. The matter has, however, not gone entirely undisputed.

Both articles which have been written specifically on the imitation of Paul have included a discussion of the imitation portrayed in Gal. 4:12. [299] Also, many commentators in their exposition of this text call attention to the express statements about imitation in Paul's other letters. [300] Michaelis, however, finds that Gal. 4:12 offers no parallel to the texts on imitation, and points to the difficulty which the clause ὅτι κἀγὼ ὡς ὑμεῖς offers to understanding the matter as imitation. [301] Michaelis undoubtedly has in mind Oepke's discussion of the matter, to whom he refers his readers. [302] Oepke in his latest discussion of the text has become even more specific in rejecting the thought of imitation in 4:12 than he was in the edition of his commentary to which Michaelis referred. Oepke has added the comment: "Die Kombination vollends mit 1 Kr 4, 16; 11, 1; Phl 3, 17; 2 Th 3, 7 . . . ist ganz abwegig." [303] It must be admitted that there are real difficulties as to just how this sentence is to be understood. Oepke, after finding difficulties in various alternatives, proposes: "Am besten unterlässt man jede Spezialisierung.... Das ergreifend schlichte: 'Brüder, ich bitte euch' lässt eher auf eine allgemeine Bitte um Verständigung schliessen.... Am natürlichsten ist es, weiter nichts zu ergänzen, als in der zweiten Satzhälfte γίνομαι. ὡς ἐγώ bzw ὑμεῖς vertritt dann ein Adj, und γίνεσθαι steht wie 1 Th 1, 5b; 2, 7 in der Bdtg 'auftreten, sich verhalten'. Pls bittet, dass die Leser sich nicht gegen ihn verschliessen, sondern ihm entgegenkommen, so, wie er ihnen." [304]

Oepke's calling attention to the importance of the appeal "I beseech you, brethren" is a point well made. This appeal indicates clearly that there is a change of tone in what Paul says. However, does an indication of a change of tone mean also an indication of entirely new content? Must the elliptical phrases "Become as I, for I also as you" be held in mind without content until one has heard Paul further and received the material with which to fill them out? This is of course a possible manner of expression. A speaker would proceed to do it only after a definite pause, and a writer would undoubtedly give some indication of it in his manuscript. The common practice of New Testament editions and versions of beginning a new paragraph at this point helps us in a measure to look ahead for the content, rather than supply the content from what we already have in mind. But did Paul mean it this way? The matter is not easily determined, and there is no possibility of speaking with definiteness one way or the other. Nevertheless, it is to be noted that

---

[299] See Eidem, *Stud. Tillägnade E. Stave*, pp. 77,78; Stanley, *Biblica*, XL, pp. 874–876.

[300] P. Bonnard, *L'épitre de saint Paul aux Galates*, C.d.N.T., Neuchatel/Paris: Delachaux & Niestlé, 1953, p. 91; Schlier, *Gal.*, p. 147; P. A. van Stempvoort, *Oud en Nieuw: De Brief aan de Galaters* (in *De Prediking van het Nieuwe Testament*), Nijkerk: C. F. Callenbach, 1951, p. 122; A. Schlatter, *Die Briefe an die Galater, Epheser, Kolosser und Philemon*, Stuttgart: Calwer Verlag, 1949, p. 109; H. Lietzmann, *An die Galater*, H.N.T., Tübingen: J. C. B. Mohr (Paul Siebeck), 1932, p. 27; Lagrange, *Gal.*, p. 111; G. S. Duncan, *The Epistle of Paul to the Galatians*, M.N.T.C., London: Hodder and Stoughton, 1934, p. 138; *et al.*

[301] Michaelis, T.W.N.T., IV, p. 675, fn. 29.

[302] *Loc. cit.*

[303] A. Oepke, *Der Brief des Paulus an die Galater*, T.H.N.T., 2. Aufl., Berlin: Evangelische Verlagsanstalt, 1957, p. 104.

[304] *Ibid.*, pp. 104,105. *Cf. N.E.B.*: "Put yourselves in my place, my brothers, I beg you, for I have myself in yours."

it is not the words "Brethren, I beseech you" which stand at the head of the sentence in Greek, but the elliptical command "Become as I, for I also as you." Had Paul proceeded immediately to pour content into these phrases, the matter would of course be clear. However, he does not. He proceeds to make further statements which to us later readers remain highly enigmatic.[305] So far as we can detect, these statements provide no definite content in regard to what the Galatians are to be or to become.[306] We have not yet examined how formidable the difficulties are which Oepke has found with interpreting "Become as I" in the light of the content which is already in mind from the previous context. However, unless these difficulties are really formidable, it would seem that Oepke's interpretation is not the most natural, as he claims; but that the most natural way is to fill the elliptical phrases with content which is already in mind from what Paul has been saying.

There would undoubtedly be little discussion of whether the appeal "Become as I" is a call to imitation or not, had Paul not added the still more elliptical phrase, "for I also as you." Although various proposals have been made as to what verbs are to be supplied in these phrases,[307] it seems most likely that the whole thought is to be read as follows: "Become as I am (εἰμί), for I also have become (ἐγενόμην) as you were (ἦτε; or 'are,' ἐστέ)."[308] The sense of the first clause can hardly be doubted, if the content which is already at hand is to be supplied. The whole argument to this point has shown Paul's exasperation because the Galatians have submitted themselves to the law and its requirements as a necessary part of their service of God. "Become as I am" can only mean, "Free yourselves of this bondage to the law; give up the idea that your standing before God is dependent on the fulfillment of certain obligations on your part; count as nothing, as refuse, as pure loss, all the righteousness that you suppose you can gain in that way; become free from the law as I am."

Paul then adds the second clause as a reason or incentive to do what he has just said. Do this, "for I also have become as you are." In the light of the foregoing understanding of his thoughts here, the content of this clause must be in effect: "For I abandoned my legal ground of righteousness and became without legal standing before God, like you Gentiles." It has often been the practice of commentators at this point to refer to Paul's words in I Cor. 9:21: "And to them that are without law, [I became] as without law, not being without law to God, but under law to Christ, that

---

305 Cf. e.g., the very next phrase: "Ye did me no wrong" (4:12b); and further such statements as: "Where then is your gratulation of yourselves?" (4:25); "So then am I become your enemy, by telling you the truth?" (4:16); "It is good to be zealously sought in a good matter at all times" (4:18).

306 Among the Reformers and some of the early Protestant interpreters (Luther, Calvin, Beza, Grotius, Calovius, Bengel, et al.) it was common to understand the passage as calling for a reciprocation of love: "Love me as I love you." While such a content for the elliptical phrases could be derived from vss. 13–20, it is difficult to see why Paul would have chosen the words γίνεσθε ὡς to express the thought.

307 For a review of the various proposals, see Sieffert, Gal., pp. 262,263.

308 So in effect Schlier, Gal., p. 147; E. D. Burton, A Critical and Exegetical Commentary on the Epistle to the Galatians, I.C.C., Edinburgh: T. & T. Clark, 1921, pp. 236,237; Sieffert, Gal., pp. 262,263; et al.

I might gain them that are without law." This gives good opportunity to show how the words appeal to the affection and gratitude of the Galatians. Lightfoot has put it strikingly: "I gave up all those time-honoured customs, all those dear associations of race, to become like you. I have lived as a Gentile that I might preach to you Gentiles. Will you then abandon me when I have abandoned all for you?"[309] Oepke is quite correct, however, when he points out that when the matter is so understood, Paul's giving up the law has no comparison with the way he is asking the Galatians to give up the law.[310] Paul's becoming as a Gentile in the sense of I Cor. 9:21 was a matter of accommodation on his part in order to have the contact necessary to communicate the gospel to them. Paul is not asking for any kind of accommodation in regard to the law on the part of the Galatians.[311]

When Paul says, "For I also have become as you are," he has in mind his far more radical becoming like the Gentiles than just the accommodation mentioned in I Cor. 9:21. When Paul came to the realization that "by the works of the law shall no flesh be justified" (2:16), he, the proud Jew, was in effect reduced to the status of the Gentiles. All on which he had relied had suddenly vanished. He was a sinner before God (2:17), without difference from the "sinners of the Gentiles" (cf. 2:15). These were the practical implications of seeking and obtaining justification in Christ, as Paul had so forcefully argued in connection with Peter's sudden misgivings about eating with Gentiles (2:11ff.). In this passage Paul had portrayed the sense in which he had become like the Galatians. In becoming a Christian he had had to become as empty of all personal and legal standing before God as the Gentiles were. For the Galatians now, as Christians, to find a necessity in legal observances was the height of the incongruous. "I beseech you, brethren, become as I am, for I am become as you are."

> Sieffert represented the matter slightly differently. He gives as the sense of the words: "Denn auch ich, als ich das Judenthum verliess, bin dadurch euch damaligen Heiden gleich, selbst also wie ein Heide 2, 14. Phil. 3, 7. geworden insofern, als auch ich ein für allemal innerlich frei und ungebunden gegenüber der Knechtschaft des jüdischen Gesetzes wurde wie ihr es waret."[312] Oepke quite correctly objects to this representation of the matter as not giving due account to the bondage in which heathendom lived; cf. 4:8.[313] Sieffert has seen Paul's becoming like the Gentiles too much in terms of a positive gain, namely, that of a release from the law. The becoming like the Gentiles is better described more negatively, as losing all standing and privilege before God. As Ridderbos says, "He [Paul] too had wished to be saved in no other way than the Gentiles, who could not appeal before God to a single work

---

[309] J. B. Lightfoot, *Saint Paul's Epistle to the Galatians*, London: Macmillan, 1884, p. 174.
[310] Oepke, *Gal.*, p. 104.
[311] Tinsley, *Imitation*, p. 140, has proposed: "The meaning of Gal. 4. 12 is probably that the apostle's willing surrender of so many things which as a Jew he personally held dear can safely be taken as a model for a similar self-denial on the part of his readers." In view of the context, however, it is hard to see what would bring Paul to urge self-denial on the Galatians. Tinsley offers no explanation.
[312] Sieffert, *Gal.*, p. 264.
[313] Oepke, *Gal.*, p. 104.

of the law." [314] Sieffert's emphasis was undoubtedly influenced by an interest in maintaining a parallelism between the two clauses. "Be free from the law as I am, for I became free from the law as ye were." But there appears to be no necessity of maintaining such a rigorous parallelism. The clauses do not stand in reciprocal relation, as though Paul had said, "Become as I am, *even as* I became as you were." Rather, the second clause gives a reason for fulfilling the first. This is nicely done when Paul's words are understood as meaning: "As Christians, be like me in rejecting all forms of bondage to legal requirements as necessary to your salvation in Christ, for it was precisely in this matter of legal advantage that I as a Jew had to learn to become as destitute as you Gentiles in order to become a Christian."

Is Paul then issuing a call to the Galatians to imitate him, when he says, "Become as I am"? Oepke scoffs at the idea and asks mockingly whether the second phrase then means that Paul took the heathen Galatians as his example. [315] His remark, however, is not really to the point. The two phrases, according to the foregoing interpretation, are not exact parallels: one is a present call for action; the other a statement of a past fact. Furthermore, they give expression to quite different situations. As Oepke's question implies, all thought of imitation in regard to Paul's becoming like the Gentiles is ridiculous. It is well to note carefully, however, what gives rise to the incongruity which makes this thought ridiculous. This lies not in the words themselves, but in the situation which they portray. Paul, in becoming a Christian, forsook the law as a way of salvation, with the result that he became like the Gentiles. Incongruity and ridiculousness arise from the thought that becoming like the Gentiles could in any way have appealed to Paul and motivated his action. Paul forsook the law not *in order to* become like the Gentiles, but *with the result that* he became like the Gentiles. However, when Paul calls the Galatians to become like him, the situation is quite different. They are already Christians and are being called from an erroneous way which they have recently taken. The thought of motivation now suggests itself. There is a call for action, not simply a statement of fact. Furthermore, the Galatians stand in a certain relationship to Paul. The context shows how prominent the thought of this relationship between himself and the Galatians is for Paul. He addresses them as "my little children" (4:19). He had brought the gospel to them and they had responded to his preaching of it (*cf.* 1:6). They are Christians which he had been privileged to beget. They had opened their hearts not only to the truth of the gospel; their personal reception of Paul himself had been most open and hearty (4:13—15). But now there are some who are trying to lead them to understand Christianity quite differently, and their efforts have been partially successful (1:6ff.; 4:17). Paul pictures the matter in most personal terms. The Galatians are moving away from *him;* his opponents are trying to get the Galatians to seek *them* (4:17). He issues the Galatians a thinly veiled reproach for their fickleness toward him

---

[314] Ridderbos, *Gal.*, p. 165.
[315] Oepke, *Gal.*, p. 104.

when he says: "But it is good to be zealously sought in a good matter at all times, and not only when I am present with you" (4:18). Lightfoot nicely lays bare Paul's thought here: "I do not complain that they desire your attentions, or you theirs. These things are good in themselves. I myself am not insensible to such attachments. I remember how warm were your feelings towards me, when I was with you. I would they had not grown cold in my absence." [316] Then comes the most touching utterance: "My little children, of whom I am again in travail until Christ be formed in you" (4:19). He is the father (or perhaps better, the mother) earnestly endeavoring to bring forth well-formed children. In such a context the thought of becoming like Paul has clear overtones of attraction, stimulation, and motivation. In regard to such a situation it is by no means far-fetched or ridiculous to propose the thought of imitation. To this end he makes his appeal to them: "Become as I am." The Galatians are being called by their father to be real children of his, and to show this by their likeness to him. Paul is pleading with them to imitate him. He hopes thus to lead them back to the truth of Christianity.

Stanley apparently understands these words of Paul not so much as a plea to return to the truth of Christianity as such, but as a plea to be Pauline in their Christianity. Stanley says: "Since it is Paul, not Peter, who has converted the pagans of Galatia to Christianity, their Christian life must be based upon his personal version of the Gospel, in which Mosaic observances have no part. The apostolic traditions as represented by Paul's kerygma and his own life provide the Galatian community with the necessary example for 'imitation'. No other type of Christianity is to be admitted." [317] This understanding of the plea to adopt Paul's ways can hardly be correct. The point at issue is not Paul's personal version of the Christian gospel, in which Mosaic observances have no part, as against Peter's personal version of the Christian gospel, in which Mosaic observances do have a part. The fact that Paul is entrusted with the gospel of the uncircumcision and Peter with the gospel of the circumcision (2:7) is not an indication of two versions of the gospel with varying contents or requirements; the reference to circumcision and uncircumcision is an indication of those to whom the gospel will be addressed. [318] If Peter's gospel differed from Paul's, it too would come under the anathema of 1:8 and 1:9. And when Peter did waver on the function of the law in relation to the gospel, Paul openly contested his position and pointed out how erroneous it was (2:11–21). The moment Peter as a Christian could not treat the observance of the Mosaic law as an indifferent matter, permitting of complete accommodation to the varying situations among the Jews and the Gentiles, Peter stood condemned (2:11). The Galatians' falling into legal observances, however, was no simple matter of accommodation. They were finding them necessary and mandatory. Paul's call to the Galatians to become like him is a call to return to the Christian gospel. It is not a case of Pauline Christianity over against a Petrine Christianity. It is a case of the Christianity Paul had taught over against a deviation which was no Christianity at all.

Bonnard also makes a comment on Gal. 4:12 which calls for comment. He observes: "Il [Paul] ne se tient pas pour un chrétien d'un genre

---

[316] Lightfoot, *Gal.*, p. 177.
[317] Stanley, *Biblica*, XL, pp. 875—876.
[318] Ridderbos, *Gal.*, p. 88; Schlier, *Gal.*, p. 44; Lagrange, *Gal.*, p. 36.

exceptionnel; ce que les Galates doivent imiter en lui, c'est la simple foi au Christ; l'apôtre pourrait tout aussi bien dire: 'Imitez tous ceux qui, comme moi et avec moi, ont renoncé à la loi pour croire Jésus-Christ.'"[319] It is undoubtedly true that Paul did not conceive of himself as an exceptional type of Christian. But, when Bonnard proposes that Paul could equally well have called for the imitation of others who had renounced the law in favor of faith in Christ, he shows that he has failed to grasp the real significance of the appeal to become like Paul. Paul does not here view himself simply as an illustration of Christianity, the same as any other Christian. The thought of imitation in Paul's writings appears repeatedly in the father-child context. The call is not simply to imitate Paul as an example of a good Christian, but to imitate Paul as their father in Christ. The real force of Paul's appeal to imitation would be lost in substituting the call to imitate all those who have renounced the law in favor of faith in Christ. An appeal to the imitation of others would have carried much less stimulating and motivating power than the appeal to imitate their spiritual father.

Along the same lines we may notice that Paul's statement recorded in Acts 26:29, while being verbally very similar to Gal. 4:12, can hardly be understood as a call to imitation in the same sense as Gal. 4:12. In this passage in Acts Paul had been making his defence before King Agrippa, and at the end Agrippa acknowledged: "With but little persuasion thou wouldest fain make me a Christian" (Acts 26:28). Paul's answer is: "I would to God that whether with little or with much, not thou only, but also all that hear me this day, might become such as I am (γενέσθαι τοιούτους ὁποῖος καὶ ἐγώ εἰμι), except these bonds" (Acts 26:29). Paul's wish is obviously that the possibility which Agrippa has just suggested might become a fact, *i.e.*, that he might become a Christian. Paul's speaking of it in terms of becoming like himself has the effect of recommending Christianity to Agrippa. It calls attention to Paul's satisfaction, happiness, and joy as a Christian. It suggests that he counts it a real privilege, and that others might well have grounds for envying him, if they only understood what Christianity meant. However, the situation is not yet ripe for imitation in the usual Pauline sense. There is not yet an underlying union existing between Paul and Agrippa. Paul stands as an illustration and recommendation of Christianity to Agrippa. But he is not yet a spiritual father to Agrippa, nor a teacher to whom Agrippa is committed and devoted. The two lives have not yet begun to flow together. One can not say that all thought of imitation in every sense of the word is foreign to this passage. However, we may conclude that this passage is not to be grouped with the other passages where Paul speaks of the imitation of himself. On this score, thus, it differs from Gal. 4:12.

\* \* \*

Paul's appeal to the Galatians, "Become as I am" (Gal. 4:12), is not an express call to imitation, but in substance it amounts to just that. The point of imitation here is not so much Paul's conduct as a Christian, but his basic Christian commitment, his doctrine, his faith. The fact that he must appeal for imitation on this score is a silent testimony of the seriousness of the situation in Galatia. The Galatians had turned to an insistence on certain legal requirements and observances as necessary to Christianity. Paul points

---

[319] Bonnard, *Gal.*, p. 92.

out that, far from being necessary to Christianity, such a position is basically contradictory to Christianity. He pleads with them to free themselves from this bondage to legalism and to become like him. It is an appeal for them to imitate him, issued entirely in the context of their being his children in Christ. Being his spiritual children, they must hold to his faith, and bring it to expression, also in their attitudes toward the law.

### VII. The Pastoral Epistles [320]
### (I Timothy 1:16; II Timothy 1:13; 3:10)

A. *I Timothy 1:16 — Howbeit for this cause I obtained mercy, that in me as chief might Jesus Christ show forth all his longsuffering, for an ensample of them that should thereafter believe on him unto eternal life.*

Timothy had been requested to stay in Ephesus while Paul went on to Macedonia (I Tim. 1:3). The Christians in Ephesus were in great need of pastoral care and leadership, for there was an invasion of false teaching infiltrating the church and corrupting its faith and its morals. Ephesus needed a pastor; so Timothy stayed behind. However, Timothy also needed a pastor. At least that is the spirit in which Paul wrote to him. Paul speaks to Timothy as a pastor and father. The letter is written with an eye to bolstering Timothy's spirit and giving him some guidance and direction in certain difficult matters. The letter begins with recalling the situation and something of the false teachings which were circulating in Ephesus. It is these which occasioned Timothy's staying there. Timothy was to serve as a witness to the gospel of Christ as Paul had been preaching it.

When Paul comes to mention "the gospel of the glory of the blessed God, which was committed to my trust" (I Tim. 1:11), he is led into a personal digression. He finds in what has happened to him an amazing illustration of the nature and power of the Christian gospel. He is living evidence of its meaning and effectiveness. What it had done for him it could do for others. He mentions this for Timothy's encouragement. Timothy must constantly face those openly opposed to the gospel or subtly enucleating it of its essence and power. He must keep in mind, then, that Paul the blasphemer, Paul the persecutor, Paul the chief of sinners was saved by an abundant manifestation of the grace of the Lord. Paul goes on to add this explanation: "howbeit for this cause I obtained mercy, that in me as chief might Jesus Christ show forth his longsuffering, for an ensample of them that should thereafter believe on him unto eternal life" (1:16). The thought of Paul as an example has here once again come to expression.

That the example of Paul as here expressed is not to be understood in exactly the same way as in the Thessalonian letters and in Philippians is

---

[320] It is not our purpose to enter into the extensive discussion in which scholars have engaged as to the genuineness of these letters as Pauline letters. Our examination of the three texts concerned is on the assumption that these letters are Pauline.

suggested already in the use of another Greek word. Here the word is ὑποτύπωσις instead of τύπος. In fact, the question may be raised to what extent the idea of example really comes to expression in this passage. As Radford has pointed out: "The compound ὑποτύπωσις ... acquires from the prefix the special idea of a form outlined as the basis for further work." [321] There is abundant evidence from classical Greek writings for understanding the word as "outline," "rough draft or form," "incomplete sketch, in contrast to the complete picture." [322] Hence, Radford suggests that "perhaps ... it is not mere fancy to regard the μακροθυμία [longsuffering] shown in S. Paul's case as an outline of God's dealings with men, 'to be afterwards filled up and coloured over with the rich hues of the Divine mercy shed forth over all the world' (Bp. Wordsworth, ad. loc.)." [323] On the other hand, ὑποτύπωσις can indicate a model or pattern. [324] Furthermore, we find this passage being understood in the sense of "an example for the encouragement of others" already in the Greek speaking church fathers. [325] Scott has found a phrase which succeeds well in combining the two ideas; he speaks of Paul as "a typical illustration." [326] Paul was a kind of sample of the Master's work. He served to illustrate and recommend it.

Paul was an illustration and proof of the supreme talent, ability, and power of Christ. [327] In the very early days of the spread of the church Christ effected this radical conversion from a most extreme antithesis to the gospel to a most wholehearted devotion to it. Thus, Christ made it eminently clear to what extent his saving power could work. Here Christ's work became typified. Paul became a sample of the Master's work. It was a sample not in the sense of one instance picked at random from many, but as a radical instance clearly illustrating the potentialities and limits of what Christ could do. Furthermore, it was a first instance. The idea of Paul's being "chief" among the saved as well as of sinners has a kind of dual meaning. As Hendriksen has put it: "The apostle considers himself not only the chief of sinners but *also*—and in a certain sense *for that very reason*—the most glorious illustration of Christ's longsuffering.... Paul is 'foremost' as an example of what Christ's longsuffering can accomplish. He is at the same time 'foremost' as the head of a procession of persons to whom that longsuffering is shown." [328]

---

[321] Radford, *Expositor*, 5th Ser., VI. p. 384.
[322] *Cf.* Liddell-Scott, *Lexicon*, *s.v.*
[323] Radford, *Expositor*, 5th Ser., VI, p. 385.
[324] *Cf.* Philodemus, *De Musica*, (ed. J. Kemke, Leipzig: Teubner, 1884, p. 77): εἰς ὑποτύπωσιν ἀρετῶν.
[325] *Cf.* Theodoret, *Interpretatio Epistolae ad Timotheum primae*, sub 1:16 (ed. J.-P. Migne, P.G., LXXXII, p. 793): ἵνα μηδεὶς τῶν μεγάλα παρανενομηκότων εἰς ἐμὲ ἀποβλέπων ἀπαγορεύσῃ τὴν σωτηρίαν. Theophylact, *Expositio in Epistolam I ad Timotheum*, sub 1:16 (ed. J.-P. Migne, P.G., CXXV, p. 24): πρὸς ὑποτύπωσιν, φησί· τουτέστι, πρὸς ὑπόδειγμα, πρὸς παράκλησιν, πρὸς προτροπήν. See also Chrysostom, *Fourth Homily on I Timothy*, *sub* 1:16.
[326] E. F. Scott, *The Pastoral Epistles*, M.N.T.C., London: Hodder & Stoughton, 1936, p. 14.
[327] "ὑποτύπωσις ist ein Tätigkeitsnomen; es nennt den Akt dessen, der formt und gestaltet" (A. Schlatter, *Die Kirche der Griechen im Urteil des Paulus*, Stuttgart: Calwer, 1936, p. 62).
[328] W. Hendriksen, *Commentary on I and II Timothy and Titus*, London: Banner of Truth Trust, 1959, p. 82.

When Paul was saved, a pattern was set; his salvation was the model and standard according to which Christ's future work would proceed.

Commentators have often pointed out that ὑποτύπωσιν is followed by the genitive rather than the dative, so that the thought is "an example of those who are to believe," rather than "an example to (or for) those who are to believe." [329] The point is then urged that the instance of Paul makes clear what kind of people will finally attain to eternal life through Christ—people who are sinners, [330] and then not only certain less extreme types of sinners, but even the very worst. [331] The point is of course true, but it does not come to expression only through some specific rendering of the genitive following ὑποτύπωσιν. To translate ὑποτύπωσιν τῶν μελλόντων πιστεύειν as "example of those who are to believe" does succeed in throwing the thought into bolder relief. But the thought that Paul illustrates that salvation in Christ is for sinners, even the worst of them, is the point of the whole passage and does not depend simply on the genitive. Furthermore, the genitive following τύποι in I Peter 5:3 is clearly to be understood as an example *to* (or *for*) the flock. We have also noticed how the same accent is strong in the use of the genitive with τύπος in I Tim. 4:12. [332] This is perhaps one of those "genitives of 'looser relation,'" of which Robertson speaks. [333] At least the grammatical construction of the passage does not preclude its being understood as "an example *to* (or *for*) those who are to believe."

Whether the passage *is* to be understood in this way or not remains difficult to determine. There are no real clues in the text as such. The only indication of any significance is that the Greek commentators were urging the comfort and encouragement of Paul's example on their readers in commenting on this text. However, to conclude that this resulted from their reading the phrase as "example for those who are to believe" is not warranted, since their homiletical purposes could also have led them to make this application of the text. And even if they had read it this way, they are still separated by more than three hundred years from the original expression of the thought. The matter finally does not make a great deal of difference in understanding the text and its context, since in either case it is clear that Paul is an illustration of Christ's saving work on sinners, and the fact has obvious implications for the encouragement of sinners in all ages.

Paul saw himself as an illustration, pattern, or model of what Christ's saving work would do for others coming after him. To speak of Paul's example in this connection is within the limits of current usage, but then it must not be thought of in the sense of an example which others are to strive to follow or imitate. He is an example of Christ's work for the encouragement and reassurance of others and not for their imitation. It is noteworthy that when the example of Paul is held up for the specific purpose of imitating, it is not the example of his having obtained mercy, "that in me as chief might Jesus

---

[329] *Cf.* B. Weiss, *Die Briefe Pauli an Timotheus und Titus*, K.e.K.N.T., 7. Aufl., Göttingen: Vandenhoeck & Ruprecht, 1902, pp. 98,99; G. Wohlenberg, *Die Pastoralbriefe*, K.z.N.T., Leipzig: A. Deichert, 1906, p. 98; Bouma, *I Tim.*, pp. 93,94.
[330] Bouma's emphasis; *cf. I Tim.*, pp. 93,94.
[331] Weiss's emphasis; *cf. I Tim.*, pp. 98,99.
[332] See above, p. 87.
[333] Robertson, *Gram.*, p. 500.

Christ show forth all his longsuffering, for an ensample of them that should thereafter believe on him unto eternal life" (I Tim. 1:16). Such an example (ὑποτύπωσις) calls for other reactions than imitation.

B. *II Timothy 1:13 — Hold the pattern of sound words which thou hast heard from me, in faith and love which is in Christ Jesus.*

The word ὑποτύπωσις appears again in the second letter to Timothy.[334] Here we read of "the pattern (ὑποτύπωσιν) of sound words" which Timothy has heard from Paul. Paul begins the letter with the customary giving of thanks, this time particularly for Timothy and his faith. He proceeds to exhort him to stir up the gift of God which is in him (II Tim. 1:6), and not to be ashamed of the testimony of the Lord (1:8) Let him also have no feelings of shame over Paul's imprisonment; but rather let him align himself with Paul in suffering hardship for the gospel (1:8). Paul points out that it is his faithful service of the gospel which had brought him to all the sufferings which he is now experiencing. In regard to it all he has no feelings of shame (1:12). On the contrary, he can make a beautiful confession: "For I know him whom I have believed, and I am persuaded that he is able to guard that which I have comitted unto him against that day (1:12). Then, speaking directly to Timothy again he says: "Hold the pattern of sound words which thou hast heard from me, in faith and love which is in Christ Jesus" (1:13).

The thought of Paul's example is to be found in the context here. Paul exhorts, "Be not ashamed," and, "Suffer hardship"; and then points out, "I suffer also," and, "I am not ashamed." That he is urging his example on Timothy is plain. Does the thought of following his example come to expression in the statement about holding the pattern of sound words which he had heard from Paul? This depends largely on what Paul had in mind in speaking of a ὑποτύπωσις.

> Radford sees in the word a suggestive allusion "to a definite form of belief ..., framed in its simplest shape for the instruction of catechumens and expanded afterwards by the councils of the Church for the protection of the faith against heretical interpretation."[335] Probably many could agree with him provided there is sufficient flexibility in what is to be understood by "definite form." As Easton has observed, we must not think of a formulated creed here, like the English rendering "the pattern of sound words" might suggest. He points out that "there is no definite article in the Greek, and 'words' [λόγων] does not mean 'terms' but 'contents of terms,' 'concepts expressed.'"[336]

The idea of a ὑποτύπωσις is basically that of a sketch, a rough draft, or outline. Undoubtedly this idea plays some role in the meaning of the word

---
[334] The word appears in the New Testament only in I Tim. 1:16 and II Tim. 1:13. It is not found in the LXX.
[335] Radford, *Expositor*, 5th Ser., VI, p. 385.
[336] B. S. Easton, *The Pastoral Epistles*, New York: Charles Scribner's Sons, 1947, p. 45.

here. However, the emphatic position of the word as the first word of the sentence suggests a more important idea than that Paul's words are to be considered for their value as a sketch, outline, or summary. They are the outline which sets the basic pattern and standard for what Christian teaching and preaching is. They are not a model to be reproduced as exactly as possible. Rather they serve as a framework within which to operate and a form which is determinitive of the overall shape. [337] Paul exhorts Timothy to regard what he has heard from him as a standard and guide for sound teaching. This was most important for Timothy's ministry in the midst of so much error.

Paul's exhortation to Timothy to "hold the pattern of sound words" heard from him is not a call to imitate him or follow his example. It is a call to give due regard to the standard of Christian teaching which Paul has set, to regulate his own teaching by it, and to see to it that it is properly passed on to others (cf. 2:2). In this text, even as in the former one, Paul's position of establishing a pattern carries another consequence than that he is to be imitated.


C. *II Timothy 3:10 — But thou didst follow my teaching, conduct, purpose, faith, longsuffering, love, patience, persecutions, sufferings.*

There is another expression in II Timothy which suggests the thought of the imitation of Paul. Paul says concerning Timothy: "But thou didst follow (παρηκολούθησας) my ... conduct." Paul had been speaking about what difficult days lay ahead. Apostasy would be not only general, but radical. Disrespect and lawlessness would rise to fearful heights; self-centeredness and passion would rule the day; morality would all but go into eclipse. The leaders and teachers at the head of this procession would present a dismaying array of falsehood and confusion. Their conduct would be utterly disreputable. These days would be difficult for Timothy, for the persecution and opposition with which he was already well acquainted would grow steadily worse, and the divergent and false teachings would become steadily more vociferous. Paul is confident that Timothy will be able to remain steadfast in the midst of the pressures and confusion of these days. When Paul writes, "But you (Σὺ δὲ)," he sets Timothy in full contrast to the false and corrupt teachers. In radical distinction from them Timothy has become a thoroughgoing follower of Paul. [338]

Timothy's following of Paul pertains to his conduct as well as his teaching.

---

[337] C. Spicq has stated it well when he says: "Paul exhorte Timothée à faire à son tour oeuvre de héraut et de didascale, avec toute la hardiesse et l'initiative que comportent ces fonctions sacrées, mais il précise l'objet de cet enseignement dont la première qualité est l'orthodoxie; il s'agit d'exposer la saine doctrine, celle-là même que Timothée a reçue de son maître" (St Paul: Les Epîtres Pastorales, E.B., Paris: J. Gabalda, 1947, p. 319).
[338] The thoroughgoingness of Timothy's following is emphasized not only by the long enumeration Paul makes of ways in which Timothy was a follower, but also by the strong verb he uses. Cf. Kittel, T.W.N.T., I, p. 216, 13—15: "[In παρακολουθέω] liegt ein starker Ton, auf der durch das Präfix angedeuteten Genauigkeit und Beständigkeit der Übereinstimmung."

It is hardly possible to determine more specifically what Paul had in mind by his conduct. The word ἀγωγή appears only here in the New Testament. However, there is abundant evidence in other Greek writings for its usage as a general term expressing manner of life—all the particular habits, customs, mores, and ways of doing things that go into making up a way of life.[339] It is synonymous with Paul's expression "my ways which are in Christ" (I Cor. 4:17),[340] which also had to do with Paul's image as it could be found in Timothy. Spicq proposes that in view of the conduct being associated directly with the teaching (διδασκαλία), the reference to conduct here may have in mind particularly Paul's missionary methods, the practical matters in his ministerial work, his way of preaching, organizing his communities, and such matters.[341] In view of Timothy's position as Paul's fellow-worker and in view of his long association with Paul in his missionary work, these aspects of Paul's life must surely be included among the things in which Timothy became a follower of Paul. However, there appears to be no reason for thinking more particularly of these aspects of Paul's conduct than of the whole range of his Christian life. It seems preferable to leave a general term general.

Perhaps it is superfluous to ask whether imitation has played a part in Timothy's thoroughgoing following of Paul. One might conceivably argue that the conduct is the Christian way of life as Paul has given formal instruction in it, but such would be an artificial understanding of the matter. In one who was first a convert of Paul's and then a long-time associate of his, there was of course imitation (cf. I Cor. 4:17). Imitation had its part to play not only in Timothy's becoming a follower of Paul's conduct; it played its role also in Timothy's becoming a follower of Paul in other matters mentioned here: his faith, longsuffering, love, and patience. Timothy learned these things as much by observing them in action as by being formally instructed in them or hearing them proclaimed. Paul served as Timothy's example both in the Christian life in general and in the Christian ministry. Timothy followed him; he learned from him and imitated him; in time he was sufficiently like Paul to be included with him in his example to others (cf. I Thess. 1:6; Phil. 3:17). We learn from this text that the pattern of Christianity as Paul manifested it had been successfully formed in Timothy through Timothy's thoroughgoing following of Paul. "Following" here is a concept which includes the phenomenon of imitation.

## VIII. Acts 20:35

*In all things I gave you an example, that so laboring ye ought to help the weak, and to remember the words of the Lord Jesus, that he himself said, It is more blessed to give than to receive.*

---

339 See Bauer, *Wörterbuch, s.v.*; K. L. Schmidt, ἀγωγή, *T.W.N.T.*, I, pp. 128,129.
340 Schmidt, *T.W.N.T.*, I, p. 129, 35ff.
341 Spicq, *Épitres Pastorales*, p. 373.

A reference to Paul's example is to be found also in his farewell address to the Ephesian elders at Miletus, as recorded in Acts 20:18—35. Paul begins by speaking of his irreproachable conduct among them from the first moment of his acquaintance with them (20:18—21). He tells them that under the Holy Spirit's leading he is returning to Jerusalem, where he is sure that there will be grievous opposition awaiting him, and that he is convinced that he will not be returning to them again (20:22—25). He exhorts them to a diligent fulfillment of their responsibilities as bishops, the more so in view of the days of error and perversion which are approaching (20:28—31). The address concludes with Paul's commending them to God, and with his pointing them to the example of hard work, personal sacrifice, and giving of himself in the service of others which he had consistently portrayed to them (20:32—35). Both the words of the address and the further description of the parting scene (20:36—38) show the deep friendship and love that exists between Paul and these Ephesian leaders.

In form this farewell address has many similarities to farewell addresses found elsewhere in the Bible and in the literature of the day. [342] Munck has noted particularly these matters in the address of Acts 20:17—35 as being characteristic: "Nous avons donc ici une figure du N. T. qui: 1° avant de s'embarquer pour le martyre, rassemble les Anciens d'Ephèse pour leur adresser comme dernières paroles un enseignement définitif; 2° il exhorte ceux qu'il va quitter et, 3° il se donne lui-même comme modèle, ils doivent imiter sa vie sans tache et son infatigable sollicitude pour la communauté, qu'il leur rappelle. Enfin 4° il prédit les persécutions que souffrira la communauté et la venue après sa mort, de faux docteurs." [343] In regard to the characteristic of holding oneself up as an example, Munck does not indicate any specific instances in the Old Testament farewell addresses, and states that even in the later Jewish literature this characteristic is less common than some of the others. [344] As we have noted earlier, there was much attention centered on being an example in the death scenes of Eleazar and the seven young martyrs in *II* and *IV Maccabees*. [345] In the New Testament Munck finds the two letters to Timothy to be in the nature of farewell addresses and points to Paul's example in I Tim. 1:16, and to the exhortations in II Tim. which picture Timothy as being addressed by his teacher and his model. [346] The element of example also is found in the farewell scene of Jesus with his disciples (*cf.* John 13:15). Apparently reference to oneself as an example was a rather standard element of farewell speeches and scenes in late Judaism. As Williams has suggested, "It is ... probable that Paul

---

342 *Cf.* E. Stauffer, "Abschiedsreden und Abschiedsszenen" (Beilage VI), *Die Theologie des Neuen Testaments*, 4. Aufl., Stuttgart: W. Kohlhammer, 1948, pp. 327—330; and J. Munck, "Discours d'adieu dans le Nouveau Testament et dans la littérature biblique," in *Aux sources de la tradition chrétienne: Mélanges offerts à M. Goguel*, Neuchatel/Paris: Delachaux & Niestlé, 1950, pp. 155—170.

343 Munck, *Mélanges Goguel*, p. 161.

344 *Ibid.*, p. 159: "Moins courant est le cas où celui qui va mourir raconte sa vie, de laquelle il tire des exhortations morales auxquelles sa personne sert de modèle ou d'exemple pour mettre en garde (cf. Test. douze Patr.; Vie d'Adam [30—44]; Apoc. Moïse [15—30])."

345 See above, pp. 45f.

346 Munck, *Mélanges Goguel*, pp. 162,163.

or Luke followed the main trend of a Farewell Discourse consciously or otherwise." [347]

In this same connection it is interesting to notice the word used in Acts 20:35 to express being an example: ὑπέδειξα. In the farewell scene in John's gospel, Christ's example was expressed with the noun ὑπόδειγμα. The same term was used in Eleazar's final words in *II Macc.* 6:28 and 31. [348] In other than farewell scenes, ὑπόδειγμα in the sense of an example is found in Heb. 4:11, James 5:10, II Pet. 2:6, and very often in *I Clement.* [349] Neither ὑπόδειγμα nor ὑποδείκνυμι are used in Paul's letters. The New Testament instances of the verb are found, with one exception (Matt. 3:7), in Luke-Acts: Luke 3:7 (parallel to Matt. 3:7); 6:47; 12:5; Acts 9:16; 20:35. In both Luke 6:47 and 12:5 the verb appears in a clause which is not found in the parallel passages in Matthew; the additional clauses apparently are to be accounted for as Luke's editorial work. [350] Perhaps, then, ὑποδείκνυμι is a typically Lukan word and its appearance in Acts 20:35 is to be traced rather to Luke's later recording of the essence of the speech, than to Paul's literal words at the time. [351] In any case, the language of the speech as a whole shows a close approximation to the language of Paul's letters. [352] Furthermore, a calling attention to his example is in full harmony with regular Pauline practice.

In bidding farewell to the elders at Ephesus Paul testifies to a free conscience. He was "pure from the blood of all men" (Acts 20:26). He had faithfully and diligently preached the gospel and the whole counsel of God. He had also been careful that his life would give no countertestimony. He had not been motivated by greed or covetousness (20:33) and had taken special precaution that no one should suspect him of this. He had engaged in manual labor to supply his own needs and those of the men associated with him in his work of bringing the gospel (20:34). It is this latter thought which calls forth the specific reference to his example: "In all things I gave you an example, that so laboring ye ought to help the weak" (20:35).

It is possible to read "in all things" (πάντα) with vs. 34, so that Paul

---

[347] C. S. C. Williams, *A Commentary on the Acts of the Apostles,* B.N.T.C., London: Adam and Charles Black, 1957, p. 232. C. F. Evans has argued against the proposal that Luke worked upon an actual reminiscence of a speech of Paul by pointing out the difficulty of accounting for the appropriateness of much of the material to such an occasion as this; *cf.* "The Kerygma," J.T.S., VII (1956), pp. 34–35. Since, however, the form and content of the speech may have been influenced by the current form of farewell discourses, Evan's argument is robbed of much of its force.

[348] In the account of the same event in *IV Macc.* 6:19 the words τύπος and παράδειγμα are used.

[349] *Cf. I Clem.* 5:1; 6:1; 46:1; 55:1; 63:1. *Cf.* further *Sirach* 44:16; *IV Macc.* 17:23; *Papias* 3:3.

[350] E. Klostermann, *Das Lukasevangelium,* H.N.T., 2. Aufl., Tübingen: J. C. B. Mohr (Paul Siebeck), 1929, pp. 85, and 133.

[351] H. J. Cadbury remarks in his note on "The Speeches in Acts": "It may also be noted that this speech [Acts 20:18–35] has the best claim to be included in the memoirs of the eyewitness, since 'we' passages very nearly envelop it" (B. Chr., Vol. V, p. 412, fn. 2).

[352] *Ibid.,* pp. 412f. For the parallels to I Thessalonians (sometimes a bit far-fetched), *cf.* H. Schulze, "Die Unterlagen für die Abschiedsrede zu Milet in Apostelgeschichte 20, 18–38," T.S.K., LXXIII (1900), pp. 119–125. For resemblances to the Pastoral Epistles, *cf.* Lock, *Pastoral Epistles,* p. xxv.

says that he supplied *every need* of himself and his companions. [353] Zahn objects to such a reading because it makes Paul sound too boastful. [354] Grosheide finds it too crass and not wholly correct, for the apostle did not refuse all aid and all friendly help in his efforts to provide for himself. [355] The variant reading πᾶσι found in the manuscripts D and *m* hints that there may have been difficulty in knowing exactly what Paul meant here already in early times. Lake and Cadbury suggest: "In either connexion πάντα could perhaps be even more appropriately rendered 'always.' Such a usage is apparently supported by I Cor. ix. 25, x. 32, xi. 2, xiii. 7 and other Hellenistic examples as well as by modern Greek." [356] It seems best to understand πάντα as indicating how consistently and thoroughly Paul had given his example.

Paul found that his laboring to supply his needs was of value for the example that it gave. This whole matter of Paul's working to support himself was a matter about which he was very sensitive. He returns to the theme several times in his letters. On the one hand, he viewed it as a completely free choice on his part, going over and beyond what was either required or appropriate, and done in order that his bringing the gospel might in no way be linked with financial considerations (I Cor. 9:15–18). On the other hand, he found that his hard manual labor set a good example of self-sacrifice and self-giving to the new Christian communities (II Thess. 3:7–9). [357] In II Thess. 3:7–9 he was pointing to his example particularly in a situation where there was idleness and where men's time and energies were being dissipated in other pursuits. Here in Acts he is thinking particularly of his example of being able to give aid to those in need.

Paul speaks of the necessity of giving help to the weak (τῶν ἀσθενούντων). The commentators at the time of the Reformation and many of the earlier Protestant commentators understood this as meaning to care for those who were weak spiritually, either in faith or practice. [358] The thought would seem to be a natural one for the occasion. However, it neither fits with the idea of manual labor of which Paul has just spoken nor with the saying of Jesus about the blessedness of giving which Paul cites by way of further stimulation to activity. The usage of the word elsewhere in Acts would seem to point toward the word's referring to the sick and physically handicapped (*cf.* 4:9; 5:15,16; 9:37; 19:12). However, there is sufficient evidence from classical sources and from the papyri that ἀσθενέω and its cognate forms were used for the economically and socially weak, *i.e.* the poor. [359] The term here is to

---

353 Such a reading has been proposed by Lachmann, Overbeck, Nösgen, Bethge, B. Weiss, and Blass, according to H. H. Wendt, *Die Apostelgeschichte*, K.e.K.N.T., 9. Aufl. Göttingen: Vandenhoeck & Ruprecht, 1913, p. 294. Lake and Cadbury, *B. Chr.*, Vol. IV, p. 263, also choose this understanding of the words, although they admit the acceptability of the other as well.

354 T. Zahn, *Die Apostelgeschichte des Lucas*, K.z.N.T., 1./2. Aufl., Leipzig: A. Deichert, 1921, Vol. II, p. 725.

355 Grosheide, *Handelingen*, Vol. II, p. 250.

356 Lake and Cadbury, *B. Chr.*, Vol. IV, p. 263. The suggestion has been followed by F. F. Bruce, *The Acts of the Apostles*, London: Tyndale Press, 1951, p. 383.

357 See the discussion of this matter above, pp. 135ff.

358 Wendt, *Apostelgeschichte*, 6./7. Aufl. (1888), p. 449 lists among those understanding the word this way: Erasmus, Calvin, Beza, Grotius, Calovius, E. Schmid, Bengel, Neander, Tholuck, Schneckenburger, Baumgarten, and Meyer.

359 Bauer, *Wörterbuch*, s.v.

be understood as referring to the needy in the broad sense, without observing any distinctions as to whether that need arose from physical conditions or from social and economic conditions.

Paul's example was, "that so laboring ye ought to help the weak and to remember the words of the Lord Jesus, that he himself said, It is more blessed to give than to receive." The needy can be helped and the words of Jesus can be applied and experienced when one labors as Paul labored. The point of comparison is not to be found in the nature of the work as such, as though Paul were here recommending manual labor to all the elders. Rather Paul is pointing to the intensity, zeal, energy, and idealism with which he labored. It was a self-giving labor, for it enabled him to give to the benefit of others needing help. It was the very opposite of selfishly accumulating things for himself or living in ease while others furnished him his needs. Paul's life as a Christian was one of radical self-giving for others and for Christ. His hard manual labor was one of the most obvious evidences of this. It stood as an example to those who like Paul were in the service of Christ and his church.

The scene at Miletus in which Paul calls attention to his example once again portrays a father and his children. This becomes particularly clear when this scene is compared to the farewell scenes and addresses found often in the late Jewish literature. In such passages one after another famous personage is pictured as sending for his family, calling his sons together, and speaking his final words to them. [360] The elders from Ephesus are Paul's sons in the Lord, and as he makes his farewell to them, he points them to the Christianity he had portrayed to them. Here once again is an implicit call by Paul, the father, to his sons in Christ to be imitators of him.

---

[360] Cf. e.g., *Testament of Levi* 1:2: "He [Levi] was sound in health when he called them [his children] to him; for it had been revealed to him that he should die. And when they were gathered together he said to them...." (ed. Charles, Vol. II, p. 304); *Testament of Dan* 1:2: "For he [Dan] called together his family, and said...." (*ibid.*, p. 332); *Testament of Joseph* 1:1: "When he [Joseph] was about to die he called his sons and his brethren together, and said to them...." (*ibid.*, p. 346); *The Books of Adam and Eve* 49:1: "And Eve perceived that she would die, (so) she assembled all her sons and daughters, Seth with thirty brothers and thirty sisters, and Eve said to them...." (*ibid.*, p. 152).

CHAPTER FIVE

# THE IMITATION OF PAUL: CRITIQUE AND CONCLUSIONS

What did Paul have in mind in speaking to Christians in various places about their imitation of him? On the basis of the foregoing study we are able to make some observations on this matter and to draw our conclusions. We are also in position to evaluate the conclusions to which others have come in their studies of this subject. We shall turn first to these conclusions of others. Our attention is directed mainly to the studies of Eidem, [1] Stanley, [2] and Michaelis. [3]

## I. Critique

Both Eidem and Stanley point to a fact which is fundamental to detecting the meaning of Paul's call to the imitation of himself: this call appears in words directed to churches which Paul himself has founded and where he is personally known. [4] He speaks explicitly of the imitation of himself to the Thessalonians, the Corinthians, and the Philippians; the idea of imitation is also found implicitly in his words to the Galatians, Timothy, and the Ephesian elders. In letters to congregations which Paul had not founded and where he was not personally known, such as Romans, [5] Ephesians, [6] and Colossians, [7] the thought of imitation and example may appear, but it is then the imitation and example of Christ or God, and not that of Paul. [8] Hence, there can be no thought of Paul's example being a phenomenon of general importance throughout all of Christendom, so that it could be recommended to one and all alike. Paul urged his example upon those knew him personally.

What was the example of Paul which he found to be so important for those to whom he was writing? Eidem is quite correct in observing that it has nothing to do with any ecstatic experiences which Paul enjoyed, or with what might be termed his personal idiosyncrasies. [9] Paul can highly recom-

---

[1] Eidem, *Stud. Tillagnäde E. Stave*, pp. 67—85.
[2] Stanley, *Biblica*, XL, pp. 859—877.
[3] Michaelis, *T.W.N.T.*, IV, pp. 661—678.
[4] Eidem, *Stud. Tillagnäde E. Stave*, p. 83; Stanley, *Biblica*, XL, p. 877.
[5] *Cf.* Rom. 1:10; 15:23.
[6] *Cf.* Eph. 1:15; 3:2; 4:21.
[7] *Cf.* Col. 1:3,7; 2:1.
[8] *Cf.* Rom. 15:1—7; Eph. 4:32—5:2; Col. 3:13.
[9] Eidem, *Stud. Tillagnäde E. Stave*, p. 83.

mend the value of the gift of continency and can wish for others to seek it and enjoy it (*cf.* I Cor. 7:7–9), and yet there is no thought of urging his unmarried state as an example which Christians ought universally to adopt. He had made it his personal policy not to receive compensation for his work of evangelizing, but to provide for his own support (I Cor. 9:6–21). However, there is no suggestion that he thought other missionaries and evangelists ought to do the same. He found in his hard manual labor an example of industriousness, self-sacrifice, and benevolence (*cf.* II Thess. 3:7–9; Acts 20:35); but there is no implication that others were bound to adopt a practice of manual labor. In spite of all the emphasis which Paul lays on giving oneself for the sake of the gospel and one's fellow men, there is no hint that he believes his readers ought to leave home, go to some far city, and preach the gospel. Paul has a personal life and a personal calling which need not be repeated in all the Christians he knows. When he calls for the imitation of himself, he is not seeking a copy which will reproduce him to the finest detail.

The various points of imitation which Paul has in mind in the different passages are as follows: joyful endurance of suffering for the sake of the gospel (I Thess. 1:6); industriousness and self-sacrifice (II Thess. 3:7–9); humility and self-giving (I Cor. 4:16); giving oneself for the gospel and the salvation of others (I Cor. 11:1); a rejection of the idea of legal righteousness and a total and continuous humbling of oneself in favor of gaining Christ and the goal in him (Phil. 3:17); freeing oneself from the bondage of legalism (Gal. 4:12); self-giving labor and benevolence (Acts 20:35). There are other references to following Paul's conduct which are too general to enable one to designate the specific point of imitation (*cf.* Phil. 4:9; II Tim. 3:10). From the foregoing list one fact becomes strikingly apparent. There is a certain accent which keeps recurring in the passages on imitation. It is the accent of humility, self-denial, self-giving, self-sacrifice for the sake of Christ and the salvation of others. This is the way of life which Paul found himself representing, and it is the way of life which he expected to find appearing in his readers. In regard to this way of life he speaks of the imitation of himself.

In two places Paul linked the thought of the imitation of himself directly to the thought of the imitation of Christ. These places speak of imitation in the matter of joyfully enduring suffering for the sake of the gospel (I Thess. 1:6) and in giving oneself for the gospel and for the salvation of others (I Cor. 11:1). These two passages are clear indications that Paul finds not only himself representing this way of self-denial, self-giving, and self-sacrifice; Christ represented it too. In fact, the way of life that Paul pictures is Christ's way. It is the way of Christ pictured in the gospels and presented as the way for his followers. In Chapter Three of our study, in reviewing the idea of the imitation of Christ, we noticed how Jesus during his earthly days called men to follow him in his way of deepest humiliation, suffering, and self-giving. This was the way to salvation, exaltation, and glorification. We noticed also how after Christ's exaltation, Christians continued to be joined to him, now no longer in physical accompaniment upon an earthly way, but in living union through faith and the receipt of the Holy Spirit. This union with Christ brought them into involvement in Christ's way of life as he had revealed it during his earthly days. Christ's commands to deny oneself, take up one's cross, and follow him continued to be applicable after Easter. The way which Paul repeatedly recommended for imitation was this way. It was Christ's way. Paul presented himself as an example of Christ's way. His readers were to imitate his Christianity.

In view of Paul's way being basically Christ's way, the question arises why Paul drew the attention so often to himself rather than to Christ. Was there something peculiar in Paul's representation of the Christian way, so that it was different from the Christian ways which other apostles and missionaries portrayed? Stanley thinks so. He says: "While Paul insists that his kerygma is essentially the same as that preached by other apostles, he is also aware that, as his personal testimony to Christ, his preaching and way of life have their own characteristic modalities, determined chiefly by his conviction that he carries on the role of Christ as the Suffering Servant of God." [10] We shall not interrupt our present pursuit with an explication and evaluation of the thesis that Paul saw himself as carrying on Christ's role as the Suffering Servant who is now engaged in the work of being a light to the Gentiles. [11] The question is whether Paul's references to imitation are to be explained in terms of some "characteristic modalities" in his preaching and way of life, which then presumably were not characteristic of the other apostles and missionaries. It becomes clearer what Stanley has in mind, when he says: "This personal character of his [Paul's] own manner of preaching the Word makes Paul refer to it as 'our Gospel' [I Thess. 1:6]. This same quality may be discerned in the various spiritualities prevalent in the Church, as also in the inspired writings of the Bible." [12] We find it questionable, however, that it is this kind of nuance and variety of expression found within Christianity which Paul has in mind in referring to the imitation of himself. What is there in the context of the passages on imitation which could lead to this conclusion? We have seen repeatedly how Paul is urging the imitation of himself in the face of outright heretical teachings being propagated among his readers. This was obviously the case in Corinth, [13] Philippi, and

---

10 Stanley, *Biblica*, XL, p. 877.

11 Cf. the development of the thesis in L. Cerfaux, "Saint Paul et le 'Serviteur de Dieu' d'Isaïe," *Studia Anselmiana*, 27—28, Rome: Herder, 1951, pp. 351—365. Stanley pursues the matter further in "The Theme of the Servant of Yahweh in Primitive Christian Soeriology, and Its Transposition by St. Paul," *C.B.Q.*, XVI (1954), pp. 385—425, and comes to the conclusion of a "mystical conception of the Apostolic vocation" (p. 420). He states further: "Aware of his Divine appointment as Servant of Yahweh, Paul perceived, more deeply perhaps than any other inspired New Testament writer, that in carrying on the work of his Lord as the Servant in gospelling to the Gentiles, he was in a very real sense identified with Him" (p. 420).

12 Stanley, *Biblica*, XL, p. 865. In accounting for the significance of the expression "our gospel" it does not appear to be necessary to go beyond the explanation of G. Friedrich: "Wenn er es sein Evangelium nennt, so deshalb, weil er als Apostel mit seiner Verkündigung betraut ist" (εὐαγγέλιον, *T.W.N.T.*, II, p. 731, 11—12).

13 It might at first appearance seem in I Cor. 4:14—16 that Paul is urging the imitation of himself as their father in distinction from Cephas and Apollos who could only be classed as

Galatia, [14] even in Thessalonica Paul found it necessary to point out the difference between himself and some other teachers who were surely not representing the same gospel as Paul (*cf.* I Thess. 2:3—6). [15] Paul's call to imitation is not in order to secure certain Pauline characteristics in the Christianity that is coming to expression in his readers. The characteristics which must come to expression are those basic to Christianity itself. Paul is not making special pleas for his version of Christianity and his manner of Christian life. We can not agree with Stanley's proposal that Paul's call for the imitation of himself arises from there being something unique about his Christianity. This leaves the question unanswered, then, as to why Paul calls for the imitation of *himself* in his attempts to strengthen his readers in their Christianity.

Michaelis looks in a quite different direction for an answer on how to understand the matter of the imitation of Paul. In his study of the terms μιμέομαι and μιμητής he finds the usage employed by Paul falling into three classes. [16] In I Thess. 2:14, and perhaps also in I Thess. 1:6, the words simply express a comparison, and there is no thought of a conscious imitation. In our study of these passages, however, we found no reason for ruling out the idea of imitation. In fact, we found the possibility of a very conscious and intentional imitation on the part of the Thessalonians. [17] Michaelis finds a second type of usage in II Thess. 3:7—9 and Phil. 3:17. Here he acknowledges that the reference to imitation can be understood in the sense of following an example. He finds at the same time, however, that these passages carry a strong accent on the recognition of Paul's apostolic authority, so that the following of Paul's example must be conceived of as including the obeying of his commands. Michaelis is correct in insisting that following Paul's example is not an alternative or substitute to acting in obedience to his instructions. Following his example certainly includes the idea of acting in obedience to apostolic authority. However, when Michaelis proceeds to draw the two ideas so close together as to make them practically synonymous, and to find the primary significance of imitation to lie in the matter of obedience, [18] we have not been able to agree with him. Our exegetical study of these two passages did not reveal that the element of obedience was as essential to an understanding of the true character of imitation in them as

---

tutors. However, the radical deviations from the Christianity of Paul, as they are reflected in the whole of the letter up to this point, and particularly in 4:8—10 (*cf.* above, p. 144, fn. 162) are hardly the kind of thing that can be attributed to Apollos or Cephas or in any way identified with them as their "characteristic modalities" of Christian teaching and life.

14  We noticed in connection with Gal. 4:12 how little reason there is to concur with Stanley's proposal that the call is to become like Paul rather than like Peter. The deviation is for more radical than a Petrine representation of Christianity (*cf.* above, p. 194).

15  In II Thessalonians Paul's distinguishing himself from an unorthodox movement becomes far more pronounced (*cf.* above, pp. 132f.).

16  Michaelis, *T.W.N.T.*, IV, pp. 674—675.

17  See throughout Chapter Four, Section I, and in particular, pp. 108, 120, 123.

18  *Cf.* Michaelis, re II Thess. 3:7—9: "Mit τύπος [ist] weniger das Muster, das nachgebildet, als das V o r b i l d, das b e f o l g t werden soll, gemeint" (*T.W.N.T.*, IV, p. 669, 26—27); re Phil. 3:17: "Es heisst zuerst: ... seid gehorsam!" (*ibid.*, p. 670, 20—21).

Michaelis feels it is.[19] Michaelis' explanation is not particularly helpful in explicating the precise meaning and peculiar significance of Paul's calling for *imitation*.

In the third type of usage which Michaelis finds, the tendency to submerge the idea of imitation in the idea of obedience becomes more emphatic. Michaelis finds that in I Cor. 4:16 the idea of example has receded completely in favor of the idea of obedience. In this passage, however, we found that Michaelis, along with many others, placed too narrow limits on the meaning of Paul's reference to teaching his ways (I Cor. 4:17), so that this latter expression precluded the idea of the Corinthians' imitating and following the ways shown by Paul's conduct and example.[20] We found that Paul's reference to his teaching in this passage had to do with the comprehensive process by which he sought to lead the Corinthians to the Christian faith and into a life appropriate to such an allegiance.[21] Paul's leading the Corinthians into an imitation of his personal conduct was an important part of this comprehensive teaching process. The idea of imitation in this passage need not be reduced simply to being obedient to Paul's formal instruction; it means following the example of Paul as seen in his personal conduct. Also in I Cor. 11:1, I Thess. 1:6, and Eph. 5:1 Michaelis finds that the idea of obedience rather than of example is the dominant idea. In none of these instances did our studies of the passages substantiate Michaelis' proposal.[22] Michaelis concludes that, when Paul calls his readers to be imitators of him, there is but little thought of their following his example, and that Paul's real thought is that they should be obedient and should act in accordance with his instructions.[23] We have not found ourselves in agreement with Michaelis' understanding of the meaning and significance of the imitation of Paul.

We are also unable to agree with Michaelis' wholesale rejection of the thought of the imitation of Christ in Paul's writings. Michaelis states the matter most emphatically and dogmatically: "Die Forderung einer imitatio Christi hat in den paulinischen Aussagen keine Stütze."[24] This statement is perhaps to be explained as a reaction against warped and unwholesome conceptions of the imitation of Christ. But Michaelis finds the references to the imitation of Christ satisfactorily accounted for as follows: "Man [wird] ein μιμητής Χριστοῦ nur ... in der konkreten Bewährung des Gehorsams gegenüber Wort und Willen des Herrn."[25] The term μιμητής has thus lost all trace of the idea of imitation. We have found no reasons, however, either in regard to I Thess. 1:6 or to I Cor. 11:1 for abandoning the idea of an

---

[19] See above, pp. 138, 185f.
[20] See above, pp. 147ff.
[21] See above, p. 150.
[22] See above, pp. 78f., 116ff., 167f.
[23] "Die Prüfung hat ... ergeben, dass diese Auslegung [die Nachahmung eines Vorbildes] mindestens sehr eingeschränkt werden muss. Wenn die Gemeinden als μιμηταί des Apostels bezeichnet werden, dann ist daran gedacht, dass sie ihm folgsam zu sein und nach seinen Weisungen zu handeln haben" (Michaelis, *T.W.N.T.*, IV, pp. 675, 16 – 676, 2).
[24] *Ibid.*, p. 676, 8,9.
[25] *Ibid.*, p. 676, 12—14.

imitation in the sense of following the conduct of someone who is seen as an example. In fact, in I Cor. 11:1 the element of example is very emphatically present in the context. When one rids himself of the idea that imitation must mean artificiality and slavish copying, and understands the idea in the sense of a child's adopting the ways he sees in his father and the other more mature people around him, the thought of the imitation of Christ is eminently well-suited to Paul's thought in these passages. The essence of imitation is not to be found at the point of obedience, as Michaelis proposes. The essence lies at the point of bringing to expression personally things that are observed in and learned from others.

## II. Conclusions

What does Paul have in mind in speaking of the imitation of himself? In the first chapter of our study we noticed a variety of ways in which the Greek word for imitation (μιμέομαι and related forms) was used. Of particular interest to our present study were the usages of the word in connection with the processes of moral growth, the development of character, and the adopting and bringing to personal expression of the ways seen in another. Imitation occurred in the parent-child relationship, the teacher-pupil relationship, the leader-follower relationship. Furthermore, the idea of imitation among the Greeks did not necessarily carry the stigma of artificiality, uncreative copying, slavish reproduction. They saw the possibilities of imitation being a most worthwhile and enriching experience for human beings. Pursuit of the fine arts could be approvingly referred to as imitation. The idea of bringing something to expression was a fundamental one, perhaps even the primal one in μιμέομαι. In imitation one could bring a person, his characteristics, ways, and way of life to living expression and personal representation in one's own life. Paul made use of this idea and activity in his work of spreading the gospel.

In Chapter Two we investigated the background and meanings of the word τύπος, which Paul used to express his personal example. We found that the root idea of the word quite likely is that of a form or mold, and that within the whole range of ideas which sprang from this basic idea, the idea of a pattern, standard, model, or personal example of human behavior has a natural and well-established place. The Greek and Hellenistic Jewish use of the word in this sense carried strong moralistic accents.

In our investigation in Chapter Three we found further confirmation of the fact that the ideas of imitation and following an example in the Greek and Hellenistic Jewish world were closely associated with moralistic views of man's goal and the attainment of it. In this chapter we sought to go beyond the express use of the words μιμέομαι and τύπος and to detect the idea of imitation and of being an example particularly in the area of religion and of morals as it came to expression in other words or was implicit in various expressions and ideas. We noticed such things as the attention given by the Greeks (and Romans) to the examples from history, the examples of the nation's heroes and leaders, the examples of teachers. We also noticed the important place given to imitation in religion. The life of God was often proposed as the ideal for man, and by way of imitating God, following him, and becoming like him man could attain his own goal and highest good, namely, divinity. We found that the ideas of imitation and of giving or following an example were practically nonexistent in the Old Testament writings. However, in the period prior to the New Testament these matters were coming to expression in the writings of the Jewish world. The influence of the contact with the Greek world is to be detected here. Much of the Jewish attention to imitation and example also showed strong undercurrents of moralism. The Greek and Jewish environments of the New Testament give much testimony of how important the ideas of imitation and learning by example are to systems of self-effort, self-development toward moral uprightness and perfection, reaching the goal of life through personal discipline and through being challenged to reach for the best. There was no particular evidence in the environment outside the New Testament of what role these ideas might play in a religion of salvation by grace through faith.

In Chapter Three we noted further that Jesus came depicting a way of life leading to heavenly glory and salvation. It was the way of self-giving, cross-bearing, self-denial, humiliation, suffering, and death. Jesus called men to follow him in this way. Jesus, however, was different from the other leaders of mankind. He not only set an example and led the way for his followers. He was the Messiah of God, the Savior; his call was the Messianic call to salvation which brought men new life and accorded to them new powers. Men were brought into living union with Christ. His followers shared his life, were recipients of his Spirit, and became participants in his benefits and final reward. He became the pattern for their lives, but this was not simply the pattern of a good life which they were to endeavor to emulate and to attain through their own effort and struggle. He was the pattern for their life because they were in living union with him, and were being formed anew according to his image. In our study of various texts we saw how, when the New Testament writers made reference to the example of Christ, it was as an example to those who knew him as Savior and Messiah and were enjoying the benefits deriving from him. His example had real significance to such people, for it was a picture of the way to which they were committed. His life was a picture of the life to which they were being transformed. To hold Christ's example before his followers was to stimulate their participation in the salvation and transformation which was at work in them by virtue of their living union with their Savior and Lord.

We noticed further in Chapter Three that the New Testament writers spoke of the imitation of God. Here too the thought of imitation was found in the context of a very personal and vital relationship which existed between God and the people being addressed. The readers or hearers of the call to imitation were seen as children of God their Father. Imitation could be expected from children. It was self-evident that children would be like their Father in certain basic characteristics. This is the nature of the relationship between God and his people. To call children to imitation was to call them to be what they already were, and to bring to expression those things which were already theirs by virtue of their birth and their life in the care of their Father.

Finally, in Chapter Three we noticed that the New Testament speaks of the imitation and example of other men. In pointing Christians to the example of the Old Testament saints the thought was in the context of emphasizing that Christianity was no break with the past, but that Christians were called to go the same way God's people had always gone. Christian leaders were also urged to be examples to the Christians over whom they had been placed. The emphasis was on presenting a living portrayal of the Christian way and of using the influence of their personal relationships with people to help them toward bringing their Christianity to fuller and more consistent expression. Hence, over against the strong moralistic overtone and emphasis in the thoughts of imitation and example outside of the New Testament, we found that these thoughts appear in the New Testament in the service of salvation in Christ. In the New Testament the appeal is not to the inherent goodness of the way, to its reasonableness, wisdom, superiority, virtuousness, and perfection. The appeal is to the fact of salvation in Christ. By virtue of this fact and this relationship of living union to Christ, the Christian is engaged in making Christ and his way a real and total part of his life. He is being brought to conformity to Christ, and in this process his imitation of Christ plays an important part.

The matter of the imitation of Paul has its role to play in this program of salvation in Christ. We noticed that the imitation which Paul was urging upon his readers concerned the basic Christian way. Paul found in urging the imitation of himself on his readers he was stimulating them in building their Christian lives. He was teaching them the Christian way and helping them to bring Christ to expression in their lives. But why did he urge the imitation of *himself*? We have noticed in our exegetical studies of the imitation of Paul in Chapter Four that sometimes his example served as a forceful illustration for pedagogical purposes. This was particularly the case in regard to his personal policy of providing his own support through hard manual labor. This hard work powerfully illustrated his industriousness, his willingness to sacrifice himself, and his eagerness to engage in works of benevolence. He presented himself as an illustration of the kind of responses a Christian makes to salvation in Christ. As we noted in connection with II Thess. 3:7–9, he gave the example with the specific intention of its leading to imitation. His recalling his example to the Ephesian elders at Miletus (Acts 20:35) points in the same direction. His directing the Philippians' attention to their leaders who were walking according to his example (Phil. 3:17) again attests to the care he had bestowed on using his personal example for pedagogical purposes. When Paul confessed that Timothy had followed his teaching, conduct, and purpose (II Tim. 3:10), it shows how much Paul had been involved in pedagogy in the fundamental sense of forming and training a boy's (παῖς) conduct (ἀγωγή). Paul found the matter of personal conduct of no less importance than the Christian doctrines and beliefs. Paul preached Christianity in his mission groups, but he also lived Christianity in their midst, giving them a clear-cut and consistent portrayal of the Christian life. As we saw in I Cor. 4:16,17, Paul saw in his conduct and personal example an important aspect of the comprehensive program in which he was engaged of teaching Christianity. In his role as teacher Paul stands as an example of the thing he is teaching. Paul points to his own example and calls for the imitation of himself, because he is the teacher who has made these things vividly real to his readers.

However, the relationship between Paul and those with whom he speaks about imitating him is deeper and more basic than simply that of the teacher-pupil relationship. Paul was not speaking about the imitation of himself to Christians in general; neither were his hearers simply Christians who at one time or another had received some Christian instruction from him. These were Christians who had been born into Christianity through his preaching of the gospel. He was their spiritual father; he had begotten them in Christ. In I Cor. 4:14–16 Paul makes it particularly clear that he is calling them to imitate him by virtue of the fact that he is their spiritual father. Others could claim to have imparted teaching to the Corinthians. But their Christian father could be found in Paul alone. From this fact and in view of this relationship arose his appeal for imitation. As children of their father they could be expected to be his imitators. We noticed further how clearly and expressly the fact of Paul's spiritual fatherhood is in the context of the speaking of imitation in I Thess. 1:6 (*cf.* 2:7–12) and Gal. 4:12 (*cf.* vs. 19). Paul's spiritual fatherhood is implicit in the farewell scene at Miletus (Acts 20:17–38). In speaking of Timothy's following his conduct (II Tim. 3:10), he is speaking of his beloved child (II Tim. 1:2). The thought of fatherhood does not come to literal expression in the context of II Thess. 3:7–9 or of Phil. 3:17. Nevertheless, we have noticed the intimate personal relationship that exists between Paul and his readers in these passages. In I Cor. 11:1 the call to imitation still carries the echoes of the former call in I Cor. 4:16. It is clear that Paul calls for the imitation of himself from those whom he has fathered in the Christian faith.

Paul's call for the imitation of himself arises from the fact that those to whom he is speaking are his spiritual children. Here we have the clue to why he can direct so much attention to himself in promoting their Christian growth. He has been a most vital link in their coming to union with Christ and a most vivid link in their learning Christ's way. He has been in a pattern-forming position. The first impressions of the shape, character, and direction of life in Christ were seen in Paul and learned from him. His position as spiritual father was determinitive of the basic shape of their Christian lives. Therefore, in his Christian nurture of them he appeals to this fact. As children of their father, they are to be his imitators.

In calling for imitation Paul is nurturing his children in Christ. As every good father, he is directing his efforts toward the children's attainment of maturity and independence from their father. The children will forever bear the stamp of his forming, but there will come a point in their lives when they will have outgrown the need of learning further by way of imitating their father. In their maturity their relationships with others and with life itself will be direct. As mature Christians their lives will be characterized by a directness and immediacy of relationship to Christ. They will not be bringing Christ to expression by way of the Christ they have seen in their father Paul. They will bring Christ to expression as they know him directly. As mature Christians it will not be the imitation of Paul that is important, but the imitation of Christ. In our study we have taken note of Paul's working to this end. Paul speaks of the imitation of Christ sometimes by way of the imitation of himself (I Cor. 11:1); sometimes alongside the imitation of himself (I Thess. 1:6); sometimes independent of the thought of imitating himself (Phil. 2:5). It is an elementary step for his children to learn to imitate Paul's Christian ways. In so doing they will bring to expression in their lives the Christianity they see and know in their spiritual father. This is a significant development. However, they must grow further toward maturity. They may not be forever dependent on their father's mediation. They must mature to the imitation of the Christian way as Christ himself presented it, thus bringing Christ and his way to direct expression. Paul is nurturing his children to a mature and direct bringing of Christ and his life to expression in their own lives. We are able to agree with Stanley's conclusion only partially, when he says: "The *imitatio Christi* which Paul proposes to his communities is a mediated imitation." [26] It is mediated during the days of immaturity. Paul is looking forward, however, to the time when he can joyfully acknowledge about the whole Christian life of his children, as he could once about the Thessalonians: "Ye became imitators of us and of the Lord" (I Thess. 1:6).

Nevertheless, Stanley does point to an important fact when he speaks of the imitation of Christ being mediated. Paul was a vital link in the process by which his converts learned to bring Christ and Christianity to expression in their lives. This is the blessed role which missionaries often are privileged to play in the lives of those to whom they bring the gospel. This role, however, is not limited to missionaries and evangelists. Every Christian has had spiritual parents, but the percentage of Christians who find these in the missionaries and evangelists is actually quite small. Most Christians find their spiritual parents in their physical parents. Their years of spiritual immaturity have been the same ones in which they were physically immature. The role of the Christian parent with his child is not dissimilar to that of Paul with his converts. Christian parents are a vital link in the process by which their children learn to bring Christ and Christianity to expression in their lives. They mediate the imitation of Christ. The church, thus, has the important duty of keeping Christian parents alert to this fact and of providing them the necessary aid and spiritual care for their task. It is very important to the spiritual health of coming generations that there should be a healthy and vital imitation of Christ in parents.

It is perhaps not inappropriate to make a closing remark on the basis

---

[26] Stanley, *Biblica*, XL, p. 877.

of Paul's ministry to his converts about the conduct of Christian leaders today in their work of evangelizing and of nurturing and caring for their congregations. Paul saw in his own example and conduct a significant means of promoting Christian nurture and growth in his converts. His example was not merely a neutral phenomenon that did not contradict his preaching. Paul made of it a positive value; it served as a part of his total teaching. People were led to a fuller life in Christ through the power and influence of Paul's life over them. The intimacy of Paul's contact with his churches is striking. His readers had an amazingly broad knowledge of his life and conduct. His stay in some of his churches was not an extensive one. Paul must have lived very intensively with those who responded to his preaching. His letters reveal how personal was their knowledge of each other. His calls for imitation reveal how extensive, intimate, and personal was their knowledge of him. In a very short time a living relationship had been established between them, to which Paul could appeal even after they had been separated from each other for a matter of years. He worked at nurturing men to Christian maturity by establishing a most personal relationship with them. He could work for the deepening of Christianity by calling men to imitate him.

The church of today has resources available in its work of evangelism and Christian nurture of which Paul could not have dreamed. There is now great opportunity of multiplying one man's voice through public address systems, microphones, television cameras, printing presses, duplicating machines, addressographs. There is much emphasis in Christianity on doing things in a big way and in reaching and serving large numbers of people. The influence of close personal relationships, of example and of imitation does not lend itself to these easy processes of multiplication. Are close personal relationships, imitation, and example to be regarded as obsolete for present-day Christianity? Is it possible that they are too time-consuming for such critical times as these? One finds difficulty projecting Paul into the present situation. However, it is noteworthy that Paul's time-consuming personal working and living with people did bring forth results which were neither trivial nor insignificant. Perhaps the church of Christ would be well served with more Christian leaders working at slower pace, limiting their contacts and activities, and opening their personal Christian lives sufficiently to permit of imitation—be it only by a few. Busying oneself with a large number of nominal Christians or possible Christians can hardly be considered more important than serving to bring Christ to real and living expression in a few. True, "the harvest indeed is plenteous, but the laborers are few" (Matt. 9:37). But Jesus points to the answer: "Pray ye therefore the Lord of the harvest, that he send forth laborers into his harvest" (Matt. 9:38).

# LIST OF ABBREVIATIONS

| | |
|---|---|
| A.S.V. | *American Standard Version.* |
| B. Chr. | *The Beginnings of Christianity*, ed. F. J. F. Jackson and K. Lake, London: Macmillan, 1920–33. |
| B.J.R.L. | *Bulletin of the John Rylands Library.* |
| B.N.T.C. | *Black's New Testament Commentaries.* |
| B.z.F.c.T. | *Beiträge zur Förderung christlicher Theologie.* |
| C.B.Q. | *The Catholic Biblical Quarterly.* |
| C.d.N.T. | *Commentaire du Nouveau Testament.* |
| C.G.T. | *Cambridge Greek Testament for Schools and Colleges.* |
| C.N.T. | *Commentaar op het Nieuwe Testament.* |
| E.B. | *Études Bibliques.* |
| E.R.E. | *Encyclopedia of Religion and Ethics*, ed. J. Hastings, Edinburgh: T. & T. Clark, 1913. |
| E.T. | *The Expository Times.* |
| H.N.T. | *Handbuch zum Neuen Testament*, ed. H. Lietzmann. |
| I.C.C. | *The International Critical Commentary.* |
| J.B.L. | *The Journal of Biblical Literature.* |
| J.T.S. | *The Journal of Theological Studies.* |
| K.e.K.N.T. | *Kritisch=exegetischer Kommentar über das Neue Testament.* |
| K.J.V. | *King James Version.* |
| K.N.T. | *Kommentaar op het Nieuwe Testament.* |
| K.V. | *Korte Verklaring der Heilige Schrift.* |
| K.z.N.T. | *Kommentar zum Neuen Testament*, ed. T. Zahn. |
| L.C.L. | *Loeb Classical Library.* |
| L.T.K. | *Lexicon für Theologie und Kirche*, 2. Aufl., Freiburg: Herder, 1957ff. |
| LXX | Septuagint. |
| M.N.T.C. | *The Moffat New Testament Commentary.* |
| M.T. | Masoretic Text. |
| N.B.G. | *Nederlandsch Bijbelgenootschap Translation of the Bible.* |
| N.E.B. | *The New English Bible.* |
| N.I.C.N.T. | *The New International Commentary on the New Testament.* |
| N.T.D. | *Das Neue Testament Deutsch.* |
| N.T.S. | *New Testament Studies.* |
| P.G. | *Patrologiae Graecae*, ed. J.-P. Migne, 161 vols., Paris, 1857–79. |
| P.L. | *Patrologiae Latinae*, ed. J.-P. Migne, 221 vols., Paris, 1844–91. |
| R.G.G. | *Die Religion in Geschichte und Gegenwart*, 2. Aufl., Tübingen: J. C. B. Mohr (Paul Siebeck), 1927ff; 3. Aufl., 1957ff. |

| | |
|---|---|
| R.S.R. | *Recherches de Science Religieuse.* |
| R.S.V. | *Revised Standard Version.* |
| S.T. | *Studia Theologica.* |
| T.H.N.T. | *Theologischer Handkommentar zum Neuen Testament.* |
| T.L. | *Theologische Literaturzeitung.* |
| T.N.T.C. | *Tyndale New Testament Commentaries.* |
| T.S.K. | *Theologische Studien und Kritiken.* |
| T.U. | *Tekst en Uitleg.* |
| T.v.T. | *Tijdschrift voor Theologie.* |
| T.W.N.T. | *Theologisches Wörterbuch zum Neuen Testament,* ed. G. Kittel, G. Friedrich, Stuttgart: W. Kohlhammer, 1933ff. |
| Z.N.W. | *Zeitschrift für die neutestamentliche Wissenschaft.* |
| Z.T.K. | *Zeitschrift für Theologie und Kirche.* |

# BIBLIOGRAPHY
(List of Works Cited)

(For the bibliographical data on the Hebrew, Greek, and English texts used without further reference in citing the Old Testament and Apocrypha, the New Testament, and the Apostolic Fathers, see p. xiv, fn. 13.)

Aalders, G. C., *De Profeet Jeremia*, K.V., Kampen: J. H. Kok, 1953.
Abbott, T. K., *A Critical and Exegetical Commentary on the Epistles to the Ephesians and to the Colossians*, I.C.C., Edinburgh: T. & T. Clark, 1909.
Allo, E.-B., *St. Paul: Première épître aux Corinthiens*, E.B., Paris: J. Gabalda, 1934.
Ambrosiaster, *Commentaria in XIII Epistolas Beati Pauli, Ad Opera Sancti Ambrosii Appendix*, ed. J.-P. Migne, P.L., XVII.
*The Apocrypha and Pseudepigrapha of the Old Testament*, ed. R. H. Charles, 2 vols., Oxford: Clarendon Press, 1913.
*Aristeas to Philocrates (Letter of Aristeas)*, ed. M. Hadas, New York: Harper & Bros., 1951.
Aristotle, *De Poetica*, trans. I. Bywater, in *The Works of Aristotle*, ed. W. D. Ross, Oxford: Clarendon Press, 1952, Vol. XI.
——, *Rhetorica ad Alexandrum*, trans. E. S. Forster, in *The Works of Aristotle*, ed. W. D. Ross, Oxford: Clarendon Press, 1952, Vol. XI.
Asting, R., *Die Heiligkeit im Urchristentum*, Göttingen: Vandenhoeck & Ruprecht, 1930.
*The Babylonian Talmud*, ed. I. Epstein, 35 vols., London: Soncino Press, 1935—48.
Bachmann, P., *Der erste Brief des Paulus an die Korinther*, K.z.N.T., Leipzig: A. Deichert, 1905.
Bailey, A., *Dictionnaire Grec-Français*, édition revue par L. Séchan et P. Chantraine, Paris: Librairie Hachette, 1950.
Barrett, C. K. *The Gospel according to St. John*, London: S.P.C.K., 1956.
Barth, K., *Erklärung des Philipperbriefes*, 5. Aufl., Zollikon=Zürich: Evangelischer Verlag, 1947.
Bauer, W., *Das Johannesevangelium*, H.N.T., 3. Aufl., Tübingen: J. C. B. Mohr (Paul Siebeck), 1933.
——, *Griechisch-deutsches Wörterbuch zu den Schriften des Neuen Testaments und der übrigen Urchristlichen Literatur*, 5. Aufl. Berlin: Alfred Töpelmann, 1958.
Baur, F. C., *Paulus, der Apostel Jesu Christi*, 2 Tle., 2. Aufl., Leipzig: Fues's Verlag (L. W. Reisland), 1866.
Beare, F. W., *The Epistle to the Philippians*, B.N.T.C., London: Adam and Charles Black, 1959.
——, "On the Interpretation of Romans VI. 17," N.T.S., V (1958-59), pp. 206—210.
Benoit, P., *Les épîtres de saint Paul aux Philippiens, à Philémon, aux Colossiens, aux Éphésiens*, in *La Sainte Bible*, Paris: Les éditions du Cerf, 1949.

Berkouwer, G. C., *Geloof en Heiliging*, Kampen: J. H. Kok, 1949.
Bernard, J. H., *A Critical and Exegetical Commentary on the Gospel according to St. John*, 2 vols., *I.C.C.*, Edinburgh: T. & T. Clark, 1928.
Blass, F., and A. Debrunner, *Grammatik des neutestamentlichen Griechisch*, 9. Aufl., Göttingen: Vandenhoeck & Ruprecht, 1954.
Blumenthal, A. von, "ΤΥΠΟΣ und ΠΑΡΑΔΕΙΓΜΑ," *Hermes, Zeitschrift für Klassische Philologie*, LXIII (1928), pp. 391—414.
Boman, T., *Das hebräische Denken im Vergleich mit dem Griechischen*, Göttingen: Vandenhoeck & Ruprecht, 1954.
Bonhoeffer, D., *Nachfolge*, München: Chr. Kaiser Verlag, 1958.
Bonnard, P., *L'épître de saint Paul aux Philippiens*, *C.d.N.T.*, Neuchatel/Paris: Delachaux & Niestlé, 1950.
———, *L'épître de saint Paul aux Galates*, *C.d.N.T.*, Neuchatel/Paris: Delachaux & Niestlé, 1953.
Bornemann, W., *Die Thessalonicherbriefe*, *K.e.K.N.T.*, 5./6. Aufl., Göttingen: Vandenhoeck & Ruprecht, 1894.
Bornkamm, G., "Paulus," *R.G.G.*³, V, pp. 166—190.
Bouma, C., *De Brieven van den Apostel Paulus aan Timotheus en Titus*, *K.N.T.*, Amsterdam: H. A. van Bottenburg, 1946.
Bousset, W., *Der erste Brief an die Korinther*, in *Die Schriften des Neuen Testaments*, 2. Aufl., Göttingen: Vandenhoeck & Ruprecht, 1908 (3. Aufl., 1917).
Brown, F., S. R. Driver, and C. A. Briggs, *A Hebrew and English Lexicon of the Old Testament*, Oxford: Clarendon Press, 1952.
Bruce, F. F., *The Acts of the Apostles*, London: Tyndale Press, 1951.
Buber, M., "Nachahmung Gottes," *Der Morgen*, I (1925-26), pp. 638—647 (= *Kampf um Israel*, Berlin: Schocken Verlag, 1933, pp. 68—83).
Büchsel, F., and K. H. Rengstorf, γεννάω et al., *T.W.N.T.*, I, pp. 663—674.
Bultmann, R., *Der Stil der paulinischen Predigt und die kynisch-stoische Diatribe*, Göttingen: Vandenhoeck & Ruprecht, 1910.
———, *Das Evangelium des Johannes*, *K.e.K.N.T.*, 11. Aufl., Göttingen: Vandenhoeck & Ruprecht, 1950.
———, *Jesus*, Tübingen: J. C. B. Mohr (Paul Siebeck), 1951.
———, *Theologie des Neuen Testaments*, 3. Aufl., Tübingen: J. C. B. Mohr (Paul Siebeck), 1958.
———, πιστεύω et al., *T.W.N.T.*, VI, pp. 174—230.
Burnet, J., "Pythagoras and Pythagoreanism," *E.R.E.*, X, p. 526a.
Burton, E., *The Apostolic Fathers*, 2 vols., Edinburgh: John Grant, 1909.
Burton, E. D., *A Critical and Exegetical Commentary on the Epistle to the Galatians*, *I.C.C.*, Edinburgh: T. & T. Clark, 1921.
Calvin, J., *Opera quae supersunt omnia*, ed. G. Baum, E. Cunitz, E. Reuss, 59 vols., in *Corpus Reformatorum* Vols. XXIX—LXXXVII, Brunsvigae/Berolini: C. A. Schwetschke, 1863—1900.
———, *Commentary on the Epistles of Paul the Apostle to the Corinthians*, trans. J. Pringle (1848), 2 vols., Grand Rapids: Wm. B. Eerdmans, 1948.
———, *Commentaries on the Epistles of Paul the Apostle to the Philippians, Colossians, and Thessalonians*, trans. J. Pringle (1851), Grand Rapids: Wm. B. Eerdmans, 1948.
Cerfaux, L., *La théologie de l'église suivant saint Paul*, 2ᵉ éd., Paris: Les éditions du Cerf, 1948.
———, "Saint Paul et le 'Serviteur de Dieu' d'Isaïe," *Studia Anselmiana*, 27—28, Rome: Herder, 1951, pp. 351—365.
Chadwick, H., "I Thess. 3:3: σαίνεσθαι," *J.T.S.*, I (1950), pp. 156—158.
Christ, W. von, *Geschichte der Griechischen Literatur*, 6. Aufl., bearb. von W. Schmid und O. Stählin, München: C. H. Beck, 1920.

Chrysostom, J., *Opera omnia quae extant Graece et Latine*, ed. Bern. de Montfaucon, 13 vols., Venetiis, 1734—41.
Cicero, *De Oratore*, ed. E. W. Sutton and H. Rackham, 2 vols., *L.C.L.*, London: Wm. Heinemann, 1959.
——, *Tusculan Disputations*, ed. J. E. King, *L.C.L.*, London: Wm. Heinemann, 1960.
Cohn, L., and I. Heinemann, *Die Werke Philos von Alexandria*, 5 Bde., Breslau: M. & H. Marcus, 1919—29.
Cornford, F. M., *Plato's Cosmology*, New York: Liberal Arts Press, 1957.
Cremer, H., *Biblisch-theologisches Wörterbuch der neutestamentlichen Gräzität*, 10. Aufl., hrsg. von J. Kögel, Gotha: F. A. Perthes, 1915.
Cullmann, O., *La Tradition*, Neuchatel/Paris: Delachaux & Niestlé, 1953.
Daniélou, J., *Sacramentum Futuri: Études sur les Origines de la Typologie Biblique*, Paris: Beauchesne, 1950.
Daube, D., *The New Testament and Rabbinic Judaism*, London: Athlone Press, 1956.
Davies, W. D., *Paul and Rabbinic Judaism*, London: S.P.C.K., 1948.
Deissner, K., *Paulus und Seneca*, *B.z.F.c.T.*, 21, 2. Heft, 1917.
Delling, G., πληροφορία, *T.W.N.T.*, VI, p. 309.
Dibelius, M., *An die Thessalonicher I. II. — An die Philipper*, *H.N.T.*, 3. Aufl., Tübingen: J. C. B. Mohr (Paul Siebeck), 1937.
——, *Der Brief des Jakobus*, *K.e.K.N.T.*, 8. Aufl., Göttingen: Vandenhoeck & Ruprecht, 1956.
——, "Nachfolge Christi im N.T.," *R.G.G.*², IV, pp. 395—396.
Dick, K., *Der Schriftstellerische Plural bei Paulus*, Halle a. S.: Max Niemeyer, 1900.
Diels, H., *Die Fragmente der Vorsokratiker*, 3 Bde., Berlin: Weidmann, 1952.
Dinkler, E., "Korintherbriefe," *R.G.G.*³, IV, pp. 17—23.
Dio Chrysostom, ed. J. W. Cohoon and H. L. Crosby, 4 vols., *L.C.L.*, London: Wm. Heinemann, 1946.
Dittenberger, W., ed., *Orientis Graeci Inscriptiones Selectae*, 2 Bde., Leipzig: S. Hirzel, 1903—5.
Dobschütz, E. von, *Die Thessalonicher-Briefe*, *K.e.K.N.T.*, 7. Aufl., Göttingen: Vandenhoeck & Ruprecht, 1909.
Dodd, C. H., "The Mind of Paul: A Psychological Approach," *B.J.R.L.*, XVII (1933), pp. 91—105.
——, *History and the Gospel*, London: Nisbet, 1938.
——, *The Johannine Epistles*, *M.N.T.C.*, London: Hodder & Stoughton, 1946.
Driver, S. R., *A Critical and Exegetical Commentary on Deuteronomy*, *I.C.C.*, Edinburgh: T. & T. Clark, (reprint) 1951.
Duker, A. C., and W. C. van Manen, *De Geschriften der Apostolische Vaders*, 2 dln., Amsterdam: C. L. Brinkman, 1871.
Duncan, G. S., *The Epistle of Paul to the Galatians*, *M.N.T.C.*, London: Hodder & Stoughton, 1934.
Du Plessis, P. J., ΤΕΛΕΙΟΣ. *The Idea of Perfection in the New Testament*, Kampen: J. H. Kok, 1959.
Dürr, L., "Heilige Vaterschaft im antiken Orient," in *Heilige Überlieferung. Ausschnitte aus der Geschichte des Mönchtums und des Heiligen Kultes ... Ildefons Herwegen dargeboten* (= Beiträge zur *Geschichte des Alten Mönchtums und des Benediktinerordens*. Supplementband), Münster: Aschendorff, 1938, pp. 1—20.
Duvenage, S. C. W., *Die Navolging van Christus*, Potchefstroom: Pro Rege — Pers Beperk, 1954.
Easton, B. S., *The Pastoral Epistles*, New York: Charles Scribner's Sons, 1947.
Eidem, E., "Imitatio Pauli," *Teologiska Studier Tillägnade Erik Stave*, Uppsala: Almquist & Wiksells, 1922, pp. 67—85.

Epictetus, *The Discourses,* ed. W. A. Oldfather, 2 vols., *L.C.L.,* London: Wm. Heinemann, 1926—28.
Evans, C. F., "The Kerygma," *J.T.S.,* VII (1956), pp. 25—41.
Ewald, P., *Die Briefe des Paulus an die Epheser, Kolosser, und Philemon,* K.z.N.T., Leipzig: A. Deichert, 1905.
——, *Der Brief des Paulus an die Philipper,* K.z.N.T., 1./2. Aufl., Leipzig: A. Deichert, 1908 (3. Aufl., 1923).
Findlay, G. G. *The Epistles of Paul the Apostle to the Thessalonians, C.G.T.,* Cambridge: University Press, 1904.
Foerster, W., κατακυριεύω, *T.W.N.T.,* III, pp. 1097—1098.
Frame, J. E., *A Critical and Exegetical Commentary on the Epistles of St. Paul to the Thessalonians, I.C.C.,* Edinburgh: T. & T. Clark, 1912.
Franke, A. H., *Handbuch über die Briefe Pauli an die Philipper, Kolosser, und Philemon,* K.e.K.N.T., 5. Aufl., Göttingen: Vandenhoeck & Ruprecht, 1886.
Franses, D., *De Apostolische Vaders,* Hilversum: Paul Brand, 1941.
Friedrich, G., εὐαγγέλιον, *T.W.N.T.,* II, pp. 718—734.
Gerhardsson, B., *Memory and Manuscript,* Uppsala: Almquist & Wiksells, 1961.
Gispen, W. H., *Het Boek Exodus,* 2 dln, K.V., Kampen: J. H. Kok, 1951.
Glueck, N., *Das Wort Chesed im alttestamentlichen Sprachgebrauch als menschliche Verhaltungsweise in profaner und religiöser Bedeutung,* (Inaugural-Dissertation), Jena, 1927.
Goppelt, L., *Typos. Die typologische Deutung des Alten Testaments in Neuen,* Gütersloh: C. Bertelsmann, 1939.
——, *Christentum und Judentum im ersten und zweiten Jahrhundert,* Gütersloh: C. Bertelsmann, 1954.
Greijdanus, S., *De Brieven van de Apostelen Petrus en Johannes, en de Brief van Judas,* K.N.T., Amsterdam: H. A. van Bottenburg, 1929.
——, *De Brief van den Apostel Paulus aan de Gemeenten in Galatië,* K.N.T., Amsterdam: H. A. van Bottenburg, 1936.
——, *De Brief van den Apostel Paulus aan de Gemeente te Philippi,* K.N.T., Amsterdam: H. A. van Bottenburg, 1937.
Grosheide, F. W., *A. T. Robertsons Beknopte Grammatica op het Grieksche Nieuwe Testament,* Kampen: J. H. Kok, 1912.
——, *De Handelingen der Apostelen,* 2 dln., K.N.T., Amsterdam: H. A. van Bottenburg, 1942—48.
——, *Het Heilige Evangelie volgens Johannes,* 2 dln., K.N.T., Amsterdam: H. A. van Bottenburg, 1950.
——, *De Brief aan de Hebreeën en de Brief van Jakobus,* C.N.T., 2e dr., Kampen: J. H. Kok, 1955.
——, *De Eerste Brief aan de Kerk te Korinthe,* C.N.T., 2e dr., Kampen: J. H. Kok, 1957.
——, *De Tweede Brief aan de Kerk te Korinthe,* C.N.T., 2e dr., Kampen: J. H. Kok, 1959.
Grundmann, W., δεῖ, δέον ἐστί, *T.W.N.T.,* II, pp. 21—25.
——, δέχομαι, *T.W.N.T.,* II, pp. 49—53.
——, δύναμαι/δύναμις, *T.W.N.T.,* II. pp. 286—318.
Gulin, E. G., "Die Nachfolge Gottes," *Studia Orientalia,* I (1925), pp. 34—50.
——, *Die Freude im Neuen Testament,* 1. Teil: *Jesus, Urgemeinde, Paulus,* Helsinki, 1932 (= *Annales, Academiae Scientarum Fennicae,* Ser. B, Tom. XXVI).
Hadorn, W., *Die Abfassung der Thessalonicherbriefe in der Zeit der dritten Missionsreise des Paulus,* B.z.F.c.T., 24, 3./4. Heft., 1919.
Haenchen, E., *Die Apostelgeschichte,* K.e.K.N.T., 13. Aufl., Göttingen: Vandenhoeck & Ruprecht, 1961.

Hatch, E., and H. A. Redpath, *A Concordance to the Septuagint*, Oxford: Clarendon Press, 1897.
Haupt, E., *Die Gefangenschaftsbriefe*, K.e.K.N.T., 7./8. Aufl., Göttingen: Vandenhoeck & Ruprecht, 1902.
Heinrici, G., *Kritisch Exegetisches Handbuch über den ersten Brief an die Korinther*, K.e.K.N.T., 7. Aufl., Göttingen: Vandenhoeck & Ruprecht, 1888.
Heinzelmann, G., *Der Brief an die Philipper*, N.T.D., 7./8. Aufl., Göttingen: Vandenhoeck & Ruprecht, 1956.
Heitmann, P. A., *Imitatio Dei*, Studia Anselmiana 10, Rome: Herder, 1940.
Hendriksen, W., *New Testament Commentary: Exposition of I and II Thessalonians*, Grand Rapids: Baker Book House, 1955.
——, *Commentary on I & II Timothy and Titus*, London: Banner of Truth Trust, 1959.
Héring, J., *La première épître de saint Paul aux Corinthiens*, C.d.N.T., Nechatel/Paris: Delachaux & Niestlé, 1949.
Herodotus, ed. A. D. Godley, 4 vols., L.C.L., London: Wm. Heinemann, 1931.
——, trans., W. Beloe, London, 1825.
——, *Histoires*, ed. Ph.-E. Legrand, Paris: Société d'Édition "Les Belles Lettres," 1956.
Hesychius, *Hesychii Alexandrini Lexicon*, ed. Mauricius Schmidt, 5 vol., Jenae: Sumptibus Frederici Maukii, 1858–68.
Heyde, J. E., "Typus – Ein Beitrag zur Bedeutungsgeschichte des Wortes Typus," *Forschungen und Fortschritte*, XVII (1941), pp. 220–223.
Hippocrates, ed. W. H. S. Jones, 4 vols., L.C.L., London: Wm. Heinemann, 1931.
Holl, K., "Der Kirchenbegriff des Paulus in seinem Verhältnis zu dem der Urgemeinde," *Gesammelte Aufsätze zur Kirchengeschichte*, Tübingen: J. C. B. Mohr (Paul Siebeck), 1928, Vol. II, pp. 44–67.
Isocrates, ed. G. Norlin, 3 vols., L.C.L., London: Wm. Heinemann, 1928.
Josephus, ed. H. St. J. Thackeray and R. Marcus, 7 vols., L.C.L., London: Wm. Heinemann, 1926–43.
Joüon, P., "Notes philologiques sur quelques versets de l'épître aux Philippiens," R.S.R., XXIII (1938), pp. 89–93; 223–33; 299–310.
Juncker, A., *Die Ethik des Apostels Paulus*, 2 Bde., Halle a. S.: Max Niemeyer, 1904–19.
Kahmann, J., "Het volgen van Christus door zelfverloochening en kruisdragen, volgens Marc. 8, 34–38 en par.," T.v.T., I (1961), pp. 205–225.
Keil, C. F., *Commentar über die Briefe des Petrus und Judas*, Leipzig: Dörffling & Franke, 1883.
Keulers, J., *De Brieven van Paulus*, 2 dln., Roermond: J. J. Romen, 1953.
Kittel, G., ἀκολουθέω, T.W.N.T., I, pp. 210–215.
Klein, G., *Der älteste christliche Katechismus und die jüdische Propaganda-Literatur*, Berlin: G. Reimer, 1909.
Klostermann, E., *Das Lukasevangelium*, H.N.T., 2. Aufl., Tübingen: J. C. B. Mohr (Paul Siebeck), 1929.
Koehler, L., and W. Baumgartner, *Lexicon in Veteris Testamenti Libros*, Leiden: E. J. Brill, 1953.
Kohler, K., *Jewish Theology Systematically and Historically Considered*, New York: Macmillan, 1918.
Koller, H., *Die Mimesis in der Antike*, Bern: A. Francke, 1954.
Koole, J. L., *Studien zum koptischen Bibeltext* (Beihefte zur Z.N.W., 17), Berlin: Alfred Töpelmann, 1936.
——, *De Joden in de Verstrooiing*, Franeker: T. Wever, 1946.
Köster, H., "Häretiker im Urchristentum," R.G.G.³, III, pp. 17–21.

Kuhn, K. G., *Konkordanz zu den Qumrantexten*, Göttingen: Vandenhoeck & Ruprecht, 1960.
Kühner, R., *Ausführliche Grammatik der Griechischen Sprache*, Hannover: Hahnsche Buchhandlung, 1892.
Kürzinger, J., "Τύπος διδαχῆς und der Sinn von Röm. 6, 17f.," *Biblica*, XXXIX (1958), pp. 156–176.
Lagrange, M.-J., *St. Paul: Épître aux Galates*, E.B., Paris: J. Gabalda, 1926.
Lake, K., and H. J. Cadbury, *English Translation and Commentary [of Acts]*, B. Chr., Vol. IV.
——, *Additional Notes to the Commentary [of Acts]*, B. Chr., Vol. V.
Lampe, G. W. H., and K. J. Woollcombe, *Essays on Typology*, Studies in Biblical Theology, No. 22, London: S.C.M. Press, 1957.
Lee, E. K., "Words denoting 'Pattern' in the New Testament," *N.T.S.*, VIII (1961/2), pp. 166–173. (This article reproduces almost totally and literally the article of L. B. Radford, listed below.)
Leeuwen, J. A. C. van, *Paulus' Zendbrieven aan Efeze, Colosse, Filémon, en Thessalonika*, K.N.T., Amsterdam: H. A. van Bottenburg, 1926.
Lenski, R. C. H., *The Interpretation of St. Paul's Epistles to the Galatians, to the Ephesians, and to the Philippians*, Columbus (Ohio): Wartburg Press, 1946.
——, *The Interpretation of St. Paul's Epistles to the Colossians, to the Thessalonians, to Timothy, to Titus and to Philemon*, Columbus (Ohio): Wartburg Press, 1946.
Liddell, H. G., and R. Scott, *A Greek-English Lexicon*, new edition by H. S. Jones, Oxford: Clarendon Press, 1940.
Lietzmann, H., *An die Korinther I, II*, H.N.T., Tübingen: J. C. B. Mohr (Paul Siebeck), 1931.
——, *An die Galater*, H.N.T., Tübingen: J. C. B. Mohr (Paul Siebeck), 1932.
Lightfoot, J. B., *Saint Paul's Epistle to the Galatians*, London: Macmillan, 1884.
——, *The Apostolic Fathers*, 2 pts. in 5 vols., London: Macmillan, 1889–90.
——, *Saint Paul's Epistle to the Philippians*, London: Macmillan, 1890.
——, *Notes on Epistles of St. Paul from Unpublished Commentaries*, London: Macmillan, 1904.
Lock, W., *A Critical and Exegetical Commentary on the Pastoral Epistles*, I.C.C., Edinburg: T. & T. Clark, 1924.
Lofthouse, W. F., "Fatherhood and Sonship in the Fourth Gospel," *E.T.*, XLIII (1931/32), pp. 442–448.
Lohmeyer, E., *Die Briefe an die Philipper, an die Kolosser und an Philemon*, K.e.K.N.T., 8. Aufl., Göttingen: Vandenhoeck & Ruprecht, 1930.
Lohse, E., ῥαββί, ῥαββουνί, *T.W.N.T.*, VI, pp. 962–966.
Lütgert, W., *Freiheitspredigt und Schwärmgeister in Korinth*, B.z.F.c.T., 12, 3. Heft, 1908.
——, *Die Irrlehrer der Pastoralbriefe*, B.z.F.c.T., 13, 3. Heft, 1909.
——, *Die Vollkommenen im Philipperbrief und die Enthusiasten in Thessalonich*, B.z.F.c.T., 13, 6. Heft, 1909.
*The Third and Fourth Books of Maccabees*, ed. M. Hadas, New York: Harper & Bros, 1953.
McCasland, S. V., "Christ Jesus," *J.B.L.*, LXV (1946), pp. 377–383.
Machen, J. G., *The Origin of Paul's Religion*, New York: Macmillan, 1928.
McNeile, A. H., *An Introduction to the Study of the New Testament*, revised by C. S. C. Williams, Oxford: Clarendon Press, 1953.
Manson, T. W., *The Teaching of Jesus*, 2nd ed., Cambridge: University Press, 1935.
Margoliouth, G., "Heroes and Hero-Gods (Hebrew)," *E.R.E.*, VI, p. 656.
Masson, C., *L'épître de saint Paul aux Éphésiens*, C.d.N.T., Neuchatel/Paris: Delachaux & Niestlé, 1953.

——, *Les deux épîtres de saint Paul aux Thessaloniciens, C.d.N.T.*, Neuchatel/Paris: Delachaux & Niestlé, 1957.
Mayor, J. B., *The Epistle of St. James*, London: Macmillan, 1892.
Meinertz, M., and F. Tillmann, *Die Gefangenschaftsbriefe des Heiligen Paulus*, in *Die Heilige Schrift des Neuen Testaments*, Bonn: Peter Hanstein, 1931.
Michael, J. H., *The Epistle of Paul to the Philippians*, *M.N.T.C.*, London: Hodder & Stoughton, 1928.
Michaelis, W., *Der Brief des Paulus an die Philipper*, *T.H.N.T.*, Leipzig: A. Deichert, 1935.
——, μιμέομαι, μιμητής, συμμιμητής, *T.W.N.T.*, IV, pp. 661–678.
——, ὁδός, *et al.*, *T.W.N.T.*, V, pp. 42–118.
Michel, O., *Der Brief an die Hebraër*, *K.e.K.N.T.*, 11. Aufl., Göttingen: Vandenhoeck & Ruprecht, 1960.
——, μιμνῄσκομαι *et al.,T.W.N.T.*, IV, pp. 678–687.
Milligan, G., *St. Paul's Epistles to the Thessalonians*, London: Macmillan, 1908.
M'Michael, W. F., "Be Ye Followers of me," *E.T.*, V (1893/94), p. 287.
Moffatt, J., *The First Epistle of Paul to the Corinthians*, *M.N.T.C.*, London: Hodder & Stoughton, 1954.
Morris, L., *The Epistles of Paul to the Thessalonians*, *T.N.T.C.*, London: Tyndale Press, 1956.
——, *The First and Second Epistles to the Thessalonians*, *N.I.C.N.T.*, Grand Rapids: Wm. B. Eerdmans, 1959.
Moulton, J. H., *A Grammar of New Testament Greek*, 2nd ed., Vol. I: *Prolegomena*, Edinburgh: T. & T. Clark, 1906.
——, and W. F. Howard, *A Grammar of New Testament Greek*, Vol. II: *Accidence and Word-Formation*, Edinburgh: T. & T. Clark, 1919.
——, and G. Milligan, *The Vocabulary of the Greek Testament*, London: Hodder & Stoughton, 1952.
Müller, J. J., *The Epistles of Paul to the Philippians and to Philemon*, *N.I.C.N.T.*, Grand Rapids: Wm. B. Eerdmans, 1955.
Munck, J., "Discours d'adieu dans le Nouveau Testament et dans la littérature biblique," in *Aux sources de la tradition chrétienne: Mélanges offerts à M. Goguel*, Neuchatel/Paris: Delachaux & Niestlé, 1950, pp. 155–170.
Murray, J., *The Epistle to the Romans*, *N.I.C.N.T.*, London: Marshall, Morgan & Scott, 1960.
Neil, W., *The Epistle of Paul to the Thessalonians*, *M.N.T.C.*, London: Hodder & Stoughton, 1950.
Oepke, A., *Der Brief des Paulus an die Galater*, *T.H.N.T.*, 2. Aufl., Berlin: Evangelische Verlagsanstalt, 1957.
Pape, W., *Griechisch-Deutsches Handwörterbuch*, 2 Bde., Braunschweig: F. Vieweg, 1880–84.
Passow, F., *Handwörterbuch der Griechischen Sprache*, 4 Bde., Leipzig: F. C. W. Vogel, 1841–57.
Philo, ed. F. H. Colson and G. H. Whitaker, 9 vols., *L.C.L.*, London: Wm. Heinemann, 1929–41.
——, ed. L. Philippson et al., in *Bibliothek der griechischen und romischen Schriftsteller über Judentum und Juden*, Leipzig: Oskar Leiner, 1870, Vol. IV.
Philodemus, *De Musica*, ed. J. Kemke, Leipzig: Teubner, 1884.
Plato, *Platonis Opera*, ed. J. Burnet, 5 vols., Oxford: Clarendon Press, 1900–7.
——, *Euthyphro, Apology, Crito, Phaedo, Phaedrus*, ed. H. N. Fowler, *L.C.L.*, London: Wm. Heinemann, 1928.
——, *The Republic*, ed. P. Shorey, 2 vols., *L.C.L.*, London: Wm. Heinemann, 1946.
——, *Theaetetus*, ed. H. N. Fowler, *L.C.L.*, London: Wm. Heinemann, 1921.

——, *Timaeus and Critias*, trans. A. E. Taylor, London: Methuen, 1929.
Plummer, A., *A Commentary on St. Paul's Epistle to the Philippians*, London: Robert Scott, 1919.
——, *A Critical and Exegetical Commentary on the Gospel according to S. Luke*, I.C.C., 5th ed., Edinburgh: T. & T. Clark, 1922.
Plutarch, *Moralia* XII, ed. H. Cherniss and W. C. Helmbold, L.C.L., London: Wm. Heinemann, 1957.
Pop, F. J., *Apostolaat in Druk en Vertroosting: De Tweede Brief aan de Corinthiërs*, in *De Prediking van het Nieuwe Testament*, Nijkerk: G. F. Callenbach, 1953.
Preisker, H., *Das Ethos des Urchristentums*, Gütersloh: C. Bertelsmann, 1949.
Prévot, A., *L'aoriste grec en -θην*, Paris, 1934.
Procksch, O., ἅγιος, *T.W.N.T.*, I, pp. 87–116.
*The Psalms of Solomon*, ed. H. E. Ryle and M. R. James, Cambridge: University Press, 1891.
Quell, G., and W. Foerster, κύριος *et al.*, *TW.N.T.*, III, pp. 1038–1098.
Quintilian, *Institutio Oratoria*, ed. H. E. Butler, 4 vols., L.C.L., London: Wm. Heinemann, 1958.
Rad, G. von, *Theologie des Alten Testaments*, Band I, München: Chr. Kaiser Verlag, 1957.
Radford, L. B., "Some New Testament Synonyms: Δεῖγμα, ὑπόδειγμα, τύπος, ὑποτύπωσις, ὑπογραμμός," *The Expositor*, 5th Series, VI (1897), pp. 377–387.
Rengstorf, K., διδάσκω/διδάσκαλος, *et al.*, *T.W.N.T.*, II, pp. 138—168.
——, μανθάνω/μαθητής, *et al.*, *T.W.N.T.*, IV, pp. 392–465.
Ridderbos, H. N., *De Strekking der Bergrede naar Mattheus*, Kampen: J. H. Kok, 1936.
——, *The Epistle of Paul to the Churches of Galatia*, N.I.C.N.T., Grand Rapids: Wm. B. Eerdmans, 1953.
——, *Heilsgeschiedenis en Heilige Schrift van het Nieuwe Testament*, Kampen: J. H. Kok, 1955.
——, *Aan de Romeinen*, C.N.T., Kampen: J. H. Kok, 1959.
——, *Aan de Kolossenzen*, C.N.T., Kampen: J. H. Kok, 1960.
Ridderbos, J., *Het Boek Deuteronomium*, K.V., Kampen: J. H. Kok, 1950.
Riesenfeld, H., "La voie de charité," *S.T.*, I, pp. 146–157.
Rigaux, B., *St. Paul: Épîtres aux Thessaloniciens*, E.B., Paris/Gembloux: Gabalda, Duculot, 1956.
Riggenbach, E., *Der Brief an die Hebräer*, K.z.N.T., Leipzig: A. Deichert, 1913.
Robertson, A., and A. Plummer, *First Epistle of St. Paul to the Corinthians*, I.C.C., Edinburgh: T. & T. Clark, 1911.
Robertson, A. T., *A Grammar of the Greek New Testament in the Light of Historical Research*, Nashville: Broadman Press, 1934.
Ross, W. D., *Aristotle's Metaphysics*, 2 vols., Oxford: Clarendon Press, 1924.
Sanders, L., *L'Hellénisme de Saint Clément de Rome et le Paulinisme*, Louvain: Bibliotheca Universitatis, 1943.
Scherer, J., *Entretien d'Origène avec Héraclide et les évêques ses collègues sur le Père, le Fils, et l'Âme*, (Publications de la Société Fouad I de Papyrologie: Textes et Documents, IX), Cairo, 1949.
Schippers, R., *De Gereformeerde Zede*, Kampen: J. H. Kok, 1955.
——, *Mythologie en Eschatologie in 2 Thessalonicenzen 2:1–17*, Assen: G. F. Hummelen, 1961.
Schlatter, A., *Die Kirche der Griechen im Urteil des Paulus*, Stuttgart: Calwer Verlag, 1936.
——, *Die Briefe an die Galater, Epheser, Kolosser und Philemon*, Stuttgart: Calwer Verlag, 1949.

——, *Paulus. Der Bote Jesu*, 2. Aufl., Stuttgart: Calwer Verlag, 1956.
Schlier, H., *Der Brief an die Galater*, K.e.K.N.T., 10. Aufl., Göttingen: Vandenhoeck & Ruprecht, 1949.
——, *Der Brief an die Epheser*, Dusseldorf: Patmos-Verlag, 1957.
——, "Galaterbrief," *L.T.K.*² IV, pp. 487–488.
——, θλῖψις, *T.W.N.T.*, III, pp. 139–148.
Schmidt, K. L., ἀγωγή, *T.W.N.T.*, I, pp. 128–129.
——, "Nicht über das hinaus, was geschrieben steht! (I. Kor. 4, 6)," in *In Memoriam Ernst Lohmeyer*, hrsg. von W. Schmauch, Stuttgart: Evangelisches Verlagswerk, 1951, pp. 101–109.
Schmithals, W., *Die Gnosis in Korinth*, Göttingen: Vandenhoeck & Ruprecht, 1956.
——, "Die Häretiker in Galatien," *Z.N.W.*, XLVII (1956), pp. 25–67.
——, "Die Irrlehrer des Philipperbriefes," *Z.T.K.*, LIV (1957), pp. 297–341
——, "Die Irrlehrer von Röm. 16:17–20," *S.T.*, XIII (1959), pp. 1–19.
——, "Zur Abfassung und ältesten Sammlung der paulinischen Hauptbriefe," *Z.N.W.*, LI (1960), pp. 225—245.
Schmitz, O., and G. Stählin, παρακαλέω et al., *T.W.N.T.*, V, pp. 771–798.
Schoeps, H.-J., "Von der Imitatio Dei zur Nachfolge Christi," *Aus Frühchristlicher Zeit*, Tübingen: J. C. B. Mohr (Paul Siebeck), 1950, pp. 286–301.
Schrenk, G., and G. Quell, πατήρ et al., *T.W.N.T.*, V, pp. 946–1024.
Schulze, H., "Die Unterlagen für die Abschiedsrede zu Milet in Apostelgeschichte 20, 18–38," *T.S.K.*, LXXIII (1900), pp. 119–125.
Schürmann, H., "Die vorösterlichen Anfänge der Logientradition," in *Der historische Jesus und der kerygmatische Christus*, hrsg. von H. Ristow und K. Mattiae, Berlin: Evangelische Verlagsanstalt, 1961, pp. 342–370.
Schweizer, E., *Erniedrigung und Erhöhung bei Jesus und seinen Nachfolgern*, Zürich: Zwingli-Verlag, 1955.
——, "Discipleship and Belief in Jesus as Lord from Jesus to the Hellenistic Church," *N.T.S.*, II (1955/56), pp. 87—99.
——, "Die Kirche als Leib Christi in den paulinischen Antilegomena," *T.L.*, LXXXVI (1961), pp. 241–256.
Schwyzer, E., *Griechische Grammatik*, in *Handbuch der Altertumswissenschaft*, ed. W. Otto, München: C. H. Beck, 1939.
Scott, E. F., *The Pastoral Epistles*, *M.N.T.C.*, London: Hodder & Stoughton, 1936.
Selwyn, E. G., *The First Epistle of St. Peter*, London: Macmillan, 1947.
Seneca, *Ad Lucilium Epistulae Morales*, ed. R. M. Gummere, 3 vols., *L.C.L.*, London: Wm. Heinemann, 1953.
——, *Moral Essays*, ed. J. W. Basore, 3 vols., *L.C.L.*, London: Wm. Heinemann, 1928.
Sevenster, G., *De Christologie van het Nieuwe Testament*, Amsterdam: Holland Uitgeversmaatschappij, 1946.
Sieffert, F., *Handbuch über den Brief an die Galater*, K.e.K.N.T., 7. Aufl., Göttingen: Vandenhoeck & Ruprecht, 1886.
Smith, H. P., *A Critical and Exegetical Commentary on the Books of Samuel*, *I.C.C.*, Edinburgh: T. & T. Clark, 1904.
Spicq, C., *St Paul: Les Épîtres Pastorales*, *E.B.*, Paris: J. Gabalda, 1947.
——, *Épîtres aux Corinthiens*, in *La Sainte Bible*, Tome XI, 2ᵉ Partie, Paris: Letouzey et Ané, 1948.
——, *L'Épître aux Hébreux*, 2 vols., *E.B.*, Paris: J. Gabalda, 1953.
——, *Agapè dans le Nouveau Testament, Analyse des Textes*, 2 vols., Paris: J. Gabalda, 1958–59.
——, "Les Thessaloniciens 'inquiets' étaient-ils des paresseux?" *S.T.*, X (1956), pp. 1–13.

Staab, K., and J. Freundorfer, *Die Thessalonicherbriefe, die Gefangenschaftsbriefe und die Pastoralbriefe*, Regensburg: Friedrich Pustet, 1950.
Stählin, G., "Galaterbrief," *R.G.G.*³, II, pp. 1187—90.
Stanley, D. M., "The Theme of the Servant of Yahweh in Primitive Christian Soteriology, and Its Transposition by St. Paul," *C.B.Q.*, XVI (1954), pp. 385—425.
———, "'Become Imitators of Me': The Pauline Conception of Apostolic Tradition," *Biblica*, XL (1959), pp. 859—877.
Stauffer, E., *Die Theologie des Neuen Testaments*, 4. Aufl., Stuttgart: W. Kohlhammer, 1948.
Stempvoort, P. A. van, *Eenheid en Schisma in de Gemeente van Korinthe volgens I Korinthiërs*, Nijkerk: G. F. Callenbach, 1950.
———, *Oud en Nieuw: De Brief aan de Galaters*, in *De Prediking van het Nieuwe Testament*, Nijkerk: G. F. Callenbach, 1951.
Stendahl, K., *The School of St. Matthew*, Uppsala: Almquist & Wiksells, 1954.
Stephanus, H., *Thesaurus Graecae Linguae*, 8 vol., Paris: Didot, 1831—65.
Strack, H. L., and P. Billerbeck, *Kommentar zum Neuen Testament aus Talmud und Midrasch*, 4 Bde., München: C. H. Beck, 1922ff.
Stumpff, A., ζῆλος, *T.W.N.T.*, II, pp. 879—884.
———, ἴχνος, *T.W.N.T.*, III, pp. 405—409.
Swigchem, D. van, *Het Missionair Karakter van de Christelijke Gemeente volgens de Brieven van Paulus en Petrus*, Kampen: J. H. Kok, 1955.
Tacitus, *Historiarum*, ed. H. Goelzer, Paris: Société d'Édition "Les Belles Lettres," 1921.
Taylor, A. E., *A Commentary on Plato's Timaeus*, Oxford: Clarendon Press, 1928.
*The Greek Versions of the Testaments of the Twelve Patriarchs*, ed. R. H. Charles, Oxford: Clarendon Press, 1908.
Theodore of Mopsuestia, *In Epistolas B. Pauli Commentarii*, ed. H. B. Swete, 2 vols., Cambridge: University Press, 1880—82.
Theodoret of Cyrrhus, *Commentarius in omnes sancti Pauli Epistolas*, ed. J.-P. Migne, *P.G.*, LXXXII.
Theognis, *Poèmes Élégiaques*, ed. J. Carrière, Paris: Société d'Édition "Les Belles Lettres," 1948.
Thucydides, trans. B. Jowett, Oxford: Clarendon Press, 1900.
Thyen, H., *Der Stil der Jüdisch-Hellenistischen Homilie*, Göttingen: Vandenhoeck & Ruprecht, 1955.
Tinsley, E. J., *The Imitation of God in Christ*, London: S.C.M. Press, 1960.
Torrance, T. F., *The Doctrine of Grace in the Apostolic Fathers*, London/Edinburgh: Oliver and Boyd, 1948.
Unnik, W. C. van, "Navolging van Christus," *Christelijke Encyclopedie*, 2e dr., Kampen: J. H. Kok, 1956—61.
Veldhuizen, A. van, *Paulus' Brieven aan de Korinthiërs*, T.U., Groningen: J. B. Wolters, 1917.
Vincent, M. R., *A Critical and Exegetical Commentary on the Epistles to the Philippians and to Philemon*, I.C.C., Edinburgh: T. & T. Clark, 1897.
Völter, D., *Paulus und seine Briefe*, Strassburg: Heitz & Mündel, 1905.
Wallis, P., "Ein neuer Auslegungsversuch der Stelle I. Kor. 4, 6," *T.L.*, LXXV (1950), pp. 506—508.
Weiss, B., *Die Briefe Pauli an Timotheus und Titus*, K.e.K.N.T., 7. Aufl. Göttingen: Vandenhoeck & Ruprecht, 1902.
———, *Das Neue Testament nach Luthers berichtiger Übersetzung mit fortlaufender Erläuterung versehen*, 2 Heft, 2. Aufl., Leipzig: J. C. Hinrichs, 1907.
Weiss, J., *Der Erste Korintherbrief*, K.e.K.N.T., 9. Aufl., Göttingen: Vandenhoeck & Ruprecht, 1910.

——, *Das Urchristentum*, Göttingen: Vandenhoeck & Ruprecht, 1917.
Wendland, H.-D., *Die Briefe an die Korinther*, *N.T.D.*, Göttingen: Vandenhoeck & Ruprecht, 1956.
Wendt, H. H., *Die Apostelgeschichte*, *K.e.K.N.T.*, 6./7. Aufl., Göttingen: Vandenhoeck & Ruprecht, 1888 (9. Aufl., 1913).
Westcott, B. F., *Saint Paul's Epistle to the Ephesians*, London: Macmillan, 1906.
——, and F. J. A. Hort, *The New Testament in the Original Greek*, 2 vols., London: Macmillan, 1907.
Whitaker, G. H., "The Philology of St. Luke's Preface," *Expositor*, 8th Series, XX (1920), pp. 262–272.
——, "Notes on the Paper 'The Philology of St. Luke's Preface,'" *Expositor*, 8th Series, XX, pp. 380–384.
——, "Additional Note on 'The Philology of St. Luke's Preface,'" *Expositor*, 8th Series, XXI (1921), pp. 239–240.
Wilckens, U., *Die Missionsreden der Apostelgeschichte*, Neukirchen: Neukirchener Verlag, 1961.
Williams, C. S. C., *A Commentary on the Acts of the Apostles*, *B.N.T.C.*, London: Adam and Charles Black, 1957.
Wingren, G., "Was bedeutet die Nachfolge Christi in Evangelischer Ethik?" *T.L.*, LXXV (1950), pp. 385—392.
Wohlenberg, G., *Der erste und zweite Thessalonicherbrief*, *K.z.N.T.*, Leipzig: A. Deichert, 1903.
——, *Die Pastoralbriefe*, *K.z.N.T.*, Leipzig: A. Deichert, 1906.
Woollcombe, K. J., "The Biblical Origins and Patristic Development of Typology," in *Essays on Typology*, Studies in Biblical Theology, No. 22, London: S.C.M. Press, pp. 39–75.
Xenophon, *Cyropaedia*, ed. W. Miller, 2 vols., *L.C.L.*, London: Wm. Heinemann, 1914.
——, *Memorabilia*, ed. E. C. Marchant, *L.C.L.*, London: Wm. Heinemann, 1923.
Zahn, T., *Das Evangelium des Matthäus*, 2. Aufl., *K.z.N.T.*, Leipzig: A. Deichert, 1905.
——, *Die Apostelgeschichte des Lucas*, 2 Bde., *K.z.N.T.*, 1./2. Aufl., Leipzig: A. Deichert, 1919—21.
——, *Einleitung in das Neue Testament*, 2 Bde., 3. Aufl., Leipzig: A. Deichert, 1905—7.

# INDEX OF TEXTS DISCUSSED

## Classical writings

**Herodotus**
1. 67 .................... 2f.
**Hippocrates: ΠΕΡΙ ΔΙΑΙΤΗΣ**
1. x ff. ................. 17f.

## Jewish writings

**Wisdom of Solomon**
4:2 ..................... 8
15:9 .................... 8
**II Maccabees**
6:27,28,31 .............. 46
**IV Maccabees**
6:19 .................... 46
9:23 .................... 45
13:9 .................... 45
**Philo: De Sacrif. Abel. et Caini**
68 ...................... 10ff.
**Testament of Asher**
4:3 ..................... 9

## Old Testament

**Genesis**
1:26,27 ............. 38, 42
**Exodus**
20:8–11 ............... 40f.
**Leviticus**
19:2 ............ 39, 43, 73
**Deuteronomy**
10:18,19 .............. 38f.
**I Samuel**
20:14 ................... 40
**II Samuel**
9:3 ..................... 40
**I Kings**
18:21 ................. 35f.
**Jeremiah**
12:16 ................... 149

## New Testament

**Matthew**
5:43–48 ............... 71ff.
**Mark**
10:42ff. ................ 54
**John**
13:15 ................. 54ff.
13:33–35 ............. 56f.
21:19,22 .............. 53f.
**Acts**
20:35 ................. 201ff.
23:25 ................... 21
26:29 ................... 195
**Romans**
5:14 .................... 22
6:17 .................... 21
15:1–7 ............ 62, 158f.
**I Corinthians**
2:4 ..................... 110
4:6 ................... 140ff.
4:16 .................. 139ff.
4:17 .................. 146ff.
7:7–9 ................... 156
10:6 .................... 22
11:1 .................. 154ff.
14:33–36 ............... 105
**II Corinthians**
8:9 ................... 61f.
10:1 .................... 64
**Galatians**
4:12 .................. 188ff.
**Ephesians**
4:24 .................... 75
4:32–5:2 .............. 75ff.
**Philippians**
2:5 ................... 59ff.
**I Thessalonians**
1:5 ................... 110ff.
1:6 ............ 92ff., 108ff.
1:7 ..................... 116
1:8–10 ............... 116ff.
2:1–12 ................ 112f.
2:13,14 ................ 98f.
3:3 ................... 94f.
4:11,12 .............. 127ff.
4:13ff. ................ 129
5:1ff. ................. 129
**II Thessalonians**
2:2 ................... 129f.

3:5 .................... 63f.
3:7–9 ................ 126ff.
I Timothy
1:16 .................. 196ff.
4:12 .................... 86f.
II Timothy
1:13 .................... 199f.
3:10 .................... 200f.
Titus
2:7,8 .................... 87f.
Hebrews
6:12 ..................... 81

11 .................... 81ff.
12:2,3 ................... 63
13:7 .................... 84f.
James
5:10,11 .................. 84
I Peter
1:15,16 .................. 74
2:21 .................... 57f.
5:3 ...................... 86
III John
vs. 11 .................... 85

# INDEX OF AUTHORS AND EDITORS

Aalders, G. C. 149
Abbott, T. K. 75
Aeschylus 2
Aland, K. xiv
Allo, E. B. 22, 140, 151, 161
Alt, A. xiv
Ambrosiaster 121
Aristeas 10, 44, 49
Aristotle 3, 6, 24, 25
Asting, R. 73
Bachmann, P. 22, 151
Bailey, A. 1
Barrett, C. K. 53, 55
Barth, K. 172, 184
Basore, J. W. 28
Bauer, W. 28, 53, 73, 75, 180, 201, 204
Baum, G. 22, 96, 161, 172, 179
Baumgartner, W. 137
Baur, F. C. 103
Beare, F. W. 21, 172, 179
Beloe, W. 18
Bengel, J. A. 177
Benoit, P. 170
Berkouwer, G. C. 55, 59
Bernard, J. H. 55
Billerbeck, P. 56, 145
Blass, F. 81, 99, 100, 102, 117, 176, 180
Blumenthal, A. von 17, 18
Boman, T. 47
Bonhoeffer, D. 69
Bonnard, P. 59, 60, 61, 170, 172, 179, 181, 187, 190, 195
Bornemann, W. 99
Bornkamm, G. 173
Bouma, C. 87, 198
Bousset, W. 151
Briggs, C. A. 39
Brown, F. 39
Bruce, F. F. 204
Buber, M. 42, 43
Büchsel, F. 145
Bultmann, R. 25, 53, 57, 72, 82, 85, 134
Butler, H. E. 25
Burnet, J. 4, 26

Burton, E. 111
Burton, E. D. 191
Bywater, I. 6
Cadbury, H. J. 203, 204
Calvin, J. 22, 40, 96, 104, 121, 161, 172, 179
Carrière, J. 150
Cerfaux, L. 105, 208
Chadwick, H. 95
Chantraine, P. 1
Charles, R. H. 9, 204
Cherniss, H. 2
Christ, W. von 6
Chrysostom, J. 61, 101, 114, 117, 177, 197
Cicero 28
Cohen, A. 43
Cohn, L. 11
Colson, F. H. 10, 11, 12, 13, 20, 49
Cornford, F. M. 4
Cremer, H. 72, 74, 79, 150
Crosby, H. L. 6
Cullmann, O. 134
Cunitz, E. 22, 96, 161, 172, 179
Cyprian 9
Daniélou, J. 22
Daube, D. 47
Davies, W. D. 161
Debrunner, A. 81, 99, 100, 102, 117, 176, 180
Deissner, K. 28
Delling, G. 112
Democritus 2, 7, 19
Dibelius, M. 59, 61, 84, 93, 120, 159, 172
Dick, K. 119
Diels, H. 2, 7, 19
Dinkler, E. 140
Dio Chysostom 6
Dittenberger, W. 19
Dobschütz, E. von 94, 96, 101, 103, 116, 119, 120, 121, 128, 129, 130, 131, 136
Dodd, C. H. xi, 64, 159
Driver, S. R. 39
Duker, A. C. 111
Duncan, G. S. 190

# INDEX OF AUTHORS AND EDITORS

Du Plessis, P. J. 72, 175
Dürr, L. 145
Duvenage, S. C. W. xii, 51
Easton, B. S. 199
Eidem, E. xii, 137, 156, 160, 172, 190, 205
Eissfeldt, O. xiv
Empedocles 18
Epictetus 28
Epstein, I. 43
Evans, C. F. 203
Ewald, P. 76, 172, 178, 179
Findlay, G. G. 103, 111, 117, 118, 131
Foerster, W. 86, 122
Forster, E. S. 25
Fowler, H. N. 27
Frame, J. E. 63, 98, 103, 109, 113, 115, 116, 121, 128, 129, 130, 135, 136
Franke, A. H. 171, 172, 177, 178, 179
Franses, D. 111
Freundorfer, J. 121
Friedrich, G. 208
Gerhardsson, B. 44, 152
Gispen, W. H. 40
Glueck, N. 40
Godley, A. D. 17, 18
Goelzer, H. 41
Goppelt, L. 22, 83
Greijdanus, S. 13, 59, 60, 61, 105, 172, 178
Grosheide, F. W. 21, 22, 53, 55, 62, 81, 84, 85, 142, 152, 161, 204
Grundmann, W. 110, 114, 133
Gulin, E. G. 26, 28, 35, 36, 121
Gummere, R. M. 26
Hadas, M. 9, 10, 20
Hadorn, W. 121, 160
Haenchen, E. 160
Hatch, E. 29
Haupt, E. 172, 179
Heinrici, G. 147
Heinzelmann, G. 172
Heitmann, P. A. 27, 28, 71
Helmbold, W. C. 2
Hendricksen, W. 109, 128, 197
Héring, J. 22, 151, 154
Herodotus 17, 18
Hesychius 23
Heyde, J. E. 18
Hippocrates 2, 3, 103
Holl, K. 104
Hort, F. J. A. 163
Howard, W. F. 102
Isocrates 7, 9

James, M. R. 145
Jones, W. H. S. 1, 2, 3
Josephus 13, 20, 33, 45, 102, 145
Joüon, P. 178
Jowett, B. 24
Juncker, A. 134, 152
Kahle, P. xiv
Kahmann, J. 97, 125, 126
Keil, C. F. 13
Kemke, J. 197
Keulers, J. 94, 121, 134
King, J. E. 28
Kittel, G. 36, 51, 52, 53, 56, 200
Kittel, R. xiv
Klein, G. 42
Klostermann, E. 203
Koehler, L. 137
Kögel, J. 72, 74, 79, 150
Kohler, K. 43
Koller, H. 2, 5, 6
Koole, J. L. 45, 48, 49, 122
Köster, H. 173, 189
Kuhn, K. G. 46
Kühner, R. 102
Kürzinger, J. 21
Lagrange, M. J. 189, 190, 194
Lake, K. xiv, 204
Lampe, G. W. H. 22
Lee, E. K. 21
Leeuwen, J. A. C. van 75, 127, 128, 137
Legrand, P. E. 18
Lenski, R. C. H. 102, 128, 172, 180
Liddell, H. G. 1, 17, 18, 75, 197
Lietzmann, H. 22, 142, 151, 190
Lightfoot, J. B. 15, 23, 63, 135, 141, 173, 175, 179, 183, 192, 194
Lock, W. 87
Lofthouse, W. F. 72
Lohmeyer, E. 169, 172, 178, 179
Lohse, W. 51
Lütgert, W. 128, 132
Machen, J. G. 105
Manen, W. C. van 111
Manson, T. W. 51
Marchant, E. C. 7, 26, 150
Margoliouth, G. 29
Masson, C. 76, 79, 99, 128
Mayor, J. B. 84
McCasland, S. V. 60
McNeile, A. H. 169
Meinertz, M. 172
Michael, J. H. 179, 187
Michaelis, W. xii, 5, 9, 10, 11, 12, 13, 31, 33, 34, 59, 61, 76, 77, 78, 79, 98, 100, 108, 116, 121, 138, 149,

151, 152, 154, 159, 167, 168, 172, 177, 181, 184, 185, 190, 206, 209, 210
Michel, O. 82, 85, 151
Migne, J. P. 61, 121, 197
Miller, W. 25
Milligan, G. 94, 96, 109, 111, 118, 122, 123, 128, 137
M'Michael, W. F. 177
Moffatt, J. 22, 140, 142, 151, 157, 161
Montfaucon, B. de 61, 101, 114, 117, 177
Morris, L. 95, 121, 128, 135
Moulton, J. H. 100, 102, 118, 137
Müller, J. J. 172, 179
Munck, J. 202
Murray, J. 68
Nauck, A. 2
Neil, W. 121, 128
Nestle, Eb. xiv
Nestle, Erw. xiv
Norlin, G. 7
Oepke, A. 190, 192, 193
Oldfather, W. A. 28
Origen 9
Pape, W. 1, 17
Passow, F. 1
Philo 10, 11, 12, 13, 20, 44, 45, 48, 49, 82
Philippson, L. 11
Philodemus 197
Pindar 2
Plato, 4, 5, 13, 14, 18, 26, 27, 128, 145, 177
Plummer, A. 22, 122, 161, 169, 172, 179
Plutarch 2
Pop, F. J. 62
Preisker, H. 120, 175
Prévot, A. 100
Procksch, O. 39
Quell, G. 122
Quintilian 24
Rackham, H. 24
Rad, G. von 30
Radford, L. B. 21, 22, 197, 199
Rahlfs, A. xiv
Redpath, H. A. 29
Rengstorf, K. 30, 143, 145, 149, 150
Reuss, E. 22, 96, 161, 172, 179
Ridderbos, H. N. 68, 72, 134, 173, 189, 193, 194
Ridderbos, J. 39
Riesenfeld, H. 152
Riggenbach, E. 85
Rigaux, B. 17, 63, 93, 98, 102, 109, 111, 117, 118, 121, 129, 131, 134, 135
Robertson, A. 22, 99, 117, 161
Robertson, A. T. 102, 135, 163, 180, 198
Ross, W. D. 3, 25
Ryle, H. E. 145
Sanders, L. 83
Scherer, J. 95
Schippers, R. 31, 34, 130, 152
Schlatter, A. 152, 190
Schlier, H. 76, 80, 95, 189, 190, 191, 194
Schmid, W. 6
Schmidt, K. L. 142, 201
Schmidt, M. 23
Schmithals, W. 132, 140, 144, 154, 173, 175, 189
Schmitz, O. 154
Schoeps, H. J. 14, 42
Schrenk, G. 145
Schroeder, O. 2
Schulze, H. 203
Schweizer, E. 51, 52, 53, 54, 57, 68, 69, 173
Schwyzer, E. 102
Scott, E. F. 197
Scott, R. 1, 17, 18, 75, 197
Séchan, L. 1
Selwyn, E. G. 74
Seneca 26, 28
Sevenster, G. 159
Shachter, J. 145
Shorey, P. 5, 19
Sieffert, F. 189, 191, 192
Smith, H. P. 40
Spicq, C. 61, 73, 79, 82, 109, 131, 133, 134, 142, 200, 201
Staab, K. 121
Stählin, G. 154, 189
Stählin, O. 6
Stanley, D. M. xii, 99, 106, 120, 165, 190, 194, 206, 208, 215
Stauffer, E. 202
Stempvoort, P. A. van 104, 105, 190
Stendahl, K. 152
Stephanus, H. 1, 17
Strack, H. L. 56, 145
Stumpff, A. 9, 58
Sutton, E. W. 24
Swete, H. B. 61, 94, 101, 117, 121
Swigchem, D. van xii, 127
Tacitus 41
Taylor, A. E. 4, 27
Thackeray, H. St. J. 45
Theodoret of Cyrrhus 61, 117, 197

Theodore of Mopsuestia 61, 101, 117, 121
Theognis 150
Thucydides 11, 24
Thyen, H. 82
Tillmann, F. 172
Tinsley, E. J. xii, 36, 37, 64, 65, 67, 68, 69, 70, 144, 192
Torrance, T. F. 67, 83
Unnik, W. C. van 65
Veldhuizen, A. van 142
Vincent, M. R. 172, 179
Völter, D. 155
Wallis, P. 142

Weiss, B. 198
Weiss, J. 147, 151, 154
Wendland, H. D. 22
Wendt, H. H. 204
Westcott, B. F. 79, 163
Whitaker, G. H. 10, 11, 12, 13, 20, 49, 110
Wilckens, U. 160
Williams, C. S. C. 169, 203
Wingren, G. 69
Wohlenberg, G. 117, 172, 198
Woollcombe, K. J. 19, 22
Xenophon 7, 25, 26
Zahn, T. 72, 182, 204

www.ingramcontent.com/pod-product-compliance
Lightning Source LLC
Chambersburg PA
CBHW051635230426
43669CB00013B/2308